TALKING VERSE

TALKING VERSE

Edited by
**Robert Crawford, Henry Hart, David Kinloch,
Richard Price**

VERSE
St Andrews and Williamsburg

© 1995 Copyright of individual pieces remains with the contributors.
Copyright of this anthology belongs to the editors.

Published by Verse, School of English, University of St Andrews,
Fife, Scotland KY16 9AL, and Verse, Department of English,
College of William and Mary, Williamsburg VA 23185, USA.

This volume forms issues 11.3 and 12.1 of *Verse*.

ISBN 1872612 05 9
ISSN 0268-3830

CONTENTS

INTRODUCTION

This volume reprints a selection of interviews from *Verse* magazine, drawn largely from issues of the 1990s, though a sprinkling of earlier interviews has been added, along with some brand new ones. From its launch in 1984, *Verse* has been international in outlook. It has published interviews with such poets as Gennady Aygi and Miroslav Holub, but to give this book some coherence the editors decided to focus on poets who write in English (or sometimes in English and Scots), with a strong accent on the younger generation of poets whose work has appeared in *Verse* and to whom the magazine has shown a clear commitment. In other words, the present collection celebrates just over a decade of *Verse* by presenting an international mixture of poets talking about their work and about what matters to them. This is where John Burnside rubs shoulders with Les Murray, where Simon Armitage and Robert Pinsky meet.

Most of the interviews here were tape-recorded, transcribed, sent for approval to the interviewee, and printed in full. They are reprinted now without alteration. *Verse* always aimed to provide extensive interviews, though in one or two cases the poets kept things brief. These conversations are often flavoursome in ways that may provide encouragement, confirmation, and recognition for other writers at the same time as affording to readers a useful commentary on the work of the interviewees.

A great number of the poems in issues of *Verse* have appeared by now in individual poets' collections. Our normal policy was to avoid printing material which had appeared already elsewhere, at the same time as publishing only writing that we really believed in. Glyn Maxwell's 'Out of the Rain', for instance, which first appeared in *Verse* Vol. 7 No. 1, is now available in his book of the same title. However, David Kinloch's interview with Maxwell in *Verse* Vol. 7 No. 3 is available nowhere else, and that issue of *Verse* has been out of print for some years. Most of the back-issues of *Verse* are sold out by now, and we receive a considerable number of requests for interviews here reprinted. *Talking Verse*, then, is a collection of material which is both a commentary on the writing of poetry in *Verse*'s heyday and a resource for future readers.

I hope that *Talking Verse* will further the kind of international, even intercontinental poetic awareness to which the magazine has been committed throughout its lifespan. *Verse* began in 1984 because David Kinloch and I wished to start a poetry magazine with a Scottish accent that would publish high-grade Scottish work alongside the best international poetry. Some self-aggrandizement was involved inasmuch as we occasionally published our own poems in early issues, before deciding to abstain. When plotting the magazine we were both Glaswegian graduate students at Balliol College, Oxford. In 1983 we'd organized a reading by fellow students at Holywell Manor, Balliol's Graduate Centre, that featured poetry in over thirty languages, and this must have whetted our appetites for more. To launch a magazine we needed a third editor — not least because between us we had £400 to put towards publishing a first issue, and it looked as if £600 would be needed. Rather nervously we approached Henry Hart (then at New College, writing a D.Phil. on Geoffrey Hill), whom I knew because we were both supervised by Richard Ellmann. Henry was enthsiastic, put up the other £200, and brought with him an excellent knowledge of American poetry as well as access to American poets. As the magazine developed, the Scottish-American axis proved invaluable, allowing us to preserve an international mixture of work that soon extended to Australian, New Zealand, and Canadian writing, as well as work from the United Kingdom and the United States. As a Francophile and teacher of French literature (now at Strathclyde University), David Kinloch brought material from Paris and other parts of France, underpinning our commitment to publishing poetry in translation. Foreign features ranged from Scandinavian to Chinese, from French to Polish verse. Our commitment to an international approach and to maintaining a Scottish accent continued and are reflected in this present book.

7

Verse began in Oxford, and was helped by the lively poetry climate there, to which the magazine contributed. In 1985, for instance 'Verse at St Hugh's' brought John Ashbery, Yves Bonnefoy, Alison Brackenbury, David Dabydeen, Douglas Dunn, and others to read at St Hugh's College where I then worked, and where the magazine had its editorial headquarters. We organized a conference on Ashbery's work, and in 1986 we ran a Festival of Australian Verse at St John's College with readings by Peter Porter and other Australian poets, as well as films of Les Murray, Porter, and Roland Robinson by the Australian poet and film-maker Richard Tipping. I have a vivid memory of sitting on the bare floor of Richard's flat just before he returned to Australia. Besides me was an unplugged matt-black video recorder; on top of the video recorder in the otherwise empty room sat Richard's pure white rabbit.

All this was great fun, but there were ways in which being based in Oxford was awkward. It stopped us getting a Scottish Arts Council grant, for instance. The Arts Council of Great Britain was a no-go area and we didn't want an English regional grant since we were worried that might commit us to publishing a certain percentage of local poets. In practice we did publish local poets, but we didn't want to be obliged to do this. We were wary of being confined by an Oxonian image. Our internationalism was in part an outflanking of Anglocentrism, not to mention Oxocentrism. The poets we published, even if they had Oxford connections, tended to be 'alternative' figures. We featured, and went on featuring the work of W. N. Herbert, for instance, though his post-MacDiarmid Scots was a far cry from the Martian School then dominant in Southern English poetry of the early and mid-1980s. By the time the first issue of *Verse* appeared Henry Hart had returned to the USA where he began the hard, successful work of establishing the magazine there. He secured work by poets as diverse as Amy Clampitt and A. R. Ammons, as well as writing by young poets such as Richard Kenney and Diann Blakely Shoaf. Henry's trust and efficiency meant that the transatlantic editing of *Verse* became as much of an epistolary treat as a chore — which, given the possible scope for budgetary and artistic scrapping, is saying a good deal.

Neither Henry, David, nor I ever got our £200 back or made any other money from the magazine. More importantly, nor did the poets whose work we published. Probably the most remarkable thing about *Verse* has been the generosity of its contributors. From the start, when such writers as Alasdair Gray, Donald Hall, Seamus Heaney, and Edwin Morgan gave us poems for a magazine that didn't even exist, we were unbelievably fortunate in the way we managed to cadge first-rate work. I think part of the reason for this was that contributors liked the magazine's international mixture, as well as our policy of publishing new or young writers alongside the Great and Good. Trusting subscribers were crucial also. They had to be trusting, since we virtually never announced in advance what the next issue would contain. Our first subscribers tended to be relatives; as the magazine developed, our subscriber base shifted to people who were absolutely sure that what they wanted was modern poetry. When we got grant money we chose to expand the scope of the magazine, rather than pay contributors a mere couple of pounds a poem, which is all we could have afforded. This may have been a questionable decision, and it would have been better to be able to pay decent rates, but we stand by what we did, not least because it allowed us to expand *Verse* from a forty-eight page hall into a one hundred-and-eighty page auditorium, making it easier to admit new poetry, more critical prose, and more of the sort of interviews which make up this book.

Verse was not a perfect magazine. Though we published poets as different as Carol Ann Duffy and Lauris Edmond, we were unable to attract as much first-rate poetry by women as we would have wished. Because we published the magazine ourselves, overseeing all the printing, finance, and marketing, we kept the cover price low, but never achieved a circulation of over 1,000 copies per issue; usually we hung around the 800 mark, selling almost exclusively to subscribers. To by-pass bookshops was perhaps foolhardy, and certainly hard to do, but postage costs and bookshops' commission made most shop sales uneconomic. The magazine wasn't perfect, but it had to be nimble.

In America *Verse* was part of literature festivals at the College of William and Mary in Williamsburg, and elsewhere. In Scotland we collaborated with the Scottish Poetry Library to bring Michel Deguy from Paris to read with Sorley MacLean at the 1985 Edinburgh International Festival. Once installed in the School of English at St Andrews University, *Verse* was a sponsor of the St Andrews Poetry Festival, and involved in such electrifying readings as that given by Simon Armitage and Glyn Maxwell in 1988 before either poet had published his first full collection. 1990 saw the launch of *Other Tongues: Young Scottish Poets In English and Gaelic* (published by *Verse* as a book) when Meg Bateman, W. N. Herbert, David Kinloch and Angela McSeveney read in the three languages, overlooking the long breakers of St Andrews Bay.

Such events were part of the life of the magazine, but not part of its actual pages. It was those pages that mattered most to the editors and we concentrated on maintaining quality at the same time as extending *Verse*'s acoustic. Throughout the magazine's life all its editors have had full-time jobs, as well as writing their own poetry and criticism, so the assistance of a business manager, Fiona Mullan, in our first two years, and the later help of U.S. editorial assistants Nigel Alderman, Ronda Holm, Elaine Sisson, Daniel Quentin Miller, John Kerr, Kriss Murphy, and Jennifer Ehlers (all William and Mary students) was enormously welcome. Between 1990 and 1992 Nicholas Roe in St Andrews was a co-editor before pressure of his academic work forced him to resign. From 1991 the poet and critic Richard Price has been a purposeful fourth editor, bringing to the magazine substantial administrative ability, and helping to publicize *Verse* in London. Without the work of these people it is highly unlikely that *Verse* would have developed as vigorously in the late 1980s and the 1990s. During this period, partly in response to favourable criticism, we expanded the length and number of interviews. What this book presents is a generous selection, taken mainly from the 1990s when several of those with whom *Verse* was associated established themselves as significant figures in the younger generation of poets. The conversations with Simon Armitage, John Burnside, W. N. Herbert, Kathleen Jamie, Angela McSeveney, and Don Paterson, among others, are in each case the first really substantial interview to be published. It was always one of our aims to try to get full interviews with poets at the start of their careers, confident that these would be of both contemporary and, later, of considerable historical interest.

At the same time, as *Talking Verse* makes clear, we wanted to publish attentive interviews with older, more established poets. So here are voices as different as those of Liz Lochhead and Robert Pinsky, Tony Harrison and Sharon Olds. To these '90s interviews a few earlier conversations from the 1980s have been added: Les Murray spoke just as his work was being published widely in Britain and America for the first time; Edwin Morgan spoke shortly before the appearance of not only *Themes on a Variation* but also his *Collected Poems*; Frank Kuppner in 1989 provided an interview unusually close to the spirit of his own poetry, perhaps because he was both interviewer and interviewee.

From October 1987, when I returned to my native Glasgow, *Verse* had a Scottish address, which seemed only natural for a magazine so committed to a Scottish-international outlook. As the number of Scottish interviews in this book indicates, *Verse* played some part in fostering a new generation of Scottish poets. David Kinloch returned to Scotland from Oxford via Swansea and Salford, by which time I was in St Andrews. Meantime, across the Atlantic, Henry Hart had moved from the Citadel in South Carolina to the College of William and Mary in Virginia. All this made for some on-the-hoof editing, but the mag somehow always appeared almost on time, and we made the most of generous, sustained support from first the Citadel, then The College of William and Mary, as well as the Scottish Arts Council. Those subsidies kept us going, and kept us affordable as far as individual subscribers were concerned. Our editorial mobility enlivened and some times complicated work, but also kept the editors aware of the wider world.

This book celebrates just over a decade of *Verse*. It marks also the departure from the magazine of the original Scottish editors, of Richard Price, and of Henry Hart in America also. After over a decade of editing, rather than puttering on into senile respectability it seems a good idea to stop while *Verse* is lively, alert, and not entirely predictable. It would have been good to reprint other prose from the mag — Seamus Heaney on Edwin Muir, Glyn Maxwell on Auden, W. N. Herbert on 'Radical Scots' — but the interviews seem to catch best something of the magazine's excitement and to offer most to the reader who may well encounter other work from *Verse* in volumes elsewhere. Several books — on John Ashbery and on Derek Walcott, for instance — are forthcoming in the United States where essays from *Verse* are being gathered with other critical pieces for publication by academic presses. This book does not come from an academic press. It is not po-faced. It is wide-ranging, and shoots off at times in unexpected directions. *Talking Verse* is what *Verse* has been about.

Robert Crawford
St Andrews, February 1995.

Readers in search of other materials from *Verse* will find them most easily by using the Scottish Poetry Library's index to the entire run of the magazine. This volume is being published at the same time as the present book, and is available from the Scottish Poetry Library, Tweeddale Court, 14 High Street, Edinburgh EH1 1TE. The editors are grateful to the SPL for producing this index. Lastly, we would like to thank all contributors to the magazine, especially the interviewees and interviewers whose work is included in *Talking Verse*.

FLEUR ADCOCK

TALKING TO ROBYN MARSACK

Fleur Adcock was born in Papakura, New Zealand, but lived in England from 1939 to 1947. After the war her family returned to New Zealand, where she finished her schooling and then took a degree in Classics from Victoria University, Wellington. She married the poet Alistair Campbell in 1952, and they had two sons. In 1958 they were divorced, and Adcock moved to Dunedin, where she worked in the university library and trained as a librarian. After a brief spell in Wellington, she left for England in 1963, and has lived there ever since. She worked as a librarian at the FCO, and left the civil service in 1979. This conversation took place on a cold afternoon in London, 3 February 1993.

RM: I thought that I'd start out with the standard *Paris Review* opening question: do you work with a pencil and paper?

FA: I always work with a pen, always. I couldn't possibly think at a typewriter, even less at a screen, I just regard that as so alien — it would make me feel like a machine myself. So pen or pencil in one hand, and anything to write on: back of an envelope, notebook, whatever I'm carrying round. Then typing it out — I haven't even progressed to a word-processor — makes it look finished, concrete, I don't want to touch it again. That's the last point. Of course I do sometimes. I feel it's still fluid when it's in manuscript.

RM: So you're not an author who makes changes even at proof stage?

FA: No, never.

RM: Never!

FA: Well, practically never. Unless I've made some terrible howler, which occasionally happens. I think I once put Nebuchadnezzar instead of Belshazzar, or the other way round. Once I've finished it's off my hands, it can make its own way in the world.

RM: Does that mean that you don't show your work to anybody?

FA: Not now, on the whole. I used to, of course. I used to go to groups and do a lot of that, as you do in your twenties, early thirties. In Dunedin we had a writers' group in the very late Fifties-very early Sixties, and that was quite useful. I'd been married to a poet, but I never showed him anything. Somebody dispassionate: other students, university staff, Charles Brasch [poet and founder of *Landfall*] used to come along, and whoever was Burns Fellow [writer in residence at Otago University for a year] at the time — it was easier to show people like that. We just used to sit around and chat — little gatherings at each other's flats. Then when I came to England in 1963, I found myself introduced to the Group — Edward Lucie-Smith's Group — so I went to that for a few years, quite a different experience. As soon as I arrived I rushed off to the readings, as you do, and at a reading by William Empson I ran into Hubert Witheford, another New Zealander, and he said was I interested in going along to the Group, so I did. I didn't know anything about it, and Hubert shortly afterwards disappeared from it, but I carried on.

RM: How was it different from the Dunedin meetings?

FA: Well, it wasn't just sitting round with a glass of beer in one hand, reading a poem and chatting. It was prepared in advance: you submitted poems and when your evening came they were all photocopied and sent out beforehand. So you'd go along, prepared to discuss Peter Porter or Martin Bell or me . . . And everyone would spend the whole evening discussing one poet's work. It was a bit terrifying, but I went down quite well on the first occasion because I had my entire life's work to choose from, and could pick out the best! They quite liked some of them though they weren't exactly what they were used to — they were poems that appeared in *The Eye of the Hurricane* [published in New Zealand in 1964]. Some of them were thought a bit romantic. After that, you had to keep writing as you went along . . .

11

RM: How long did you keep going? Were there any other women?

FA: As long as it lasted — I forget when it fizzled out, 1966 or '67. There were very few women. There was a core of regular people and then a floating group. I became a regular: Friday nights in Chelsea, in Edward Lucie-Smith's flat in Sydney Street. Margaret Owen used to go, but hasn't written since. There were quite often women there who didn't participate.

RM: What kind of changes would you make to your poems as a result of these discussions?

FA: I probably wouldn't make a change to the actual poem — I'd just realize that a particular device wouldn't work, or that I'd failed to get my meaning across. They were very hot on clarity and meaning, very sensible.

RM: Were they much under the Movement's influence, then?

FA: They thought not, no; they considered themselves very different. I wasn't quite sure in what way. More adventurous, possibly.

RM: Would it be about that time that people were talking about Lowell and Plath?

FA: No, not until the Seventies. I read Lowell and Berryman in the early Seventies, that was when they were being published here and visiting England. I heard Berryman read at the Poetry International — well, that must have been in 1967, I think — I heard him read but didn't know anything about him, he was just this strange guy with a long beard who tottered around the stage, very drunk.

RM: What did you think of the Americans? Were you bowled over?

FA: Yes, I was rather, but I don't think I was influenced. We just talked about them — Lowell and Berryman, that is — the way they used their own lives as material; and Berryman's personae — Henry, Mr. Bones. My enthusiasm for Plath had worn off by then. The more people imitated her, the more it waned.

RM: I wondered, because there is an early poem of yours that I thought might have been influenced by Plath.

FA: The answer will be no! Which one? Oh, it may not be no, there's one . . .

RM: 'Gas'?

FA: No! No, that's much later. There is one in which I think I recognize some Plath, looking back. A very early poem, written before I left New Zealand: 'Unexpected Visit', which I wrote in 1962. But I didn't realize there was Plath in there, otherwise I would have eliminated it, of course.

RM: Why do you say 'of course'?

FA: Well, I don't go in for imitating people. If I see influences, I cut them out. But you don't see them at the time, only afterwards. And I can see some early Plath, at that point. I bought *The Colossus* when it first came out, just before I left Dunedin.

'Gas' was in fact a sort of Group-influenced poem, in the sense that George Macbeth, who was a stalwart member of the Group, said, 'We're all writing science-fiction poems this year, where's yours?' So I thought, oh, what a good idea to fill up the long winter evenings — I must have led a quieter life then, no commissions or commitments. I wrote 'Gas' out of two ideas: one of them was about identity, the question — I don't know how to put this, I tried to put it in the poem. When I was about seven, I remember suddenly coming to and thinking, 'Have I always been me, or was I somebody else once, and I've just turned into me and that's why I'm thinking about it, because otherwise why would I be wondering?' So, are you always the same person? In 'Gas' the physical bodies are the same, but who knows what the mental contents are: they all have the same memories, I suppose. And the other thing was just one of those odd incidents. I remembered another childhood memory: I woke up and thought my little sister had got into bed with me and was tickling the palms of my hands, and wondered why she was doing that; then I realized that my own hands were touching each other — but if it had been somebody else in there with me, I thought

12

how would you identify a person just from the hands? You'd do it all by feel — a broken nail, things like that. So I had them waking up from this gas attack and trying to work out who they were. It was a bit of an exercise, a bit cold-blooded.

RM: Speaking of exercises, it's noticeable in your last collection, *Time-Zones*, that there is quite a bit of commissioned work. Is this something you especially like?

FA: I think I need to be kick-started sometimes, just to get me going. I quite like a commission because you don't know what's going to come out. You're asked to write a poem about whatever it is — say, the Tate Gallery — but you have quite a lot of latitude. It depends what's waiting around in the subconscious asking to be written about. The Tate Gallery poem is based on an idea I'd often had, that when you went in and looked at pictures you came out and looked at the world differently, so that was waiting to be written. There was one for a charity called Birthright ['Counting'], and that was just something I should have written years or decades before, at the birth of my first son, but I never had. The fact that I was asked to write a poem on the subject of mother and child somehow got it going.

RM: What do you mean, 'should have written'?

FA: Well, I think it's an obligation upon women to write about important female experiences like giving birth. It took me a while to realize this — I was rather a late starter as a feminist, it didn't really happen until the Eighties. But if you don't realize or recognize the obligation until years after the event, then you don't get round to it. And at the time, young mothers are far too busy. I wasn't really writing in those days: you have babies or you write.

RM: You don't write much about your children, in fact: was that a deliberate decision?

FA: There have been points when I've written about them, but I became inhibited when I discovered that they could read what you'd written about them when they were five. I gave a reading at my son Andrew's school once — fortunately he was off with German measles and spared the embarrassment. There I was, reading to all those boys, and it struck me that my book was in the library. Poor Andrew, all the boys flipping through the book out of sordid curiosity and saying, 'Oh look what kiwi's mum's written!'

RM: Is this a more general problem, the problem of exposure?

FA: When I was younger, I didn't notice it. New Zealand was so gossipy, of course, that everyone knew what was going on whether you wrote about it or not. No point in concealment there! People quite often say to me at readings, 'Don't you feel you're exposing yourself in your poetry?', and I say, 'You've no idea what I'm holding back!' I'm only exposing what I'm prepared to expose; there are things I'd like to write about but simply wouldn't — I've got much more discreet as I've got older.

RM: What do you think, for example, of Lowell's using other people's letters in his poetry?

FA: I use other people's experiences, sometimes. Things they've told me or things I've observed. If I think they're the kind of people who read poetry, I'd hesitate to publish it. I've written about the next-door neighbours, and about East Finchley . . . I'm sure the barbers wondered what I was doing, peering in their window and staring at their Durex posters whenever I passed.

RM: What about the sequence 'Meeting the Comet'?

FA: Well, that's fiction. It's based on a child I knew and that did cost me a lot of thought and emotional agonising. It was the little child who lived in the flat above me when I lived in Newcastle, 1979-81. I started writing the poem much later, when I was travelling to the Adelaide Festival in 1986, and other things come into it, like Halley's Comet. It was something I wrote in little bits, as a way of keeping myself sane and having something to work on during a rather complicated tour, away from my normal desk and working environment. I thought about this little girl and what she would feel like as she grew up, but she isn't the girl in the poem, and anyway I'd lost touch with those people. I made her student-age, and I was also thinking of a niece of mine who is a lesbian, and some of her

13

ideas got into the poem. Then the mother of the child happened to write to me, asking me to write something for a cause she was interested in, and it turned out that she'd become a keen reader of poetry magazines. So I confessed and sent her the poem, afraid that she might find it upsetting or hurtful, or that the child might. However she seemed to approve of it, so I was deeply relieved. As it went along, various things cropped up: for example, there's a quotation from an Adelaide newspaper about the result of research into malformations, that they could be caused by chemicals in insecticides, and that was coincidental while I was working on the poem. In fact the mother had done all the right things during pregnancy, but they were in Africa where you had to use insecticides.

I did worry about the poem. I write about all these gruelling subjects — illnesses, dying, cancer, heart attacks — and there's always someone sitting in the audience whose father has just died of a heart-attack or whose mother has cancer. Afterwards they come up and say that they're glad I was able to write about it. Once in a school I read 'The Soho Hospital for Women', in which a woman has cancer, and the teacher said that a girl whose mother had cancer had really opened up in class, had never talked as much.

I don't know why I do it. I suppose it's just a sense of the vulnerability of the world, and of the human body in particular. I haven't written an awful lot about Alzheimers yet, but that's coming! I suppose I'm getting towards that part of life where it's dementia rather than birth defects which is haunting me.

RM: Do you not think that's one of the functions of poetry, anyway, to speak for people who can't speak?

FA: Yes — or who can, but haven't got round to it, or don't quite like to. As long as you don't feel you're invading their territory. I think there's something very unsavoury about writing the kind of thing D.M. Thomas writes, about Auschwitz, when he has no right to do so. In a sense I have no right to write about serious things occurring to other people, but death and illness are common to us all, so I'm morally justified in that sense. And of course if you're in contact with them, you want to write about them.

RM: Thinking of recent events in Germany and Eastern Europe, I wondered whether your translations from Romanian were a way of coming to terms with these things creatively but not, as it were, voyeuristically?

FA: No, I think it was more a way of doing a duty to some friends, whose poetry I wanted to make available to a wider audience. They were all people I knew: Daniela Crasnaru, Grete Tartler — one I didn't know, Ioana Craciunescu, whose poems I translated for the *Child of Europe* anthology, whom I've met since. Their books weren't easily available, and went out of print quickly. I learnt the language as a way of getting into their world, of making discoveries and passing them on. It had practical results: most of the time poetry does make 'nothing happen', but these translations brought two Romanian poets first of all to Scotland, to the Edinburgh Festival, then to England once or twice, and opened up their lives for them, just towards the end of the regime. Especially Grete, whose book was translated before Ceaucescu fell.

I was fascinated by the language — it's a Romance language, so it wasn't too alien. I had Latin, Italian and French so it wasn't impossible. As I worked my way through the grammar books — the verbs and the awful, awful pronouns — I practised on their poems. I showed them to the poets when I went back to Romania, and they were very excited. They're all very well-educated and could understand what I was doing. Daniela went through the whole manuscript; Grete couldn't, as the post was unreliable and dangerous, so I had to rely on a Romanian lady here. I feel closer to Daniela's personality — she's much less of an optimist than Grete, more vulnerable — but Grete's poems I think were more suited either to my style, or the English language, or the fashions in poetry at the time. They were less obscure and seemed more accessible, not written in quite such an impenetrable code as the other poets'.

RM: Daniela Crasnaru uses rhyme quite often.

FA: Yes, I used rhyme where she did — that's fun. I like re-creating rhymes — in the medieval Latin poets, too. Their sentiments aren't terribly original now, so you can really only contribute to the form.

RM: Were the translations in *The Virgin and the Nightingale* also a commission?

FA: No, that was another obsession. I have obsessions — that was my twelfth-century phase, when I was in Newcastle. I had a fellowship there for two years, and I had time. I picked up one of the Oxford books of medieval Latin verse in a secondhand bookshop, and then I had the entire resources of two university libraries — Newcastle and Durham — and could get all the editions, in German. It was also connected with Eleanor of Aquitaine, another of my obsessions. Gillian Whitehead and I wrote an opera about her.

I don't know what it is that attracts me to the medieval — I'd also written about Hotspur: the starkness, the dawn of learning, those efflorescent springs when everything comes to life after you've been starving. And the singing voice that comes into poetry — that's when rhyme enters, because classical Latin didn't rhyme. You have to re-write these poems for every generation.

RM: Do you enjoy the act of translating?

FA: Yes, I like having something to get on with. It's there in the morning when you get up and you don't have to have any inspiration. The last thing I did was a bit of Ovid's *Metamorphoses* for the collection Michael Hofmann is putting together. Mine isn't very literary because I feel a duty to the text to be absolutely accurate.

RM: So not along Lowell's lines?

FA: Not at all! I feel that's what you do when you don't know the language very well — like Pound, sometimes.

RM: Among your commissions have been several anthologies, one of contemporary New Zealand poetry and one of women's poetry — they're in rather fraught areas!

FA: I'm doing a safe one now — safe but impossible. I didn't realize what hatred the New Zealand one would arouse — I feel I would have been lynched if I hadn't left the country! Who was this Pommy woman coming out and thinking she knew about our literature? That was the point: I was someone who was interested in New Zealand literature and had kept up with it, read *Landfall* and the books that came my way, and could go out with a fresh eye and read more of it, without being involved in all their feuds. Perfectly reasonable. And the way I saw it, I realize now, was probably not the way the publishers saw it. I saw it as a showcase for New Zealand poetry, as a way of introducing it to a wider world; as one of the 'Oxford Books' people would buy it. But no one bought it overseas, it was too expensive; in New Zealand it wasn't expensive, everybody bought it and hated it, wrote to *The Listener* about it, stopped speaking to me . . . I'm despised in New Zealand because of my 'British' style — rhymes, making sense and all that.

RM: Do you feel that New Zealand poetry has taken an American direction?

FA: Yes, but of course you can't say that because it's pointing out that they have another form of colonialism!

As for the women's anthology . . . ! I loved reading for it — far more discoveries to be made there. Josephine Miles, for example. I was very ignorant about American poets except for the ones who get published here. I just read my way through the alphabet in the Arts Council Poetry Library, and in the UEA Library, and read things people recommended. Craig Raine, my editor at Fabers, then went through the script and I lost about twenty per cent of the contents. Jenny Joseph was very upset about my choosing her poem about being old and wearing purple, which of course is a masterpiece — the price you pay for writing such a good poem. Originally I had chosen two of hers, but Craig made me cut one out, saying we mustn't have anything to detract from 'Warning', it was so good. She would have forgiven me for two poems! I hadn't wanted to do a universal English-language anthology, just a British one, partly because I thought the big Americans were over-exposed already, but Craig wanted everything. Most of the interesting Scottish poets were too young.

RM: When you were reading so much women's poetry, were you writing much?

FA: No, not when you're taking so much in. I think that's an inhibiting factor in general in my writing life — the more you read, the less you write. If you're reading for an anthology, everything you're reading has been published and a lot of it is very good, so that's offputting — why add to it? If you're judging a competition, which I do quite a bit, most of it's terrible, and that also puts you off.

RM: What do you feed your poetry on?

FA: As much as possible, I suppose. I read so much poetry in the course of duty that I want to read other things for pleasure. At the moment it's history — I've been researching my family and going so far back that I can read history books and come across my ancestors. I've just discovered that we're descended from Edward I. A lot of people are, of course, but they don't all *know*. I love doing the research — the thrill of detection. Most of my families were very humble, and it's impossible to identify all the ploughmen and kitchenmaids. Only the noble families are traceable before a certain date. A lot of my nineteenth-century ancestors worked in mills in Manchester and gradually struggled upwards, but some of them had actually come down in the world. I've traced one line back to gentry families, the ones who left wills and evidence, and then to the medieval aristocracy. Suddenly you get a historical figure, like Peter Wentworth in the sixteenth century, who was put in the Tower of London for displeasing the queen by wanting more freedom of speech. I wish my father had known this — these are his ancestors — but I didn't find out about them until after he was dead. It was partly instigated by that, going through his family papers and finding letters from my great-grandfather, and just a few things that had been saved in the move to New Zealand. I've written poems about this but I don't know whether they're any good as poems, because I'm always tempted to cram in all the facts and add footnotes setting the record straight. One delightful thought: being descended from Edward I means we're also descended from his ancestors, including Eleanor of Aquitaine! I can't get over that.

RM: A lot of New Zealanders come over here and trace their family histories — is yours part of that looking for roots?

FA: I suppose it's a sort of anti-New Zealand thing, because it says look how I belong here, and have done all these centuries.

RM: So New Zealand was an aberration in the family history?

FA: Well, it was an interesting venture on the whole for my pioneering ancestors, and I'm glad they did it; on the other hand, it was quite brief in the scale of things. Much more than half my life has been spent here. I spent a bit of my childhood in New Zealand, then a really formative part of my youth in England, and then New Zealand again.

RM: In an interview with Harry Ricketts in 1985, you said that you took on the New Zealand background 'very deliberately. It was like an arranged marriage, deciding that I must feel an affection for this place, and I did develop an affection for it but it hadn't been instilled in me before.'

FA: Yes, I remember that. We did a tour of the North Island when I was fourteen, and I was looking out of the car window and thinking 'I *do* like that hill over there.' Whereas with

16

England there was no problem. I was torn away from it at a very romantic age, at thirteen, like Juliet from Romeo.

It was an accident that we were stuck here, because of the war. My father came over to do a PhD, as you couldn't do a PhD in psychology in New Zealand then; it was only supposed to take two years, but we came in 1939. I think my mother realized what going back might do to us; she has certainly realized since and has said that she felt quite guilty about it, but it was just one of those insoluble things. Everything to do with here and New Zealand is insoluble. My life is full of these irreconcilable things: I can't bear to be away from my grandchildren but I can't bear to live in New Zealand, and even if I could bear to, I couldn't earn a living there.

RM: Your poems about Cumbria are about the northern landscape, but refer back to New Zealand.

FA: Yes, especially the poem to my ex-husband, 'Letter to Alistair Campbell', which talks about his landscape. I got to know when we were both working on a fruit farm in Central Otago. When I came to England first, I wasn't interested in landscape, I thought that was a New Zealand thing: New Zealand was beautiful but Europe was ancient and interesting, had art galleries and churches — buildings. I think the Lake District was the first bit I discovered, to my astonishment. It hit me, and meant something to me. There were a lot of things there that I had lost from my childhood, like wildflowers and woods and unpolluted streams. I'd been living in London and didn't know there were such places — it was a revelation. The literary aspect was incidental. When I was there on the fellowship [FA held the Arts Council Creative Writing Fellowship at Charlotte Mason College of Education, and lived in Ambleside 1977-78], I did read all that crowd but especially Dorothy Wordsworth. When I got to the end of her journals I just went back and started at the beginning again. She's marvellous.

RM: Did you feel yourself writing a different kind of poetry there?

FA: Yes — happy! I was rather embarrassed by it; who wants to read happy poetry? If you're stuck on the tube in a tunnel, who wants to think of some woman up there, strolling round the fells, breathing clean air? Still, it didn't last very long. I could sit around all day writing a poem, instead of all the usual things you do with a job and home and family. I also wrote a lot of rubbish. I wrote about thirty-six poems that year, which is three times the usual amount.

RM: New Zealand doesn't appear very much in your poetry, in terms of place-names, say, or particularised landscapes. Is that because you didn't grow up there?

FA: No, I didn't take it in. New Zealand friends go into ecstasy about the smell of the bush; to me that's just an interesting smell such as you might encounter in a hothouse at Kew, but not something that means anything to me. I had a lot to do with the sea when I was young, because I spent my teens in Wellington where there isn't much bush. We had a boathouse at Paremata, and used to row and swim. When I was in England I was a woods child — I transferred that allegiance to the sea and then switched back when I returned.

RM: Was your family literary — did they encourage you to write?

FA: Not exactly literary, but there were books in the house. I think they both read, not anything high-powered. My mother used to read poetry to me when I was little, as a bedtime story, and that was very influential — Rupert Brooke, Harold Monro — 'Nymph, nymph, what are your beads? / Green glass, goblin . . . ', all the Georgian poets. And she wrote little verses about us, and she'd sing them. So I thought of writing as something it was possible to do. My father had a lot of books which I worked my way through — H.G. Wells, socially conscious books. When we came to England, we were sent off to the country and lived on a farm. I was six and Marilyn was four, and we wrote letters to our parents who were working at an ambulance station in London. I think perhaps writing became our means of communication. Marilyn couldn't write, she drew the pictures and I wrote little stories.

17

I wrote a Book called 'The Blue Flower', which consisted of one sheet folded over and a picture on the cover. I started writing, composing, making up things.

When we were at school they got us to write poems — I was nine when I won a gold star for one!

RM: So there wasn't an influential English teacher?

FA: No, it was just us, Marilyn and me, living in our fantasy world. As soon as she could write, she did; she did what I did and that's what we did — no television, so there were drawings and games and telling yourself stories in your head and writing them down. We moved around a lot. I went to eleven schools in England, and each time I didn't have any friends so I reverted to an interior world. Back in New Zealand I wrote one or two poems about spring in England, which didn't go down very well. Then adolescence happened, and of course you write in adolescence even if you didn't before or after. Then I went to university and got married in my second year, so I wasn't writing. Alistair was a poet — very much published, terribly famous, in his third edition — so that daunted me. I stopped writing and so did he — maybe he had stopped already. Jim Baxter used to come round — he was at teachers' college then — and say that domesticity had destroyed Alistair's creativity, but I think he'd just got to the stage when he wanted to settle down anyway and it wasn't a romantic, poem-writing phase.

RM What made you start again?

FA: Getting out! Going and beginning my own life. I was divorced by the time I was twenty-four, and I had to start learning it all. I had learnt a lot from Alistair and his friends — Baxter, Louis Johnson, Denis Glover who lived round the corner for a while. Baxter was a great talker. I didn't show him any poems until long afterwards, when he came down to Dunedin for a teachers' conference and got in touch. Then I showed him poems and he showed me some.

But my influences were out of books, of course! We heard about this quaint thing called creative writing teaching in Dunedin, when Ian Cross came down as Burns Fellow, and we were vastly amused by the idea of a lot of Americans sitting round in a classroom learning how to write. I expect it is a help, but these people end up writing like their teachers, and who wants a lot of clones? I prefer to do it the way everybody else, I like to think, has done it — Milton, Marvell, Donne — reading books.

RM: What were you reading in Dunedin?

FA: I read my way through the contents of the university library, where I was working for three years: English and foreign literature, Proust and Gide in French, Rilke in German, all the English-language poets I could find. And psychology, history, bits of physics — all kinds of mad enthusiasms. I've never read so much before or since, most of it forgotten now, of course. I was still keen on Eliot, Pound and Auden; and Donne and Milton. Strangely enough, Edwin Muir was one of the people being read and talked about then. I permitted myself to read Yeats — I'd never dared read Yeats before because Alistair was so influenced by him. I read a lot of Robert Graves. Then all the Movement poets started appearing: the *New Lines* anthology, Larkin, Elizabeth Jennings. It was a very good university library and they took magazines — the *London Magazine* was very interesting in those days.

RM: Did you feel that it was all happening somewhere else?

FA: Yes, I did. Most of the poets in New Zealand I had actually met, and none of them had died — even Ron [R.A.K.] Mason came down as a Burns Fellow — none of them had had time to die! It was such a tiny society and so recent; nobody much you could call a poet had been published before the 1920s. There'd been two editions of Curnow's anthology, causing great rage and uproar. I was interested in it all, but that wasn't enough to keep you going.

18

RM: Who are you interested in reading now?

FA: Dead poets! I've really enjoyed this last summer, reading my way through dead poets and looking for creature poems — Jacky Simms and I are doing the *Oxford Book of Creatures*, she's doing the prose and I'm doing the poetry — I wallowed in it! People like Skelton, whom I'd only read in anthologies; Michael Drayton's *Polyolbion*... One of my pleasures when I was young was reading my way all through people's works: nearly all of Shakespeare, *Paradise Lost*, all of Blake's prophetic books — that was when I was fourteen or fifteen.

RM: In my experience this is more typical of men — the systematic method of reading.

FA: Well, as I've said before in interviews, I didn't realize I was female for quite a while — apart from in life, I mean I didn't realize that my literary approach might be gender-formed. Now I think it is, in a lot of ways, but there's a pernickety, masculine side to me which may be partly because of my classical education, or maybe that was why I chose it. I wouldn't have wanted to read English, I don't think — look what happens to people who do!

RM: You quite often write in a two-line stanza, or did at one time . . .

FA: It's what came into my head at the time! I find I go through phases about rhythm: at the moment my basic rhythm is roughly a four-beat line, though it used to be the pentameter. It can be very rough: if you look at 'Libya', you'd only hear it in reading aloud, on the page you wouldn't realize there was rhythm at all. There's always a rhythm in my head, otherwise the poem wouldn't occur.

RM: It starts with a line?

FA: It starts with a line or a phrase, but it always begins with the sound of it. Some people begin with a visual image. Bunting said, about *Briggflatts*, that he drew a sort of graph — mountain peaks — and it was based on that, on music. But for me it's something I hear my voice saying. Sometimes something quite mad — a phrase from a dream; when I wake up I jot it down. Then it goes on to attach itself to whatever are my preoccupations at the time, and I realize that the phrase has some connection with the subject, and it begins to turn into a poem. I don't always know where it's going to lead me; the end is often not in view when I begin. It's a process of slowly extracting the poem from my subsconscious, where I sometimes feel it's lurking, ready-made and waiting to be discovered. The act of concentrating on technical problems, particularly if a poem seems to need a strict form, sometimes lets the meaning develop of its own accord.

I do enjoy using rhyme and strict metres, if I think I can get away with them and not sound too frivolous or too mechanical. These things come and go in phases. Sometimes strict form can distract from the content, in a serious poem. I have to trust my instincts.

I did a reading in a school not long ago, and a teacher suggested that my poems tend to take a little wander in the middle. I'd been reading from *Time-Zones*, and I think he was commenting on a poem about my father. Afterwards it occurred to me that Horace's poems do this too. I spent a lot of time on Horace for my MA — perhaps I caught something from him.

RM: I wanted to ask you about 'From the Demolition Zone', which suggests an exalted view of poetry: 'Come, literature, and salve our wounds . . . '

FA: That's a bit obscure. I suppose it was written under the influence of Romanian poets, because I was thinking about them and about other places where terrible things were happening. I was thinking of my friends who wrote to keep sane, when it was too cold and they were too hungry and there was nothing that made life worth living, and they'd write or translate. One woman, who must have been about seventy, talked about sitting with her coat and scarf and boots and gloves on, translating Iris Murdoch. What could be the point of getting up in the morning if you didn't have this work to do? And they couldn't speak out. So that poem seems a little bit over the top for me — it hasn't much of the tight-lipped British.

19

RM: I was thinking of it in contrast to 'Leaving the Tate', which ends 'Art's whatever you choose to frame'.

FA: That line is being trotted out all the time, but I didn't know that was what I thought. Well, I thought of it in that context at the time: a poem is something with white space around it. And that is another thing I say when people ask me what a poem is, what the difference is between poetry and prose when you come down to it: something that you choose to frame with white space. I remember having a great argument with Antonia Byatt when we were judging the TLS/Cheltenham competition, and disagreed over one of the entries. Some of us thought it was a good poem; she thought it was just a little bit of description such as, she said, any decent novelist would have on every page. She's so wonderful at that sort of thing, of course, she has brilliant bits of description on every page. She said, what makes it a poem? In the end we had to say, well, it's the white space. You've got only twelve lines, so the reader has to think about it more, the end is connected back to the beginning, and so on. It stands alone: something cut out and placed separately.

RM: So everything is possible as a subject for poetry?

FA: Yes, if you could do it. But you wouldn't want to read poems about everything!

SIMON ARMITAGE
INTERVIEWED BY JANE STABLER

Simon Armitage was born in 1963 in Huddersfield, West Yorkshire. He read Geography at Portsmouth Polytechnic before returning to North West England to train in Social Work. In the late 1980's he published three pamphlets and was recognized almost immediately with an Eric Gregory Award in 1988. The following year his first book *ZOOM!* (Bloodaxe Books) appeared as a Poetry Book Society Choice. He now lives in Marsden in the Pennine Moors above Huddersfield and works as a probation officer. In 1990 he read with Glyn Maxwell at the St. Andrews Poetry Festival. This interview with Jane Stabler was conducted by post between November 1990 and January 1991.

JS: Your childhood does not feature very prominently in *ZOOM!* — what aspects of your early years would you say have influenced your writing? So much contemporary poetry depends on infant experience: are you suspicious of poetry which uses early memories?

SA: I can't work out whether I'm mildly envious or faintly sceptical of authors, poets, who can dredge up bucket after bucket of personal sediment from way back, sift it, then hold up certain items said to be of immense psychological significance. I suppose ZOOM! is very much a here and now book. Flicking through, the one poem which does cast backwards in that manner is *Greenhouse*, though if there is any direct psycho-analysis going on, it's simply this; that in many ways, for better or worse, I seem to have followed in my dad's footsteps, tested my shoe size in his footprints and so on. Ultimately, I should say it is a poem by a son, celebrating rather than grumbling about parental influences. O.K., tell that to Larkin, but to be honest I've had a belly full of the other type, you know, how much the poet would have liked to sneak into the master bedroom and murder his/her parents in their silk pyjamas. In any case, I always remember the details of other peoples earliest memories more clearly than my own, like Auden seeing his parents dressed in drag and bursting into tears, or in Church, another choirboy or somebody whispering to him ''come here, you little bastard.'' Or Lowell remembering his mother ill in bed, surrounded by gardenias. Maybe if I ever get to the biography stage, I will have recalled or invented something for myself, or Peter Ackroyd will have invented something for me.

JS: What did you read when you were very young?

SA: Well, having said all that about having no memory, I'm now going to thoroughly contradict myself. I remember reading *The Wind in the Willows* sat in the airing cupboard at home, where it was warm and very comfortable on top of the clean towels. I also remember reading a book called *The Frightened Boys*, I can't remember who it was by or what it was about. The first book I actually bought was the *Observer's book of Grasses, Sedges and Rushes*, mainly because it was at the front of the rack and I didn't have the gumption to ask for anything else. So for that particular Summer, while all the other kids were rattling off F.A. Cup Winners since the War or first class County Cricket grounds, I was throwing in the odd comment about sheep's fescue or crested dog's tail. I also remember being very much enticed by catalogues, instruction manuals or lists. But little or no poetry.

JS: Your first degree was in Geography (as opposed to English) and you refer wryly to the ''[instinctive] . . . friend in English Literature'' in 'Dykes': what was your experience of poetry or literature as taught at school?

SA: Much as you'd expect in a cattle market comprehensive content on getting the maximum number of pupils up to school leaving age with the minimum of fuss. But it worked both ways: I was a very poor student up until the final push in the Upper Sixth, and I certainly didn't capitalise on whatever opportunities did exist. I suppose I was out every night, "squandering the substance of my soul on riotous living". I remember one incident when the Head of English really took me to task for saying that Greene's *The Power and the Glory* was "crap". Honestly, I shudder now. He should have taken me outside into the car park . . . but I also remember him pointing out that it wasn't my opinion that he objected to so much as my choice of language, and that turned out to be a valuable lesson. Importantly, though, school did clue me in to some poetry, mainly Hughes and Larkin, which I couldn't help enjoying. And Shakespeare of course.

JS: After Portsmouth polytechnic you worked with young offenders before going on to Manchester University for an M.A. in Social Work — what were you reading at this time and when did you start writing poetry?

SA: I did write poetry as a student at Portsmouth — uninformed teenage nonsense really. I still have it hidden away under the bed, and look at it if I ever feel like melting with embarassment. Then when I came back up North, I began going to Peter Sansom's writing workshops, and really got stuck in. That would have been 1985, and amongst other things I particularly remember reading Geoffrey Moore's *Penguin book of American Verse*, which took the top of my head off. I literally read it until it fell to pieces, then took it back, got another copy and practically did the same again. Poems like, *The Death of a Ball Turret Gunner*, or *Relating to Robinson*, or *Dirge*, suddenly seem to open up great new possibilities. Also Williams, Lowell, Berryman and the rest of that crew, but not much of the Beat stuff. Well, bits and bats. Douglas Dunn's *Terry Street* was another book I'd just cottoned on to, but by no means knew. That line "his trowel catches the light and becomes precious" embodied for me much of what I was looking for in poetry: observation and detail, strong visual imagery related to a larger theme, a nice turn of phrase and something I can only describe as a surprising sensitivity. Funnily enough, I once asked Douglas Dunn if he was alluding to diamonds, as in the shape of the trowel becoming precious with the light on it . . . and he seemed genuinely surprised. Harrison, Muldoon, McMillan and Murray as well from the contemporary scene, plus all the Faber and Faber crew. When you're home made, and shopping for books in Huddersfield and Halifax, it boils down to what you can get your hands on.

JS: Are you conscious of any particular mentors or influences?

SA: I think it is extremely difficult to talk about influences. Pick any star in the firmament and I'm sure I'm indebted to him or her in respect of something or other. In some instances, it's obvious. Take the line "they were quizzed, thumped, finished off and dumped", from my poem *The Stuff*. That's Auden's "tipped, found weeping, signed for, made to answer, topped" *(Venus will now say a few words)*. The techniques are harder to trace; favourite poets aren't necessarily the ones to learn from. It all goes into the melting pot and it is impossible to pick out clear, unadulterated flavours. I should say that it's more to do with the serving than the supper. And with poets from further back it's more about picking up ideas or philosophies. As for mentors, Peter Sansom still forms a big fraction of the composite critic/audience sitting on my shoulder, watching the words as they land on the page, falling backwards off his chair or curling his nose up!

JS: What sort of a difference did winning an Eric Gregory Award make?

SA: I have to say that it made all the difference in the world. In terms of confidence mainly, it somehow legitimised what I was trying to do, and gave me the guts to go on doing it. To be given the O.K. by a group of people I'd just about hero worshipped, (well, perhaps not hero worshipped, but only thought of in terms of names rather than faces) was very exciting. And it wasn't long after that when Bloodaxe signed me on, so yes, I have to say it was very important. The money came in handy as well.

JS: Your work as a probation officer seems to inform much of your writing: how do you feel about a biographical approach to the reading of your poems?

SA: I don't know, I haven't really thought about it. The only thing on that score which comes to mind is a chap (this has got nothing to do with the question) who once approached me after a reading to say how disappointed he was that I didn't drive a Lada and wear a snorkel parka. Oh yes, and another chap who asked me what I thought of such and such a car, and when I passed on the subject he looked, well, cheated. I do like writing about cars but I don't know a thing about them. Honestly, I know it's very modish to be mechanically inept, but I really don't know the hub cap from the oil pump.

JS: What is the relationship between your two careers? Where and how do you find the time to write?

SA: I'm not sure about the relationship, but as for the writing, I tend to do that mainly in my head, and only commit things to paper at a later stage. I think that's a consequence of not having a lot of free time, so I find myself composing in the car, on the train, in the bath, even when I am supposedly talking to people, which must be very rude and will have to stop. There's probably some giveaway sign, such as rapid eye movement or the tapping out of syllables on the left hand. If I do have spare time, I prefer to read, but I must say that one of my favourite pastimes is listening to poetry on cassette in the car while driving. God help the poor sod who steals my car, and cranks up the stereo and gets Ezra Pound at full tilt . . . As for work itself, the firm have been surprisingly flexible about letting me have time off but eventually it might well be a case of "when an immovable body meets an irresistible force, something has to give" But I don't know what, when or how.

JS: Many of your poems embrace local personalities and family businesses — do you feel part of a particular community?

SA: Yes, I do. I am.

JS: Do you feel there is a danger in being type-cast as a "Northern Voice"?

SA: Well, I don't think it's a case of being typecast because I do have a Northern voice and I try to speak with it. Whether I'm celebrating the North or poking fun at it. Lawrence Norfolk in the T.L.S. said ZOOM! couldn't have been written in Hampstead: I'm not entirely sure what that means but I like it. Another reviewer said I had the voice of Philip Larkin but without the marbles . . . No, no, I'm sorry, I've just made that up.

JS: Your poetry blends a distinctive West Riding urban decay with wilder moor landscapes: Is this a dual source of imaginative power or do you see yourself as more inclined to the modern idiom of the city?

SA: The place where I live offers the urban and the rural, both at very short notice. The moors behind our house are some of the bleakest and most extreme in the country, but at the same time we are within an hour of about five major cities and a handful of big towns. Perhaps that's why a lot of my poems exist at that uncomfortable linguistic intersection where the back street meets the sheep dip. The swineherd talking backslang.

JS: What about the "importance of elsewhere"? Your poem 'It Ain't What You Do It's What It Does To You' is defiant about staying and working in the North whilst a poem like 'The Peruvian Anchovy Industry' recognises the imaginative resources of abroad. Are you drawn to travel?

SA: If the poems in ZOOM! appear smug or self-satisfied or whatever, I suppose that's because they are "insider" poems. They are written from inside the subject, which I hope affords them that certainty or sureness. I suppose I do want to travel, to write "outsider" poetry, but this is my territory for the moment and I haven't finished with it yet.

JS: You have written a dissertation on the psychology of television violence. Many of your poems (I'm thinking of the ones like 'Angoisse') describe barely contained force — or energy, to give it a more neutral name: are you conscious of making another exploration of violence in your poetry?

SA: Perhaps, although I always think that the most important thing is to avoid the "collusive grin", and to refer to violence or whatever through exlusion or refraction. To run alongside. And . . . I was just about to make a point about the use of language and suggestion, which escapes me now. Something about elementals. No, sorry, it's gone.

JS: Would you see your empathy with displaced figures as a continuation of any particular tradition or as a new departure?

SA: No, it's as old as the sea, but I do try to overlap the voyeurism inherent in this type of poem. That's something which isn't always admitted. In the poem *A Painted Bird for Thomas Szasz* for instance, the idea of observation from a safe distance is (I hope) more crucial than empathy for the fictional protagonist.

JS: Would you like to comment on your use of dramatic monologue? Do you find it a helpful way of mediating autobiographical experience?

SA: Again, it's hardly my invention, and in my case I would also acknowledge that in some instances it is most definitely the case of the poet failing to deal with his own feelings. Sending someone in to do the job instead. Quite dishonest, really.

JS: One of the most welcome aspects of your work has been your carefully pitched sense of humour which often seems to be located in colloquial understatement. Do you think that you can develop this line of response?

SA: Yes.

JS: *Zoom!* has been linked to the sound of an American voice and intelligence. Would you perceive any such affinities? What sort of contact have you had with American poets?

SA: Well, I've spoken earlier about my liking for American poets and their work, but I suppose the embryonic coming together of West Yorkshire and the U.S.A. is a somewhat surreal and cumbersome concept. As for being likened to the American Intelligence, rightly or wrongly that brings to mind American nationalism and American foreign policy, so I would have to take that as an insult. Like many people, I suppose I'm always enticed and seduced by a great deal of American culture as perceived through books, films etc., and I'm fond of the American voice because it's so dynamic. I heard someone the other day talking about "psycho-toxic personality" as a possible entry in the next Collins dictionary, meaning a character likely to socially poison someone in close proximity. That could only be American, and I like it. Reversely, other issues, mainly political ones, are equally indigenous but extremely uncomfortable for me. Lets call it a fatal attraction.

JS: Are painting and music important to you?

SA: Probably, I'm a big fan of both, but I would find it difficult, no, impossible to say how one thing has categorically influenced another. Maybe the music hall component in some of the poems or the rhyming or phrasing has an ancestry in amateur operatics, or maybe such antecedents are more philosophically rather than technically important, and have a bearing on what I feel is fair game for subject matter, or what I feel able or prepared to tackle. With painting, I always swore never to write around a particular canvas, after Auden's *Musee des Beaux Arts* and Lowell's *Marriage?*, because they are both so bloody good. But there will be a piece called *Millet: The Gleaners* in the next collection, which is something of a political poem I'm afraid. But hopefully not a poem which simply describes a picture.

JS: How has recent acclaim and joining the establishment (in the form of being asked to judge poetry competitions) affected both your careers?

SA: Well, this is the kind of question I'd prefer to expand on in the pub, where I could take up more time and less paper. I suppose I have some fairly strong views, not about the establishment (whatever that is) but about the anti-establishment, and about the fact that I apparently went to sleep one night in one bed and woke up in the other. However, if I could stick to the question and just say if I have committed this adultery and become a card carrying member of the official Poetry Politburo, then I don't think it's changed either my mind or my poetry. As for probation, and regarding the competition, most colleagues don't know the National from the Derby and aren't bothered either way, and that suits me just fine.

JS: In his book *Under Brigflatts* (Caranet, 1989), Donald Davie has argued that "worth in poetry cannot be determined by the committee" (he was refering to the Arvon Competition). What is your response to this claim?

SA: I'm afraid I don't know the context of that remark. If that is a comment about collective judgements as to the merits of a poem or poet, then my experience in the National Poetry Competition would lead me to agree with him. Otherwise, this seems to be a quote which says more about Davie's position in relation to the Committee, rather than his opinion about its existence. It's easy to knock the Poetry Society, the Arvon Foundation, etc., but there are other, more furtive and less desirable fraternities where the making of corporate and covert judgments are common practice, and that whole thing gives me the shivers.

JS: How would you distinguish your own work from the vast number of contemporary publishing poets?

SA: This is a good question which could only land me in hot water. Luckily, being the poet and not the critic I can satisfy myself with just writing the poems, and let other people bother about that. That said, I am extremely inquisitive as to what other people are up to, and largely in relation to what I am doing or attempting to do myself.

JS: What do you read now? Are there any contemporary writers whose work is especially important to you? What do you think of the proliferation of poetry anthologies?

SA: Going with the second half of the question, I love anthologies and think they are extremely good value. I also feel that they are usually very well edited in the way that many collections aren't (less padding) and just as a simple equation it seems to me a perfectly logical idea to have the best of many, as opposed to the varying quality of just one. I'm not saying that so as to try and put down the worth of a collection by an individual, which obviously has other merits: just simply trying to say that I find anthologies an attractive proposition and worthwhile investment. Going back to the first half of the question, W.D. Snodgrass is my current obsession. *The Selected Poems 1957 - 1987* was far and away the best book I read last year.

JS: Your own work has a remarkably traditional shape in the sense of formal appearance. Would you like to expand upon your ideas of rhythm and rhyme?

SA: Briefly, I prefer order to chaos, I think, and I find the structured and organised poem easier to read and easier to write. More approachable, I suppose. There might also be an element of superstition in terms of syllable count and verses adding up to a significant number (ten syllables per line, ten verses in ten pence story) and also, if I didn't limit myself through using such a framework there's no telling where some of the lines or indeed poems might finish. The rhymes are usually slant/near/para/loose/or half, or whatever. This gives me more scope, it seems more realistic, and full rhyme always seems like sticking the boot in. The rhythms are more variable, except to say that in some of the longer narrative pieces I easily fall into a canter which combines two metres: let's call it deacapestic, or anatylic.

JS: How do you compose your titles and what is their relation to the poems?

SA: I don't really recall. Differently every time, I suppose. Sometimes the title comes first and conceives the poem, then sometimes it comes afterwards and acts as a nail on which the poem hangs. Their relationship is often a refracted one and perhaps I look for a string of words or a word which performs any number of functions. Take *Newton's Third Law*. For a kick off it sounds good: it appears knowledgeable and weighty enough to announce the poem, and it's an established arrangement of three words. It has a direct meaning (for every action there is an equal but oppositive reaction) which importantly in the case of this poem can be applied to a social as well as a scientific context, and sets the scene, i.e. the physics lab. In the past, I've occasionally called poems ''Poem'', but not because I was trying to be fly or obtusé or Beatish, but usually because anything else would have adversely offset the piece, or would have appeared too smart, or because I have wanted to acknowledge that poetry is exactly what is about to follow, written and read for the sake of writing and reading. Nothing more. So, in terms of relations, not parents or siblings exactly. More like kissing cousins.

JS: What effects do you hope to achieve by your revitalization of cliche? (eg ''The seals took it badly'', 'Remembering the East Coast', ''he was sodding this for a game of soldiers'', 'All Beer and Skittles').

SA: I do have a long and prepared speech which defends to the hilt my use of idiom and catchphrase in relation to idiolectical poetry, and para-phrased it goes something like this:

1. It's my voice: that's how I speak.
2. It allows me to get nearer, or associates me more closely with the speaker in the monologues.
3. Most idioms or catchphrases are images of some type, and whilst I'm not exactly ''revitalising'' them I am asking them to work a little harder, not just perform their common function, but introduce a second, sometimes literal or sometimes punning element.
4. They contain a good deal of music and rhythm which isn't disharmonious with the way I'm trying to construct poems.
5. I've said before that I don't hold with the view that cliche represents a bias against the truth, in terms of there only being one truth, or poetry owning the franchise on truth.
6. I should very much like to coin an idiom. ''Bored like the man who married a mermaid'' is forthcoming and probably my best shot so far. I like to think that in poems such as those you have mentioned, my own efforts sitting alongside more established turns of phrase do not look out of place.

JS: What sort of political thrust is in your poetry?

SA: I was about to say ''vaguely lefty'', until I remembered what Sean O'Brien had said, about that second word being used in a pejorative sense by the Right. So I should say ''vaguely leftish'', although I hope in a way that doesn't come across in the poems. I'd get my head knocked off by some people for saying this, but I can't bear poetry that takes a very obvious political attitude, or party political poetry, or consensus poetry. I wrote a poem about the poll tax, against the poll tax I should say, which isn't dishonest in terms of what I think, but is deceitful in terms of how a thing should be expressed, or how I want to express things in poetry.

JS: How would you describe the role of the reader in your poems about personal relationships?

SA: To be honest I don't think I have ever given it a thought. Or if I have I have never come up with an answer. For an on the spot response, perhaps I see or imagine the reader as some type of arbitrator, especially in the cases where the so called relationship poems involve a dispute. As for the poems which reaffirm or describe the consolidation of a relationship, I don't know, perhaps I have a similar sub-conscious idea of the reader, somehow wanting his or her seal of approval. I don't know. It's a good question.

JS: Several of the poems in *ZOOM!* describe plumbing or car maintenance. Do you see any metaphoric link between poetry and practical skills as in Seamus Heaney's early craft poems?

SA: Maybe. The car thing seems to present an endless and I hope tireless abundance of imagines, common to almost everyone and therefore communicative in some sense. The plumbing has served a similar function in a number of poems, but as I mentioned before I know nothing about cars and even less about plumbing on the technical side, despite having the name Armitage. My dad was a plumber at one time, though it isn't as if we've ever talked about it much, except for me to check out the accuracy of my metaphors. But the choice of items and ideas are important, and (I hope) I am not just posturing, just as I hope I'm not retreading old ground.

JS: How do you see your work(s) evolving? What are you working on now?

SA: I've just about put the icing on the next collection, which should be punctuated with a number of ''Robinson'' poems, which I'm very pleased with. Robinson was Weldon Kees's disenfranchised character who obviously went missing when Kees did, and I don't know where I stand in terms of copyright, but I've resuscitated him and delivered him into the 1990's. Hopefully the poems will be spread throughout the collection, much as they were in Kees's collected poems. I'm also working with BBC2 on a programme scheduled for October with the same team that made Tony Harrison's Blasphemer's Banquet — documentary style with poetic commentary. That's fairly challenging because it means writing to order, rather than writing about whatever takes my fancy whenever I feel like it. But as an exercise in concentration and collaboration I think it's useful. Other than that and the usual sidelines, I've got what I think is a great idea for a two act play, but I don't have the time (or the ability more likely) to write it. Unfortunately, I have blabbed this idea to so many people I shouldn't be surprised if it's already been written.

JS: Have you ever considered writing a novel?

SA: No. The very idea upsets my stomach. Just the effort — terrifying.

JS: How do you regard the present vogue for poetic translation of or variations on classical poetry?

SA: I enjoy reading it but wouldn't want to do it myself until I had absolutely nothing left of my own to say. Not that translations don't incorporate the translators own thoughts and feelings, they do, obviously, but I don't think I'm in tune with anyone enough so as to want to recreate their whole canon in another language. The odd poem perhaps, but I like to think I have enough trouble with my own language without inflicting my difficulties upon another.

JS: Would you like to offer any introductory comments on the poem 'Not the Furniture Game'...

SA: Yes. The Furniture Game of course is that writing exercise where one person, usually famous, is likened to a particular car or drink or piece of furniture etc., etc. I wrote the poem not long after seeing a theatrical production of Hughes's *Crow* in Glasgow and I also had Heaney's *The Grauballe Man* at the back of my mind, as well as the two poets mentioned. More than that, I was interested in taking the cataloguing of likeness or similitude a stage further . . . to see how far I could push it. I wanted each likeness to be something other than an image or a metaphor or a simile: more of an equivalent. Finally, when I read it, I read it as I imagined Whitman might have read *To A Locomotive In Winter* head back and full-throated, like a sermon: ''Launch'd o'er the prairies wide, across the lakes, to the free skies, unpent and glad and strong.''

JS: Simon Armitage, thank you very much.

JOHN ASH

TALKING WITH DAVID KENNEDY

JOHN ASH was born in Manchester in 1948, and published two collections with Oasis Books, *Casino* (1978) and *The Bed* (1981). He was recognized as a prominent British postmodernist poet in the 1980s when Carcanet published his collections *The Goodbyes* (1982), *The Branching Stairs* (1984), *Disbelief* (1987), and *The Burnt Pages* (1991). He lives in New York.

DK: In his review of *The New Poetry* in *The Guardian*, Peter Forbes called you the acceptable face of postmodernism. Is that a definition you're happy with?

JA: Obviously not — who wants to be acceptable?

DK: Does the reception of your work in England matter to you very much?

JA: Well, the reception of my last book makes me feel like not publishing another book in England. I don't know whether I'm coming in for a touch of Auden syndrome.

DK: Is postmodernism a term you like to be associated with?

JA: I don't really care! I guess if anybody's postmodern I probably am.

DK: Do you find it an interesting idea, a sustaining idea?

JA: No. (Long pause) I may have done at some stage. I thought it seemed kind of chic (laughing) or something but, no, I don't really know what people mean. I'm postmodern in the sense that I come after the great modernists, whoever they were, so to an extent that's all it means to me.

DK: The lines in *Every Story Tells It All* ''we value music because of its ability to say something and not say it'' might be a better approach to much of your work?

JA: Yeah, but, you know, there's nothing new in that statement; it's a very ancient statement by now. It's Pater, it's Mallarmé, and Ashbery is very much of that aesthetic as well. In fact, of course, he borrowed a whole chunk of Pater for one of his best known poems and didn't acknowledge it. Bad boy!

DK: Would you agree with the Wallace Stevens remark that the poem should resist the intelligence almost completely?

JA: Oh, I'd agree with anything that Wallace Stevens said. (Laughing) Like Oscar Wilde, he's always correct.

DK: It's possible from an English perspective to see your work as avant garde, experimental.

JA: I think of my work as being pretty middle of the road in terms of French literature and American literature and Italian literature. If you think in terms of English poetry then it's probably fairly advanced or modernist but it really isn't. It's only experimental in the sense that I will try things out that might appear totally daft. Fooling around with risk. *Disbelief* is my most experimental book in that sense. There are several poems in there which use techniques of varied repetition which have some kind of relation to the sestina or the villanelle or the pantoum but in fact don't obey any rules whatsoever apart from my own. (Laughing) And they're clearly an attempt to write poems which are structurally musical rather than poems making loopy lilting musical noises like Swinburne's; actually trying to write something like that. Or sonata form or variation technique.

DK: Can we expand a little on the importance of music to you and your writing? John Ashbery said it's almost a constant background for him — is it the same for you?

JA: I don't think I write to music as much as John does. I probably used to do it more but once I've got on a roll with my writing then I'll listen to music. But I don't really know what the connection is. I certainly follow contemporary classical music very closely . . . Oddly enough, that's one of the things I love about England. England has a lot of wonderful composers at the moment: Oliver Knussen and Jonathan Lloyd and Robin Holloway and Mark Anthony Turnage when he's good. The list is fairly endless. There are certain things in contemporary music that I think have some relevance to my work but I don't know what they are though really, just now. (Laughs).

DK: Do you have a set way of working?

JA: I sometimes start with what I think Mandelstam called — I've forgotten the exact term — something like 'the given line', the line that is a gift and you kind of go on from there. That often happens, though I might actually get rid of the given line when the draft is finished (laughing) with typical perversity. I never set out thinking I must write a poem on this subject but then as a poem will go on it will become clear to me that I am writing about some subject. For example, in *The Burnt Pages* the theme of early death to do with AIDS and so on keeps cropping up all the time and obviously I became aware of that. But I didn't set out to make a statement.

DK: Not even in "Following A Man"?

JA: No, not really. It happened. It's all true — like many of my poems. (Laughs). The one that seems to me to speak most clearly about AIDS is "Twentieth Century" and that just began with an observation of the boys from the gym walking down Eighth Avenue, all looking *excessively* healthy and thinking that for all I know all of them could be dead in five years. I didn't have a program, it's just something that happened.

DK: What about the relationship between being gay and your poetry . . .

JA: Oo, 'ere we go again! (Laughs).

DK: In the interview you gave *Bete Noire* you said the answer was 'an infuriating yes and no'.

JA: Yes.

DK: I thought we might talk about it by looking at James Schuyler's poetry. It seems to me that what is happening there is that there's a different sensibility at work and it's what I would call a more integrated sensibility. There's the pleasure principle, but there's also good manners and civility. There's a reorganisation . . .

JA: And the size of Doug Crase's cock! (Laughs). Oh, one of the great things about Jimmy's poetry is he says all that kind of stuff without making any fuss about it and without having an agenda. It's completely a part of his life, his daily round, and he writes about it. And for some reason, the English don't seem to get Jimmy's poetry, some of which I think is hauntingly beautiful. Some of it is sentimental and a bit self-indulgent but so what! He's a natural poet with, at his best, a wonderful musicality . . . He never wrote a dishonest word in his life.

DK: There's a sense in which he's suggesting new ways that a male poet, not necessarily a gay one, might write and express emotions and feelings. Like the poem where he spends most of the time telling us how he's splashing expensive cologne all over himself and his apartment.

JA: If you're gay you're forced to be more self-conscious about your sexuality, to think about it more. And so, in a way, it's more literary even before you start to write about it. It's not something you can assume and you can't assume that people will accept it. And so being gay you have to construct, much more than I think straight people do or straight men, you have to construct a personality. You have to construct ways of dealing with it and ways of presenting yourself to the world. And ways of disarming potential hostility. Jimmy certainly does and so does Ashbery. So, John's kind of obliqueness and retiringness and his sudden startling honesty and then his goofiness and gorgeous lyricism . . . John would hate me to say this but I think the way he writes is a lot to do with him being gay.

DK: I've never read a piece about you yet that didn't mention the fact that you live in New York, that you were heavily influenced by Ashbery. Is all that something that's very boring to you now, something you feel you've moved on from?

JA: I haven't moved on from John so it's not boring. John is inexhaustibly fascinating as a person and I still value his friendship and his opinions enormously. I don't give a shit about whether people think I'm too influenced or not. I owe John a lot but on the other hand by the time I got to John I'd already been reading a lot of the poets he was influenced by: Wallace Stevens, Marianne Moore, Elizabeth Bishop, Rimbaud and a bunch of other French poets. One French poet I discovered through John and I'm very grateful is Max Jacob whose prose poetry I think is just wonderful. And very funny.

DK: Do you see yourself as having any particular place on the American scene? Are you seen as an English writer there?

JA: I seem to have been accepted as an American writer within about six months of arriving there in the sense that I started being included in anthologies of contemporary American poetry almost immediately which I found a little odd.

DK: John Ashbery said in an interview that he felt the American scene was very regional — are you perceived as an American poet or a New York poet?

JA: New York poet. Oh, you know, you live in New York and you write poetry. There's some kind of shared sensibility and, you know, the original New York school group which is Ashbery and Schuyler and Koch and O'Hara. But even when you think of that group which was very intimately connected socially and still is, the surviving members of it anyway, they're completely different. O'Hara seems to me the kind of unifying poet of that group in the ways you can relate things in the other three's work to things in his work because it's so oceanic and contains everything.

DK: Schuyler's interesting, isn't he, because he's a transitional figure between that generation and people like Berrigan who came after?

JA: In a way, Jimmy is kind of the confessional poet of the New York school though he'd probably have hated the label. It's as confessional as anything, reveals the most intimate details of his life and yet it's worlds away from Robert Lowell because it's not self-dramatising. And it's witty and self-deprecating. And that, I guess, is one thing they all have in common. And then there's a second and third generation of writers, many of whom are brilliant. Tony Towle, for example, and Charles North who I like a lot. And then there's a group who are, I guess, roundabout my age or a little younger. And there is some kind of connection but it's very difficult to . . . In a way, it just simply has to do with living in New York, so you're kind of writing about the same things, you're surrounded by the same phenomena, and there is really no correct New York school to tow, which is one of the great things about it. You can write the most obscure stuff or you can write the most utterly direct and kind of ludicrously funny stuff. One of the great things about the New York poets is they're *very funny*. You know Paul Violi?

DK: Yes, yes . . .

JA: He's a wonderful comic poet. Because of that of course he isn't taken seriously enough because critics still have this ludicrous idea that comedy isn't serious. Kenneth Koch suffers from the same thing too. (Pause) One of the great things about New York is that if you give a poetry reading, you can be fairly sure you'll have a big audience. There are people who go to poetry readings on a regular basis. So you read to large, appreciative audiences. And you even get paid for it as well. (Pause) New York is a very visually exciting city on the simplest level because you have all these enormous buildings and it's so varied. Everything is crammed next to each other. You get scummy little buildings three storeys high and gigantic skyscrapers. It's never dull. It's too noisy and it's too hot in the summer and it's smelly and people go crazy there. But apart from that it's wonderful.

DK: Byzantium's something that continues to be very important to you and I know you're just finishing a book about it — what was it that attracted you to that culture, that period of history? Was there a sense of being a kindred spirit to it?

JA: Yes. Actually, this kind of links in with the music thing earlier. I get particularly obsessed by composers who I think have been unjustly neglected. With Byzantium, you have a whole historical — to call it an episode is insulting since it lasted for 1100 years — you have an entire civilization that was routinely slandered . . .

DK: For its decadence presumably?

JA: Oh yeah decadence. So being gay, you can relate to that as well probably. Being decadent and effeminate and corrupt and conniving and all the rest of it. Whereas, in fact, through most of the Middle Ages it had a much higher standard of civilisation than Western Europe and just glorious art until the day it died. And passed on the whole of Greek literature to us. So it's a civilisation we have an immense debt to and, obviously, I love its art and its architecture and I do feel some kind of strange connection with that . . . I'd always wanted to write about Byzantium and I couldn't think of a way of doing it because I'm not a scholar, I'm not an historian, I can't read Greek, so it seemed ridiculous to tackle the entire span of Byzantine history or even attempt a scholarly study of a century. So what I decided to do was talk about Byzantium in terms of place. Reading a lot of the standard historical accounts one does constantly come across references to places in Anatolia and it was very difficult even to locate some of them. And so I decided I would set off into Anatolia and find them and write about them and the history would spring from the place so that the reader would have the impression of how it was now and what I was doing there and then I could kind of take off and tell you about the personalities or the historical events connected to it. The problem with this technique is it's completely unchronological so you're switching back and forth through time all the time.

DK: It seems like a very personal technique.

JA: Yes, but it was also a way of making it more accessible to people and I thought that was necessary. And, in fact, at the moment we do need to know a lot more about the history of that area. What is happening in the Balkans, what is happening in Turkey, what is happening in Armenia and Azabyjan, all go back to that period really. You can't really understand it unless you know that history. And the thing about Byzantium that I find so haunting is that if you think of all the medieval kingdoms or nations like France or Germany or Spain or Italy, they're still *there*. Byzantium is the great medieval civilisation that didn't make it. It expired just at the birth of the modern era.

DK: Is there anything that could be of particlular value to us now?

JA: A high valuation of literacy.

DK: You wrote in "World's Floor": "the issue is exile, how far we have come and will go in a spirit of inquiry and despair . . . Can any song be sustained?"

JA: I guess lines like that would connect with my love of ruins which is why I love Turkey so much. I try and travel there whenever I can. I'm at my happiest when I'm travelling around a ruined city somewhere on the high Anatolian plateau and one of the things I like about the book I've just written is that though I was kind of fairly ecstatically happy throughout this journey, underneath, the story I'm telling is desolatingly sad, so you have those two strains throughout the book.

DK: You said in "The Future Including The Past": "My civilisation has ended and I liked it so much . . . " That feeling of nostalgia can be detected throughout the whole body of your work.

JA: That statement is heavily ironic.

DK: And in "The Burnt Pages" where you talk about "the pangs of a new nostalgia" — is that heavily ironic too?

JA: Oh yes. Nostalgia, I think, is a very destructive emotion.

DK: And yet your work is full of this kind of wistfulness, isn't it?

JA: Yeah. It's not purely ironic. I kind of like the idea of nostalgia as part of an aesthetic but, as a person, I am extremely unsentimental and extremely un-nostalgic. When I'm in a place I make the best of that place and don't pine for something else.

Edited interview *c* David Kennedy 1993

JOSEPH BRODSKY

TALKING WITH WILLIAM WALSH

In 1987 Joseph Brodsky was awarded the Nobel Prize for Literature; however, years earlier, in March 1964, he was sentenced to five years in exile in northern Russia. Because of internal and international protests, his sentence was commuted to two years. On June 4, 1972 he was involuntarily exiled from the Soviet Union, and after a brief time in London and Vienna, he settled in the United States.

Brodsky was born in 1940 in Leningrad and began writing poetry at the age of eighteen. His five volumes of poetry in Russian are unavailable in the Soviet Union, but his first collection of poetry to appear in English emerged in 1973. In 1986, *Less Than One* won the National Book Critics Circle Award. His other books include , *Elegy for John Donne and Other Poems, Selected Poems* (1973), *A Part of Speech* (1980), and *To Urania* published by Farrar, Straus and Giroux. In 1992, *Watermark*, a book-length essay on the city of Venice, was published.

Joseph Brodsky currently lives in New York City and South Hadley, Massachusetts, where he is Andrew Mellon Professor of Literature at Mount Holyoke College.

This interview was conducted at West Virginia University, in Morgantown, in 1992 when Joseph Brodsky was Poet Laureate of the United States.

Walsh: There are many in the literary community who don't look at literature as beauty or expression of meaning, but as a representative of chauvinistic ideals — the canon, why read Dostoyevsky, let's read Kate Chopin . . .

Brodsky: This is pure bunk. I know all about that. I think books are written to move hearts, to change. There is that terrific line from Rilke, "With every muscle, with every turn, this story tells you change your life." That's what it's all about. Yeah? This rather substantial increasing deafening noise about the changing requirements of the canon, it's a cry from the future. It's a demographic cry, because the demographic composition of the country is going to change. Yeah? Those groups which we regard as minority are going to have a substantial part if not the majority. They try to cater to themselves. It's a mistake to go on the assumption that this will simplify the task, but indeed, you have in practically every school (and I believe in yours as well) ethnic slices, block status for instance through which the individual may graduate with a degree in I really don't know what, and he will not be able, she, very often, not exactly to read and write, but maybe even that. You graduate from that sort of program but you haven't read a line of Shakespeare. You've read Bharati Mukherjee up to your nostrils but that has a very small yield. The best thing you can say about that is that it has a sort of therapeutic-narcissistic value for the individual to read those things. But education is not therapy. It is, if you will, a rape.

Walsh: But then, Mr. Brodsky, do you think that maybe the Nobel Prize for literature is being limited by the same considerations, when they've given the recent Nobel Prize to an Egyptian for literature and the Nobel Prize in Literature to a Latin-American, and this year the Nobel Prize to a South African? Are they pandering to the groups to enlarge the canon, and we should hold the line?

Brodsky: No. That's not true. It's easy for me to speak. I'll have to answer your question directly. Obviously, some sort of geo-political cultural matters do play a role in those considerations. I remember about three or four years ago I was in Stockholm and I saw a man who reads everything. He's just astonishing. As I walked into his office I saw on his desk several books by Octavio Paz. He asked me what I though of Mr. Paz. I began to do a song and dance — I told him he was a wonderful poet. I told him actually the truth, what I think. I told him Paz was a wonderful essayist, far greater essayist than a poet. Still, a wonderful poet. He [Paz] considers himself a poet. Yeah, well, that's simply the ego of the gentleman. A wonderful gentleman in my view. Also, you have to take into account the role he plays in Latin-America, in the Latin-American culture, and in Latin-American letters, because it was sort of dominated by people like Neruda, and later by Marquez, whose political sympathies are quite clear cut and stupid. Pernicious in many ways. And then this gentleman said to me, "I wish considerations of this sort didn't have any play in our operation." But that was a wish that they didn't. Obviously, they do. Particularly this year — it was awarded to Nadine Gordimer, who politically I admire, like, respect, etc., and she's done a tremendous amount of good, so to speak, social work in her country. That is, working against Apartheid. But to give it to Nadine Gordimer — it was in my view a bit erroneous, because there is a tremendous South African writer far better than Nadine Gordimer. It's like giving a prize to nineteenth century versus giving it to twentieth century. There's a wonderful book, *The Life and Days of Michael K.* I think it's one of the best books I ever read in my life, at least in the last twenty or thirty years. Well, but there's Bishop Desmond Tutu, and there's this and that, the relevance of South Africa itself, and so forth and so forth. So presumably they do. On the other hand you have to take into account something, how should I say, less appealing than the considerations of that sort of thing. The truth is, there are not that many great writers around. The very fact that I've been given the Nobel Prize is the best illustration to that. *(laughing)* Yeah. Now I'm trying to be cute. Or elegant, even. The last time I think it was given deservedly was to Czeslaw Milosz. But then figures of that magnitude, they don't exist. What you have is several orders below. Those several orders below I can stand. Well, I regard myself as being there, if you will. *(laughing)* That's what I think. It's an obvious temptation to go a little bit global. They've done it before. They gave it to Tagore. You remember that? They gave it to Soyinka, though he writes in English, of course.

Walsh: The widening of the canon that everybody is talking about is similar to your notion of reading everything that is written, that you admit there are two other cultures. How would you see a conflict between the two?

Brodsky: I don't see a conflict. And indeed I would change the canon, but I would change it in some different manner. Because the canon that does exist, in a sense, has one tremendous shortcoming, it's not even a shortcoming, it's a very dangerous thing building the canon. How does our canon go? It starts, let's say at best, with the *Old Testament*, then the *New Testament* if at all, then we get the Greeks, a little bit of Rome, then the Middle Ages, the Enlightenment, then whatever's in the nineteenth century, and pretty soon we are here now. All that tradition, with the exception of the *Old Testament*, and I know the canon is very seldom figured this way, but it starts normally with Aristotle and becomes a pickle forever for the individual. Well, all that tradition puts a tremendously high premium on one thing, on the reason, on the rational operation [Aristotle's rational operation]. Obviously, an individual grows up and is lead to believe that the reason is the main tool of operation for the human being in this world. Well, I'd question that to begin with. But even without questioning, you have to take into consideration that there is a substantial part of the world where reason plays a second fiddle. The whole point is about our civilization as it were, and I'll get back to this, because I have lost your question . . . *(laughing)* but the whole point is about civilization at some point of doubt drawing a chalk line through Moscow, let's say, and whatever was lying beyond that straight line was almost equitable in existence. That's of course, efficient and sensible and perhaps the only way to run your own affairs. You sort of build that wall around yourself, your intramural civilization with the laws etc. etc. based on reason and you can implement them and enforce them. The whole point is that right now in a global, geo-political manner, in a practical manner, we get into all sorts of inter-deals with the realms which don't abide by our books. Increasingly that realm makes inroads and all sorts of ruckus within our ranks. Take Iran or Iraq, you name it. My idea is that an individual in the course of his life always bumps sooner or later into somebody who behaves in a manner which couldn't be interpreted in a solely logical manner. Rationally we should all be happy, shouldn't we? And yet, she goes away. Why is that? The next thing you do is run to the shrink or seek this advice or try to remedy it in some sort of way. Or you're thinking you made a mistake. What would be sensible to try, and this is what I do in my small way with my students. Though it's not my direct responsibility to supply them with the canon, I give them a reading list for two years. They may do with this list whatever they wish. But it starts not with the *Old Testament*. It starts with a little bit of Gilgamesh, and a little of the Sumerian text. Then I give them the *Old Testament*. The reason is the choice, the choice mankind has made. It's not the given. It's one of the options. This way at least later on in their lives they will be less prone to get hysterical when something doesn't work the way they intended it. *(laughing)* In this way I would indeed change the canon. I would sacrifice, perhaps not Blake, but Aristotle, and I would replace him with, I really don't know who, but I would introduce Batuta into the canon, a tremendous Arabic traveler who is better than Marco Polo any day — far more observant and covered far greater territory.

But on the other hand, I would either expand the canon or change it in the deliberate manner to introduce the reader of the canon to a greater display of the rational, the human affairs. That's what I would do. That would be the goal I would keep in mind. But to do it simply for the sake of putting in — I really don't know whom, well. I think for that matter I won't include Tagore.

Walsh: Would you keep its historical spread or maybe even broaden that?

Brodsky: I would do something else if you want to know. The idea which I've had for a long time, but I don't know how to implement it . . . I was trying to talk with the National Endowment for the Arts, but the thing is that when the authority of the state is in decline or nonexistent practically, when the authority of the church is compromised or whatever, then under those circumstances the authoritative philosophy is simply not available for the masses. The ony sources of the ethical education and the purpose of every society is to save the efforts of the members. Hence, ethics. The only source of moral education are presumably the arts and history. Now about history, universally in this country, people know it very sketchily, if at all. What I would try to do, is to produce a canon of historical material, that is, that we know, all that exists on record, but every event — the uprising of Spartacus, the Battle at Waterloo — you name it, I would supply it with three very succinct possible interpretations. Every phenomenon would have three interpretations. One would be the traditional, conservative la-de-da. Second would be Marxist. The third would be Freud and I don't know what. This way an individual who reads that sort of event would be presented with the equivalent of multiple choice. He *will* make his own choice. In the first place this enables him to think. Otherwise what happens is this — you go to high school, a good high school, a private school, whatever it is, and you get a general notion of history, a skeleton of what transpired, feudalism, capitalism, Middle Ages, and then you go to the university and the professor of most likely a particular political persuasion tells you: No, what happened was this and for this set of reasons. And you think, "Of course. In high school I was a kid. Now it's a serious matter. Now I'm being told the truth." For the rest of your life or for a substantial number of years, you just ride on that? It's another illusion, if you will. It's not exactly of your own choice. Maybe you will prefer this interpretation yourself. But that's the chance. The thing is that you have a choice. Of course, it may result in some unyielding encyclopedia. I don't believe it can be done in a compact manner. That sort of thing should be distributed nationwide.

Walsh: It appears that you've taken morality and ethics directly back to aesthetics.

Brodsky: Well, no. This is the way I'm talking about the arts. Indeed, I do think and I've written that, said that, and I can repeat that — aesthetics is the mother of ethics. Of course, yes. This is why the arts are so crucial. It turns one into an aesthetical being, a person with taste. They are quite unlikely to make a wrong ethical choice. I'm perfectly convinced of that. What kind of example can I produce? Take for instance a child, a little babe in your arms. You have guests and the child smiles to somebody, yet cries to another person. Well, what is that? He doesn't have yet the ethical apparatus, judgement or experience, but maybe there's some other consideration. Or better yet. How do you choose your beloved? On what basis? An ethical basis? *(laughing)* If you do that then you can wind up with a rather peculiar-looking spouse. *(laughing)* How do you choose a mistress?

Walsh: Could we move back to the issue of the canon? It seems to me the purpose of a canon is to create a community, a communication system of shared preferences. But the danger of the canon is that it leaves out whole chunks of experience that are not part of a particular paradigm of established reality, and although the canon you described is one which is more historically deep than one partly of the western tradition, nonetheless, even with that canon there are literatures of primitive histories that would not be part of the perception of that reality that that canon would dictate. It would seem to me there could be certain indigenous groups that might be left out, and the richness they might add to our understanding of their experience is therefore lost.

Brodsky: The very fact that you speak about indigenous groups that don't have a vast reach themselves is fact that we are fully capable of appreciating these indigenous groups through the prism of our own refinement. There is part of the answer. The very apprehension you have is already the answer, you see. The richness they can offer, the moment we spot it we will be able to appreciate it. In this country we are very fond of the Indians and their heritage. We begin to appreciate their heritage because it is rendered into English, and perhaps, and I'm just jumping over several hurdles here, but perhaps the better we manage our own language, the better we will render the Indians, the more we will be moved.

Walsh: One of the issues is that you never render anything without a bias, and that is the big thing now-a-days. People talk about how always in translation you make certain choices and present their stories or poems in a particular way. Hiawatha is an example of making it more palatable, accessible, and in some ways you might claim, distorted. A lot of the movement today is saying there is a distortion in all translation.

Brodsky: Yes, but it's better to have a distortion of translation than an absence of the material. Secondly, very often distortion is a promotion of the material. I think our civilization as it is rests on the translation. The Bible has been translated. The *New Testament* has been translated. Everything we know practically has been translated. We haven't generated that much ourselves, have we? *(laughing)* We just translate quite a lot of things and notions. Our languages are composite languages. And to bemoan that is simply a mark of immaturity of undualish realness on the part of those people. It's so funny, because I find myself in the position very often, increasingly so, well me a Russian at least by origin, playing a particularly English role, trying to talk common sense. *(laughing)*

Walsh: I quite agree with you that the distortion is a kind of promotion. For example, the Chinese philosophical work has enjoyed many versions, and many scholars who were unhappy with the translation, translated the material themselves. I think the distortion is much better than absence. The biggest enemy is ignoring a certain work . . .

Brodsky: Before you ask your question let me say this. I believe in bad translations, because you know what's good about bad translations, they awaken the reader's intuition. Whereas, a good translation confines the material to its own achievement.

Walsh: The biggest enemy to literary creation in China and also in Russia used to be totalitarianism.

Brodsky: It wasn't the enemy of creation — it was the enemy of distribution.

Walsh: As well, yes. In ten years of cultural revolution, there were only eight plays, dramatic plays, of so called revolutionary models, and I also know that in Russia many writers, poets were persecuted. Similar things happened in China, and elsewhere in the world. Many people feel the enemy has changed now, and it's not really so much totalitarianism as commercial profit.

Brodsky: I can shorten the trip for you. The real enemy is not totalitarianism or commercialism, the real enemy always was and always will remain the vulgarity of the human heart which produces either totalitarianism or commercialism. This is essentially what art is up against. Always. Always was and will remain. Given the size of the Chinese population, given the size of the Russian population, I profoundly believe that those nations will produce out of their own bowels somebody who will say "NO" to this and rather loudly. And will be heard. It's divine economy versus diabolical economy. I'm not trying to operate under these vague categories. But when a certain idiom becomes the domineering idiom of the state, idiom of the church, idiom of the clergy, idiom of commerce, etc, the balance within the language becomes tilted. Every society has a high pitch towards the positive, life-affirming, ensuring the inevitability or necessity of the success of the society. Well, a keen ear will always detect that imbalance and try to produce the antidote. Hence, for instance, the genre of ballads, English ballads, the emphasis on the war, the dark, getting your comeuppance. But why are they so bloody? Because the official idiom, the domineering idiom is not blood, it's too pristine. Why do we get a foul language? Why, when a young man of the age fifteen, sixteen, seventeen, eighteen, nineteen, twenty with no experience whatsoever in this life starts to write his poems he's predominantly dramatic, dark, dissatisfied with his life though he has no experience whatsoever. He speaks out of linguistic necessity to produce a counter balance. That's how it works.

Walsh: You mentioned earlier that you would like to make poetry more accessible to the masses, and as Poet Laureate, would like to put all the old poetry recordings of Eliot, Stevens, etc. on compact disk. How accessible can we make poetry when so many people simply cannot read and, of course, there are greater problems facing them? What other changes would you try to make?

Brodsky: Perhaps now we have more reason to make this observation than normally, because of the means of communication are in the hands of God-knows-who. I start with a very simple premise. Basically, my central idea . . . well, it's not my central idea, it's just simply born out of experience, but it harks back to the notion of original sin, that man is radically bad. His soul is number one — that is the idea that man is inherently good and what makes him bad are the bad institutions; therefore, let's improve the institutions. You know there is some disturbance because the improvements to the institution, the logical result is to politicize that and so forth. Well, it simply has to do with human nature, and you can't really change the human nature, but you can press a different button in the human nature. It's most grievous in the United States where theoretically you can read anything you like. It's terribly sad because illiteracy is practically universal. Okay, there are twenty-five per cent who are functionally literate. It can be given to the people, but they don't have an access, and if you don't have an access you do all those things that result subsequently in the statement that the modern culture will take against human nature. It's one thing to teach in the university and try to convince students. It's getting harder and harder to convince them, mind you. For a variety of reasons, actually there are some logistical reasons as you know, they have to do too many things, etc, etc. One thing that is troublesome, in a sense, is that our universities are rather free universities and the kid can study anything until the very last year, taking courses in whatever. There's one course he takes in literature, another in micro-biology and so forth. It's good that he becomes a renaissance type. Essentially, it means no concentration in one thing. I think the rigors should be higher — more rigorous. Or perhaps they should stay longer in the school. An indivdual emerges and acts according to the well-being of his fellow citizens at the age of twenty-three or twenty-four. This is all fine and dandy, but it's just idiotic. There was a great shudder when I saw the line-up of President Carter's administration. They were kids. Somebody barely the age of thirty-five or thirty-eight was running our policy — Hamilton Jordan.

Walsh: I notice a number of observations you have made and a number of people have made about you over the past three days, is that you consider yourself a private person. We're in a society that we like to believe is private, but I see an anomaly in that a man of letters in an open society such as ours has a difficult time being a private person.

Brodsky: No, he doesn't. I can speak, let's say, for my humble self. I came here twenty years ago and I enjoyed something extraordinary. I enjoyed fifteen, perhaps seventeen years of peace. I was completely left alone. And I liked it enormously. Then something transpired and I got into the public eye. One of the manifestations of that is my stint here, and indeed now it has become a little bit difficult. But it's not difficult in the final analysis. It's not that difficult. Though you may advance this and that thesis and explain this or that to the public, defend this or that . . . you can be blinded or confused by your public role. The only thing is — it claims time. Well, I think I've been given quite a lot in a sense, and I just may in a sense pay back. I'm not doing that on a daily basis or a weekly basis, but it's this year that happened to be hectic that way. Maybe just as well. If I can suffer as a writer for this, so much for my writing. *(laughing)*

Walsh: That contradicts your own notion that good writers are good and that suffering should not matter.

Brodsky: No. No. It doesn't contradict that at all. Big deal. If I suffer, so much for that. No, I don't believe that I can lose. All I can lose is time. I somehow am inclined to think maybe I dilute myself, but at a certain point I'll shed all this garbage. And, well, I'll just do my own thing. What's happening in no way changes my ear, my sense of what should rhyme with whtat. I think, God willing, I'll last a while and I'll just return to that. This [the five days in Morgantown] is just an escapade, an episode.

Walsh: I'd like to return to your phrase — the vulgarity of the human heart — and ask you about the impact of electronic media and computers on society and writers.

Brodsky: I was talking with the kids [undergraduate and graduate students at West Virginia University] today about that. I've been teaching for twenty years, and with the advent of the word processor I began to notice the quality, rather the [different] texture of my students' writing now that they compose all their papers on the word processor. Some go for the fancy printout and this and that. But what they unanimously have in common, well almost unanimously, universal — they all write in equal chunks, paragraphs of the same length. My explanation to that is, presumably, they are sort of mesmerized by this screen. I'm not trying to say anything funny. It's terribly sad and terribly dangerous. What's happening is that they are mesmerized by that screen, a hypnotic, mechanical thing. It's not the paper. It's not disposable, you see. So therefore, they try to fill it up.

You can't find in anyone's writing anymore a sentence-long paragraph, one that occupies two lines. It's almost gone entirely. And not only with student papers. It's gone on to newspaper articles, magazines and everywhere. Everybody writes like this. The saving grace, the most remarkable aspect of prose is its rhythmic nature, the way it is about human speech. That's entirely gone. We are adding some unnecessary things. We are getting sort of fuzzy. The great virtue of American writing always was a succinctness. That was always a telling sign of who was the author. That's my experience. They get straight to the business in the first paragraph. Now it's getting fuzzier and fuzzier. That should be somehow addressed I believe. I'm not trying to say "Let's return to the good old days to the quill and the paper". Though it would be ideal in a sense, but I don't believe that many of the people who are twenty-two, twenty-three, twenty-five have their own handwriting. But that's something else. The whole point about writing is that it's a great investment of your body, because it takes your arms etc. etc. Yeah? Or dipping into the ink pot, or if it's a fountain pen then fine. The whole point is that with the word processor it's all with your fingertips, almost no touch at all. Some animal link is being lost between what you are doing and the results, not to mention the mesmerizing effect of the printed word [on the screen]. You believe that you have said something, though you may have said very little. The printed word has this hypnotic thing.

Walsh: I've noticed that my students, even the very bright ones, choose less and less to read, preferring more film experiences. I'm wondering what your opinion is on the future of books.

Brodsky: Well, there is the future. There's still the future. I know what you are talking about, and I could be quite eloquent on that subject because we indeed are getting into the culture of ideograms, of the pictorial realm. That, I can practically say, is back to the caves, to the wall paintings. It essentially is. It's ideograms. I do believe there is a future for books, because I think pretty soon, if not this generation, the next, the television will become like the wall paper. It won't be as significant to the individual as it is today, as it was to our generation. They will watch less and read more. I think. One develops. Your question itself betrays a certain disillusionment with television and perhaps you read more than you watch. But there was a period in your life when you watched quite a lot — not quite a lot, but you did. You shouldn't deny it. *(laughing)* It has something to do with the individual growth, not growth in that positive terms, but simply in relation of the years, and pretty soon one gives up watching television so much for a simple reason: one realizes he is watching someone else's job being done by someone else, while not doing his own. This is my sense of it. If I don't watch it so much it's not because it's not interesting, but I know I'm watching someone else's job. I'm not doint mine. I could have done something else. I could have written something. Maybe I would read. Not necessarily read. I would do something different. I would write something or perhaps I would court a dame or I would just build a bench. I don't really know what. But you don't do that. It's a medium of impotence. Well, we know all that. It depends on the perception of the individual himself, whether he feels he's impotent to practice anything qualitative, to do something at this given point. Or he is. And if he is, then he will switch the television off. That's how I think it's going to be. I think literature in the final analysis is fairly safe. The whole point is that the great revenge of literature comes not from television but from our swelling numbers [to overwhelm television's impact]. We can very well expect a coherent discord of any literary matter in the foreseeable future; however, we will definitely read.

Walsh: What then, according to your definition, is the difference between a live performance of *Hamlet* and a two hour movie on television where in both cases you are watching someone else work?

Brodsky: I'm against either way. On those two occasions that I taught Shakespeare I expressly forbade students to watch it either on the tv or to go to the cinema, or for that matter to the theatre, because I think they should read. When you read, a great deal of adventure occurs in your mind. Take the simple line, "How have you been doing, Prince? Well, well, well, well." When you read it, you invest, and you have four or six interpretations. When you deal with an actor it's one interpretation. If he's subtle, he may convey ambiguity, but that's about as much, whereas, there's far more. Not to mention that when you watch something you follow the plot line inevitably, or you invest in this or that character with your own sympathy and identification with that character. When you read, it's all you.

Walsh: Two poets you've mentioned who you admire — Hardy and Auden — were masters of sound. I'd like to hear you read your work in Russian because the Russian I have heard you read is very rhythmic; yet, when I look at your poems they seem more for the eye. You know Auden's musical selection. Every one of them has drive, beat — "Desires of the heart are as crooked as corkscrews, not to be born is the best for man . . ."

Brodsky: Now your are talking about something which I think I can at this point defend. What you were talking about with those syncopations are wonderful. I'm not going to defend my Russian record. That I will leave. I know what I'm doing in Russian. But now after some point I know what I'm doing in English. It's indeed for the eye, although I think I can read it out loud as well, not all because I'm a lousy reader of English. I have to keep my eyes on the text because it's difficult to memorize. Today, and this is perhaps my delusion, I am the next generation after Auden, if you will. I'm not trying to say . . . but you brought this comparison. I think now you have to deafen your mute or musical aspects. I'm interested, myself, in verse in monotony of the sound rather than an emphatic acoustics of the words. When I was younger I tried to produce all the sound effects I could. But it's a matter of ageing, you see, and what you try to do is impart to your verse a certain aspect of time itself, and perhaps a romantic vision of time or sense of time is rather monotonous — it's not emphatic. It's even tone. I still believe those caesuras and the syncopations can be hinted at. Here, Auden comes to my support in a sense, to my side. He once said Bach was terribly lucky because in his day if you wanted to address the Almighty you'd write directly to Him, whereas nowadays if an author wanted to praise the Lord, he has to use the indirect speech. To a certan extent, what I am saying to you is more or less in the same vein — I'm not defending myself here so much, I'm just trying to explain it to you.

Walsh: Tomorrow will you read your poems in Russian as well as English?

Brodsky: Well, I read some in English and some in Russian. I read them both [the same poem] in English because the audience is predominantly English.

Walsh: Could you discuss the future of poetry as you see it.

Brodsky: I can't talk about the state of poetry in the future.

Walsh: Then the health of poetry.

Brodsky: You can only talk about the individuals and there are going to be enough individuals to make their mark. It's inevitable. It's inevitable because I believe in the human genius. I believe the material that exists already will push individuals far. Human genius.

JOHN BURNSIDE

INTERVIEWED BY W. N. HERBERT

John Burnside was born in Fife, Scotland, in the mid-Fifties, and was educated in Catholic schools in Scotland and England. He now lives in Surrey, England, where he works as a Knowledge Engineer in computer systems design. He has published three books: *The Hoop* (Carcanet, 1988), *Common Knowledge* (Secker and Warburg, 1991) and *Feast Days* (Secker and Warburg, April 1992). *The Hoop* and *Common Knowledge* both received Scottish Arts Council Book Awards. He is presently working on a prose poem sequence, provisionally entitled *Another Loneliness*, from the Emily Dickinson poem:

> There is another Loneliness
> That many die without —
> Not want of friend occasions it
> Or Circumstance of Lot

> But Nature, sometimes, sometimes thought
> And whoso it befall
> Is richer than could be revealed
> By mortal numeral —

This interview was recorded in Bramley on 7 September 1991.

WNH: What I was very impressed by when you were reading in Oxford was the concept of Palestine as a fictional landscape and the way that related to biography, because I don't know if that's one hundred per cent clear from the poem ["Palestine"]: why Palestine?

JB: That's from the next book which is going to be called *Feast Days*, coming out next April. What always got me about the Palestine thing was that it existed and it didn't exist: what was Palestine? My father was actually based in Palestine after the war. He was an Air Force man.

WNH: This was while it didn't exist?

JB: Well it was called "Palestine" by people like him; he was based in Palestine and of course in 1948 "Palestine" ceased to exist and became "Israel". When I asked at school about it they said "There's no Palestine". There never was a place called "Palestine" according to the teachers that I had. But it was on the old maps in the Bible; I was at a Catholic school and we had all these prayer books and Bibles with a little pink country called "Palestine" where Jesus walked . . .

WNH: That's the point, isn't it? That's the Holy Land, it's where Jesus actually walked. If it doesn't exist, then maybe Christ also has a sort of fictional existence.

JB: It causes that sort of confusion when you're a twelve-year old Catholic child. You want to know about these kind of things. I actually had a map which had the marks of paths which Jesus would have taken, like double jagged lines, broken lines where he walked from here to here. So it became a mythological country.

WNH: This is where it interests me. It seems to me that it's a real Scottish theme, because in Scotland historical fiction is a kind of literary unit of the dispossessed; you recreate your country, you create an independent space for your country in fiction. One of the things which interests me in your work is the use of fictional space. Again referring back to that reading: in "The Annunciations" [from *Common Knowledge*] you're entering a painting, you're conjecturing about that space in which a painting can have meaning.

41

JB: Also that encounter happens in that space. It's like the space you have in dreams, where you're dreaming you walk into a landscape or a house or whatever.

WNH: Right, and how integrated that is. I had quite strong dreams when I was about twenty of a kind of New York, where I was reading a lot of American fiction and I began to dream . . . because I was keeping a reasonably good diary of my dreams, it began to take on coherence, because the more attention you pay to it the more information you get back. And so you actually begin to build up a geography.

JB: Oh yes. Did you ever draw a map of the country in your dreams? Because I had a long period where it was actually an identifiable place which I'd never encountered in the outside world. And I actually ended up drawing a map with a river down the middle of it, and it was like two sides of a track, with this wonderfully rural, beautiful landscape with a town in the middle of it. This town actually had a bit of the river running through it, and all these bridges. It was like an old German or Dutch university town. And across the other side of the river there was a place — and I called it the Snakelands at the time — I used to walk through this in the dream, frequently, looking for somebody, a child I thought. This area was very very rough, it was like a bad part of a modern industrial town, you know, tough guys coming out of the buildings. It was this wonderful contrast.

WNH: Hemispheric. Did you live in that sort of halfway landscape?

JB: When I was having that dream I was living in Cambridge actually.

WNH: Where I grew up as a child there was fields at the end of the street, but the other end of the street you were into an estate.

JB: When I was a kid, we lived right at the edge of Cowdenbeath. I moved at ten to live in Corby, which is a sort of industrial new town. It was a horrific shock getting there, it was a horrible place. I refused to speak to people for about two years. [laughter] I sulked. I beat up one kid on my doorstep and busted his nose, just because . . . he did something to offend my mother, actually, but there was this whole thing. I was so angry about having left Scotland and coming to live in this horrible new town in England. I didn't like the English. I did like history. When I was a kid I was really interested in history; it was Scotland, of course, being parochial, we'd study Scottish history, which I thought was wonderful; it was really wonderful stories. There's one story in history I always remember, I think it was Catherine Douglas but I'm not sure, where they were beating down the doors through the castle to get the king and kill him and the woman put her arm through the door and held it just long enough for the king to escape. Scottish history is full of strong women, and women are ignored in English history.

WNH: When they're not actually being beheaded.

JB: When they're not queens or Florence Nightingale. I was brought up by women, my father worked away, and my mother and my sisters made a very female household. My memory of my childhood's always strong women, strong Scots women, you know, they hulk these huge bags around and do all the heavy work. And there's something about working class Scots women and that history that when we came to England there was no parallel.

WNH: How did you fit in eventually? What was the thing that enabled you to get on with your life? You seem to be hankering back there to a kind of ideal childhood.

JB: I certainly have a very strong nostalgia for that time. My childhood was probably really like yours, but we didn't have the estate at the end of the street, we had the woods, and a field on the other side. It was relatively rural, there was actually a pit, it was a coal mining town. How did I? Well, eventually you just have to, don't you. I stayed in Corby for the minimum amount of time, I ran off when I was sixteen. I finished my A-levels but I went and lived with my girlfriend in a town, Kettering, which was not much better but at least it wasn't Corby.

WNH: So how do we get to Spain then? [laughter] It seems a very strong theme for you; you speak Spanish and you talk of Spanish poets. If you say you build up a series of significant landscapes, what would be the transition from Kettering to Spain

JB: There are certain countries, Italy is another one . . .

WNH: Well, Italy for me was a very very strong imaginative experience. I'm actually trying to analyze at the moment why a foreign country should say something to you about your own.

JB: It's like Italy is a space in your mind, and also a country. And you look at the country and you're really looking for some kind of correspondence to the space in your mind. When I first went to Italy, my first trip there was looking for that space where the annunciation happened, always in the paintings. In fact all the trips that we have gone to Italy have been to look at art. We don't go thinking "How do people live in Italy?"

WNH: Really? When I first went there it was art, but I was also obsessed with the way they went about because it was the first foreign lifestyle I'd seen. What they did for breakfast, what they bought, and just the whole question of the packaging of things, the amount of neon in their shops. It seemed to me to be harking back to a more childlike image of what the shops had been like when I was small. So I found that aspect really evocative, emotionally engaging.

JB: I actually see Italy as a big museum. I relate to Spain as a place where real people live. But I don't relate to Italy now, I only relate to the Italy of Giotto or Baldovinetti or whoever. It's like Japan, you see these [indicating prints and porcelain around the room], I would refer to Japan or to Japanese art in what I was writing, but I wouldn't want to go to Japan now; the idea terrifies me of going to somewhere like Kyoto or Tokyo, because I would be looking for that space again that means something to me. I shared a house with a Japanese student for a year in Cambridge, and during the time we spent together we went through a lot of haiku poetry and other Japanese poetry. And he read it to me in Japanese and gave me translations which explained some of the nuances. You cannot translate Japanese. He was trying to explain to me all the nuances that go on in one word, and also the cultural background.

WNH: I often think that Japan is a very strong alter ego for Britain. I quite frequently find that the reserve of the English and the reserve of the Japanese when they're being described to me as different things actually sound very similar.

JB: And the crafts actually, if you look at that whole period when Hokusai, Kunisada, Hiroshige were working, you see a little bit later in Britain the PreRaphaelites and the Arts and Crafts movement. There's a really lovely quote, I can't remember it exactly, about Japanese pottery. These things [indicating pottery in the room] would be made by young apprentices often, and they would sit down and do them for hours, and they actually believed in cultivating a sort of boredom, a vacuity where eventually they'd paint that pot with "empty mind", where they actually making a piece of art.

WNH: Are you interested in the crossovers like — what's his name? Leach, and St Ives.

JB: Bernard Leach? I don't find European ceramics very interesting.

WNH: What's the quality that you're particularly looking for?

JB: I don't know but that's got it! That one there. [laughter]

WNH: [to imagined audience] Can you see that on the tape?

43

JB: One of the nice things about ceramics was that those were usable objects. The same motifs come up again and again and therefore they could be really boring and dry, or else you could do something really interesting, and that one seems to succeed for me. That's about late eighteenth century, Japanese. They didn't go in for anything experimental, though they did experiment, but not a lot. The Chinese even less so because, in fact, in the Imperial kilns, they didn't do a lot of experiments. They actually had experimental kilns, where they destroyed everything afterwards. They found one recently, actually, where they had been doing experimental stuff, but it was very bureaucratic there, the Emperor's inspectorate — every single piece that was to be used by the Emperor had to be inspected by these guys — and it had to be perfect. They did stuff for export that they despised really. The blue and white pattern was not popular in China, but for export to the Middle East. That was the original market, then Portugal after that, then the rest of Europe.

WNH: The difference with Scotland being that, having invented something that we can sell to the rest of the world we also manage to sell it back to ourselves. We're also bought by the gimmick of the shortbread and the tartan.

JB: I fall for that every time when I go back home. I come back with shortbread for my friends. But that would be running in parallel with Chinese taste, and the stuff they made for themselves would be quite different.

WNH: The things that I like in the Ashmolean are very, very simple pieces which usually aren't at all decorated. I like the teabowls or something like that where the concentration is on the shape and the form itself, or the glaze rather than any actual image.

JB: The most important thing with that was to display the spontaneity of the artist working on it. And those tea bowls, some of the most beautiful ones, they look like crude pieces from an external point of view.

WNH: There's one eighth-century something-or-other I just . . . I've bought a minimum of literature which I haven't really read because I find that I'm not really interested enough: what I actually want is the experience of going in and looking at the thing.

JB: It's nice to know the history of the traditions just to see the context in which people were working. It's like you talk about the biography of a writer, I don't think it matters very much — it certainly doesn't matter much to me whether Jimenez for example was some wonderful guy or not. I don't really care about his personality, I'm interested in his poetry. But you need to know a cultural framework to get the most out of his work.

WNH: I quite get off on that at one level, but I think perhaps it's a separate level from that at which I'm engaging with someone's work. For instance, we were talking about Capra: I love film biographies, I devour film biographies — and it seems to me when I'm watching the films it's actually in a separate compartment, like Montgomery Clift: I see a Montgomery Clift film I'm watching the particular presence, the acting, whatever, and the fact I know all these dreadful things about his private life doesn't seem to be impinging on it at all.

JB: You don't think so?

WNH: It seems to me — I'm sure it isn't — that it's quite compartmentalized in my mind. And I sometimes get this impression about writing as well, that these things, they sort of threaten each other, they bulk upon each other, but they don't necessarily . . . the actual act of reading, the actual act of watching, presumably the act of examining a cup or a dish, is almost discreet, it's almost distinct from all that, it's almost a thing in itself.

44

JB: Well, looking at that [back to the porcelain], of course, it's an anonymous person who made it, the artist is unknown. But with a man like John Ford, as a moviemaker; are you never watching a John Ford film and suddenly realise "I don't like this guy's politics."

WNH: I think, to be more accurate, what I'm saying is I prefer the routes by which I know something about this person, the routes by which that affects how I'm watching it to be secret, to be unknown to me. I like to have the information, but I don't want to know in what way it's affecting my viewing.

JB: It's like . . . you remember the late interview with Orson Welles? Very late on. To me, he emerged in that particular interview as being this wonderful, generous, charming old man who still felt perhaps a little bitter about everything, but laughed . . . he had this wonderful laugh. And he was talking about vicious and bitchy attacks on his work, running him down and trying to make him not responsible for *Citizen Kane* for example, and he just laughed, it was wonderful. He told the story, and he told it all against himself, then he just laughed. I really love *The Magnificent Ambersons*, you look at it and you have this wonderful shining image on the screen, and then suddenly it goes all dull, and you say "That's where the studio cut their bits in". And his friends at the time, Joseph Cotten, Robert Wise, the rest of them, while he was in Brazil they all worked with the studio, not thinking; it was just part of their job. This is a mythical country as well if you like; *The Magnificent Ambersons* before the studio made their cuts.

WNH: The other side of it is that it's from this very crucible of all the mediocrities, the studio, the hack work, that something like that arises. Presumably what he is doing is accepting that this is the nature . . . from these ingredients either it comes off, or . . .

JB: And he worked with that all his life, it was the hack movies that often paid the money to make the real movies. I mean *Chimes at Midnight* was paid for by hack work in advertizing and grotty movies. That is where you need your context. Somebody two hundred years from now will look back at Orson Welles and they will need that biographical context. The thing is there's this wonderful charming bear of a man, because you like him so much, will you like his work more or not?

WNH: Ah, but if you'd found out the opposite, would you have simply built that into a picture . . . Aren't you saying again that you've got two things which prop each other up, the personality and the art, and the way they prop each other up can be directly contrary.

JB: I did this thing which was called "English Speaking Board" Because — I had this strong Scots accent, and the school I was at got us to do this thing. You had to read various things, and then deliver a little essay or something you'd written, and then you were questioned afterwards. I chose to do my little essay on Wagner who I was very interested in at the time. I didn't know anything about Wagner's life and I loved the music — I was about thirteen, fourteen; it was like that adolescent passion for that sort of music — and I still like Wagner now. But I researched part of his life and I thought "What a creep this guy is! He's horrible, I hate him!" And for a while, actually, it tainted my appreciation of the music. I mean, he was a bit of a creep, but he wasn't as much of a creep as various people would like to see him as. But would you be able to appreciate . . . again, alright, another example: again, another passion — I refer to these things as passions, I suppose they're obsessions — During a period of my life I was interested in Heidegger, and Heidegger's a pretty dubious guy in terms of his politics and how he managed to accommodate the Nazis. And you found the work wonderful, and then you found out about the guy and you think "Hmm". And does it taint your appreciation of the work?

WHN: I have the same experience with Pound, when you're reading about the fascist broadcasts, and he delivers all these statements in the 1960s, he tells Ginsberg that he's terribly sorry about this and that and says of his wife "Of course, she knew I was talking shit".

JB: Well he was, and I think he did know that he was. I don't have any problem actually with Pound.

45

WNH: The interesting question about Pound is whether it's justified for somebody to really create a fictional mode of the reality around him in order to get at his ideal, which is what he did; he created a fictional Mussolini, he created a fictional fascism, that fitted, that fitted Confucianism, that was going to be closer to the ideal.

JB: But Yeats did as well.

WNH: Yes indeed. It is a whole argument that the early Modernists were basically engaged in a literary fascist act, necessarily, the regimenting and ordering of a culture.

JB: We find it easy to condemn people like Yeats for working around fascism, but until recently people who were on the Left and were able to actually countenance Stalinism were "acceptable".

WNH: This is getting more and more extreme, actually. The whole concept of being politically correct, in a university environment, it becomes more and more clear inflexibility of thought is a kind of qualification, is becoming a qualification, a certain kind of inflexibility, which is every bit as dangerous as somebody like Pound setting himself up and saying "In order to understand Kulchur you have to accept certain principles". I find that a difficult, troubling area, because there are a lot of views you might feel sympathetic to, unless you're allowed to think about them very much. And this is very much my experience, I think, a version of it goes on in Scotland. The whole nationalist ethos is very politically correct in a limited sphere.

JB: When I hear that the English government won't allow the planting of trees on English uplands, but will give grants or tax exemptions to people planting trees on Scottish uplands, I'm almost livid with anger. Even although I've been away from Scotland for so long, and couldn't really claim to be Scottish Nationalist, or really in touch with Scotland at all now, that made me so very angry. But it's those sorts of things, the abuse of the landscape.

WNH: Would you call yourself an exile?

JB: No, I just don't live in Scotland any more [laughter]. I'd like to go and live there again, not necessarily in Scotland — I'm not really too hung up on the Scottish thing — but I am very interested in the Gaelic or the Celtic thing. When I move around in Scotland, or even Cornwall or wherever, it's a feeling of relaxing. Here in the Home Counties with all these Anglo-Saxons who have these materialist attitudes — it really is that, it sounds ridiculous, harking back to something that's been mixed out pretty well now, but there are certain attitudes, materialist attitudes, which are very Anglo-Saxon. This is what we were saying, about the attraction to Spain, and the Spanish poets, they're not afraid to talk about the soul, or death, or these abstract things that bother the English.

WNH: Right, so you're talking about metaphysics in a sense, aren't you? You're saying there's a whole aspect of metaphysics as opposed to a conventional . . .

JB: I find the word "metaphysics" disturbing because of my interest in philosophy.

WNH: The unification of metaphysics and philosophy may be a while off, but what I'm saying is that metaphysics is a very traditional Scottish notion, and what you're doing is placing a metaphysical conception of, maybe, what a poet does?

JB: I think the English would be happier with poems about vacuum cleaners.

WNH: [laughing] Oh the vacuum cleaner can be a beautiful object, and the Hoover Building is becoming an icon.

46

JB: It's just that there's this feeling that you shouldn't really talk about the soul. The soul doesn't exist, it's a metaphysical thing. I like early Wittgenstein more than the later Wittgenstein, and the thing that interests me about the early stuff is about showing, the whole idea about showing. And it seems to me that the activity of the poet as opposed to the prose writer is, the prose writer is concerned with what Wittgenstein says you can say about the world, and the poet is trying to get into that area, and work in that area where you can't say about the world, you can only show. And an interesting poem for me is one that shows, and that's why I would be interested in Geoffrey Hill rather than whoever. Jimenez and Guillen and other Spanish poets who interest me, their poems are about showing.

WNH: So is it a visionary poetry? What you seem to be saying is akin to the idea that there is information which is useful, and then there is a work, be it an artwork or an actual artifact, which is a kind of expression, a kind of event. These pots are events rather than something which is purely limited by whether it was intended for a foreign market or an internal market. What you are saying reminds me quite strongly — as I say I came with a few bits and bobs in my head — and one of the phrases which struck me quite strongly is a poem "Psyche" — in *The Hoop* where you say "the soul is a dialect, perhaps". This concept of taking something which is not part of normal discourse, the soul, the metaphysical reality, and putting it with the difficult linguistic entity, whatever that is. For me, the word "dialect" in this country always means Scots dialect, but that's clearly not generally true . . .

JB: But it's about marginalized language, it's a local form of communication. The traditions that have always been parallel . . . there's the orthodox, prose if you like, view of the world, in terms of organisation, where people who are interested in intellect or pride or assertion of something can operate within that framework. So you have the church. And then there's the parallel tradition of *gnosis*, or that sort of Buddhism . . .

WNH: Or the Franciscans.

JB: . . . or the Franciscans — well, the Franciscans did some pretty dubious stuff . . .

WNH: Ah but there's a great film about St Francis, was it Visconti?

JB: Ah, I hate that film! It's horrible!

WNH: I stood and watched almost all of that film in a shopping centre in Glasgow. Silent movie, because I couldn't get at the script. I was waiting for a train, and I noticed it was on. I watched the whole thing on Radio Rentals. Maybe the dialogue was not important, but it was full of very lovely images.

JB: You know what? As far as I'm concerned there's really only one religious film. *The Gospel According to Matthew* by Pasolini. Superb film. Wonderful wonderful wonderful film. But there's those two traditions, yeah? And the poetry that interests me will always belong to that other tradition, the Gnostic tradition if you like. And every now and then, the main tradition, the power-based tradition, gets up stomps all over the other one, and tries to get rid of the Gnostics and the seers and the poets.

WNH: Do you feel this is what happens in a small way when you are described as a nature poet, or when you are described as a poet of the suburbs?

JB: Well I think they are to a certain extent valid at that particular time, I mean *Common Knowledge* was about living in a suburb, a lot of it anyway. Though I wrote about the Annunciation there, which has nothing to do with suburbs. But I think if people want to have a categorisation, they want sort of a handle . . . but it would be very difficult to put in a blurb or a newspaper review "This book's really about the soul". Also, because the things which get marginalized are actually very dangerous because they attract the people who are going to use that area to bring out their own spiritual materialism, if you like. There's a wonderful book called *Cutting through Spiritual Materialism,* by Rinpoche Trompe, all about all those Western people who go out there and become Buddhists.

WNH: Is that the one with the thing about washing dishes in it? He's talking about washing up in a monastery and you've got these piles and piles of bowls from all the monks and you've got a couple of husks and cold water to wash them in, and whether you're going to wash the bowls, or whether you're going to try and get through this so you can get on with the next part of your life. He's saying "Just wash the bowls". There's a wonderful image there of the self being like a bottle tossed into the water, and the person who is not washing these bowls, you're just a bottle tossed in the water. It's such a beautiful image because it's an image of lack of control, but also for us, very strongly, the Western cultural image, the cartoon image, is of the bottle with the message in it. I find that a very powerful expression of what we do when we're engaged in writing as opposed to living.

JB: I see writing as a work. They used to talk about the Great Work, magicians and alchemists, and the Great Work was . . . and there were various metaphors. And the Great Work was realising fullness. And to me writing is the discipline that is given to me as making those pots were to that person. And I'm not concerned to write clever poems that will please everybody and look like poetry, I'm interested in writing the poems that come. I don't actually write any of the poems that I write anyway, I let them happen, I don't stop them. The Great Work as far as I am concerned is moving myself out of the way of the poems so that they can come and they end up on the paper. It's not me trying to say anything, like me saying "Here I am, in the late twentieth century, with certain preoccupations". Occasionally it bothers me that I don't write poetry that's more political. And then I think "I can't do anything about this". Except impose, or superimpose, on a poem, political concerns that I have. I've done it, and spoiled poems, or else concocted poems which don't actually work, and thrown them away. I wrote a three-piece poem about Palestine, which a certain editor was smart enough to see that it was not really a poem at all. It's very important to have that discipline, and that is discipline.

WNH: In a sense this comes back to the resacralization of things. Are you saying there that the topics, the painting, the suburbs in the early morning, whatever, are the things that are left in the way?

JB: No, not at all. It just so happens that at this period of my life the most valid moments that I have happen to be, mostly, in the twilight times, in the early morning and late at night, when I'm on my own. And I live in a suburb, so it's happening in a suburb. I could live in a desert and it would be something different perhaps. But what really matters to me is when I feel real, sort of full, only happens when I'm alone, really. Authenticity is happening then, you're in touch then. With other people around, it's very difficult because they cloud things, they get in your way, they draw you back to you.

WNH: The point I'm trying to make is just whether you're heading for a kind of absolute idealism of the poem, you know, the Wallace Stevens' "Notes Towards a Supreme Fiction", or whether there is a kind of experience, a reality, which is simply usefully expressed in a verse, in a given moment, in the way that a pot is a useful instrument.

JB: Guillen's work, all of his work, is treated as far as he was concerned as one big book, actually one big poem. It wasn't the fashioning of artefacts, like with pots, but actually a continuous process. And that interests me, in some of the things he said about that process for him. From your own point of view — from my point of view, your point of view — you make the poem, and when it's finished, it's on the paper, other people are consuming it, as it were, it's gone by for you, it's like a wave, a ripple that's gone downstream and you're here. The only thing that matters, really, now, is the poem that's happening now, or the moment that's happening now. And the freezing of that into an artefact isn't the main concen; obviously there's something there, something that you do want to communicate to people . . .

WNH: Again, you're not trying to make a by-product of the experience, though? You know, the excreta of the experience is the poem.

JB: [laughter] No, not at all. But if you got attached to the product, to the artefact. I think that's where you would fail. When you started looking at the poem as an expression of you, as an event that's somehow to do with your ego. I really like the idea of ego-free poetry. Ego-free anything actually.

AMY CLAMPITT

INTERVIEWED BY EMILY B. TODD.

Amy Clampitt was born in New Providence, Iowa, in 1920, and lived on a farm in that same town until leaving for Grinnell College. After graduating with a degree in English in 1941, Clampitt moved to New York City, where she worked as an editor at Oxford University Press, a reference librarian at the Audubon Society, and also as a freelance writer and editor. She began writing poetry and prose early on in her life, but did not begin publishing poems until the 1970s when her first collection *Multitudes, Multitudes* was brought out by a small press in 1973 and her first poem was accepted by *The New Yorker* in 1978. It was the publication of *The Kingfisher* by Alfred A. Knopf in 1983, however, that marked Amy Clampitt's debut as a well-respected and highly-praised contemporary poet. The collection met immediately with great critical acclaim and was followed by three other books of her poetry, also brought out by Knopf in the US and by Faber in the UK: *What the Light Was Like* (1985), *Archaic Figure* (1987), and *Westward* (1990); *A Silence Opens* will appear in 1994. Amy Clampitt has also written several essays, many of which are collected in *Predecessors, Et Cetera* (The University of Michigan Press, 1991), and a play about the Dorothy Wordsworth circle entitled "Mad With Joy," which was produced in March 1993. A recipient of a MacArthur Fellowship, as well as a Guggenheim Fellowship and an American Academy and Institute of Arts and Letters Award, among many other awards and honors, Clampitt, over the past decade, has combined her writing with teaching, holding writer-in-residence posts at several universities and colleges including the University of Wisconsin, Milwaukee, The College of William and Mary, Amherst College, and Smith College. Amy Clampitt lives in New York City.

This interview was conducted through the post in June 1993.

EBT: Could you talk about the writing — and other kinds of work — you did before the publication of *The Kingfisher,* which seemed to mark the beginning of a prolific decade for you?

AC: By the 1960s, I had reluctantly concluded that I must be a poet if I was a writer of any kind, but I had little confidence about ever getting anything published. I had written a fair number of poems — dozens, scores, I don't know — by the time Howard Moss happened to accept one for *The New Yorker.* That was in 1978. I don't think that anything I had written up until then was vastly different from what I have written since, though I would like to think I had gotten more economical with phrasing.

EBT: In your collection of essays *Predecessors, Et Cetera,* you write about Wordsworth in 1990, quoting verses from Wordsworth's poetry that bear relevance to contemporary events. The essay brought to my mind, of course, Wordsworth's own address to a predecessor: "Milton! thou shouldst be living at this hour: England hath need of thee." How do you conceive of a poet's role in (or contribution to) society?

AC: At least since the 1960s, I've had an urge to refer in some way to public issues — which is not the same as speaking for any identifiable group or point of view. There's a lot of fractious poetry being written; I've written some of it myself. What I'm really concerned with — as I think most poets are — is with keeping limber, with maintaining what I have to call a subversive attitude, the opposite of going along with anybody's program whatever. It amounts to wariness about being co-opted. Since part of being co-opted means having to accept somebody else's language. I see this wariness as a particular function of poets.

EBT: On the subject of Wordsworth again, I know you have taken an interest in William and Dorothy Wordsworth (you've even written a play about Dorothy) as well as the other Lake Poets. Could you talk about your interest in this circle of people — and why Dorothy seems especially to have captured your imagination?

AC: All along, without having thought about it all that much, the English Romantic tradition is the one I must have felt I belonged to. Wordsworth and Coleridge and especially Dorothy have been a special concern of mine for a decade now, ever since my visit to Grasmere in the spring of 1983. And for much of that decade I found myself thinking about, and getting ready to undertake, and finally — with many, many revisions — actually writing a play with Dorothy as its central character. Under the title "Mad with Joy," it was given a staged reading by the Poets' Theatre in Cambridge (Massachusetts) on March 1 of this year. A lot of care went into that one evening — sets, costumes, direction, and the performances themselves — and I look back on it as about the most thrilling thing I ever had a part in.

Some people who saw it told me they saw a lot of *me* in the character of Dorothy. I hadn't been aware of anything but a reader's delight in her transparent rendering in her journals of the way she lived, close to the world of the seasons and flowers and the changes in the weather. But there were also entries — like the one where her brother has just left on a journey, and she's feeling desolate, and she writes, "Here is one of his bitten apples. I can hardly bear to throw it into the fire" — entries hinting as well at a huge repressed tragedy, which found expression only later in her life when she went mad. The Wordsworth household was a real pressure cooker, with or without the presence of Coleridge (who turns out to have been no less tragic). All kinds of people left records of what went on there, including Thomas De Quincey, who becomes the narrator of the final — or, anyhow, current — version of the play.

The kind of thing that I love about opera — people belting it out at the top of their voices — has a perverse fascination for me, I guess, and has something to do with my wanting to write a play. And it's counter to the advice I've more or less absorbed from the whole Brooks and Warren approach to writing poetry: that it's a bit vulgar to make that much noise. I'm naturally noisy, a trait nobody appreciates in a small child, so a painful part of my education has been trying consciously not to overdo things, to avoid being excessive. But part of me is still a rebel against that education. A play in which the central character goes mad is a sort of license to cut loose. So maybe the people who saw the author in the character of Dorothy may have been right, after all.

EBT: Where or how does a poem begin for you? Is it in a moment you observe? Or a phrase you overhear? How do your poems grow and take shape?

AC: I suppose every beginning is more or less fragmentary. More often than not, the fragments I try to bring into a poem never really cohere, so when they do there is some coming together of things that have no ostensible connection beforehand. Sometimes I have a kind of story to tell. As a one-time would-be writer of fiction, I'm generally aware of narrative possibilities — what happened before what — or, anyhow, a sequence of some kind. It's always easier for me to finish a poem once I find that sequence. Sometimes the links are not syntactically expressed: there are gaps, silences on the page. On the other hand, recurrences, images, or even phrases that link up and come full circle are the kind of things that often seem to come to me naturally as a poem gets itself finished.

EBT: You have described yourself as a "poet of place" ["Interview," *Predecessors, Et Cetera,* 1991], yet your poetry does not strike me as particularly regional as much as rooted in a variety of places — Maine, New York, Italy, England, Greece, and the Midwest. (*What the Light Was Like* even names its sections according to various places — "The Shore," "The Hinterland," "The Metropolis.") Do you feel particularly connected to any one of these places? Are there places that have been especially important to your poetry (maybe have lent themselves easily to metaphor)? And are they the same ones that have been important in your life?

AC: No, I don't think of myself as a regional poet — I'm too much of a nomad to be rooted anywhere. In fact, I'm ready by now to revise that earlier description of myself and to declare that I'm not a poet of place but of *displacement*. The one thing I've written lately that (I think I can say) more of me went into than any other is a poem called "Sed de Correr." The title comes from Cesár Vallejo, and its theme is precisely this increasing sense of displacement that I've had as the century comes to an end. Not that the displacement is new — it's what our entire history is all about; but it's just that I myself got grabbed by it.

This isn't the whole answer to your question, of course. I have been grabbed by particular places, some of them because they were entirely new to me, as the coast of Maine was; sometimes because I'd read about them beforehand, as in England and Greece. I love remembering places where I've been and may never go again. The Midwest is special because it was where I started, where my earliest memory is lodged, and for that very reason the hardest of all to write about.

EBT: Many of your poems reflect a naturalist's eye and are very grounded in the physical, natural world. How does it feel to be a contemporary poet who writes about nature, when so many other poets today do not?

AC: I'm not really a naturalist, but from an early age I was encouraged to notice what grew and to want to know the names of flowers and birds. I can't imagine growing up without all that. I haven't really thought of myself as exceptional in writing about the natural world. In fact, there are enough readers who get turned on by the same kind of things that I do, so I don't terribly mind having people say, as they sometimes do, "Where do you get all those words from?" since quite a lot of them turn out to be botanical ones.

EBT: You also play the part of an archaeologist, observing artifacts, finding signs of the past. (I'm thinking of "Beach Glass" and "Salvage," which ends with the phrase "The pleasures of the ruined," as well as the poems in *Archaic Figure*, which look at both ancient lives and objects.) What are the "pleasures of the ruined" for you?

AC: Living as I have for most of my life in New York City, I've been exposed to a nature that has a lot of junk ground up in it — a vacant-lot, pigeon-roost kind of nature. I do have a fondness for discards, human and otherwise. It comes out of my resistance (which is any poet's) to other people's versions of what is worth noticing.

I suppose there is an anomaly when it comes to my wistfulness towards the great monuments of the past, in that it, that wistfulness, has a component of taking someone else's word for what's important. But in any case, as one who has felt uprooted from an early age and conscious of the thinness of the culture around me, I've yearned for a connection with whatever in the world has endured in whatever condition, and that means a fondness for ruins, I think.

EBT: The titles of your poetry — "Dancers Exercising" or "Vacant Lot with Tumbleweed and Pigeons," for example — sometimes resemble titles of paintings, and the poems themselves abound in minute detail and careful observations and framing. Do you feel that your work is akin at all to that of a visual artist?

AC: I've always gravitated toward painting and the visual arts generally. During my early years in New York, I had more to do with painters or, at any rate, felt more at home with them than with most literary people. I always had an eye for light and colour that ran in tandem with my ear for language. Not being able to draw, to render the texture of things I saw, such as the way the branches of a particular kind of tree are just not like those of any other, I found myself exploring what words could do as an equivalent to drawing and brushwork. Giving a descriptive poem a painterly title may also be a cue to the reader that it's just a sketch, and not to expect anything more than that.

EBT: The section of poems about Keats in *What the Light Was Like*, "Voyages: A Homage to John Keats," and the poems "George Eliot Country," and "Margaret Fuller, 1847" all represent imaginings of other writers' lives. I'm interested in the composition of these poems. Do you find yourself imagining what would have happened to your sensibility in their circumstances?

AC: Like most bookish people, I've been drawn to whatever I could learn of the lives of the writers whose works thrilled me. In fact, I find it hard to separate the work from the person. That being so, I've long seen the novels of George Eliot as a gloss on the life of the actual Mary Ann Evans. I have a great reverence for the actually experienced as opposed to the merely imagined. That's why a really good biography can be more thrilling than any fiction. Elizabeth Bishop (I think it was) once said that the letters of Keats were better than the poetry. There's something in that, even for a total admirer like me. I wouldn't love the poems quite so much if I weren't so devoted to the person I know to have written them. When it comes to a figure like Margaret Fuller, it's the life that remains the inspiration. I suppose it's the would-be storyteller asserting herself — but it's an intense personal identification with a person who in some sense is still alive that led me to write these poems.

EBT: Your notes at the back of each book so thoughtfully anticipate your readers' questions (as well as suggest an extraordinary amount of research). Do you imagine your readers when you write? Who do you imagine?

AC: The idea of notes came from a friend who said she would find a particular poem of mine "easier to get into" if it had marginal glosses. I wasn't about to go in for those, but it occurred to me that I'd been helped by back-of-the-book annotations myself, so why not? In a sense, I've been writing notes for that same friend from that day to this. But those notes are also tributes, homages, reminders to myself of a debt incurred, often to rather obscure sources.

EBT: There seems to be a tension in your work between honoring continuity yet feeling exiled from your roots, always changing, being propelled forward. "Black Buttercups," to my mind, speaks to this exile most powerfully; whereas other poems mark strong connections with nature and the past. What do you feel exiled from? And what, conversely, provides the continuity?

AC: I've hinted at an answer to this in what I've said about being, or not being, a poet of place. There's a paradox, as you suggest — but the human psyche is a bundle of paradoxes. Poems such as "The Woodlot," "Imago," and especially "Black Buttercups" go very far back into my particular childhood experience. I've given a more circumstantial account of that experience in a prose piece called "Providence," one of a collection of essays edited by Michael Martone and published by the University of Iowa Press a year or so ago; the book is called *Townships*. My own particular feeling of uprootedness is centered on the experience in my tenth year, of moving from one house to another, three miles apart. It was, on the face of it, as simple as that. But, of course, that isn't all. The sense of not being at home in the very landscape that contained my earliest memories is something I seem to have been living with from the start. I was conscious of trying to understand that feeling, by going back to the lives of my pioneer grandparents, when I wrote the long poem "The Prairie." I can't be sure how many native Midwesterners share that sense, but it's hardly too much to say that it made a writer of me.

MARK FORD

TALKING TO GRAHAM BRADSHAW

Like his poems, Mark Ford is not easy to pin down. Born in Nairobi in 1962, he studied at Oxford and Harvard, taught English at Lincoln College Oxford and University College London, and is currently living in Japan and teaching at Kyoto University. A selection of his poems first appeared in *New Chatto Poets Two* (1989); in 1992 Chatto & Windus published *Landlocked*, Ford's first full collection. In England, the poems seemed to Michael Hoffman ''unmistakably mid-Atlantic'' (*TLS*); in the United Stated, John Ashbery related them to a ''specifically English'' tradition ''which bubbles up everywhere'' (*P.N. Review*). After hailing *Landlocked* as ''one of the most refreshing books of poetry I have seen in years'', Ashbery observed that ''Ford's poetry is light and agile and sometimes sweet, but it also has a disconcerting way of turning sharp and naughty and even sinister — the turns, and not their direction necessarily, keep it alive on the page and sometimes aloft over it.'' In other words, landlocked it isn't. Rather, as Ashbery put it, *Landlocked* alludes to ''the imaginary world of geography books where, as Baudelaire said of Constantin Guys, 'the observer is a prince who enjoys travelling everywhere incognito.'' This interview was conducted in Kyoto in July 1992.

G.B.

GB: I'd like to begin by asking about Hugo Williams's admiring but rather strange comment on the backjacket of *Landlocked*: ''Mark Ford does for the 1960s what T.S. Eliot did for the 1890s. . .'' What do you think he's getting at here?

MF: I'm not exactly sure. I am, I suppose, obsessed with certain aspects of the sixties but I do try and keep this very much to myself, as a sort of dark secret — I really don't want to impose it on anyone else. I don't think there's anything specifically about the sixties in the book — you know, there are no references to Haight-Ashbury or Woodstock or The Factory — but probably I listen so much to music from the sixties that a general impression of the era may have filtered through into some of the poems. The sixties are a very unhip decade to be evoking so I probably shouldn't be admitting all this. In fact I was only eight years old when they ended so I don't know much about them first-hand — the only sixties-ish memory I have comes from when I was about five and we were living in Chicago and a neighbour's son came back from Vietnam without a leg. Of course a lot of things from then haven't worked well, *Easy Rider* and psychedelia and so on, but, still, if I had to pick the art of any decade since the war it would probably be the sixties. In both politics and culture there's been a rather numbing reaction against that time — Thatcherism sometimes seems the final gruesome antithesis of all that radicalism. . . But I'm no good at this sort of cultural generalization, and don't really believe in it either. I suppose all you can say is that pretty well all poetry reflects the spirit of the time at which it was written, whether consciously or unconsciously.

GB: A lot of the poems in the book seem to me to be dramatic. Would you agree with this?

MF: Yes, they're all dramatic really, at least in that I think it would be impossible to identify me personally with any thing expressed in any of the poems. I guess that's just a way of saying that they're not confessional. Nothing specific that has happened to me as an individual has ever seemed important enough to be put in a poem. . . or maybe it's that my personal experience is *too* important for poetry. . . Well, for whatever reason, I never write directly about myself. Also poetry, like any other art, is a way of escaping from the boring conundrums of everyday life, the loops of one's consciousness, and an opportunity to be someone else. But I've never used specific *dramatis personae* like in a Browning monologue either — it's more just a question of the delight I get from using types of diction I'd never myself normally use. . . An example of this would be, say, in "High Performance" when the poem has the phrase "a super intelligence." I would never myself say someone had a "super intelligence", but I know people who might use that phrase and there is a terrific liberation and excitement for me in employing it in a poem. . . Don't ask me why.

GB: Might this be connected with Keats's idea of "negative capability"? Is the "chameleon poet" your ideal?

MF: It might come from there, I suppose. Keats has always been one of my favourite poets since I first read him at school when I was about fifteen. This is a very common thing. I've just been teaching a Romantic poetry course for the British Council out here in Kyoto and once again at the end of it everyone said they liked Keats best. . . He does have this amazing ability to create lives utterly different from his own, yet not in a deliberate calculating way. And yet it's not as if he's thereby concealing his own life. In a bizarre way you get both the love story of Madeline and Porphyro in "The Eve of St. Agnes" *and* Keats himself having an ordinary evening in Winchester. . . I chose the epigraph for *Landlocked* from Keats — it's a tiny poem he wrote probably when he was very young, though the date's not known: "O grant that like to Peter I / May like to Peter B. / And tell me lovely Jesus Y / Old Jonah went to C." It somehow captured everything that I like about his poetry, the joy it takes in other identities as well as the impossibility of ever really escaping one's "sole self", which tied in with the idea of being landlocked and so on.

GB: How thematically coherent is the book then? Is the concept of being landlocked operative in every poem?

MF: Well, I hope not, in that I'm not that keen on collections that are *too* carefully organized. Paul Muldoon is probably my favourite of all younger poets writing today, but I sometimes wonder if some of his books, which are all wonderfully intelligent and humorous, aren't slightly overplotted. Everything fits together with an almost sickening thoroughness — but that's probably his point. The links between the poems in *Landlocked* aren't nearly so deliberative. . . Actually I was joking about this with my editor Mick Imlah the other day, and we agreed that whatever unity our books had derived more from recurring personal weaknesses than artful manipulation of significant themes. As T.S. Eliot once put it in an interview, "One wants to get something off ones's chest. One doesn't quite know what it is that one wants to get off the chest until one's got it off. . ." That one's own personal problems surface again and again in poems isn't particularly strange. The thing really is to hold off recognizing the psychological or emotional dilemma which is prompting you, because once you've located it and thought about it consciously, it may stop motivating you to write poems about it. . . Anyway, looking through the manuscript when I was wondering what to call the whole collection I realized that a lot were about entranced states of solopsism, characters paralyzed by some kind of fantasy from which they can't move on, and which no one else can understand. As Jamie McKendrick pointed out in a very perceptive review in *The Independent*, there are lots of comically displaced images of frustration in the book, the "bull charging around in its paddock," "an angry young / mattress nailed to the floor," the salesman thrashing around in his swimming-pool full of peanuts, the corpse of the narrator's friend in "Christmas", the young boy in "General Knowledge" who traces on his atlas the veins of the Mississippi delta "winding dubiously towards the sea." Actually, when I started noticing this and decided to call the book "Landlocked" I thought I should take out all mention of the sea, but in fact I noticed that the three or four references occur only in the imagination, and, as I said, I don't like to be purist about such things. But I did change "sea-breeze" to "sudden breeze" in "Street Violence".

55

GB: Many of your poems have wonderfully arresting beginnings. . . Are these first lines normally the initial inspiration of the poem?

MF: Yes, pretty well always, though once or twice I've added the opening lines after I've more or less finished the poem. I think I did that with ''Resting Up'', which has a rather epigrammatic opening, ''Every high-rise has a special feel to it'', and also I added the opening lives of ''A Swimming-Pool Full of Peanuts'' after I thought I'd finished it. I remember they seemed a terrific stroke at the time, probably because this was more or less the first poem I'd ever written at the quite ripe age of twenty-one, and I was amazed at how easy it was. That's in fact the only poem of mine that always seems to go down well. Beginner's luck, I suppose. I'm pretty suspicious of it myself, but I've come to accept that I'll never come up with anything that hits the spot in quite the same way again. A Japanese friend of mine started speculating the other day about what the poem was really about, which I found very alarming. I told him I just didn't want to know.

GB: That poem comes rather late in the volume as a whole. . . What determined the sequence of the poems?

MF: Well, I took the business of ordering the poems very seriously. I guess there are various ways of doing it — there's Hardy's 1912-13 volume, all of whose poems deal with a central theme from different angles and using different forms, or there's the kind of mix you get in a Larkin collection in which you never get two poems alike next to each other. I tried to use a bit of both methods — for instance there are about four poems in a row (''Cross-section,'' ''Kid Crazy,'' ''Super Black Thursday,'' ''Demise'') which all deal with the theme of men without women. But I followed Larkin in trying to get a balanced mix — I was absolutely terrified at the thought of the reader getting bored, so I spread out the poems in similar forms very judiciously.

GB: Could you elaborate on your ''forms'' a little bit?

MF: For instance there are, say, three poems with three stanzas of three lines each (''General Knowledge,'' ''High Performance,'' ''Ledgers'') and three poems which I think of as sonnets and a half with twenty-one lines each (''Stocking Up,'' ''Resting Up,'' ''Outing''), and there are quite a few, perhaps too many, with thirteen lines which are almost sonnets, and there's the one called ''Then She Said She Had To Go,'' which has three six line stanzas in sort of two columns with a shared word in the fifth line. . . There are quite a few one-off forms like that one or ''Sneaker Dot-to-Dot'' or the six couplets of ''Policing Beaconsfield. . . And then there are those sort of almost talking blues poems which are the first I wrote, ''Night Out,'' ''Christmas,'' ''A Swimming-Pool Full of Peanuts'' which have quite a strong narrative drive. They probably came out of my reading Frank O'Hara. I was on a great Frank O'Hara kick when I wrote those.

GB: In terms of your poetry, what exactly do you expect to come out of your time in Japan?

MF: I've no idea. . . Certainly I'm not the type who can write poems about lying on the *tatami* in a *minschuku* eating *sashimi* wearing a *yukata* feeling *genki* and looking at Mount Fuji. . . To tell you the truth I don't really understand Japanese culture much as yet. It's a very complex, multi-layered place — even the most elementary exchanges seem full of very precisely coded messages which a foreigner can never really hope to pick up. One must be content with the surfaces of Japanese life, but these surfaces are utterly entrancing. For months I was high on just the look, the feel, the smell of the place. . . I'm also continually surprised by Japanese eclecticism — the nightlife for instance has a real pick 'n' mix feel to it. A single building will house bars specializing in almost anything you can think of — Country and Western, Reggae, Russian folk, Jazz, House, Greenwich Village circa 1963. . . you get in the elevator and take your choice. . . and then there's *The Pig and Whistle*, a British pub complete with dingy patterned carpet, darts board, an eight-man rowing boat suspended upside down from the ceiling, on the walls there are beer towels advertising Tetley's and so on, plus all sorts of hideous etchings and floral plates, and as you leave and enter you're confronted by a dummy in full Scottish dress in a glass case, kilt, sporran and all. I have to admit I like the way such a place parodies Western notions of authenticity, but at the same time it has you doubting the reality of all you hold most dear.

GB: How do you respond to being surrounded by the Japanese language? Do you enjoy it?

MF: Well, at first it was alarming, frustrating, exciting, then I sort of got used to it. In the end I find it pretty constricting. But of course English — Japanese English — is everywhere out here, as you'll have noticed. I once went to my local supermarket and copied down some of the slogans on kids' sweatshirts on sale there. You get the bizarrest amalgam of Western clichés. One actually had a glorious composite poem on it — it ran something like:

I wandered lonely as a cloud that
floats on high o'er vales and
hills, the evening comes, the fields
are still on the pure horizon far,
see pulsing with the first born
star, the liquid sky I celebrate
myself, what I assume you shall assume.

In a sense it's hard not to feel pre-empted by Japan — it's unconsciously done things to the English language in particular that make the most radical post-modern experiments look tame, and I've rather reacted against that. I sit at home reading Matthew Arnold and Geoffrey Hill!

GB: Who would you name as your major influences?

MF: Well, I'm not sure I've written enough to qualify for that kind of question. But I can tell you the twentieth-century poets I like: Auden, Wallace Stevens, Elizabeth Bishop, Louis McNeice, John Ashbery (on whom I wrote my doctoral dissertation at Oxford), Paul Muldoon, as I said, Robert Frost, Frank O'Hara, Hobsman, Wilfred Owen, Marianne Moore, Larkin, Rilke (in the Stephen Mitchell translation). . . I could go on. . . Of non-poets I like the early plays of Harold Pinter enormously — everything up to *No Man's Land*. *The Homecoming* I think one of the funniest plays ever written. I also read Edmund White pretty obsessively — I find myself going through his novels over and over and over again, and just wish he'd hurry up and publish a new one. And I also like Paul Auster's fiction a great deal. Who else? Of European writers, Georges Perec, Raymond Roussel, Calvino. . .

GB: What do you think are the main dangers confronting poets writing now?

MF: Well, I can only speak for myself. . . Self-parody is one great danger, you start writing poems that mimic your own verbal habits, though your audience may not guess this. I read the other day that Larkin felt "To the Sea" in his *High Windows* collection dangerously close to self-parody, but I bet not many readers feel that way about the poem. You never really know, as author, what you can get away with. Strangely, it's probably *more* disappointing and depressing to have a poem that you feel verges on self-parody praised than to have it disparaged. It implies that your readers can't tell your good stuff from your bad. . . And then content is a problem as well. I can't bear poems about grandfathers, or fishing expeditions, or what it's like to move into a new house, unless they're very *very* good poems. I mean I start off prejudiced against them because I find the subject matter so boring, and such poems normally seem so phoney to me, so obviously worked up. My response tends to be, "So what? Who cares?" I guess basically I'm always looking for gaps, little fissures where "a thought might grow," to use Derek Mahon's phrase. Bishop is the best at this — "The Man-Moth", "The Gentleman of Shalott", "The Map", and so on. . . And then there's form! What should the poem look like, should it rhyme? The course is pretty well all hazards. . . The only way to do it is by not caring. In the end all of these things take care of themselves, and at the same time even the strangest-seeming poem often turns out to be about the most standard things. There's no escaping them. I've certainly not managed to.

GB: What sort of things are you talking about?

MF: Oh you know, the usual ones. . . Love, language, time, and so on. Concepts so grand there's nothing you can say about them, certainly nothing original, yet you can't evade them either, however hard you try. Hopefully they don't intrude too much, but. . . In the end I suppose it's a question of being content with what you get given — you scoop up a bucketful and enjoy as much as you can the various life-forms that happen to be in it. And, well, they seem wonderfully individual and autonomous at first but of course in time just get to seem representative of the age-old dilemmas. That must be just the way it goes.

DANA GIOIA

INTERVIEWED BY ROBERT McPHILLIPS

Dana Gioia, who was born in Los Angeles in 1950, is unique among contemporary American poets. He does not have an MFA in Creative Writing. Nor has he made his living teaching poetry workshops whose burgeoning in American universities Gioia has criticized in his attention-getting 1991 article, "Can Poetry Matter?" Instead, like T. S. Eliot and Wallace Stevens, Gioia chose to eschew academia and pursue a career in business while simultaneously establishing himself among the most significant poets and critics of his generation. His poems and essays have appeared in *The New Yorker, The Nation, The Hudson Review*, and *Verse*. His first collection of poetry, *Daily Horoscope*, was published to much acclaim in the United States in 1986 by Graywolf Press. In 1991, Graywolf issued his second book of poems, *The Gods of Winter*, which was simultaneously published in Great Britain by Peterloo Poets. *Gods* was the Fall 1991 selection of the Poetry Book Society. In addition, Gioia has published a translation of Eugenio Montale's *Mottetti*, has edited a selection of short stories of the poet Weldon Kees, and co-edited two anthologies of Italian poetry.

This interview was conducted in Gioia's office at General Foods USA in White Plains, New York in December, 1991 and then revised in transcript.

Robert McPhillips

RM: What was it like to grow up in Los Angeles in the 1950's and 1960's?

DG: I was born and raised in Hawthorne, California — a working-class town set in the middle of Los Angeles' megalopolitan sprawl. The town was a mix of Mexicans and Okies with a few Irish to run the police and politics. Most people worked in the airplane factories for Hughes and Northrop. Hawthorne was extraordinarily ugly in the cluttered, haphazard way of factory towns, but it did have gorgeous Southern Californian weather, and the beach was only twenty minutes away. We were poor but the weather was free. Since no one we knew had much money, we never considered ourselves underprivileged.

RM: What was your childhood like?

DG: I had a happy, solitary childhood. Both of my parents worked. My father was a cab driver and later a chauffeur. My mother worked as an operator for the phone company. I was left alone a great deal. I was raised in a tightly-knit Sicilian family. We lived in a triplex next to another triplex. Five of these six apartments were occupied by relatives. Sicilians are clannish folk. They trust no one but family. My grandparents rarely socialized with anyone who wasn't related. My mother (who had been born in Hawthorne from mainly Mexican stock) had to become more Italian than the Italians to fit in. All of the older people had been born in Sicily. Many of them spoke little or no English. Conversations among adults were usually in their Sicilian dialect. It was an odd childhood by mainstream American standards but probably not too unusual among immigrant families.

Living in New York now, I often hear people describe Southern California in the typical Hollywood clichés. These popular images of glitz and glamour have little to do with the working-class Los Angeles of my childhood, which was quite old-fashioned, very European, and deeply Catholic. No, "European" is the wrong word. Very *Latin*. The Sicilians blended very easily into the existing Mexican culture.

RM: Was Catholicism important to you?

DG: Catholicism was everything to me. Growing up in a Latin community of Sicilians and Mexicans, one didn't feel the *Roman* Catholic church as an abstraction. It was a living culture which permeated our lives. In parochial school, we attended Latin Mass every weekday morning, in addition to the obligatory Mass on Sunday; so for eight early years I went to Mass six days a week. The hymns we sang were still the classics of Medieval Latin liturgy. As altar boys, we learned all the ceremonial responses by heart. Our nuns scrupulously drilled us in liturgy, ritual, and dogma — which we tolerated — and recounted the flamboyant folklore of saints and martyrs — which we adored.

This world seems so distant now. The Second Vatican Council unintentionally killed it. Working-class kids in Los Angeles today do not have the benefit of this sectarian but nonetheless broadening and oddly international education. In my Catholic high school the Marianist brothers drilled us relentlessly in Latin and Theology. We worked our way through most of St. Augustine and St. Thomas Aquinas' arguments. We also read Horace, Catullus, Virgil, and Ovid. We even translated the bawdy and beautiful songs of the Wandering Scholars. I was in the last generation that experienced Latin as a living language. Some of my teachers had attended ecclesiastical colleges in which all instruction was done in Latin. This cultural heritage opened new worlds to kids like us whose everyday lives were otherwise so narrow.

RM: What was it like to go from this working-class, ethnic background to an elite university like Stanford?

DG: Going to Stanford was a great shock. I had never been around people my own age whose parents had gone to college. At Stanford I experienced the shock of meeting the children of America's ruling class. It took me years to sort out my own reactions. I was simultaneously impressed and repelled by the social privilege my fellow students enjoyed. I was also naively astonished at how little their education meant to them. I felt then, as I do now, that in the circle of my friends in a working-class Catholic high school there were more serious intellectuals than among my contemporaries at Stanford. Of course, I was then — and continue to be now — most naive of all in thinking that being an intellectual has some value.

RM: And yet you fit in fairly well as an undergraduate. Weren't you chosen as editor for *Sequoia*, the literary magazine?

DG: I did well at Stanford because I was so hungry to learn. I often took six courses a quarter rather than the recommended four. I was also hungry after my own kind. I wanted friends who were interested in the arts. I joined the staff of *Sequoia*, Stanford's literary magazine. As a junior I became the editor of this tottering enterprise. I took the magazine from bankruptcy to become the largest small magazine, if that doesn't sound like too much of an oxymoron, on the West Coast.

RM: What did you do on *Sequoia*? I know your association wth the magazine was extensive.

DG: I had two stints on *Sequoia*. As I said before, I served as editor-in-chief for my last two years as an undergraduate. Then, a few years later, when I returned to Stanford for business school, I became poetry editor and did literary interviews. While in business school I also began writing book reviews for the *Stanford Daily*. They let me do long pieces about whatever new books interested me. In retrospect, I'm amazed by the freedom they gave me. I was able to write at great length about authors like Pound, Cavafy, Eliot, Montale, Nabokov, Rich, Burgess as well as younger poets. I wrote a review every other week for two years. I probably learned more about writing by reviewing for the *Stanford Daily* and by editing *Sequoia* than I did in my English classes. Writing for publication makes you very serious about what you are doing. Learning to put sentences together, to develop a line of thought, to select one good poem from a hundred mediocre submissions teaches you a great deal about literature. That sort of practical experience is invaluable to a young writer.

you a great deal about literature. That sort of practical experience is invaluable to a young writer.

RM: What kind of courses did you take? What literary figures interested you most as an undergraduate?

DG: Although I was a voracious reader, literature mattered less to me at first than music. I came to Stanford planning to be a composer. After a short time with the Stanford Music Department, however, my passion for music was frustrated. I wanted to compose tonal music, but my teachers believed that tonality was a dead tradition. They ridiculed or dismissed as minor most of the living composers I admired — figures like Samuel Barber, Benjamin Britten, Michael Tippett, Walter Piston, William Walton, and Ned Rorem. I spent my sophomore year in Vienna studying music and German. I escaped to Europe because I was so disappointed intellectually in Stanford. I wanted to try something else. Luckily, the California State Scholarship, which helped pay my way through college, was also applicable to the Vienna program because it was administered by Stanford. In Austria my primary interest gradually shifted from music to poetry. By the time I returned to California I wanted to be nothing else than a poet. I had this change of heart in Austria for two reasons. First, I began recognizing the limits of my musical ability. Second, speaking German so much of the time somehow changed my relationship to English. I found myself writing poems in English, and spending much of my time reading poetry in English and German.

RM: What literary courses did you take after returning from Europe?

DG: My formal coursework at Stanford was less important to me than the books I read on my own, the private passions I fostered without any sensible academic supervision. My course curriculum seems to me, in retrospect, quite haphazard. I was terribly naive as a student. I had the mistaken impression that one took the *courses* that interested one most. What I soon discovered was that the only way to get an education was to seek out the best professors, regardless of what they were teaching. I was lucky as an undergraduate to have a couple of really terrific teachers, most prominently Herbert Lindenberger, who headed the Comparative Literature program at Stanford, and Diane Middlebrook, who has since achieved fame as the biographer of Anne Sexton.

RM: Did you study a great deal of contemporary literature as an undergraduate?

DG: I attended college in northern California from 1969 to 1973, and I don't think that my development as a poet can be separated from this bizarre period of American literary history. For example, my freshman English composition teacher assigned us the following books: *Notes of a Native Son* by James Baldwin, *Soul on Ice* by Eldridge Cleaver, *Invisible Man* by Ralph Ellison, *Native Son* by Richard Wright, *Trout Fishing in America* by Richard Brautigan, and *The Plum Plum Pickers* by Eugene Barrio, a clumsy Chicano labor novel. A curious list for a class in *composition*. My first survey course in American literature assigned us Robert Creeley, Robert Bly, Allen Ginsberg, Lawrence Ferlinghetti, Gregory Corso, and Amiri Baraka. So I was never able to think of Beat poetry as non-academic or revolutionary. By 1971, it was already canonized as part of Stanford's approved version of American Literature. Coming to maturity as a writer in the California of Haight-Ashbury, one was engulfed in waves of fashion. I found myself resisting. My literary sensibility tends to be contrarian. Had I grown up in a period when people wrote sonnets and villanelles, I would probably have gone off to Black Mountain College.

RM: How did you move from studying contemporary American literature to reading earlier writers?

DG: Before college, I had what, in one sense, was a very bad literary education. I never had a historical survey of either English or American literature. I had not read most of the major British or American poets. I was, however, fortunate to have had teachers who communicated both the pleasure and personal value of literature. Athough my education was academically inadequate and historically lopsided, it was psychically valid. When I came to college, I discovered

Ezra Pound's *ABC of Reading*. That book filled me with determination to learn as much as possible about poetry in English and foreign languages. I systematically tried to fill in my gaps as an undergraduate. But going to college in the early 70's, one was always hit with the notion of relevance — "relevance" usually being defined as what one's teacher felt was morally correct and timely. The situation seems farcical in retrospect. I wanted to read the classics, and my teachers encouraged me to pursue the latest trends. Being up to date, to misquote Oscar Wilde, is America's oldest tradition.

RM: When did you read the *ABC of Reading*?

DG: I had never heard of Ezra Pound before I came to Stanford. Pound was not allowed in the American high school anthologies of the 50's and 60's because of his indictment for treason. My best friend from high school, Jim Laffan, who knew much more about literature than I did, showed up at Stanford one weekend with a paperback copy of Pound's *ABC of Reading*. I remember noticing the serious, bearded author on the cover, and I listened to Jim spout all sorts of fascinating generalizations about literature that he had discovered in this book. I asked to borrow it. I read and reread that book for the next two years and started reading through all of Pound's work. Pound shamed me into learning French, which I immediately started when I returned from Vienna, as well as teaching myself standard Italian, and keeping my Latin more or less current. Pound did American literature an invaluable service by reminding us that poetry is an international art.

RM: Did reading Pound's *ABC of Reading* change your personal reading list or did it make you seek out different types of courses to take beyond contemporary literature?

DG: It did both. I consciously took courses in earlier periods to broaden my education with writers like Chaucer or the Elizabethans because of Pound's suggestions. I also audited a Dante course. I've always been comfortable learnng on my own, and even when I was taking five or more classes in a single quarter, I still found time to do outside reading. This ability to work on my own proved my salvation in later years.

RM: Did Pound influence you to study comparative literature in graduate school?

DG: My Poundian bias made me feel, possibly unjustly, that comparative literature was the only adequate way to study literature. When I applied to graduate school, I applied only to comparative literature programs. At that point I planned to be a professor of literature who also wrote poetry. The few living poets I had seen — Edgar Bowers, Kenneth Rexroth, Christopher Middleton, Donald Davie — had all been professors. I had never really known a poet, only caught passing glimpses at a reading or a lecture.

RM: Did you take any poetry writing courses as an undergraduate?

DG: I did not take creative writing classes as an undergraduate. In fact, I had a certain unfair prejudice against creative writing. The writing majors at Stanford didn't seem to me as serious as the literature students. I looked on writing courses as a kind of self-indulgence. It never occurred to me that one needed classroom instruction to write poetry. I concentrated on learning literature and foreign languages while writing poems on my own.

RM: Journalists and critics often compare you to Wallace Stevens. Has Stevens influenced you as a poet?

DG: Stevens' importance to me has been two-fold. First, he demonstrated that it was possible to work in business and develop as a serious writer You have no idea how important — psychologically and spiritually — Stevens and Eliot were to me in my mid-twenties. I had left the university for business. I knew few writers, and those few were all based in the academy. I didn't even know of a living writer who worked in business. I felt immensely isolated. Coming home each night after ten or twelve hours at the office, I had to find not only the energy to write but also the conviction that it was possible. One needs a great deal of faith to work for years without any external encouragement. Stevens and Eliot became my patron saints. I'm sorry to phrase it in such Catholic terms, but that's the way my mind works. Second, Stevens has represented a standard of artistic integrity to me. Stevens wrote only what he believed in. He stayed away from the literary marketplace. He never courted fame or popularity. He trusted poetry absolutely. He achieved this absolute integrity at great human cost. I don't envy or admire that side of him, but his personal isolation doesn't diminish the value of his artistic example.

RM: But did Stevens influence you stylistically or thematically?

DG: Not all literary influences are best measured by comparing texts. Stevens has profoundly shaped my poetry in ways that are mostly invisible on the page. He reminded me that a poet is free to do what interests or delights him — no matter what the literary or ideological fashions of the times. In that sense, perhaps, Stevens contributed paradoxically to my conviction that form and narrative needed to be brought back into American poetry. His influence was more spiritual than stylistic or intellectual. I have, however, always admired Stevens' sheer verbal extravagance — exactly those features which Donald Davie can't abide. Stevens' over abundant diction and quirky elegance have occasionally given me the courage to exploit the possibilities of the language. Stevens reminds us that poetry should not be ashamed of being magnificent.

RM: Who are the poets who have most influenced you?

DG: There are several kinds of influence, and it is important to distinguish among them. First, there are the writers whom one imitates at the beginning. Nowadays, many young poets — at least in America — begin by imitating their teachers. That isn't altogether bad if your teacher is Theodore Roethke, Elizabeth Bishop or John Crowe Ransom. But with a mediocre master, such imitation may stunt a young poet's growth. My early models all came from books. I have been reading poetry as long as I have been reading, but I'm not sure the enthusiasms of my childhood like Poe and Kipling have influenced me as much as the writers I embraced in late adolescence when I was beginning to think of myself consciously as an artist. Those early "singing masters of my soul" were Auden, Eliot, Pound, Rilke, and Graves. I often think, however, that a young poet isn't influenced so much by poets as by individual poems. In that sense, I was fascinated with particular poems by many other writers like Wilfred Owen, Archibald MacLeish, Elizabeth Bishop, E. E. Cummings and Randall Jarrell.

There is another kind of influence, however — namely writers whose ideas and examples shape one's sense of what it means to be a poet. At different stages of my life there have been poets to whom I have looked as spiritual examples. They have helped me lead my life. Stevens, Eliot, Rilke, Auden, and Jeffers have all been important to me as spiritual guides at particular times in my life.

RM: Did any poets influence your technique?

DG: I have consciously studied the verse technique of a great many poets, especially Yeats, Eliot, Auden, and Frost. But the single most influential experience I had was in my early twenties when — God help me, I'm not kidding — I scanned every line in half a dozen major plays by Marlowe, Shakespeare, and Webster. I wanted to learn the secrets of blank verse from the poets for whom it was a living *spoken* art rather than a codified *written* form. I learned some valuable lessons about how poetry is heard from those masters, observations I have never seen in any book on prosody. I patterned much of my own verse technique on those poets. I was amused when a conservative critic attacked my prosody as too loose. Augustan critics made the same complaints about Elizabethan dramatists.

RM: I presume you hadn't been East before studying at Harvard. Was Harvard a different type of experience for you from being at Stanford?

DG: The most important thing to remember about my earlier years was how naive I was. I had virtually never been outside of California except for my brief stint in Vienna. (Even when living in Vienna, I didn't have enough money to travel much and see Europe). I had never been to New England before I arrived at Harvard. I had imagined Cambridge to be an idyllic New England town. You can imagine my horror when I arrived in Harvard Square expecting a tranquil village green only to discover a dilapidated subway stop in the middle of a traffic circle. Yet Harvard was the most exciting intellectual experience I've had in my life. Harvard was the first time I had ever been in a milieu of serious writers and intellectuals. But my two years at Harvard were also extraordinarily lonely. I was quite poor. My first year I lived in a dilapidated basement studio on a dead-end alley. The squalor was unbelievable. My life became like something out of Dostoyevsky's *Notes From the Underground*. I also suffered a serious back injury and fractured a vertebra of my spine. I didn't receive proper treatment, so during most of my time at Harvard I was in constant pain. I wasn't psychologically strong enough to deal with this protracted injury. There was a point when I grew suicidal. But, as awful as they are to live through, suffering and isolation do clarify your life. During this time I learned what was most important to me. I clung to poetry as a means of sanity.

RM: You've published a memoir of Elizabeth Bishop with whom you studied at Harvard. You and she became friends, then corresponded afterwards. What kind of influence did Bishop have on you?

DG: My first year at Harvard I took standard academic courses in French, German and English literature. I learned a great deal. But I knew no other writers and had few close friends. During my second year, however, I was fortunate to meet Elizabeth Bishop and Robert Fitzgerald as well as two younger writers, Alexander Theroux and Robert Shaw. These individuals were extraordinarily important to me. They were the first dedicated imaginative artists I had ever really known. Bishop was less important to me as a writer than as a friend. When I studied with her at Harvard, her reputation was in eclipse. My advisor, a noted literary theorist, scoffed at the notion of my taking her class. He told me bluntly that her course would be a waste of time. Luckily, I ignored his counsel. There were only five of us in Bishop's course on modern poetry. Harvard students did not consider her a literary celebrity like Robet Lowell or William Alfred. Almost immediately, Bishop and I struck up a relaxed and rather intimate friendship. We would go off to tea after class. Our talk was almost never about poetry, but about other things that we liked in common — music, novels, cats, flowers, travel. Bishop was a remarkably strict, indeed often discouraging teacher. She covered any work we submitted with corrections and suggestions, but she was extraordinarily encouraging to me. She believed in me both as an aspiring critic and a poet to a degree which no one had before. Her encouragement was entirely private. I never asked her for any help in the literary world, but her unsolicited personal endorsement came at a crucial time since I had just made the decision to leave academia for business.

RM: Your relationship to Bishop seems a bit like hers with Marianne Moore, who was notorious both for her generosity in reading her early drafts but also with a kind of real strictness in suggesting revisions. Do you see any parallel between that relationship and yours with Bishop?

DG: My relationship with Elizabeth Bishop was neither as longstanding nor as intimate as hers with Marianne Moore. But she did hammer into me the notion that every line one writes must be relentlessly considered, revised, and perfected. Every essay or translation I gave to her — because hers was not a course in creative writing — she would return to me scrupulously copy-edited and covered with suggestions for revisions, expansions, and deletions. Her example came at a crucial time because I, like all graduate students, was being encouraged by my other professors to write in a formal academic style. Bishop insisted that I write clearly, intelligently, and unpretentiously. I quickly realized that one had to make a choice between writing for the academic profession or writing for the common reader. I have chosen to write for the common reader. But the common reader, as both Samuel Johnson and Virginia Woolf remind us, does not mean an unintelligent reader.

RM: You also studied with Robert Fitzgerald, the classicist and poet. What type of influence did he have on you?

DG: Robert Fitzgerald was the single most important influence I had as a poet. Once again, his influence was not so much encouragement to write in a particular style or about particular subjects. Rather, Fitzgerald's influence was of writing to the highest standards with a knowledge of tradition and a respect for the craft of poetry. Quite by accident, I ended up taking two courses with him simultaneously my second year at Harvard. The first was a class called, in the inimitable Harvard way, "Studies in Narrative Poetry." We read Homer, Virgil, and Dante. In order to be admitted you had to be able to read at least two of these writers in the original. Everyone in the class but me was an expert philologist. I squeaked by with reasonably good Latin and minimal standard Italian. It was a wonderfully intimate and enthusiastically learned course. We did close textual analyses of selected passages from each author and tried to build a general notion of the epic tradition that bound the poems together. At the same time, I took another graduate course from Fitzgerald called "The History of English Versification." I enrolled assuming it was a class in historical prosody. To my astonishment, I discovered that, in addition to the historical and theoretical reading, we were also expected to write a verse exercise each week in whatever meter we were studying. Fitzgerald did not ask us to write a poem — only to produce verse which scanned and made sense. These exercises were the most valuable learning I had as a young poet. I had always written in both free and metered verse, but my formal work was halting and uncertain. Versification is a craft which one can learn more quickly and better from a master than by oneself. Under Fitzgerald's tutelage I learned in practical terms how the traditional meters worked. Fitzgerald also provided an important personal example. He had come to teaching later in life. He had worked as a journalist, had served in the Navy during the Second World War, and had spent years as a writer in Italy where he first translated Homer's *Odyssey*. I saw in him a representative man of letters, a person who had dedicated his life to poetry.

RM: You dedicated the title sequence of your first book *Daily Horoscope* to Robert Fitzgerald. I take it that the poem is not directly based on your relationship with him. It's one of your most sophisticated works and yet it has gotten very little critical attention.

DG: I consider "Daily Horoscope" one of my best poems, but I suspect that many people find it intimidating. The two critics who have written on it at length tried to interpret it as an elegy for Robert Fitzgerald. The sequence, however, was published while Robert was still alive, so it certainly was not intended as an elegy. I dedicated it to him because he was my most valuable teacher as a poet, and I had come across a wonderful passage in the *Inferno* in which Dante saluted Virgil as his master and teacher in poetry. I put those lines as an epigraph under the dedication to Robert, not realizing that by quoting the *Inferno*, some critics would then read the sequence as a Dantescan poem about the afterlife. Perhaps it can be adequately read that way. That was not, however, the way I intended it.

RM: How did you intend the sequence to be read?

DG: I don't believe that a poet is the best judge or interpreter of his own work. A poet knows things that aren't in the text, and, blinded by his own intentions, often misses things which are there. I know, or think I know, my intentions in writing "Daily Horoscope." How well those ambitions are realized in the final text is not for me to judge. The only observation I would make about the poem is to explain its title. I borrowed both the title and the style of the sequence from the horoscope columns you find in most daily newspapers. I was fascinated by the way astrologers addressed their readers in the second person and used the most intimate tone possible to tell what will happen to "you" each day. I also loved the way these columns create a brooding sense of mystery and danger. They tell you what to do and what to avoid. I decided to use that style in a lyric poem, and slowly it grew into a sequence. It was my intention that all of the poems were spoken to a single protagonist in the course of a single day from morning to night, but that intention may not be apparent to anyone but the author in the actual printed text.

RM: When I first read the poem, it reminded me of John Ashbery's work. I know another poet who feels the same way. I've always admired the sequence, but it remains pleasingly elusive, like much of Stevens' or Ashbery's poetry. Do you want to comment on the resemblance?

DG: "Daily Horoscope" may remind some readers of Ashbery's work, but I had read virtually nothing of Ashbery's when I wrote it. I suspect the elements in "Daily Horoscope" you noticed come from my debt to European Modernist poetry, a tradition Ashbery and I share. My own poetry draws on two somewhat contradictory traditions. One part comes out of the heritage of Anglo-American writers like Auden, Hardy, Jarrell, Larkin, and Kees, a sort of novelistic type of poetry. The critics who have written about my work with the greatest enthusiasm usually respond most deeply to this side of my sensibility. But there is another side to my work which comes out of European High Modernism. "Daily Horoscope," to the degree that it is written in any tradition, comes out of the Modernist lyric as exemplified by poets like Montale, Rilke, and Valery. Perhaps this European heritage makes the poem puzzling to critics who are more attracted by the Anglo-American aspects of my work.

RM: It seems to me that the other work closest in tone to "Daily Horoscope" is your translation of Montale's *Mottetti*. I have been struck by how different the poetry that you translate from the Italian is from most of the poetry that you write in English.

DG: Surely the great joy of translation comes from making a beautiful but alien poem your own. Why translate an author similar to yourself? As a translator, I am drawn to poets with whom I feel a deep imaginative sympathy but who also seem mysteriously foreign. Translation is a way of reconciling those opposite reactions. The period of literature which exercises the greatest fascination on me is European Modernism — not just in Italian but also in German and French (which I can read) as well as in Russian, Greek, and Spanish (which I don't know). I have been besotted with Modernist poetry since my teens. My own poetry is permeated with Modernist elements, but they are not the conventional ones, so readers don't necessarily recognize them as such.

I consider the first half of the 20th Century the greatest period of American poetry. Modernist poetry may even be the high point of *all* American literature. The incredible cluster of talent, which began with E. A. Robinson and ran through Frost, Jeffers, Eliot, Pound, Moore, Cummings, Williams, Stevens, and up through Crane, Ransom, and Tate, seems unrivalled in American literature.

RM: But some critics would argue that your poetry rejects Modernism.

DG: My poetry is shaped by Modernism but not imprisoned by it. I have tried to assimilate what is still useful to an artist, but I am writing poems for today, not for Paris in 1913. Modernism is dead. Its historical moment has passed. Although it still influences what any serious American poet hopes to do, it is no longer a viable tradition. Of course, there is a group of poets and critics who pretend Modernism is still the vital mainstream. They desperately try to perpetuate the theory that the avant-garde remains a living force. To me, being avant-garde in the 1990's is a kind of antiquarianism. The central task for poets in my generation is the perennial challenge of reinventing poetry for the present moment. We must find a way to reconcile the achievements of Modernism with the necessity of creating a more inclusive and accessible kind of poetry.

RM: The poets that you list as part of the Anglo-American Modernist movement is much broader than the standard academic canon. Most academics would exclude writers like Robinson and Frost. They would see them, and Jeffers also, as traditional poets who happened to be writing during the Modernist period.

DG: Our Father's house has many mansions. Modernism was a complex and inclusive movement. Any definition of American Modernism that does not include Frost or Jeffers is an inadequate one. Let me give you an example. If you took Frost's narratives in *North of Boston*, which was published in 1914, and compared them to the short stories that were written about rural America at that time, you would find in Frost's poetry a startling compression an unnervingly cold realism, and an absolutely Modernistic sense of the narrator. I've always wondered if Ernest Hemingway did not develop his notion of the short story by reading *North of Boston*. In some respects he and Frost are amazingly similar. Jeffers' obsessive and powerful use of violence, sexuality, and myth is also quintessentially modern. No one could have written with that force and that raw candor before 1920. In that way, Jeffers' poetry parallels D. H. Lawrence's prose. So to reduce American Modernism to a certain stylistic school such as that of Williams or Stevens or Eliot is a gross and untenable simplification. I wonder if the most valuable parts of Modernism today may be those less acknowledged aspects like Frost and Jeffers rather than the Poundian or Williamesque traditions which have already been so well-mined.

RM: That brings us around to the question of the New Formalism. You've been identified with a movement in American poetry called the New Formalism. Would you care to give a definition of the New Formalism?

DG: One can't define New Formalism without discussing the origin of its name. New Formalism was a term given by unfriendly critics in the mid 80's to young poets who had begun writing in forbidden techniques — rhyme, meter, and narrative. The name was intentionally reductive and uncomplimentary because these critics felt American poets should not write in rhyme or meter. The name New Formalism inadequately describes a genuinely vital movement by a group of poets of my generation. Our work has several similarities. We write in rhyme and meter, though not usually exclusively in rhyme and meter. At least half of my poetry, for instance, is written in free verse. Second, many of us are interested in reviving narrative poetry — not autobiographical stories, but stories about other people. Third, we differ from what one might call the New Critical poets, the post-war academic formalists, in that we consciously borrow elements from popular culture. We often appropriate style, subject matter, and even whole genres from popular culture. And our work is less self-consciously intellectual and academic than some of those earlier writers. We belive that writing can be intelligent without being pedantic. We are trying to regain for poetry both a variety of techniques, which had been forgotten in the free-verse era, and a kind of public voice which in some ways has been lost since Modernism.

RM: What other poets share this aesthetic with you?

DG: There are a number of poets whom one might classify as New Formalists. My short list would include R. S. Gwynn, Charles Martin, Gjertrud Schnackenberg, and Timothy Steele. Each of these poets is different, but what they have in common is an impressive sense of formal accomplishment. They have created a new kind of music by mixing contemporary speech and formal meters. These poets are consciously using the line and the stanza as musical elements in their poetry. R. S. Gwynn, who is a Southerner, writes very much out of popular literature.

He has a poem called "Among Philistines" which retells, brilliantly, the Samson story from a suburban American perspective. Charles Martin is very conscious of his Modernist roots and his poetry plays with Modernist paradigms with verve and ingenuity. Gjertrud Schnackenberg bears the strongest resemblance to a formalist of the older generation, but her poetry has an emotional accessibility and gorgeous musicality which seem both personal and new. Timothy Steele is an accomplished lyric poet, who writes in the plain style, but in a direct and memorable way, which I greatly admire. There are other poets one might mention like Paul Lake, Robert Shaw and William Logan or narrative poets like Robert McDowell and Andrew Hudgins. These poets share a sense of concentration and musicality. They write with a sense of tradition, but without being burdened by tradition.

RM: Recently I've read a book by a young academic critic on Post-Modernist poetry which concluded with an attack on New Formalism. Specifically, he attacked Gjertrud Schnackenberg's poem "Supernatural Love" — which I think is an exquisite poem — by comparing it to a poem by Allen Tate. He said both poems were filled with certain determinate images and that once you figure out those images, the poems' meanings are exhausted. Poems not self-consciously composed in "open" forms are denied canonic Post-Modern status.

DG: This critic looks at poetry as a puzzle, and he esteems only those puzzles he cannot solve. The major problem of contemporary poetry is that it has become the slave of contemporary criticism. Criticism values texts that generate critical discussion. I, however, subscribe to the quaint and discredited opinion that poetry is an art which is not created primarily for critics. There are enduring masterpieces of poetry about which very little can be said. Critics have a tendency to overpraise what they can talk about and to ignore wonderful works about which not much can be said. For years, Thomas Hardy's reputation as a poet languished because he wasn't very interesting for critics of a certain generation to discuss. It is not coincidental that Hardy's reputation was revived largely by poets — by Auden, Larkin, Davie, Ransom, and Reeves. The most influential Anglo-American criticism now concerns itself mainly with theoretical issues. If it addresses contemporary poetry at all, it is often to make an ideological analysis. Consequently, one often finds voluminous discussions of contemporary poems of minimal artistic merit. Some of this current criticism is interesting, but it does not have a great deal to do with what matters to me as a poet or as a reader.

RM: This leads us around to your own criticism. The first piece I ever read by you was a critical piece on John Cheever. What attracted to me about the article was that it was written in a clear and personal style. I read it at a time when I was finishing an extremely academic dissertation. It came as a revelation to me that there were young critics writing seriously about literature in a non-academic way. I subsequently discovered that you had written a series of critical essays not from within the academy but while a businessman at General Foods.

DG: One of the major problems of American poetry today is that most poets have abandoned criticism. If one goes back several generations to the early Modernists, most of them were also accomplished critics. Even if they wrote criticism as irregularly as Frost or Jeffers, they could still write compellingly about poetry. And the central poet-critics — Eliot and Pound — rank among the greatest critics in the English language. The next generation — Blackmur, Winters, Ransom, Tate — not only continued this tradition but also helped transform the academic study of literature, as did their students, the generation of Jarrell, Berryman, Schwartz and Shapiro. Ironically, once poets entered the academy to teach creative writing, they began to write less criticism. Donald Justice once commented that while teaching literature develops a critical mind, teaching creative writing somehow does not. He has bemoaned the failure of his generation to produce many distinguished poet-critics. In my own generation, there are few poets of note who take writing criticism seriously. Consequently, for the first time in this century, American poets have conceded critical discourse on contemporary poetry to literary theorists and academics.

I don't mean to belittle academic scholarship or criticism. I only insist on making a distinction. The concerns of an academic will by definition be different from the concerns of an imaginative writer. Academic critics write for their professional colleages. Poets write for their real and potential readers. Academic criticism arises out of studying the past whereas criticism by artists emerges from a vision of the future. Criticism by poets has historically educated and nourished a broader audience.

I have taken my role as a critic seriously. I have worked hard to find the right tone to discuss poetry responsibly, intelligently, but accessibly. One does not compromise a critical essay by writing it for general readers. I have probably impeded my reputation as a critic by writing in a public idiom and by discussing figures outside of the contemporary canon. A young critic can make a reputation much more quickly by writing conventionally on well-known figures than becoming an advocate for worthy but forgotten writers. But what's the point of writing another essay saying the same things on the same writer? Why write unless one has something new to say? I'm not interested in writing on major figures unless I have a dissenting opinion. Since I have made my living in business, I have the freedom to write only about what interests me. Consequently, I've devoted a great deal of critical energy and research to some forgotten or misunderstood figures, like Weldon Kees or Robinson Jeffers. I believe Kees is a major poet, although he appears in no literary histories and few anthologies.

RM: You've been the primary advocate of Weldon Kees of our generation. You've written several essays on his work and edited the selected stories. What attracts you to Kees? His work seems so different from yours.

DG: What is the use of art if we can't admire writers different from ourselves? From the moment I read Kees's work, I felt that I had come across a master. There were so many things to admire in Kees's work. First, he was able to get all kinds of heterogeneous material into his verse. His poetry was equally informed by Shakespeare and the movies, by jazz and Joyce, and yet he put them together in an exciting and satisfying whole. Second, Kees was a relentless experimentalist. He invented at least a dozen new poetic forms, most of which he used only once or twice. Usually when we talk of experimental poets, we talk about poets who leave us interesting messes, poems which are more satisfying to talk about than to read. But Kees's experiments are almost uniformly successful. They get sensibilities and subjects into poetry that were never successfully assimilated before. Kees was an accomplished visual artist. He exhibited with the Abstract Expressionists. It wasn't until I knew his work for many years that I understood the connection between these two sides of his sensibility. His central visual medium was the Modernist collage. He does the same things in verse. He combines surprising and unlikely material to illuminate the arcane connections between dissimilar things. Isn't that the way poetic metaphor operates? Kees fits as much of American experience into poetry as any post-War American poet has managed.

RM: Many would argue that John Ashbery is also doing that. Certainly he's notably influenced by the Abstract Expressionist painters and the collage method. You yourself once pointed out that Kees was an unacknowledged influence on the New York School poets.

DG: Kees is never classified as a New York School poet, and yet he seems the very model of a modern New York School poet. He was the first poet to integrate the techniques of Abstract Expressionism into verse. When I compare Kees's work with Ashbery's, however, I feel Kees is more concise, more emotionally direct, and more accessible than Ashbery. I know when I use the word ''accessible,'' I sound like a Philistine to some people, but ultimately one must judge art by a subjective reaction. Art either registers on one's imagination or it doesn't. And so by ''accessible,'' I don't mean ''simple.'' Kees is a complex, challenging poet. He is probably the bleakest, most apocalyptic poet in American literature. He is also among the most allusive.

But the sheer emotional desolation of his work is redeemed by his imaginative brilliance. The closest counterpart to Kees in American poetry is Hart Crane.

RM: Do you like Hart Crane's poetry?

DG: I came to Hart Crane's poetry relatively late. I never read him seriously until I was in my late twenties. At first I found him difficult but alluring. Then I noticed I couldn't get certain lines of his out of my head. I kept going back to his poetry with increasing esteem. I now think that *White Buildings* is one of the greatest books of American poetry ever published. I am less impressed by *The Bridge*, which seems a fascinating failure.

RM: Let me return to an earlier subject. Why did you leave Harvard graduate school in 1975 to make a career in business?

DG: I'm not sure that anyone understands entirely why one makes important decisions in life. Decisions are always complex. They involve both rational and emotional factors. I believe that I left Harvard for two reasons — the first economic, the second literary. I was the oldest son in a large working-class family. I had absolutely no money, and I felt a great deal of responsibility to provide an economic basis for the rest of the family. So, in one sense, I entered business because I needed to make a living and wanted some modest control over my life. The other reason I left academics was to become a poet. That sounds paradoxical, but I felt that I was becoming a worse writer with each passing year in academia. My poetry was becoming too studied and self-conscious. I was writing poems to be intepreted rather than to register on the imagination and emotions. As a critic, I felt I was being — I didn't feel, I *knew* I was being — encouraged to write for other specialists versus a wider audience. Why write in a style that your most intelligent friends outside the university can't follow, when you can say everything with as much accuracy in a more accessible way? My writing was changing for the worse.

Perhaps the reason I had to leave the university was because I liked it so much. I was too susceptible to its intellectual blandishments. I found the intense atmosphere of Harvard too interesting. I couldn't shield myself from the influences as well as somebody who didn't like the scholarly environment. Watching my friends who stayed in academics, I notice that they are under constant, external pressure, because they're surrounded by so many intelligent, self-conscious, critical people. It's hard for innovative or unconventional ideas to have the time and privacy to gestate under those circumstances. It's like living in a fish tank.

RM: How far along were you at Harvard when you left?

DG: I left Harvard after having completed all the course work for my doctorate and most of the language requirements in French, German, Italian, and Latin. On departing I was awarded something appropriately called a "terminal" Masters.

RM: Your departure from Harvard seemed to coincide with the rise of literary theory in the universities. In 1975 was literary theory already a presence there?

DG: In comparative literature, literary theory was already gaining dominance in the early 70's. At Harvard, one of my pro-seminars was conducted by Edward Said. For Said, we read books by Foucault and Barthes in French before they had been translated into English. We also read Lukacs, Goldmann, Hirsch, and other theorists who since have become influential. Most were already prominent in Europe. The two theorists who influenced me most were an unlikely pair, George Lukacs, (especially his *History of Class Consciousness),* and E. D. Hirsch, (for his *Validity in Interpretation).* That was before Hirsch achieved national fame with *Cultural Literacy.* In other words, the areas which interested me most in literary theory were Marxist dialectics and hermeneutics. As a critic, I seem to have a very Germanic imagination.

RM: It's somewhat ironic, then, for you to move from Marxist theory to business. Isn't the type of criticism that you are doing now the antithesis to the type of literary criticism that is being done in the universities?

DG: Is it ironic for a poet who later became a businessman to have been influenced by Marxism? I don't think so. Marxism would not have dominated a great deal of European thought if it did not have some basis in truth. As an analytical technique, Marxism gets at certain social realities better than any other philosophical school. I have never agreed with the *prescriptive* political conclusions of Marxism, nor its claims at being a *scientific* political methodology. But, as an analytical tool, Marxist dialectic can be profound. One of the things that Lukacs taught me was how institutions work, and by institutions I mean not only political or economic institutions like the government or industry, but institutions such as the legal profession or academic literary studies. One of Lukacs's major *apercus* was that there comes a point when an institution becomes so inwardly focused in perfecting its own methodology that it loses touch with its original social function. Academic literary study has fallen into what Lukacs would have called a contradiction. It has become so obsessed with its own methodology that it no longer serves its primary educational purpose. So I would, ironically, use Marxist analysis to criticize many university theorists who themselves are Marxists. The general audience for serious literature in America is dying, even as the academic profession thrives. Much of the country is sinking into illiteracy. Literature means less every year to the educated classes. And what is the response of the academy? To burrow more deeply into intricate and arcane theory incomprehensible to anyone outside the profession. I deplore this smug parochialism. I naively believe that poetry still has value for a society.

RM: I was surprised to hear you speak so eloquently on behalf of literary theory. As a critic, you often seem to be battering the dominance of theory.

DG: It will surprise some people to hear me say that I have, in principle, a high regard for literary theory. Literary theory is an essential branch of humanistic study. But one must recognize what theory can and cannot do. It's important to understand where literary theory fits into an academic curriculum. In America the academy grossly overemphasizes literary theory in its curriculum. I personally regret the shift in literary study from reading primary texts to reading critical and theoretical texts. The major problem today among students is that they simply have not read enough literature. Consequently they do not have the necessary background to take a critical attitude towards literary theory. One needs to test every abstraction against experience.

RM: Literary theory's other sin is that it has placed a layer of critical jargon between a literary text and the critics' own emotional and intellectual responses to it. Critics who try to speak clearly to a general audience are dismissed as journalists or failed academics.

DG: In America, there is an unprecedented cultural situation. Academic critics and imaginative writers not only possess no common set of concerns, but they no longer even share a common language. Neither side respects or even fully understands the other's language. Consequently, American literature is suffering the effects of an enervating bifurcation. At least one reason the poetry audience has declined in the United States is that there are no longer many first-class critics writing in a public idiom. One can point to only a handful of writers (ironically, often very scholarly ones like Hugh Kenner or Guy Davenport), who still write seriously in an accessible manner. Bruce Bawer is one of the few strong young critics who has continued the tradition of the public intellectual. Not surprisingly, he has had to make his career outside of the university. What we now posses is an impoverished public culture. If mass circulation journals cover poetry at all they do so only in short journalistic pieces dumbed-down to reach the lowest common denominator. Meanwhile, the many academic journals and presses publish work written in a kind of professional

71

jargon. Someone told me that the average American academic article is read completely by 0.9 readers. I believe it. That sort of criticism, as far as I can tell, is frequently written not to be read but to be weighed by a promotion committee.

Isn't it interesting that in the entire history of the world, there have never been so many people paid to profess poetry as in America today? We have tens of thousands of poetry professionals. And yet there's never been a culture in which poetry has played so small a role, in which poetry has been so alienated from the common educated reader. Surely that cultural paradox must reveal something about the failure of our literary enterprises.

RM: Surely working outside of the university has been important to you. How has working in business affected your writing?

DG: I am not sure I can answer that question accurately. Our professions mold us gradually in many ways that we ourselves can't see. Whenever I get together with old friends who have become teachers or lawyers, I marvel at how their work has accentuated some parts of their personalities while allowing other parts to atrophy. I would offer only two observations about the impact my job has had. First, unlike most university poets, I spend all day working with adults — most of whom are smart, mature, and practical. That experience differs from spending your days teaching the young. I think that the experience of working with peers rather than my juniors has shaped the concerns of my poetry in many ways that I only half understand. Second, by making a living outside of literature, I have been able to be quixotic about poetry. I can spend (and, alas, sometimes *have* spent) years working on a poem or essay. I have been able to write about whatever subjects I want without worrying about the commercial consequences. I can send work to small magazines, including long prose pieces that took months to write. Poets who must support themselves as writers could never afford that luxury. They must write for the marketplace. Even though my work appears in mass circulation magazines like *The New Yorker* or *The Atlantic*, I feel more allegiance to smaller journals like *The Hudson Review* or *Verse* whose central mission is literature and the arts.

RM: What did you hope to get out of business?

DG: One attraction of business was the privacy it gave me as a writer. There are so many conflicting claims on young poets today that they develop very slowly. They have to sort through more possibilities, more influences than ever before. I felt that I needed anonymity to discover myself. I needed a time with no external pressures for publication. After leaving Harvard, I did not send any poems out for nearly eight years. But I wrote virtually every night after work and on the weekends. Much of the time I spent revising. I would sometimes rewrite a particular poem off and on for years only to discard it. But the process of submerging myself utterly in my imagination and my medium was invaluable. I could never have borne the sheer loneliness of those years if I had not had an office full of people to go to each morning. Not worrying about publication gave me the freedom to make mistakes, to follow odd impulses. This period of public silence let me discover my own voice, develop my own set of concerns, without worrying about anyone outside approving or disapproving.

RM: Did your colleagues at work know that you wrote poetry?

DG: Of course not! I kept my writing a secret from them as long as I could. I felt that being known as a poet could only hurt my reputation inside the company. I also didn't want the people I worked with every day — good but very conventional middle-class folk — to know what I was writing. Offices are just like villages. People poke their noses into each other's affairs. For years I never sent work to *The New Yorker* because I was afraid someone at the office might see my poetry there. I wanted the freedom to write about whatever I wanted, and that required absolute privacy.

RM: Was that a difficult time for you?

DG: Absolutely. All young writers crave praise and recognition. I was no exception. I felt, however, that isolation and anonymity were the necessary price for self-discovery. I had to shut off the distractions in my life. I had published a great many poems as an undergraduate and graduate student, but I found, at this beginning stage, that editors did not publish my "best" work. They would often select the poems in which I imitated some other writer. To an editor, those poems were more obviously accomplished than the clumsy, inchoate musings in which I was struggling to define my own material. When I had these early exercises in other people's styles accepted, I found myself encouraged to write more in those borrowed mainstream styles rather than to work out my own murky destiny. Consequently, I felt I needed *not* to publish. I was not strong enough to resist the unintentional influence of editors. I also knew that I was not yet strong enough to make a career in business while writing *and* publishing. One of those things had to go, and it was publishing.

RM: Could you be more specific in terms of characterizing those early poems? What poets influenced you? What type of poetry were you writing as a graduate student and in your early days as a businessman?

DG: My strongest early influences were Eliot, Auden, Pound, Roethke, Rilke, and sometimes anyone I happened to be reading at the time. By the time I completed my first quarter in business school, I had made the decision to stop publishing. So what I'm describing is my early work.

RM: How many, if any, of those early poems made it into *Daily Horoscope?*

DG: The earliest poem in *Daily Horoscope* is "The Burning Ladder," the first draft of which was written when I was studying with Robert Fitzgerald. There are only one or two other early poems which made it into that book. "Four Speeches for Pygmalion," for instance, is based on a long dramatic monologue I wrote for Fitzgerald. All of the other poems were written after I had gone into business. Virtually none of my early work has been collected.

RM: Didn't you take one poetry writing seminar as a business student at Stanford?

DG: Yes, paradoxically, the only creative writing I ever took while I was in business school. I took Donald Davie's graduate poetry writing seminar, which was officially open only to the Masters candidates in Creative Writing, but Donald bent the rules and let in two outsiders — myself and an Indian student from the Food Research Institute named Vikram Seth. Donald's seminar was one of the most interesting intellectual experiences I've ever had. It was full of bright people — like Vikram, John Gery, and Vickie Hearne. It was a first rate course in practical criticism. I felt, however, that Donald's course was extraordinarily damaging for me as a poet because the work I was trying to write was at odds with the sort of poetry that he wanted.

He had strong preconceptions of the traditions an American poet should follow. Perhaps the work we brought him was still half-formed, but too much deviation from the schools of either Pound or Winters was not encouraged. In retrospect, I am grateful to Donald for being so discouraging. It toughened us up. It let us know that, if we were going to do something different, we had to expect the worst from critics.

RM: It's odd that the type of poetry that Davie would encourage was not the type of poetry that you were writing. A number of the poets you mention — Seth, Gery, and yourself — were later associated with New Formalism. I am struck by the parallels between New Formalism and Davie's early allegiance, The Movement. Davie ended up reacting against The Movement. Was he going through a phase when he was very influenced by Pound?

DG: Donald is one of the great living literary critics. But he was so English that he approached — half correctly, I think — American poetry as a foreign tradition. At that stage, Donald did not believe that Americans should be writing metrical poetry or narrative poetry. He also rejected any stylistic elegance or overt musicality. He encouraged us to write free verse about what he considered authentic American experience. I still remember the poem he praised most generously during the entire term was a formless memoir of Midwestern childhood. This poem had no redeeming quality except its Americanness. But, once again, when you have a poet-critic as strong as Donald Davie for a teacher, you must recognize that he will have his own agenda. What interests him may not interest you. One fine thing that came out of this class, however, was that several of us established our own informal writing group. John Gery, Vikram Seth, Vickie Hearne, Gail Lynch, and I formed a weekly poetry group. We would get together at someone's house or a bar and show each other our poems. John, Gail, and I were the most loyal members. Vikram and Vickie were more irregular. But that experience of non-academic writing group, which was entirely new to me then, helped me a great deal.

RM: When you left Stanford, didn't you work for a year in Minneapolis?

DG: No, I worked for a large company in Minneapolis the summer of 1976 between my two years in business school. I had never been in the Midwest before. I knew no one in Minneapolis, and it was an extraordinarily lonely period for me. I spent my days analyzing trade budgets and charting trends. I found the work and the environment most unsympathetic, and living in isolation, I spent most of my free time reading, writing, walking, and fretting. It was my first experience working for a large corporation. It made me a nervous wreck. But gradually one learns to fit in.

RM: Did you write much poetry at that time?

DG: I wrote a great deal of poetry in Minneapolis. Several poems in *Daily Horoscope* came out of that brief sojourn, such as "My Secret Life," and "An Elegy for Vladimir de Pachmann." In Minneapolis I also began a long poem called "Pornotopia", which was a kind of sexual nightmare in the tradition of Eliot and Thomson. I discarded most of this poem, but a few sections survived in *Daily Horoscope* — "Pornotopia", "The Memory", and "Speech from a Novella". "My Secret Life" was a parallel poem I wrote at the same time. I wanted to explore the fantasy worlds which some people use to escape life. The most important experience for me in Minneapolis, beside the unbroken solitude of my summer there, was discovering Weldon Kees.

RM: Both "Pornotopia" and "My Secret Life" seem quite different from the domestic themes in the first section of *Daily Horoscope* or the love lyrics there and in *The Gods of Winter*.

DG: I don't think of myself as a domestic poet. I have written very few autobiographical poems about family life. When I read the reviews of my first book, I was surprised at the difference between how the critics saw me and how I saw myself as a poet. *Daily Horoscope* is a diverse book of poems. I consider diversity a virtue in a poet, though not everyone will agree. But most critics focused on only one part of my writing, the narrative or semi-narrative poems about everyday life. They linked me to the tradition of Larkin, Frost, and Hardy. I consider that a great and perhaps undeserved compliment. But there's another side of my work, which is more private, more apocalyptic, that is also central to my sensibility. In addition to lyric and narrative poetry, I am interested in an exploratory kind of cultural and political poetry. Poems like "A Short History of Tobacco," "My Secret Life," "An Elegy for Vladimir de Pachmann," "The Lives of the Great Composers," "My Confessional Sestina," "News from 1984" represent an equally central part of my sensibility. I also believe that poems which have a lyric element, such as "In Cheever Country," "In Chandler Country," and "The Next Poem," are not simply lyrics, even if that is sometimes the easiest way to approach them critically. But an author always has grandiose visions of his own work! I'm interested in creating a lyric poetry which operates ambitiously, which reflects the aesthetics of concentration, allusiveness and even the impersonality of the Modernist lyric, but which nonetheless doesn't borrow the style of Modernism.

RM: Perhaps I used the term "domestic" too quickly. I used it with reference to what I perceive to be the narrative movement, if there can be said to be one in the first section of *Daily Horoscope*, which concludes with a vision in "In Cheever Country" of suburbia as a type of paradise. Certainly some earlier poems in the section, like "Insomnia" demonstrate that a suburban home doesn't necessarily provide a sense of security.

DG: Wouldn't that make it anti-domestic?

RM: Well, no, it seems to me that there's a tension in the poems between being a poet and living in the modern world, between being a businessman and a poet. There is also a sense of psychological tension in poems like "The Man in the Open Doorway" and "Men After Work" that business life can be unfulfilling for many people — balanced by the final poem, "In Cheever Country" where you write: "If there is an afterlife, let it be a small town/gentle as this spot at just this instant" that suggests at least a temporary sense of solace, resolution.

DG: A poet must be honest to experience. Whatever I write must somehow be grounded in my actual life. Contemporary American poetry does not have nymphs and shepherds, but it has its equivalent clichés. Most American poetry takes place in prefabricated literary landscapes, be they redwood forests or working class bars — conventionally poetic places where poets have poetic experiences. I have tried to write out of the range of my actual experience, which means the suburbs as well as nature, which means books and music as well as the family. If some of that subject matter is domestic, it's usually a kind of imperilled, precarious domesticity. My practical theory of poetry is based on tension. Any poem I write that moves comfortably along in one direction doesn't satisfy me. Good poems have unexpected leaps and turns. In the same way the language of a poem should stretch against whatever form one lays out. There should be lines and turns of phrase that surprise the reader. Unless a poem contains some surprising contradiction between its subject and its form, between its departure point and its destination, it doesn't interest me much.

RM: If one can identify, however problematically, one persona, connected with all of the poems in the opening section of *Daily Horoscope*, this persona achieves, especially at the end of "In Cheever Country," "a momentary stay against confusion," which is what Frost thought a poem should do.

DG: I believe that it's the poet's job to redeem the ordinary world around us for the imagination and the spirit — even if that world is the suburbs and office life. But the poet cannot attempt this redemption at the price of simplifying or distorting it. One must see the world for what it is. One must present all of the burdens and miseries of this common life and still see the value in it. This spiritual challenge is at the root of my notion of poetic tension. It's hard for me to see beauty without somehow acknowledging the fragility of it. If I am a transcendentalist, it is of an austere and unillusioned sort.

RM: Has Frost influenced your poetry?

DG: I consider Frost a pivotal figure in American poetry. He redefined the possibilities of our literature. Whitman and Williams created an authentic American voice only by discarding the past. That led to a very narrow definition of American art, one that was progressive and yet oddly provincial. But Frost found a way to be American without rejecting tradition. He quietly and masterfully transformed it to suit new purposes. He was our secret Modernist. He reinvented formal prosody to fit modern American speech. He used traditional genres like the narrative poem and the pastoral in startlingly innovative ways. But because he stressed his continuity with tradition the novelty of his efforts were not recognized during his lifetime. No later poets pursued the rich possibilities his work opened up. That neglect is why Frost is so attractive to me.

In the mid 1970's when I tried to write narrative poetry seriously for the first time, I found no contemporary models. Modernism had declared narrative poetry defunct. Poets still wrestled with the epic — the massive culture poem in the tradition of Pound or Crane. There were lots of poets writing anecdotal, autobiographical poems in the confessional vein. But no one seemed to be exploring narratives about other people's lives. I wanted to write what I once called in my essay "The Dilemma of the Long Poem," "poems of middle length," verse narratives that were equivalent in scope to a short story. After discarding a few aborted poems, I began searching the past for a usable tradition to draw on. Browning seemed too remote; Tennyson lovely but inert. Early Eliot was attractive but too idiosyncratic. Robinson came close, but his language and manner were too severe for my sensibility. Then I looked at Frost, and all sorts of possibilities occurred to me. He had found just the balance between lyric tension and narrative credibility. He had created a style whose full potential had not yet been realized.

RM: You have extended your range as a narrative poet in your second collection. The tension between lyric epiphany and violence is even more emphatic in "Counting the Children" than "The Room Upstairs" from *Daily Horoscope,* and in "The Homecoming" it is most emphatic of all. Are you consciously invading the territory of prose in these longer poems?

DG: Absolutely. By the end of the 1970s American poetry had been reduced to a few lyric genres. The potential of the art had been diminished. The main contribution of the so-called New Formalists has not been the reintroduction of rhyme and meter. That was only a manifestation of a deeper change in sensibility. Their most important accomplishment was the reinvention of traditional genres in a viable and unpedantic contemporary form. We wanted workable forms that went beyond the autobiographical and surrealist lyric. Some poets like Charles Martin, Tom Disch, and R. S. Gwynn have focused mainly on satiric and discursive genres. They want to steal some of the energy and flexibility of prose without necessarily giving up formal strength of poetry. My own interests have been largely focused on finding a way to tell stories memorably in verse, to create something that works both as a compelling narrative and a forceful poem. That hasn't been easy. It requires a different kind of poetic language from what the lyric needs. The reinvention of the narrative poem seems to me the most important thing now happening in American poetry. It is also the clearest signal that Modernism is dead, and that poets are creating a new aesthetic.

RM: Did the death of your first son alter your development as a poet?

DG: It utterly transformed my life. How could it not also transform my consciousness as a writer? Tragedy simplifies your vision. It sweeps everything away that isn't essential. Losing my first son made me realize how little most things in my life matter to me — and how desperately important the few remaining things were. There was a searing clarity to the grief. I stopped writing for a year. It took all of my energy to get myself and my wife through each day. When I gradually began writing again, I saw poetry differently. Writing took on a spiritual urgency I had never experienced before — at least in so sustained and emphatic a way.

RM: How was writing these new poems different for you?

DG: I was no longer concerned with what the reader would think about the poems. I wrote them for myself. I trusted my intuition and emotions. In one sense this made the poems more difficult. I didn't worry about explaining an image or situation, if it had a private resonance to me. But, in a different sense, it also made the poems more emotionally accessible. I admitted my obsessions and allowed myself to be vulnerable. I no longer cared if critics thought I was morose or sentimental. Perhaps all I am saying is that I wrote the poems that my life dictated without trying to turn them into something else.

RM: Most of the poems in *The Gods of Winter* are directly or indirectly about death, including some poems written before your son's death. How do you account for that eerie coincidence?

DG: Some of the poems were composed earlier. "The Gods of Winter," for instance, was written for my wife after she had recovered from some potentially serious surgery. But some of the poems were reconceived and recomposed after my son's death. When I began writing again, I grew dissatisfied with some of the poems I had written after *Daily Horoscope*. I no longer felt the impulse that had created them. Since I normally work on poems for years before publishing them, it was natural for me to revise these poems-in-progress into something which spoke to my new situation. I could never have finished them in their original form. My Rilke translation, "The Song," for example, seemed elegant but evasive. I rewrote it into something quite personal. When I looked at "The Homecoming" (which was then titled "The Killer"), I suddenly saw the theme of the poem differently. It wasn't about religion but about family. I rewrote it from beginning to end. I took the narrative poem I had been working on the night before my son died — "Counting the Children" — and turned it into a longer, darker poem which eventually resolved itself into a vision. The episode I had originally planned as the ending became instead a turning point at the middle. That poem especially became a kind of spiritual self-examination for me. There was no other way for me to finish it except to transform it into something new.

RM: Has the immense public response to your essay, "Can Poetry Matter?" had any effect on you as a writer.

DG: Yes, for several months it kept me too busy to write. I knew it would prove a controversial piece. I was prepared for criticism, but I was utterly defenseless for praise. Hundreds of letters arrived. Reporters called at the office. Radio and television producers booked interviews. Critical rebuttals and endorsements poured in. I made the mistake of trying to deal with the publicity responsibly. I answered a great many of the letters personally. I spent countless hours talking with reporters who knew very little about poetry. I wanted them to understand why the issues at stake were important. Meanwhile I had to maintain my normal business schedule. The whole experience drained me. I should have run for cover.

RM: What are your plans for the near future?

DG: To write poems again, if the Muse will still have me.

LAVINIA GREENLAW

TALKING TO RAYMOND FRIEL

Lavinia Greenlaw was born in London, where she has lived for most of her life. She studied literature and printing, before working in publishing and arts administration for several years. She is now a freelance writer. Her publications are The Cost of Getting Lost in Space (Turret Books, 1991), Love From a Foreign City (Slow Dancer, 1992) and Night Photograph (Faber & Faber) which was shortlisted for the 1993 Whitbread Poetry Prize. She received an Eric Gregory Award in 1990. Lavinia Greenlaw was interviewed by Raymond Friel on Tuesday, 24th May, 1994, in Covent Garden, London.

RF: When did you start writing poetry?

LG: I began as a teenager when I think poetry attracted me for all the wrong reasons. What appealed to me was the mystery, the enigma, the romance: a morbid introspection more than anything. And then I got really excited about, in particular, American and east European poetry. And as I began to try to write, I began to find out about the craft that lay behind it.

RF: Did you have an experience of "finding your voice"? Some people talk about a kind of Road to Damascus experience: they can almost remember the afternoon this happened to them. Did you have an experience like that or was it a more evolutionary process?

LG: Just after my daughter was born in 1987, when she was about nine or ten weeks old, I began to go to workshops run by Fred D'Aguiar. I was exhausted and completely wrapped up in parenthood. I also had this very strong desire to try and reclaim something of myself and I suddenly found that perhaps due to the upheaval that I was undergoing that I was writing with what felt like a voice that came straight out, that wasn't a separate poetic voice, but was mine.

RF: So the birth of your daughter was a key moment in your writing life?

LG: I think it probably shifted me away from the centre of my own world. Only recently have I written directly about her at all. But I'm sure the experience was profoundly important.

RF: Do you think it's important to share your work as it develops?

LG: Yes, I do. There's a balance to be struck between getting a critical response from people you trust to be rigorous and honest, and also having an eye to what is yours and what should be there.

RF: Who are you reading at the moment?

LG: I'm re-reading Elizabeth Bishop and frequently read Robert Lowell. I read Miroslav Holub . . . And Akhmatova, earlier this year I was reading Akhmatova.

RF: A number of those involved in the New Poetry Generation have cited Bishop and Lowell as influences on their work. Why do you think these writers in particular are so important to the present generation?

LG: Maybe, of the writers who were available to us when we were beginning to write and wanting to read, they offered something of more relevance, something that seemed more alive than their British counterparts, to our experience and our generation.

RF: Is there something in the poetry of Elizabeth Bishop about travelling and the poetry of elsewhere which appealed to you expecially?

LG: I don't think I'm a good traveller. I want to be a good traveller. I am intrigued by her use of distance, geographical poetic and emotional, which she manages to employ without any lack of commitment or involvement from herself.

RF: At the moment you're involved in the Poetry Society's New Generation promotion. What are your feelings about that generally? Good idea?

LG: Yes, I think the time is right for it because publishers are more actively addressing the need to promote poetry, to make it seem possible, even more than accessible. Poets themselves are also paying more attention to the need to be able to perform their work well and communicate their ideas to a wider audience. I think that if it can achieve anything it will be that a few of those many people who write and read poetry but don't connect what they do with organised literary activity, might begin to see a way in to the formal world of poetry.

RF: In becoming accessible is poetry in danger of giving up too much, of becoming over-diluted?

LG: It could be if the poet let it but I don't think a good poet can. Why do we write poetry? I think we like the layers and the knots and so on but I do think that a poem has to be accessible to the extent that there are enough clues and signposts within it to draw your reader in and to make them want to come back and work out what's going on and what they can take away from it.

RF: So poetry can live with publicity?

LG: Yes, so long as the publicity takes into account that it is poetry and it's not rock'n roll.

RF: If we could turn to Night Photograph, your most recent collection. To what extent do you see yourself as a London poet? I'm thinking about "River History" and "Love from a Foreign City".

LG: I do write a great deal about the city. I've lived here most of my life and I find that it addresses many of my preoccupations about location, place, the paradoxical freedom of being in a crowded place and being able to be entirely alone within that. And also the physical image it projects of both the historical and current economic, political and industrial state of this country.

ARF: Has London, as a subject for poetry, been overlooked recently do you think?

LG: No, I think the urban experience is written about very widely and I don't really think of it in terms of London, only that London is my city. So that's the one I write about. ·

RF: Apart from the local, I find in your work as well a sense of yearning for another place or way of life, particularly from the female characters, who often appear to be trapped. I'm thinking now of "Galileo's Wife" and "The Patagonian Nightingale" and "Anchorage". Would you like to comment on that?

LG: I never think about or approach my work consciously from the perspective of gender. I think the three characters you've mentioned . . . the fact that they're female is probably incidental and purely because I am. In "Galileo's Wife" I'm particularly interested in the human compulsion to map and make sense and what we accept as proof of, in this case, the fact that the world is round. The other two poems are about locating yourself or not and probably unconsciously I have attributed the desire to locate yourself to men more than women.

RF: You don't consider yourself then primarily as a woman writer?

LG: No.

RF: What about women's writing, women's anthologies and so on; do you think they're helpful?

LG: I think that I wouldn't be able to do what I'm doing now if there hadn't been a conscious move by women to collectively address the fact that their voices were not being heard and their work was not being represented within literature. On the other hand, I do not feel bound to an agenda or an experience or a perspective because I'm a woman.

RF: Is there then, as a reaction to this sense of confinement in some of the poems and the need to map and measure, a desire for the "wild grammar" you refer to in "Boris Goes Fishing". There seems to be a regret there, too, that the narrator cannot pronouce "revolution" in Russian. Would you like to comment on that?

LG: "Boris Goes Fishing" was about my frustration at being confined by my limited knowledge and ability to using a language in order to describe something that to me was terribly vivid. I think it's quite an interesting illustration of the confines of voice versus the needs of the subject. I've found since finishing Night Photograph, which was almost two years ago, that I am writing with quite a different voice and I have quite profoundly changed my ideas about strength in a poetic voice and perspective. In the past, quite naturally I have used what has been described as the controlled, detached "scientific" voice and I think partly I was concerned about allowing myself too much emotional space within my work. I now believe that there is a way of writing more directly from yourself, of allowing myself to come through it without it collapsing into self-indulgence. I'm not sure I can do it but that's what I'm beginning to explore.

RF: Would you like to talk a little about what has brought this change about?

LG: I think it came about partly from a desire to make sure that I wasn't confined . . . sorry, I keep using that word confined . . . to ensure that my work wasn't dominated by scientific subjects and also a desire to address things closer to home. I didn't write for a long time after finishing the book and if a poem began to unpack itself in a way that I considered almost formulaic according to how I was writing in Night Photograph, I stopped myself. So I didn't finish any work for a fair while; and it just seemed to arise: one day I wrote a poem that to me seemed to be more direct, more subjective and hopefully lighter and more alive in some way than my more detached work. I'm writing about things that are more local, that are more immediate.

RF: The overwhelming, the menacing in nature seem to feature in certain poems in Night Photograph. Is there a vision at the heart of that book of us as human beings fumbling around in darkness, not really knowing what we're doing with these forces.

LG: Yes, very much. I'm interested in the fact that although we live in an increasingly secular society, most of us have a blind faith in technology and science. We depend upon them every day and never question, or rarely question, their reliability except when there's some kind of catastrophe. We're at a very interesting stage, when science is revealing its variables and its subjectivity and the potential for technology through things like Internet and satellite are becoming quite overwhelming. Science and technology, instead of being perceived as tools for order and constraint, now seem like some kind of Pandora's Box. That's an over simple comparison but it interests me the way our perspective on these things changes.

RF: There's also a sense of impending natural catastrophe in some of the poems, for example "The Recital of Lost Cities". Do you feel that nature is exacting her revenge on us?

LG: I do feel that we have a tendency to think that once we have located, identified and labelled something it is under our control, even though it has been repeatedly proved to us that this is not the case and this is something that I've explored in poems like "The Innocence of Radium" and "The Recital of Lost Cities," which is about a desperate attempt to keep place-names alive after pieces of the earth have been submerged by the sea. I don't consciously think about the environmental future as being a central theme of my book but I do wonder about the finite time we have left to us as being in apparent control of our planet.

RF: It strikes me, thinking back to "River History", that there is a strong feeling for the importance of archive in your work. Is there also a sense of preserving through naming?

LG: I've not thought of it like that. I find that history attracts me when it collides with the present. When I wrote "River History" I was working in a fairly derelict area of the docklands and I would walk by the river and see Canary Wharf, Traitor's Gate, HMS Belfast and Tower Bridge, which brings together centuries of the city's history and politics. In a poem like "In the Time of Elizabeth R" I was simply struck by the parallels in the reigns of the two Queen Elizabeths.

RF: Are the new poems you've referred to earlier consciously set in London or is the place less significant?

LG: They're not consciously set in London. Most of them seem not to be set in London. I think what I'm identifying as being different about them is the voice more than the subject. I'm asking more questions, I'm allowing myself to show more of how I feel rather than concentrating on providing a conduit.

RF: Has this new emphasis on personal feeling had any effect on the form or style of your writing?

LG: I think, well I hope, that my use of form is developing. I have been conscious in the past of writing a lot of work with regular four-stress lines and I've enjoyed most the poetry I've written that has more lightness to it. I'm persisting in trying to find a light touch. I'm also quite intrigued by internal rhyme and certain plays of meaning.

RF: I'd like to go back to Night Photograph and talk a bit more about one of the big themes in the book which you've alluded to, namely science: what draws you, or what drew you then, to science as a theme?

LG: My family are all doctors and scientists and like most people of my generation I had to make the choice at thirteen about which discipline I was going to study, and so to my later regret gave up science at a very early age. When I began writing poetry I found that scientific subjects and perspectives came up again and again and this is probably due to the fact that I grew up with scientific ideas being discussed around me. I also came back to science through reading, particularly, the works of Beckett and Shakespeare and thinking about the necessity for the human scale: what happens when you step outside the human scale and the illusory nature of it. Looking into that through Hamlet and Endgame I did find I then came back to literally the mapping of the universe and the mapping of the world. So science has come up partly because of my personal background and partly because it is the discipline that most clearly addresses my preoccupations. I have been concerned that it has been construed as a subject I'm using for its novel appeal and that may be partly why I'm reacting by trying to write about terribly simple subjects.

RF: Do you feel there's a sense in which the scientific and the artistic in recent times have come closer together as science's old certainties have been questioned more and more?

LG: Yes I think there is a greater understanding between science and art, and scientists and artists, as they are both trying to make sense of and articulate abstracts and that the rigour that's applied to a scientific hypothesis should be applied to a poem. I also think that scientists have learned from artists how to tell their story in recent years. I don't just mean the proliferation of popular science books, but more a way of communicating through image and anecdote. Artists also feel a greater sense of affinity with scientists because of their increasing understanding and experience of technology.

RF: What do you mean by the rigour that's brought to bear on a scientific hypothesis being applied to poetry? How does that work?

LG: That any contention in a poem has to make sense. I think I was referring back indirectly to the start of the interview when I mentioned my weakness as a teenager for something that sounded profound and mysterious and melodramatic. When you chase a poem into a corner, it has to stand up and fight. It has to make sense when you take it apart, to be properly constructed.

RF: You've no time for the mystical then?

LG: I don't mean that poetry should be neither mystical nor dramatic. I mean that a poet should not be so enchanted with their subject that they can't distance themselves from it enough to have an objective eye to how they're constructing their poem and ordering their matter and I think that's where the scientific analogy arrives, the ordering of matter; just as scientists have learned to trust their imagination to an extent I think artists have had to learn to treat reality and the imagination with equal suspicion and not be seduced by "wild enlightenment", while letting it come when it will and doing what they can with it.

RF: Lavinia Greenlaw, thank you.

TONY HARRISON IN CONVERSATION WITH MICHAEL ALEXANDER

This conversation was recorded on 14 February 1991, the morning after Tony Harrison had read in St Andrews.

MA: When I bought your volume *Continuous* at your reading at Stirling eight years ago, you kindly inscribed it 'In Homage', which greatly puzzled me at the time. Then I wondered if you had read some of *The Earliest English Poems*.

TH: I loved those translations, it's a wonderful book. Is it still in print?

MA: There's a third edition coming out in August, with one or two new ones in it.

TH: The reason I went back to 'The Ruin' in *The Earliest English Poems* is partly because I've been drawn a lot to fragments. *The Trackers of Oxyrhynchus* is a reconstruction of fragments, but also keeps honest to the idea of it being a fragment.

MA: Yes.

TH: And I also spent a lot of time on the Roman wall and looking at the bits and pieces of the Roman wall and how it's been used for pig troughs and barns and that kind of thing; and then thinking about the whole business of the Saxon world, seeing the ruins of the Roman, and the idea of mortality and transience with a culture that built such big edifices — almost softening them up for Christianity.

MA: Yes, I used to think that it [*The Ruin*] was all to do with what the Saxons felt when they looked at those ruins, but I think to some extent their giants do come from Genesis. Now, I never used to think of that.

TH: Oh really?

MA: Well, the race of giants was drowned by the Flood. The Saxons keep on about giants in their poetry, and monsters. I think they were very puzzled about how these huge buildings could have been built.

TH: But isn't it so that if a culture that could build big things in stone like that has passed away, what hope is there for anybody? I started thinking about it, I suppose, when the Wall was coming down — the Berlin Wall — and all those things: wondering what was the new faith that would come out of the ruin.

MA: Yes. As for fragments, in some ways your work is very unlike that of people like Eliot and Pound who, in their early work anyway, wrote in fragments, while you really like things to be finished.

TH: Yes, but I am very drawn to fragments. When I was an undergraduate I translated some of Sappho, and I was drawn to the fact that it was just fragments, but you could actually reconstruct the stanzaic form just by the rhythmical fragment that you had. That's always intrigued me.

MA: I wondered if that detail in the *Kumquat for John Keats* about the girl reaching up to take the apples came from Sappho. You know, there's the fragment about the topmost apple on the tree.

TH: Oh, right! No, not necessarily. I think it's from the idea of Eve, really . . . I suppose, the first bite as well. The idea of the woman offering fruit is very central to me, I think. I remember my mother, the way she gave you fruit as though it was the most special thing that had been created.

MA: It *was*, after the war!

TH: Yes, it was, sure, and the things that you hadn't seen, even apples . . . She presented them with such a sense of a special quality, and it was to do with after the war, but also that so many . . . I mean not only Christianity but I remember the Tibetan Buddhist thing uses man picking fruit as an emblem of futility, whereas for me it's the richest emblem of life.

MA: Another point about translation. I was interested to read in the Bloodaxe book[1] your address to the Classical Association where you write about 'Vacate the thoroughfare' instead of 'Move along there'. You're right, that strikes a bell with me — that's exactly the kind of style that we were supposed to translate into. When I was at school, if you were clever you had to do Latin and Greek. It broke down halfway through my career and I was allowed to do English in the end, but against the will of the school, really.

TH: Yes, because I was considered a bright boy, I was put to do Latin and Greek . . . it was still the tradition then.

MA: Well, I remember 'vacate the thoroughfare'. One of the reasons that Pound's *Homage to Sextus Propertius* was so upsetting to people was that it did call the bluff of all that sort of artificial English.

TH: It did, it did. And Pound was important to me for that reason.

MA: I thought I would ask you about one thing which probably people don't usually ask you about: The first poem you read us, 'Thomas Campey and the Copernican System': in the last stanza you have the Imperial Host (of angels) and they are 'squat on their thrones of Ormus and of Ind'; which is from Milton, and they are of course devilish angels in Milton. Elsewhere you say 'I believe life ends with death and that is all.' I wondered about religion. Obviously you don't believe in God, but religion seems to trouble you, both in your early work in *The Loiners* and also in that thing about Salman Rushdie, which I also read in this Bloodaxe book —

TH: You didn't see the film?

MA: No, I didn't. Like many literary people, I don't watch enough television.

TH: Well, you see, I think television has great possibilities for poetry.

MA: I was glad that the only poem you didn't read last night, which you read eight years ago, was 'Nuptial Torches' — although you mentioned it.

TH: I was inclined to read the 'Nuptial Torches' . . . Dresden was bombed on Valentine's Day and then this Valentine's Day the news of bombing that bunker in Baghdad, all the news of 400 roasted bodies . . . It brought 'Nuptial Torches' back to me, although I hadn't read it for a long time just because it's been so anthologised. I got a little tired of it. But I am fairly hostile to religion, it's true. Religion is hostile to life . . . There's another poem, which hasn't been collected here, although it's in my last American book, called 'The Pomegranates of Patmos', which is, I suppose, an attack on the Armageddonism of America and people like Reagan. I remembered how Lawrence at the end of his life wrote a book on the

---

[1] Bloodaxe Critical Anthologies: 1. *Tony Harrison*, ed. Neil Astley, 1991

Apocalypse and he said how they longed for the end of this world, how they 'lusted for the end of the world those early Christians'. That lusting for an end to this life I find so undermining of the real fulfilments that there are to be found in life.

MA: You're very interested in extinction, not as regards just the planet and our threatened egos, or a lot of ordinary pieties, but also of art. Obviously you're very interested in what's going to happen. Shakespeare seems to have believed to some extent in a kind of posterity, but he keeps on talking about time and death.

TH: I think that in all art there is a gamble against time. It's not so easy for us now though, is it, to imagine posterity, I think. Since nuclear weapons came into the world the idea of a memory-less future has been with us. As Robert J. Lifton wrote in a book on the future of immortality, the idea of immortality no longer is a certainty — never *was* a certainty — but it is now actually questioned by the idea of human extinction.

MA: That makes us more mediaeval, doesn't it?

TH: Yes, absolutely.

MA: 'So long as men can live and eyes can see, So long lives this, and this gives life to thee . . . ' It's not something that somebody would have written in Chaucer's time, and certainly not before.

TH: Well, what I like about, for example, the *Trojan Women* of Euripides is that everything is . . . the whole culture is being destroyed — men have been destroyed, the city has been destroyed, the one future is the grandchild . . . he's been thrown off the top towers, the place is put to the flames, women are going off into slavery, and it's always left to the oldest woman, Hecuba, to find a reason for going to pluck some kind of hope from this terrible despair. And all she comes up with in the end when everything's been taken away is 'Had we not suffered, we would not be stories for future mortals.' It is said that history is for those who come later, and the idea of becoming stories, I think, is for me the only hope of going on after death.

MA: Another thing you probably do get asked about is metre. Your consistent liking for regular metre is there before you thought of the stage, as far as I can see. [H: I thought of the stage pretty early] . . . but looking through your books there are poems which are more allusive and ingenious and not suitable for declamation from the stage, whilst obviously some of your later work is plainer and simpler partly because of the discipline involved in getting it to the back of the stalls. However, so metre was there even from the beginning. Was that at all a conscious decision in the very beginning for you, or was it just something you thought that poetry ought to be written in?

TH: I was always drawn to metre. I think it's partly instinctual but also when I talk about 'We'll occupy your lousy leasehold poetry', I had the idea of being able to do it very well: that I'd actually *learned* how to do forms through the long process of imitation and translation, none of which I cared to publish. But I did that when I was very young. The idea of becoming a master of something, of learning skills, was very important to me, and partly to show off to *them*. But also I wanted it to be real work — in the sense that my father's work was real work.

MA: You speak in 'On Not Being Milton' of smashing the frames of the looms. You haven't smashed the frames, although you understand those who did. That is to say, you might want to smash some social frames but you're very happy to keep some artistic frames and regular metre.

84

TH: Yes, but I like also to subject them to a sort of maximum strain as well, as, for example, in *V,* where I take a very classical form but inhabit it with the most profane language so that it's as if you take the forms which have been in English literature for many centuries and subject them to all the stresses and strains of modern existence, modern thought, modern attitudes.

MA: That is like some very conservative people like James McAuley, A.D. Hope — Australian poets of a formal sort — who very much believed, particularly Hope, in trying out all the old forms, learning how to do it, using those forms — although they don't try to fill it with resistant untraditional material, so that is a big difference . . . We've been talking about you and your poetry, but do you think free verse has no longer been a useful line for people to follow?

TH: I don't find it very useful because, having said what the earlier attractions were for metric, the later are first of all the iambic beat. For the iambus is something close to the heartbeat, as Jean-Louis Barrault said 'le coeur bat l'iambe' (the heart beats iambically). And I think that the darker my subjects the more I wanted somehow the reassurance of the heartbeat. I mean, I can sit here looking out at the sea and brood about what's happening in the world at the moment and feel pretty pessimistic about it, but the heart still beats, I can't tell the heart to stop beating, so the actual beat of the iambus is very important to me in the sense of it being a reassurance that celebration in life is still possible even with the darkest thoughts and the darkest vision. So for me it's got that importance. And the way in which speech does fall often naturally into the iambic means that you can set up something where the formal had the warranty of the centuries but you can include in it only those things which put it to maximum stress in the sense of the aggression of the person who feels art is just a pile of shit. But also you can measure the speech, just ordinary speech, against the line, the literary line, the poetic line, and that you can then include . . . The iambic pentameter allows you to set speech absolutely in a context where you don't normally expect it, and therefore highlight it, so that you can pass the whole range from the most formal, the most literary to the most colloquial. I like to play off that colloquial energy against something extremely formal, and I do that in the theatre.

MA: Yes, you read — more, I noticed, last night than previously — you read with care to articulate very clearly, which is probably very necessary. But I remember you reading it more as 'a man speaking to men' eight years ago — this may be because you are even more experienced as a reader now — but you spoke very clearly, I noticed, last night. I think that's very helpful to people in getting them to notice.

TH: I think you've got to. I think the more reading I've done, the more I feel you have to use it as a way of making things clear, getting things through. I mean, sometimes you're reading to people who don't know the work at all, so you've got a chance to win some readers for the future.

MA: You explain more allusions, too. This seemed to work very well with the audience. I was very interested to see how many of the jokes which in some ways will become obsolete, like the prohibition on ending sentences with 'by', 'with' and 'from', were still taking tricks, at least in St. Andrews, which is a very old-fashioned place. People remember being taught that . . .

TH: . . . Such a strange thing, it came from moulding English according to Latin.

MA: Yes, and it was used for showing that you know how to 'speak proper', as much as anything else.

TH: The grammar schools were also founded within the belief that English couldn't measure up to Latin. I mean, that's terrible. Within that there are all kinds of gradations that certain kinds of English can't measure up to other kinds and so on. I mean, I remember somebody finding a sentence with at least five prepositions at the end. The story is of the little girl: the father reads a story to the little girl in bed every night, and like children do she wanted the same story every night, and the father got tired of this and brought a different book upstairs to bed, and the little girl said, "What have you brought the book I don't want to be read to out of up for?" It's perfect English.

MA: It's just one isn't used to seeing it written. But it works. There are quite a lot of puns in your poems, sometimes multilingual puns or plays on words, some of them simply on one word like 'Righting' [at the end of 'On Not Being Milton'].

TH: That's a found pun which comes out of illiteracy. That one particularly has all kinds of tensions around it.

MA: You've got a lot of very good concluding oneliners in your poems. That seems to me perhaps something you would need on the stage, I suppose.

TH: Well, I think I learned that as well. It's actually something I learned from my earliest days of going to the theatre, the comedians I admired, the way that a joke is structured; the last line, and the way the lines — pauses betwen the lines — are structured, in the way I remember comedians telling jokes.

MA: Yes, 'Timer', ending on 'eggs' is a very good point to end on. A terrible thing to think of — that's the most upsetting of your poems, as far as I'm concerned, although I suppose that the title poem of *Continuous* has more in it artistically. Douglas Dunn's *Elegies* was very successful, and a lot of people seem to respond very much to your poems about the death of your parents.

TH: They do, they do.

MA: I certainly do. Like you, I've lost my parents, and it makes a difference to you. Although I wasn't an only child, and I hadn't got that distance away from my parents.

TH: No, I have a sister.

MA: Oh, you have. Sorry, I didn't know. It's a funny question . . . Sometimes people are moved by things they know about and can understand, and that is on some scale that's not connected necessarily with the merit of what they're reading. I'm not suggesting that your poems or Douglas Dunn's poems about the death in the family are not good poems — on the contrary, I think in both cases they are very good — but it's a strange thing, that.

TH: I think that people need such poems. My feeling about those poems, one reason why I do read them, is that I, and they, often move people to tears. I'm very aware of that, and people have often sobbed aloud at those poems, and I realise that somewhere there is a need for such poetry, because we don't have any social forms for grieving and articulating grief any more that we rely on. You go to a funeral and they're sort of peremptory and no-one has the community belief any more in Christian funerals and so on, so I think that poems about such things people feel a very need for, and they're surprised by the depth of their own remembered grief and reaction.

MA: Yes. That's right. Yes, I'm sure you're right. People do have a need for them. A colleague of mine was saying the other day how all these literary theorists and their strange views about how language works seem to deny the possibility of such a thing as the consolatory power of poetry, or of people joined together in a poem in order to know something.

TH: Someone came to me last night and burst into tears. It happens a lot with that particular group of poems and I think that that is a good reaction to the poem.

MA: Yes, of course it is.

TH: And I think that to exclude that from literary theory is throwing the baby and the bathwater out.

MA: Yes. Speaking for myself, I'm sometimes interested by what the theorists do, but in the end it seems to have absolutely no real connection with what literature is about. A more obvious question is about elitism and speaking for the dumb. I mean, you had the high-powered education that you talked about, and I had not quite such a high-powered one because I was allowed to give up Classics and go on to English — which was a bit easier. But I don't know if you got your idea of composition and imitation and development, experimenting in modes of translation and copying things out, showing you can do it too — was that something you got through having to do Greek and Latin composition at school? You do mention that in one poem about Cicero's prose.

TH: Yes. I think it's a poem called 'Classics Society', about having to translate Hansard into Ciceronian Latin.

MA: That's right.

TH: And then I think it ends with a quotation from Burke on the Irish question, where he says, 'A dreadful schism in the British nation'.

MA: You must have thought about every possible angle of this business of having had this separating kind of education, putting one into a very different bracket from one's parents, and not just them but virtually everybody else in the school too, not just people in the street. And of course as time goes on you begin to feel stranger and stranger, in that half the things you learned . . . It must seem very strange to you to give an address to the Classical Association — I mean, I know you've done great things in the National Theatre, but that's more imaginable than giving an address to the Classical Association.

TH: Right. Becoming President of the Classical Association.

MA: There seems to be an absolutely unremoveable problem about using old, high, rare kinds of skills that are getting a lot rarer . . . to speak for those and to those to whom it all is very strange and doesn't mean very much. Do you find that's getting worse?

TH: Yes. In some ways it is, I think, when you make certain inroads into it. I've also tried to use television in simple ways to reach wider audiences, still writing the same, using the same styles, but you're reaching maybe 5 million people. Somewhere there are possibilities there which I'm hoping to go on exploring. It's more complicated than the theatre, where the choice of going out and paying money and coming to a place which is called the National Theatre makes for an audience with a different kind of composition. And the sort of people who would go out and buy a book of poems again is small. I think that what I've done is to always be fully conscious of that. Perhaps one of the reasons I don't spend a lot of time with other literary people is that there's a kind of mutual support society which often pretends to have more significance than it really does.

MA: A poetry magazine is a very strange world.

TH: Yes, a very strange world, and I tend not to send poems to poetry magazines. I prefer, if I've got a poem to publish, to have it in the newspaper. One of the things I really enjoyed about the controversy over *V* was that it was finally printed full page in *The Independent*, and I thought, that's a good place for a poem to be [MA: . . . for a public poem]. So that I've tried to move into public arenas but at the same time I'm always aware that I'm using an art form that seems to have diminishing returns. Now if you use it knowing you're a doomed species . . . The poet is also probably a doomed species, so it's a kind of affinity in that sense that you do feel that the role is continually threatened and under threat from media with more power, more kudos, more access to people's minds than poetry . . . *but*, I think there's still a need for poetry.

MA: You are getting quite a lot of exposure — you are getting through to quite a lot of people and a lot of the main organs of communication are to some extent open to you. You have been able to get hold of them, to use them.

TH: It's been a deliberate effort to claim back some of the range of poetry which is lost — first to the novel, then to cinema, television and so on. Why not find if these new media can take poetry? . . . and I think they can.

MA: Do you think there's anything to be lost? I remember reading a sentence ten years ago that a certain literary man had made a Faustian bargain with the media which he seemed to be getting away with so far. But he of course is a journalist.

TH: I think the dangers of being a television personality are something else. I resist — I don't do anything except be a poet. I don't review books, I don't go on chat shows, I don't do any of that, I only write poetry, whether it's for the page or the stage or the opera house — all poetry — and that's all I do. So that I think that whatever the . . . if you say, Is there a compromise involved in the public medium? What there is, is a real struggle with what does it mean to address people. And that for me is a very healthy one for poetry because it's often been ignored.

MA: Yes. I mean, I'm a great admirer of Ezra Pound and yet in the end, after he left Britain he wasn't really talking to anybody.

TH: No, absolutely. You can tell it in his writing that he wasn't talking to anybody but himself.

MA: Those later letters are really alarming because they're really just conversations with himself.

TH: Well, I think that he's a good warning example. He's someone I admired — what he did with classical literature — and was drawn to him. And then I suddenly thought, if this is the road of poetry, I don't want to go on it. And I guess I did react very strongly against the example of Pound.

MA: Geoffrey Hill is an interesting knife-edged case at the moment. He also has got a Leeds connection, hasn't he? And I thought that in *The Mystery of the Charity of Charles Péguy* he was getting to be a bit more accessible, but I'm not sure if that's being continued.

TH: No. He sort of gets quite difficult, and I think, if I can't understand somebody's work then who can? I think I'm a fairly intelligent reader of poetry.

MA: I know, it's very worrying seeing that happen. I was thinking not so much in terms of your getting lost somehow, more, do you think there's a steady movement towards greater clarity and accessibility in the style of your own work? Do you see any dangers from that in the end?

TH: No. On the contrary. On the contrary, I think that I work to make it more so. You know, I think that one of the worlds of the artist that has got rather buried in modernism was that sense of responsibility of the artist to make complex experience accessible without doing a disservice to its complexity in making it accessible. I think that's an important function of an artist.

MA: In some of your work there's a kind of savage Gothic satire on and caricature on what you hate or recoil from or want to see changed in religion or politics or people's behaviour. I haven't seen the thing on television that took place in the Indian restaurant, to do with Salman Rushdie [*The Blasphemers' Banquet*], but some of your work is more consciously, as it were, pamphleteering journalistic verse. I don't see any deterioration in the verse of *A Kumquat for John Keats* type, the more personal type. That's what I suppose I was wondering about.

TH: I think that's part of the range. I think that what you do on the page is one thing. As for *The Banquet*, I wouldn't normally think of publishing that. It belongs on a video tape — it's a film. Because someone was writing about it I allowed them to reprint it, and so it's on the page. It was never intended to be printed, just as I'm not very interested in the printing of my plays. I work on them all the time, I'm rewriting them until the play's on the stage. No publisher can actually print the text quickly enough for it to be the text which is performed. And now that *Trackers* has got the Delphi text and the National Theatre text together — because they're so different — and yet even those are now out of date. And I get so locked into the metre that I simply write out of my head. And it's written down by somebody else. I tell it to the actor, he learns it, and I'm sure that's how they worked when they didn't have scripts in the mediaeval plays. In the Greek world they didn't sit round reading a script, they taught it . . . the poet was the *didascolos*, the teacher. I'd love to do a play where I had the whole play in my head and I simply . . . [A: You probably could.] Yes. I'm going to experiment with it because I've done the idea of doing one performance only, which I originally did with *Trackers*, the idea you do a thing once. A wonderful new energy it brings to the idea of the celebration, the ephemerality of performance and knowing that it's ephemeral is the whole key to its celebratory nature.

MA: I did a lot of work on the radio — literary programmes for the Australian Broadcasting Commission — once, and I enjoyed it, but there was something rather funny to a literary person in thinking — when it stopped, 'that's it'. I mean, I can't read it again.

TH: I love that. I love the ephemerality of the stage and I'm sure that you know that Shakespeare didn't really care about his plays being printed, and there's something wonderful in that. And so we shouldn't worry — it's a long answer, but what I'm saying is that we shouldn't transfer the idea of page poetry to stage stuff or things for television. I think that they're doing different things, but they're nonetheless still poetry.

MA: Yes, I do think they are. And it's true that the world of the poetry magazine is . . . I mean, after all, half of them must be bought either by libraries or by other people who write, people who've appeared in that issue . . . I was quite interested by the time you spent in Africa, because a lot of our generation (although you're a bit older than me) went to Africa then. Is that part of your life any more?

TH: I still think a lot about Africa. I haven't been back since the seventies, and I would like to go back again, and you know I haven't kept up my connection, it's very hard to.

MA: Well, the world has changed, hasn't it? People who hoped for better things, who'd been to universities, went out to Africa in a spirit that cannot have been completely removed from that of Scottish missionaries a hundred years before . . . without perhaps the same . . . But it's changed now — they don't need or want us in a certain way. Why should they?

TH: No. I went at the time when there was still some of that atmosphere about, and I think I learned a lot about Britain in a curious way by being there. Not pleasant things, and when I came back my eyes had been opened to a lot of the unpleasant things about Britain, by actually being away from it in a post-colonial Nigeria. It was an eye-opener.

MA: Yes. A lot of things that were well hidden at the time.

TH: And that was what was interesting about the experience.

MA: I wonder if you feel that the collapse of regimes in the East and all these changes that are going on now in the world mean that your themes will be more British. Will they still be international? Because they always had quite an international side to them, the political things that you've written about, particularly American imperialism.

TH: Well, we'll just have to see what happens in the world. I think, when I was talking about reading your version of *The Ruin*, it's that I went back to that idea because I also live near the Roman Wall, which is a ruin of a past imperialism which you can see requarried into the limekiln or made into pig-troughs or barns and I am interested in the way things are recycled — that's one thing — not only how material things are recycled but how spiritual things become recycled and political ideologies become recycled, so there's all that waiting to be explored, but there's also the idea of the ruin of socialism, just as the ruins the Anglo-Saxon poets talked about, which somehow gave such a strong image of human transience and ephemerality to a later generation that didn't build in those lasting materials and softened them up in a sense for Christianity as described in Bede's *History of the English People*, when they talk about that wonderful . . . I'm actually writing a poem about the sparrow . . . the idea of the soul as the sparrow, the *passer*, that comes from the night into the lighted hall and [into] the night on the other side — all those images I've been looking at precisely because of the crumbling of one of the main twentieth-century ideologies. What new things are those ruins going to make people turn to, just as the Saxons turned to Christianity in the presence of the mortality and decay of a past generation? In a way, I hope that people are strong-minded enought not to go back to the same thing in the sense that they are in fundamentalism — whether it's Islamic fundamentalism or Christian fundamentalism — people panicking about the loss of the old certainties. They're undermined — they're old certainties which have become uncertain. And I think that fundamentalism is a reaction to that — it's a desperate reaction to that.

MA: We both share an interest in translation, although you say you haven't kept, published, your old original ones, but of course you're doing it all the time with the Greek and some mediaeval things too. And I like what you say, that you're making it available again in a different form — to people. It's not academic translation. In America, did you notice in your time there, that academics have a much more open attitude to translation? Many British academics think that it's a great mistake to translate anything, partly because it does them out of a job and partly because . . .

TH: Well, that's sometimes the priesthood not wanting to surrender its function, its control. That's absolutely the situation.

MA: What do you think about things like the national curriculum? There's a sense in which unless things are kept up, though they've probably not chosen the right things, then the doom of the species 'poet' is going to be even shorter, because the pressure of commerce upon education is colossal. It's into the University level now.

TH: Yes, but the pressure of commerce — the pressure of the ugly materialism, (I think at its ugliest in the Thatcher years, and we're still suffering from that) — I think that, for me, has made me finally accept that it's a good thing to be a poet. Because it's had the paradoxical effect of making me feel a threatened species. If *this* is the alternative, that to write a poem . . . [A: No need to feel guilty any more] no need to feel guilty any more. And oddly enough the Thatcher years had that effect on me.

MA: This is a very paradoxical parallel which perhaps wouldn't occur to most people. I remember at the beginning of Evelyn Waugh's *Sword of Honour* trilogy the hero, when he hears about the Molotov-Ribbentrop pact, he *knows* he wants to join up. Finally it's become clear.

W. N. HERBERT

TALKING WITH RICHARD PRICE

Widely regarded as the most adventurous of the new generation of Scots poets, W.N. Herbert has just shared with Robert Crawford a 170 page collection, *Sharawaggi* (Edinburgh: Polygon, 1990). Born in Dundee in 1961, Herbert grew up there, going to Brasenose College, Oxford as an undergraduate, and has recently completed his doctorate on Hugh MacDiarmid. With Richard Price, his present interviewer, he co-edits the magazine *Gairfish*. This interview was recorded in Oxford on 6 June 1990. It is the first published interview with W.N. Herbert.

RP: I think that it is very interesting that Edwin Morgan is middleclass yet through no fault of his own he is seldom considered in class terms. He is a ''Glasgow poet'' almost as if this 'forgives' his class, and of course belonging to Glasgow often means having a spurious honorary membership of the working class anyway.

WNH: Well this is a thing I'm always so suspicious of in Glasgow writing in people like Tom Leonard where you have this sort of hard macho image coming from the intellectuals. I'm never clear why they have to do that, apart from the difficulty, presumably, of being an intellectual in Glasgow. But I've no idea what the experience of that is. Robert [Crawford]'s the same — essentially from a middleclass background, and his poetry has a bit of that quietness about it.

RP: In Scotland 'reality' and 'being working class' have almost become the same thing?

WNH: I think so.

RP: And the result is a squeeze on middle-class identity.

WNH: Well this is what attracts Morgan to fictional modes like science fiction in which the class structure dissolves. [. . .] Morgan said in an interview that some of the experiences that the poet writes about they may not have experienced themselves, and the reader cannot tell which are which. I'm not entirely clear that that is true. I tend to think that the reader treats some things as fiction and other things as something more than fiction. It is the more-than-fiction area that most often attracts attention in terms of poetry.

RP: And I suppose there is another category of fiction made of other people's fictions —

WNH: Well of course this is quite an important issue about Scottish poets, because people like Ashbery 'steal' all the time. They lift things with gay abandon, and this is something which Scottish poets have been doing with slightly more dour abandon for ages. And yet it's meant to be an issue when MacDiarmid does it. Twenty years later people notice Ashbery lifting from Pater and so forth. It's interesting actually because we [Robert and I] were reading and talking a lot about Ashbery when we were writing the Scots poems that went into *Sterts and Stobies* [Obog Books, 1985 reprinted in *Sharawaggi*] and that was probably quite a main influence on those poems, which is strange because there is not an immediate or obvious influence.

RP: Were you very much working *together*?

WNH: We were working together in the sense of wanting to produce a collection that was rounded and balanced. I remember Robert had the Vietnamese poems, and I'm not really that interested in translating but I needed to get some together to balance it up. I'm more interested in the texture of language, maybe. For translating I have to have a really strong interest in the poem that's being translated, and I think that the Luzi poem wasn't very interesting [Mario Luzi, ''As it must'', in *European Poetry in Scotland*]. That came about through a workshop that Nigel Thompson ran. He had a translation workshop in Oxford for a couple of years where we happened to be dealing with the Luzi poem and so I did a translation of it into Scots. I was never very committed to that poem. I don't think it's very good. I liked the Cavalcanti one much better because I liked the subject of it, and I was able to play with the language more. I think that one comes off a lot better. It was very funny — I actually won a competition for that. There's this magazine here, called *Oxford Poetry*, which started up almost immediately when we started up *New Poetry from Oxford*. Suddenly *Oxford Poetry* emerged, and they never would print me. They never would take anything by me and finally they had Nigel judging a translation competition and the subject was the Cavalcanti sonnet. So I did a translation into Scots which I think must be the deepest injury I could possibly have done them and [laughter] submitted it, and of course Nigel thought that it was the best that he had. So I won the competition and they were obliged to print it. My only venture into *Oxford Poetry* so far. I was very pleased about that. A small victory. [Laughter]

RP: You are very much a poet from a working class background, but now living in Oxford. How do you feel about class?

WNH: Well, I get teased about that constantly from people who say I've joined the middle-class willy-nilly. It is of course a major theme. I remember once in the Poetry Workshop [the Oxford Poetry Workshop, which WHN has run since 1981] there were several poets who were strongly interested in this, with Tony Harrison for example, with the whole sort of angst of becoming middle class through education. I never felt any angst about it! I never felt there was any sundering whatsoever. The most that would happen would be that you would get an adverse reaction from people in Dundee. I mean most of the people I knew as a child were very pleased because I managed to get to Oxford. A lot of them have a kind of paternal/maternal interest in me. It's like you get the extended family of aunts and uncles, you know ''How's Billy doing, has he got his doctorate yet, how's he getting on'' and all that sort of stuff. And it's quite supportive. I once nearly got into a fight about it in a bar. Somebody I hadn't seen for several years, who was a bit of a bampot really, he took something I was saying amiss because he thought it sounded a bit 'educated'. I remember having exactly the same relationship with that person when I was twelve. [laughter]. He was always a bampot.

RP: There isn't a sense, when you write in Scots, of having got rid of your middleclassdom?

WNH: I don't think in the act of writing, particularly in Scots, the question of class comes up in the same way. The kind of thing you're creating linguistically is such a strange unit anyway. I remember John Glenday [editor of Blind Serpent Press] saying that my Scots was a ridiculous mixture of Chateau Lafitte in the snug at the fit o' the Hill Toun. He was trying to find some way of describing it in class terms. But you are creating a fictional realm. I don't know if it's the same fictional realm as Morgan creates, the ''Republicum Scotorum.'' I hope it's something ''more-than-fiction,'' as that sonnet seems to be [''The Coin'' in *Themes on a Variation*, Carcanet, p162]. I have been able to assimilate some *aspects of the middle class*, and in my Scots poetry I write a working class poetry which has done the same. That in itself is a shocking thing. I think that's why I've had such a strong reaction. It's not keeping in its place, basically. It's being intellectual at the same time as it's being 'authentic'. I think middle class people are very much obsessed by authenticity.

RP: When one reads your poetry in Scots, it comes across as a gathering of old and new, of anything that has at any time existed as a word —

WNH: Yes, I also have a lot of difficulty because I find myself using some quite strange English vocabulary as well in the Scots poetry, which then puts me in the difficult position of wondering whether I should gloss the English words for an English audience! But I think that's because the basic medium is looser. You just have a greater freedom because there is a less definite idea of what Scots should be. I tend to parallel it to the amount of distortion or freedom of the use of colour you get in early modern art. Like the Fauves were able to paint a face green and the Cubists were able to present the profile on the full frontal face. And similarly in Scots, because you're denying the dominance of English as a mode. You're able to place words in a context they do not normally go, and you're able to bend language in a way you do not ordinarily think of doing.

RP: Perhaps coming at it from the other way, do you not think that there's a tradition in Scottish writing of making anything with an accent comic? In a sense you may be exacerbating the problem by having videos and Iggy Pop in your poetry? Modern art is often seen as comic by those 'who know what they like'. Are your poems in Scots in danger of becoming comic anomalies?

WNH: Well that depends on whether you find Iggy Pop a comic anomaly! Or video for that matter. I mean my experience has always been that, perhaps again because I'm working class, perhaps because of my generation, I'm aware of areas which are not ordinarily part of the poetic medium. I'm very very aware of popular culture — it is simply what I grew up with. It couldn't be said that the Beatles or Captain Beefheart were in any way more or less important to me than pop art or the more extreme agitational art forms of the sixties. These things came to me with an equivalence, and when I looked at poetry I realised this equivalence did not exist, that there were a whole series of subjects that were shut out — in the same way that an extended Scots vocabulary had been shut out. It seemed like the only way you could write an intellectual Scots poetry and be accepted in Scotland was if you could find yourself a Glaswegian patois, in which case you were allotted a kind of role as a sub-Tom Leonard, and so you get all these Wee Malkies and the hard men poems of the seventies (which I find petty dire). It's a very limited persona, a very limited use of language.

So having brought one thing in, all these other things came in too. With the language came the sensibility. Punk had an enormous influence on me. I was sixteen in 77, and that was like Year One. It was like a mini Dada movement for teenagers in Britain. I don't know how far the intelligentsia of the poetry-writing class, the middle class, are aware of that. I still think Mark E. Smith of The Fall is a very exciting writer — for England. I suppose I've got a rather daft fondness for Iggy Pop —

RP: Why not!

WNH: Why not.

RP: What I'm saying is your 'gathering' of different cultures, of different 'levels' of culture, isn't actually subverting any single component in the culture except for the idea of poetry. This is not quite the same as being deliberately provocative — it's much more of a comprehensive vision.

WNH: I've always thought about admitting more things. I've never had a lot of theoretical difficulties about what I've been doing in Scots because there's always been a strong background of elements that I wanted to introduce, play with. I mean, I've never been dry for a subject. Sometimes I don't write in Scots because my English poetry is doing something.

RP: What do you think your English poetry does that your Scots doesn't?

WNH: I think it does a lot of the work. I think that the Scots is the result of a lot of work that is done in English. Sometimes it's possible to be very fluent in Scots, but sometimes you want the quickness of writing in English. There's a different rate of production possible [laughter], which is not to say — I mean one of the first things I ever wrote in Scots, *The Doldrums*, I wrote incredibly quickly [of *Akros*, 1982, no 51]. I mean they just poured out of me. That was a week for about twenty or thirty poems, and that was quite a complicated thing because I was actually going all over Dundee for the different bits to write the poems there. They started out in English and then I realised I was admitting a lot of Scots. I never really contemplated writing in Scots until I found myself writing things which made more sense in Scots. It was a very hectic week!

RP: I find myself writing in English with a Scottish *inflexion*, more than a Scottish vocabulary, and it is often just a tiny unconscious matter of idiom which English friends will be puzzled by —

WNH: It's not so much that you make what they consider to be the slip, because of course you're probably speaking reasonably normal Scots grammar in an Anglo-Scottish form. The thing that always amazes me is the kind of instinctual correction that people make as though they cannot bear the variation. People I have only just met will sometimes correct me — because they're in some way alarmed or threatened. Language is a powerful tool, and people are sometimes not aware of how much faith they invest in it.

RP: How was *Sharawaggi* put together?

WNH: It was a bit haphazard really. We both wanted to do an extended version of *Sterts and Stobies*, but when it came to ordering the material it proved rather difficult to find a coherent order. So we decided to make *Sterts and Stobies* a historical document as it were — it was five years ago, so we just left it in its own structure. And then we tried to provide a kind of moving on from that. Robert had a certain amount of material in Scots which more or less dictated the size, because what I then did was provide an equivalent amount of material. There was a number of follow-through themes — we were attempting to balance things up. I remember having enormous difficulty in establishing an order for my poems. I'm not sure that the order they're in is necessarily the optimum.

RP: It strikes me that you're not a very political poet, and certainly not nationalistically.

WNH: I think that's probably because my politics are too radical to easily fit into the accepted structures. I find it inordinately difficult to fit into a party line. I just won't write a nationalist poetry. I feel there are too many easy assumptions about being a 'nation'. I remember having a minor argument with Douglas Dunn about that several years ago in which he put it to me that it was impossible to be writing in Scots and not to be a nationalist poet. I held that that was one of the tyrannies that MacDiarmid had imposed upon us. I don't believe that there's any problem about celebrating the nature of your culture without necessarily being a paid-up member of the SNP. I don't know what I would do if there was a referendum — I mean I've never voted in my life. I'm an anarchist. I don't believe in the structure of the democratic system. I might make a special journey north to spoil my voting card! [laughter] but I probably wouldn't vote. I don't think it's going to solve Scotland's problems. Though I do think it's a perfectly reasonable time to press for independence — we could certainly do it.

RP: Do you think that poetry itself is anarchic?

WNH: Yes, I think it is fundamentally, and I think that is why it is the most underrated artform. People are frightened of it. I'm sure you've experienced the same thing: there is a reaction against poetry almost everywhere you go because almost everybody is involved in it at some level. Everyone has written. I recently went to a friend's house, and she suddenly produced writing which she had done between the ages of thirteen and seventeen. It's extremely common — everybody does write. It is a response to experience which our society wants to put outside of experience. I'm living with the editor of a current affairs journal, and he's very keen to put poetry into it, but he's got a lot of opposition because people just don't trust it. They come up with excuses — like the problem of getting lots of trash sent in, which is true, of course they will. But that only proves there are an awful lot of people around writing an awful lot of awful poetry! It was a whole mode of response to world issues that is generally passed over. I was at a dinner party the other night where I had an argument with someone over the question of being taught creative writing. We were having the old argument — music is taught in a college, art is taught in a college, but for some reason if we teach creative writing in any kind of institute this will reduce the standards! That's true enough if you look at the American way of teaching, but that doesn't mean there isn't a mode of teaching it, a mode of accepting it into our society as an equivalent art. Why are people so suspicious, why are people so doubtful? What is it about poetry that frightens them? It's because it has dangerous aspects, aspects of play, aspects of moral structuring — whatever people dread. It's the same business as having your English corrected.

RP: I want to go on to MacDiarmid. For someone you've lived with for —

WNH: Papa!

RP: Six or seven years, at least — earlier you talked about him being tyrannical with the Scots language — that seems a striking thing to say. What is your relationship with the Big Man?

WNH: Well he is a heavy paternal presence. I think poets who set themselves up as pater familias, in the way that MacDiarmid did, are going to have a lot of people rebelling against them which is what happened in the subsequent generations. Those who wish to follow on and take up the positive aspects are going to find it a difficult thing to do, and this is what I've been trying to do in my book [WNH is working on a critical study, *To Circumjack MacDiarmid*] and in my own writing. I think that Morgan of all the poets of the subsequent generation did something with MacDiarmid's English writing. Morgan was predominantly English-writing and interested in scientific areas — I think that he took up and carried on a lot of the principles of MacDiarmid's English, but I think that the Scots writing didn't really evolve. You had all these disciples. I mean I don't know what to make of people like Sidney Goodsir Smith. They seem very small fry. You're down to an anthology in which the various poets are able to contribute only two or three pieces. He's had every bit as disastrous an effect as Burns did on Scots writing in that respect.

I think that MacDiarmid made a gamble on the future with Scots. The Scottish language may not survive, or not in this form, but the leap in the dark had to be made. I think by continuing to write in synthetic Scots I'm assuming the same thing. That we have to do this if we are going to create a language. That we have to assume all possibilities. We may never create a language — stranger things have happened (Norway, for instance) — but the gesture of faith has to be made. You can see that as a nationalist statement — that this culture should not die, that it should continue to meet the frame that the modern world is putting it in. I respond to MacDiarmid's faith. He's a prophet figure. He lays down the law. He was very wrong about concrete poetry, for instance. I think that is another area where Scottish writers have done something signficant, in world terms. I think it's about time we honoured Morgan in a similar way to MacDiarmid. People should consider a twentieth-century tradition which has a relation to the eighteenth century, and the Makars, but which is a modern tradition in Scotland. I think that we're closer to a modern line than a lot of other nations, particularly England who've thrown that away quite deliberately.

RP: When you use a phrase like "twentieth-century tradition" isn't that oxymoronic?

WNH: The point where extremes meet! This is post-modernism, if I can use that much lambasted term. Post-modernism to me is getting things which cannot fit together, which should not fit together, and fitting them together willy-nilly. I think its one of the perennial artistic efforts. Surrealism, the metaphysicals — its what Dr. Johnson didn't like so it's alright by me! I think that paradox is a great giver of energy. It appeals to me that we should say that there is a line through Davidson, through MacDiarmid, through Morgan to the present generation and we should go with that line.

RP: The idea of continuity again. Something doesn't quite fit. You talk about post-modernism, but then you say "Well of course everyone's always been post-modernist. The best artists are by definition post-modernists, all the way through history."

WNH: It's a Platonic argument about the relationship of the artist to society. Are you supporting the order, are you against it? It's the Shelleyan argument about legislating society at a remove. Of course post-modernism is simply the term that we've arrived at at the moment to cover some aspects of the artistic endeavour. You know, you've got to use the jargon! [laughter].

RP: Your relation to critical theory, then, is oblique?

WNH: Yes. I'm not interested in the Stalinists of literary theory, people who think that there are certain orthodoxies that must be satisfied whether they're feminist, or Marxist. That process of creating the right position — I'd rather be right off. Not because I necessarily disagree with the theories, it's nothing to do with that at all. I'm extremely sympathetic to a lot of theories which people are throwing up. It's when they try to dictate art by them that I find myself leaving. It's the same with nationalism.

RP: There's a quotation from John Davidson: "no great poet can work at all except on the assumption that the next thing he writes will out-distance all previous composition completely — so completely that all other poetry becomes negligible in comparison."

WNH: I think that was to do with Davidson's egoism. His egoism got in the way of his receptivity. I think that he was a great poet, he was probably the primary modernist. There was an astonishing statement that Eliot made, that in the first decade of the century no single mature living poet, in either England or the States, was capable of pointing the way to a young poet conscious of the desire for a new idiom. [From *To Criticize the Critic*]. Davidson was a profound rival to Yeats, and I think his influence on MacDiarmid is quite important. One of the things that Davidson imparted to modernism was the cult of the ego. The ego of Pound is what makes *The Cantos* flawed. The poet announces that they're going to deliver at such a pitch. If they're not heard or appreciated then they start to accrue significance, they start to bolster themselves up. As Davidson hit his own unique form, which was probably *The Testaments* he became less and less popular, and so he made more and more extravagant statements about himself, and so he ended up with the quotation you've quoted. I think it's more important to have purity of reception, actually. The ego is not the issue. There is a difference between being egoistic and being 'personist'. I borrow the view from Frank O'Hara of personism, of accepting that there is an ego actually writing something, rather than taking up the role of the great classical author who is outside the piece and dictating from on high. You accept that there is a self or a personality and a social and cultural location.

RP: I'm interested that you've focused on O'Hara. He comes across as very modest.

WNH: I'm attracted to O'Hara in the same way that Robert is attracted to Ashbery. He's a very shy poet yes. When they collected his poems everybody was completely flabbergasted. No-one had any idea that he'd written so many, and it's a very sizeable achievement because it went on in private. He was considered a dilettante poet who was seen as not quite getting to grips with the issues, whereas his whole approach was a means of getting to grips with issues! [Pause]

RP: They say that Glasgow is the fifty-first state of America.

WNH: Do they! [laughter]

RP: At least I do. Do you think Dundee has a cosmopolitan atmosphere?

WNH: I think MacDiarmid had the right idea when he said that if Dante had seen Dundee he would have added another ring to Hell. Dundee is lucky because it hasn't had the attention that Edinburgh had throughout history, and Glasgow has had in recent history. I think the kind of Scottishness which is now possible in Dundee is getting to be impossible in Glasgow. The number of people my father knows still amazes me. I cannot go into a pub with him without him acknowledging a vast number of people. One of the most interesting experiences of my teens was listening to my father and a close friend of his talking about their childhood, their working life, their service in the merchant navy, and I remember them reconstructing a street in Dundee. Simply going up a street in their minds and totally reconstructing it as they walked up it, going back to 1946, 47. I think that's quite magical. The way Dundee contains these layers. I like to photograph Dundee even in its appalling state of evisceration. I'd like to make a video in Dundee, of the Doldrums.

RP: Do you visit often?

WNH: It's not necessary, but I do visit it several times a year. And a lot of it is to reassure myself about places, the texture of the streets, the way the buildings have changed.

RP: I suppose finally we have to get to a pet subject of mine, which is *Gairfish*. How long have you been involved in magazines?

WHN: I've always had magazines, since I was seventeen I've been circulating them 'samizdat' format. It's good to get something a little nicer looking, but I've never been terribly interested in the appearance. In 82-83 I was probably fairly much under MacDiarmid's thumb in that I felt that all one needed to do was to make a cultural statement, to assume a quasi-political role. The role hasn't changed (it's developed in some respects). I started *Gairfish* then with very much the idea of encouraging writing in Scots and having that kind of responsibility for Scottish writing. In subsequent years I realised I was impoverishing myself and the person I was living with at the time on a variety of projects of a similar kind, and I retreated from that role. I rejected the Messianic aspects of MacDiarmid, but I never abandoned the idea of representing a nascent voice of Scottish criticism. It's the one thing that we're very poor on in Scotland. It began and it hasn't got very far. In the same way that there is a feminist and a Marxist criticism. I think that there should be an equivalent. I wanted *Gairfish* to be a platform for Scottish writing, for Scottish criticism, and in neither case do I want to lay down any kind of orthodoxy or critical or literary canon. I want it to be sufficiently far away from the groves of academe in order to get some energy, ideational energy, and structural energy (which you've talked about in relation to the essay form — and I agree very strongly with you that it's a crucial question). So when you started talking to me about doing a kind of *Gairfish* which incorporated these aspects you were coming up with a position that I had come round to. One of the reasons why there weren't any *Gairfish* for six years was because I'd stepped back from the role of being the Magazine Editor, the Person Who Dictates Taste. With *Gairfish* as it now stands there is a chance to provide space without dictating in that fashion. I think that's what interests me in *Gairfish*. How does that square with your view?

RP: I think that's right on.

WNH: Oh, right off, please.

KATHLEEN JAMIE

INTERVIEWED BY RICHARD PRICE

Kathleen Jamie was born in Renfrewshire, Scotland, in 1962, and grew up in Midlothian. She studied Philosophy at Edinburgh University. At eighteen she won a Gregory Award for her poetry, and in 1982 she was awarded the Scottish Arts Council Book Award for her pamphlet, *Black Spiders* (Salamander Press, 1982). Since then she has had two collections published: *A Flame in Your Heart* (Bloodaxe, 1986; written with Andrew Greig), and *The Way We Live* (Bloodaxe, 1987). A travel book about Northern Pakistan will be published by Virago in 1992. She is currently Writer in Residence at the University of Dundee. This interview was conducted by post in September 1991.

RP: Just some background information first. Where were you brought up? What sort of upbringing was it, do you think?

KJ: We lived in Paisley, my people are from Ayr. I was the firstborn of three. The photos show my mum in drindl skirts and glasses with flying eaves. My dad, grinning with me in his arms. We had a garden. My mother had escaped the dingy tenement where she was brought up; the two rooms, gas-lit, shared lavvy on the stairs, the one miserable tap and a jaw-box at the kitchen window. My mother works for a firm of solicitors. Had she had my opportunities she'd have been a lawyer herself. Her mother, my Nana, is the part of me which is working class Scotland, she is the source of my Scots language. She makes me laugh and cry at once. *Philosophy, hen? Is that some kinnae medical thing?* Dad's side were wealthier, respectable, slightly eccentric. Hoteliers, master plumbers. It was a moral rather than religious upbringing, that high moral ground that Scots take at times. No church, but we wernae Catholics either. We moved to Teesside, one of the filthiest places in Britain, Dad's an accountant. Say accountant and people think of city dickheads with carphones. Not true. He works for a company that digs holes and hires skips. When I was 7 we came back to Currie, suburb of Edinburgh. There was a council scheme and a Wimpey scheme. We were Wimpey scheme. I went to the local comprehensive. I enjoyed primary school, as I recall, but high school. . . I do resent what happened there, nobody was interested, I had no guidance. I just left. It's taken me years to find my feet. At home there weren't any literary books. Some encyclopedias, solid stuff like that. No art, music, literature. Certainly no hugging and talking about how we felt! I have a friend with a similar background. He left Scotland and read a lot of Alice Miller, but I don't feel damaged, like him. I was secure. That matters. So now I feel West Coast urban, Edinburgh middle class, English liberal — an outsider everywhere. Sometimes I feel so constrained with this palaver of labelling I just bugger off abroad where nobody knows and nobody cares.

RP: How did you start writing poetry?

KJ: Song lyrics. Simon and Garfunkel, I ask you! When I was 13 or so. In the clearing stands a boxer/ a fighter for his trade. A pocketful of mumbles such are promises. I thought, I could do that. I always wrote wee stories at school, and got good marks for them. It was probably that crippling desire to please that made me keep writing; I got praised for it. I think I've sloughed that off at last, the need to please, but it's taken this long.

RP: When you won a Gregory Award, what did this do for your poetry, and for you in general?

KJ: I still feel my toes curl when I say the words 'my poetry', 'my work'. Pretentious, ken? For a long time I didn't think of 'my work', didn't consider its development. Now I'm starting to. The Gregory money was good, though. I got £1000, I was 18. I bought a bike, a typewriter, a ticket to Istanbul. I went to Israel, alone. These things are still, how to put it, my touchstones.

Now I have a word-processor, a better bike, make farther, more challenging journeys, but these things still matter. What I studied at university, my ongoing interest in Islam, my first book all came about because of the Gregory Award. Yes, I suppose it set me up.

RP: How did the *Black Spiders* pamphlet come about? Are you interested in the pamphlet format for further smaller collections?

KJ: I can't be bothered to say how it came about. It came about. Pamphlets: I'm interested in radically different ways of presenting poetry, I don't think the slim volume does poetry any favours.. It would be good to move away from the printed word altogether. I'd like to work with artists, Exhibiting, rather than publishing. But yes, pamphlets. So long as production is quick. It's this business of waiting 18 months for a production, it kills any topicality stone dead.

RP: How did your collaboration with Andrew Greig in *A Flame in Your Heart* come about? To what degree did you revise each other's work? How did you feel about imagining yourself into the summer of 1940 as a 'widow-to-be'? What sort of research did you do?

KJ: We decided we wanted to do it, No we didn't revise each others work. How did I feel? Daft question, the whole book is about how I felt. Research: read books, Enough. If I said I didn't like that book you'd no doubt ask me why, so I won't. Still, it's apprenticeship.

RP: In the poem 'Riba' in *Black Spiders* a woman with fortune-telling qualities predicts that you 'think too much, and will make journeys'. The often exotic elements in your work, from 'Women in Jerusalem' in *Black Spiders* through the Pakistan mountains in *The Way We Live* to your most recent work on Tibet, suggest that, if not thinking too much, certainly you have found insight in journeying. What is it, do you think, that seems to keep you on the move? What would you say are the qualities which mark out the best poems of travel from that lesser but more popular creature, the poem of holidaymaker?

KJ: A strange thing happens to me when I begin to think about what you call my journeying. I feel the defences come down, I feel myself open, grow warm. I begin to remember incidents, people, smells, and start to smile. What can I say? I love it. It's wonderful. To be stuck in the middle of the Takla Makan desert, it's brilliant. The farther I go the more I like myself. No-one's getting at me, telling me I should be this way or that, talk like this or the other, think thus. The stresses of daily life are gone, and of course and you're not engaged enough to feel those of the people around you. That little voice that goes *Pretentious, ken. Its awricht fur you, you're hale life's a holiday. Tibet hen? Is that near France?* shuts up as soon as I'm on the plane.

I like solving the practical problems of travelling, and benefit no end from the self-confidence it's given me. I'm not frightened as I once was, not of bank managers, bosses, old geezers in suits or kilts telling me what I should be doing. I like to write out of that sense of strength and liberation. Plus, I have a dark longing to bring chaos out of order, (like the Princess in the poem). You learn to let go, but you don't fall. It's a holiday from class, identity, mortgages. You learn a sense of proportion. Having said that, there are grievous ethical problems to consider when travelling. It's the ultimate western privilege, and I'm beginning to think twice about it. The politics of tourism, of cultural imperialism, of despoilation, the way dependencies are created. These things happened to Scotland, years ago. In other places it's happening now. Western trekkers are ruining the Himalaya; the Chinese are turning Tibetan monasteries into theme-parks. These things matter too. You get people saying 'what are you running away from'? I think 'small minded little rats like you.' I say 'You're missing the point, we can be many things, we can be multi-faceted people.' I can be Scottish and go other places'. *Bas!* It's Urdu, means 'enough'. Pretentious, ken?

RP: You have talked before about not having access to the work of the female poets. Do you think this a Scottish problem, or is it much wider than that? How has this affected your work do you think, and now that some re-discoveries, at least, are taking place, do you anticipate any tangible re-adjustments in your poetry or in the poetry of those younger than you?

KJ: Most of the poetry I encountered at school and the few years after was from the 'yes but is it a poem' school of literary criticism. It's wonderful to know there are whole other traditions, whole other cultures coming on stream now. In the future, maybe people won't have to spend ten years waiting, they'll find themselves young, get their confidence up. Won't waste their time producing things suitable for the geezers in kilts/suits, in the belief that's what poetry has to be. Did I do that? I think so.

RP: In 'Things which never shall be' in *The Way We Live* you draw, ironically I think, the picture of a kind of 'perfect' lifestyle and relationship. What I find *not* ironic, though, is the expression of a wish for artistic space — a sense of private space to write and to be alone but to reach out to other lives, too. Whether or not that's a fair interpretation, in what ways do you think being a poet compromises other ways of living?

KJ: Artistic space, Ah, now. Yes. Travelling is a means of getting some space, of course. The problem is physical space. A room of one's own. I would give my eye teeth for a study. I've had one for the last 8 months, it's been brilliant, but now it's back to a corner in the living room. Having a room with walls and door has made a great difference to myself and my work has changed. I could talk a long time about relationship to space, rooms, geomancy — it comes into quite a few of my poems. It's all money, of course. If I could afford a big space I'd have one, and no apologies, with a room for me. It's a symptom of, what? When we sabotage ourselves — women take note! when we were too self-belittling to say 'I need space to work.' It's taken me ten years to be able to say that without embarrassment.

Relationships. The myth: The relationship as compromise. To be an artist you must suffer. Be lonely/alone. There are few female role models, which is a blessing in a way. We are free to create them, even become them. Sylvia Plath and Virginia Woolf are not good role models! I want to be a good writer, even an important writer, *and* have a loving and supporting partner (a whit? hen? Aw aye, a man). But everyone's entitled to a relationship which doesn't compromise them, whatever their job or sexuality. Everyone should insist on it.

In what ways do I think being a poet compromises other ways of living? Having so little money; the insecurity. I don't think a poet can live a lie, hence our reputation for unstable relationships. In a way it is an uncompromising life.

RP: Your reception in the English poetry media has been very favourable indeed for any poet never mind a 'new' one. How have you been received elsewhere? Has Scotland paid much attention, do you think? What do you think is the most perceptive thing a critic has said about your work?

KJ: I don't think the English press was all that impressed. They were looking for a woman, any woman. I got some nice reviews, but certainly haven't taken the place by storm. I'm afraid you've still got to be male, white, and on the spot. The reviews pleased me at the time but now they worry me. It's high time I did something wacky. Peter Porter didn't like my last book, I felt a certain relief.

Scotland, well. It's a contradiction, but in one way I feel Scotland's too small. It's easy to be a big fish in a small pond. On the other hand it saddens me that no Scottish publisher has approached me, and asked if I was interested in doing a book for them (the English have). No Scottish magazine has asked me for an interview until today — I've done them for English mags and American students. An Australian University wrote out of the blue, could they buy my manuscripts? No Scottish institution has done that. They can't claim poverty, because to ask costs nothing. Then folks moan at you for going south. This isn't a money problem; that comes in afterwards, this is a problem of attitude. The SAC are very good at supporting writers, myself included, but something is missing, some other structure. I think that Scotland has some excellent writers but few good editors, that level of literary activity seems to be missing.

What I'd really like, really long for, is a proper review, a critical essay. (Sean O'Brien, are you interested?). I need help to know where I am, what I'm doing; and pats on the head, though gratifying, don't give that help. Someone said I was too concerned with what a poem ought to be. I'm more confident now, less anxious to please.

RP: In poetry terms, despite the very productive middle third of the 1980s, you seem to have paused over the last couple of years. How did you come to stop writing, and how did you restart?

KJ: I didn't stop writing, I stopped publishing. In '89 I had one of the most exciting and creative periods of my life; my work went off at a tangent, I found new ways of working, new modes of expression, it was a great, exciting time. For once, I thought 'I don't give a tuppenny fuck if it's poetry or not'. But I shoved the results in a drawer. I stopped publishing because I was scunnered with the small magazines. Waiting nine months for a wee slip of paper saying, 'Not quite'. Or getting no reply at all from the likes of *Edinburgh Review*! My life took a difficult turn, and I moved to Sheffield, and there discovered I spoke Scots and English both, so then I got into a linguistic fankle, and couldn't write, couldn't find a voice, a language. (I'm beginning to understand that it's okay to have several, Scots do have several, people are beginning to talk about this, the babel, the Scots Polyphony). Then Virago asked me to do a travel book for them and I went out to Pakistan for the summer, and spent the winter writing that, in teaching myself how to write prose. They're pleased with it, we're talking of another. I might make some money, buy a house with a study.

RP: Your return to Scotland after a good deal away is due to take place when you become Creative Writing Fellow at Dundee University. What changes, if any, in Scottish culture are you aware of since you left? How do you think a sense of Scottishness informs your work, if indeed it does?

KJ: Changes in Scottish culture. You're joking! You cross the border and what do you get? A wild exhilaration — the space! the sky! the radicalism! And then you see this rash of bumper stickers 'I'm a real Scot from Granniesoxter' and you think, Aw God, I'm home. Yesterday I had a letter from an Australian friend. He's travelled a lot and said Scotland was the best country he'd been in so far. He said it was 'strikingly handsome, uncrowded, historic, romantic.' That's a lot to put up with. I'm glad I've had a rest.

The volume of debate about things Scottish has increased, on the radio, the T.V., but I still see a definite poverty of imagination. The question: is it going to go? How I wish people would shut up twittering and act. Do it. If they want a Scottish Free State or whatever, just get on with it. The country can't move and develop as it should. We feel threatened and therefore hang on to anything and everything Scottish, even the bad old junk that should have been ditched years ago. Change will mean chaos and we're feart of chaos, we don't know it can be glorious.

Having said that, do I detect a quiet investigation going on into the damaging effects of Calvinism? Emotional repression? I hope so. I think we're very good at articulating the problems, without demanding and creating the solutions. We like our art and literature to be about problems; the exploration of despair and futility is a necessary phase but itself ultimately futile. We should pass on quickly to the answers. Do I think a sense of Scottishness informs my work? Phew. I don't know. It must do. I think about it a lot. This place winds me up. I want to take it by the thrapple and shove it headlong into the next millenia. Though part of me feels I ought to, I don't want to contribute 'a poetry of National Service'. There are more ways of being Scottish than writing in Scots about Scottish things (O heresy!) I mean, what is a 'real Scot' for God's sake, what is 'a sense of Scottishness?' Whether or not a sense of Scottishness pervades my work should be a matter of fact, not of worth.

FRANK KUPPNER

INTERVIEWED

In the upsurge of Scottish writing in the 1980's few poets have acquired their reputations with the almost dreamlike ease of Frank Kuppner. Utterly unknown before Carcanet published his cunning dislocation of Chinese art and poetry in *A Bad Day for the Sung Dynasty* (1984), he was, after his second book *The Intelligent Observation of Naked Women* (Carcanet, 1987), already a curiously familiar part of the landscape. Recently his third volume, a trilogy mingling poetry and prose *(Ridiculous! Absurd! Disgusting!* — Carcanet, 1989) appeared, by which time he had, frankly, become difficult to avoid in literary magazines. The following interview — which is actually the first extended interview he has ever given — was conducted just after the publication of his third volume. The interviewer, a friend of the author, wishes to remain anonymous.

AM: Let's start with the name. Kuppner. It's not exactly a Scottish name, is it?

FK: Well, it is now.

AM: But not in origin, surely?

FK: That depends on how far back you want to go.

AM: Let's go back to one year before you were born. In many ways a blessed time. Is it a German name, or a Polish one, or what?

FK: I believe the first three letters are Polish, and the last four German.

AM: I see. And is this background important to you? Is it something you're aware of?

FK: I think it comes in useful. To have both parents from a single culture is a little repetitive. I suppose my family background is a sort of European stereo.

AM: Good for the spiritual health.

FK: Oh, I should think so, yes. It's harder to delude yourself into believing that you are at the absolute sole centre of the universe when you are actually in two places at once. As the old German proverb puts it.

AM: How good is your German?

FK: It's not bad. Nor is it sensationally good. I still have to use a dictionary when I'm reading the more high-powered stuff. Which is not often.

AM: So much for the German literature.

FK: So much for *any* literature.

AM: What German author did you last read?

FK: Peter Altenberg. Actually, he was Viennese. Little prose sketches. Some of them are highly appealing. Particularly the late ones — after he had cottoned onto the improbable fact that he wasn't going to live forever. Pound didn't discover that until he was about 80.

AM: I didn't know that Pound was German.

FK: No; neither did he. His real name was Pfund, you know. Actually, it might have been better if he *had* been German. He might have written the Cantos in English then. Actually, on reflection, I'm not sure what a good idea that would have been.

AM: So much for what's generally held to be the greatest long poem of the twentieth century.

FK: Well, it might be — though I doubt it. If it is, God help the twentieth century. It has its moments, I'll give you that; but it's one of the most obvious failures I've ever seen. Pound realized that himself. Eventually.

AM: Let us discreetly pass on. How's your Polish?

FK: Utterly non-existent.

AM: Really? But I seem to remember reading an article of yours which clearly suggested you had that difficult language totally at your command.

FK: Not a word of truth in it. I more or less know how to pronounce Polish orthography, and I have some knowledge of Russian. That's really all it amounts to.

AM: How much Russian do you know?

FK: Ever so slightly more than I think I know. I can just about see what's what in a parallel text, with a favourable breeze. I limped halfway through Nabokov's version of *Eugene Onegin* not long ago, before I realized that I had more urgent things to do.

AM: And so much for Pushkin! Any other languages you want to claim to be in control of, while we're here?

FK: Better not. I don't want to compromise my worldwide reputation for charm and modesty.

AM: A wise move. But you've translated from the classical Chinese, haven't you?

FK: Oh, how kind! Yes. Slowly. With the aid of some wonderful dictionaries, which do all the work for you. It's the only poetry there is, really. If you are interested in poetry, you have to be interested in Chinese poetry. Just as, if you're interested in art, you have to be interested in Chinese art.

AM: And are you interested in either of those subjects?

FK: Well, one likes to pretend.

AM: Is that why you scribbled graffiti all over Chinese art in *A Bad Day For The Sung Dynasty?* Because you loved it so much?

FK: Well, I hope there was a little more to it than that. Anyway, a lover is allowed to talk nonsense. How else is he to express his love?

AM: Well, I'm with you on the nonsense. But do lovers usually write up their sweet nothings into books?

FK: I assure you, you haven't seen the half of it. This is the real thing, and no mistake. And besides: to see no faults in someone is mere infatuation, not genuine love.

AM: I'm afraid I don't quite follow you.

FK: Good. That is one of the things I have learned from Zen Buddhism. Another Chinese invention, by the way.

AM: You mention Zen once or twice in *Lost Work*, in *Ridiculous! Absurd! Disgusting!* I wasn't quite sure how to take that.

FK: Oh, better and better. Certainty will kill us all.

AM: So, pardon my naive curiosity. Are you a Zen Buddhist?

FK: No-one who says "I am a Zen Buddhist" is really a Zen Buddhist. However, yes, I am. Actually, what I am most is a rationalist — a critical rationalist, in the Popperian sense. Most of whatever philosophy I have has been quite straightforwardly lifted from Karl Popper.

AM: Fascinating. But don't feel obliged to tell us about it.

FK: I'll be merciful. But it is a fact that, as far as I can see, pointing outwards, for other people, I am a critical rationalist, and maybe, for myself, pointing inwards, I am some sort of Zen Buddhist. But what other sort is there? The thing is: I'm a critical rationalist first. Such Zen as there is has to fit into a rationalist mould. Wake up!

AM: What? Well, thank you very much for not telling us about it.

FK: I haven't said a thing; believe me.

AM: Oh, I believe you. It all sounds like a bizarre combination of enlightenment and The Enlightenment to me. Would that be fair?

FK: No.

AM: Oh, good. But you once wrote a play about David Hume, did you not?

FK: I did. I once wrote many, many plays.

AM: Is Hume someone you particularly admire?

FK: I suppose so, yes. He was a brilliant, tolerant, witty, civilized man, who was unrelenting in pursuit of a line of thought. How could I not admire him?

AM: How indeed? Why, that could almost have been a description of yourself!

FK: Striking, isn't it? He was grossly overweight too.

AM: All in all then, he was a fit representative of all that is best in Scottish culture? Was he?

FK: Well, he certainly had the intellectual extremism.

AM: A quality not entirely missing in Kuppner too, if I may be so bold. *Lost Work*, for instance, contains a distressing amount of wallowing about in the basest aspects of human sexuality and physicality. Or am I being unfair?

FK: No more so than usual. However, any real attempt to come to terms with what we are here for and what is it all about —

AM: Just slow down while I write this down, will you?

FK: If you absolutely must. But what other phrases can we use? Any serious attempt to come to terms with all that, whatever it is, must involve facing squarely up to such things as, how do we actually, what is the actual physical process, by which we come to be here? What are the actual, unavoidable, utterly normal daily processes by which life continues? Whatever else we are, these are the foundations we are built on. It seems to me at times that one could almost define the essential as being that which gets overlooked in literature.

AM: Yes, I see all that. But isn't intellectual extremism rather dangerous?

FK: "Extremism" is a poor choice of word, I suppose. Perhaps I simply mean "honesty". In the end, I'm talking about little more than a refusal on principle to run and hide behind the inherited mental furniture at the first loud noise your hear.

AM: So, you would dismiss out of hand the virtues of fine old English compromise, would you?

FK: Not at all. The vital thing about Hume, as I understand it, is that he was a tolerant man. I don't know that he went so far as to welcome counter-arguments, but at least he was prepared to leave others free to say or think whatever they liked, provided they returned the compliment and allowed him equal freedom. What's the alternative? Either that or someone forces his view onto someone else by intimidation or violence. Ideas don't bleed. Let the ideas do the fighting.

AM: But might some not claim that the very act of arguing against someone's cherished beliefs is itself an attempt to limit their freedom?

FK: Some might claim all sorts of things. I presume they don't *have* to listen. To me the difference between dialogue and diatribe is a fairly clear one. As is the difference between blowing up an argument and blowing up a house. People are physical objects, and they live and breathe inside houses, not inside arguments. Who ever knocked on the door of an argument at three in the morning?

AM: But what can you do if people simply refuse to accept all that? After all, it's perfectly likely. Some people — it might even be most people — think that what they believe is certain truth. Why should they tolerate dissent? After all, to them dissent is error.

FK: I know, I know. It's the old paradox of tolerance, isn't it? In that case, as far as I can see, you just have to defend yourself as best as you can, using force if necessary. Intolerance must not be tolerated. It sounds like a joke, but it isn't. Otherwise the intolerant just get to wipe out their opponents unopposed. Terrific for them, no doubt; but not much fun for everyone else.

AM: How would you describe your politics, by the way?

FK: I wouldn't. How would *you* describe my politics?

AM: What?

FK: Well, that's accurate enough, I suppose. Next question.

AM:· Oh. Right. Where would somebody like MacDiarmid fit into all this?

FK: "Somebody like MacDiarmid"? What do you mean, "Somebody like MacDiarmid"? Don't tell me there was more than one of him!

AM: But did he not describe Hume as being Scotland's greatest son?

FK: Yes, I believe so. MacDiarmid is a subject which I am rather reluctant to revert to.

AM: Oh good. Tell us all about him. Did he not have that extremism too?

FK: No, I rather think he was characterized by another sort of extremism entirely. For instance, it's impossible to imagine Hume saying, "If I were a dictator, I would do such-and-such a thing" — except perhaps as a good-humoured joke. But when MacDiarmid says that — and he did make such remarks — he does not seem to me to be entirely joking. If at all.

AM: But is this not, in the end, a political disagreement that is working itself out here?

FK: No, I don't think so. I grant you I think his politics were appalling, but I'm not exactly besotted with Hume's politics either. As a bourgeois liberal humanist, how could I be?

AM: What do you think about his scientific socialism?

FK: Well, since you ask, I think it would make as much sense to talk about Scientific Fascism. Or as little sense. But that is not really the main point, is it? The point is, how did they react to criticism? What, ideally, you should do, is be willing to investigate it for what it is worth, and try to see what can be learned from it. I doubt if Hume missed this by much, if at all. MacDiarmid, however, seemed to view criticism as a sort of betrayal, a personal affront. For him, the important thing was to silence it, by whatever means. Ridicule; vituperation; misrepresentation. I get a sense, from his writings, of a man who had practically no tolerance whatever. He continually sought, deliberately, to intimidate dissenting voices into silence. Don't you agree?

AM: But wouldn't we all do that, if only we could?

FK: No.

AM: Oh well. Clearly, he has had a great influence on you all the same.

FK: Has he? I'll gladly leave that to others to decide.

AM: But hasn't he? I mean, you have read quite a lot of his work?

FK: Yes, of coure. He's not a figure you can easily ignore.

AM: And surely, in a technical sense, some of your work derives fairly directly from his?

FK: Does it? Could this possibly be a reference to a poetry produced by arbitrarily cutting prose up into lines?

AM: Well, some of the passages in the *Five Quartets* particularly seem to me to be stylistically very close to MacDiarmid.

FK: Yes. I know what you mean of course. Certainly, I have never been greatly worried by the thought that my lines might seem prosaic. Which is perhaps just as well. What matters most is the content.

AM: But you don't dispute the similarity?

FK: Up to a point. Actually, I am conscious of major differences. It seems to me that I use the link-break more. As a means of continually keeping the pressure wound up, where pressure is needed to force the contents out. Whereas our favourite Stalinist — and I'm sure you would agree with me in this —

AM: Just waken me up whenever you reach a full stop.

FK: Well, his habitual rhythm, such as it is, reminds me of someone walking up and down an old sprung mattress. There is practially no individuated use of the line-break. And I get very little sense of rhythm. It looks to me — in some sense like the *Cantos* again — that it is quite clearly technically not working. There is the occasional

106

AM: and FK: dialogue:

FK (continued): decent rung, but no ladder. It is, in the end, obviously just not on. And I can't help feeling that this must have been obvious to Pound and MacDiarmid too. It is the absolute pit of bad faith to persevere with something that you know deep down isn't working.

AM: You never do that yourself?

FK: No. But sometimes to admit openly that something is failing in a strange way at once starts turning it into a success. You just have to try to be honest.

AM: Wait a moment while I write that down too. But surely there are also similarities of content?

FK: With MacDiarmid? I can't say it particularly occurred to me.

AM: I should have thought it was quite blatantly evident. Particularly in the *Autobiography of a Non-Existent Person*. What price the 'poetry of fact' now? All those excerpts from natural history books. At times it sounds so like MacDiarmid as to seem intentional parody.

FK: I suppose it did cross my mind from time to time.

AM: But where does it come from, if not from MacDiarmid?

FK: Oh, there's an easy answer to that. Lautréamont. I forgot to mention the Frenchman earlier. Rimbaud gives *Ridiculous! Absurd! Disgusting!* its name — pretty inadvertently, I should say — but if the whole book had a single presiding spirit, that could only be Lautréamont. Or Ducasse, to give him his proper name.

AM: He was a Surrealist, wasn't he?

FK: No. He most certainly was not. For one thing, he died in 1870.

AM: But he originated automatic writing, did he not?

FK: I doubt it. There is nothing less like automatic writing than Lautréamont.

AM: I can see I have been reading the wrong textbooks. And he used to incorporate vast chunks of natural history in his writings, did he?

FK: Indeed he did. He lifted them straight out of an encyclopedia. Why not? After all, facts are facts, whoever first finds them out, and whoever quotes them.

AM: It sounds like a rather narrow base on which to build a reputation.

FK: Well, that wasn't all he did, of course. Given that he died at 24, it's astonishing what he managed to achieve.

AM: And it's in the *Autobiography* that his influence is most apparent, is it?

FK: No. Much more so in *Lost Work*. That must seem far more original than it actually is to anyone who doesn't know Lautréamont. Which is almost everyone, I suppose.

AM: Lighten our ignorance. Briefly.

FK: Such ignorance is too vast to be lightened briefly. His two major works — his only two works, in fact — were a sort of rhapsodical prose sequence, and a strange collection of reworked epigrams. *Lost Work* rather combines these two attacks. Of course, it isn't a slavish imitation . . .

AM: Well, far be it from me to insist that you are genuinely original. But I don't want to lose sight of the scientific aspect. Science and technology have always been Scottish strongpoints, have they not? I'm wondering how you fit into a line that must go back at least to —

FK: Look: I don't particularly care. I don't want to bore other people with my holiday snaps. I may be part of a Scottish line. I may be a Scottish dot. I may be a hyphen. I may be a comma. Let's leave that to the pedants. I feel a more pressing need to try to get the best flowers out of the garden, rather than to trace the exact sequence of events whereby its possession devolved to me.

AM: But it *is* a Scottish garden, is it?

FK: Well of course it is. It's in Scotland, isn't it? What else would it be?

107

AM: Not a British garden?

FK: There ain't no such thing. A British garden would simply be an English garden where thistles were tolerated. Mind you, many of the thistles would be trying to transmute spontaneously into roses.

AM: Well, here is a question. Is it a Glasgow garden rather than a Scottish one?

FK: Well, obviously it's both. Actually I couldn't care less about gardening.

AM: I think we could have gathered that from your writing. But you *do* have a scientific background, don't you?

FK: Not particularly. Until quite recently the chief colours in my background have been the various calm greys of the DHSS.

AM: I refuse to be sidetracked.

FK: Then you will never be a poet. In fact, that could almost be a definition of poetry. The ability to be sidetracked down many roads at once. I suppose they should all, ideally, be major roads. I'm not entirely sure of that.

AM: Can this not be equally well done in prose?

FK: It doesn't really matter what it is done in. The important thing is that it gets done.

AM: I persist in believing that you have a scientific background.

FK: If you like. We all have a scientific background whether we are aware of it or not. But I would regard it as a matter of basic intellectual literacy to get hold of and read through a basic guide to astronomy. You have to try to get an idea of what is actually known. It doesn't take much. Something about the brain; something about prehistoric life. Half a dozen introductory textbooks and you are intellectually infinitely better off. The facts themselves are pretty irresistible — which is why they are so ignored, I suppose. And they are so utterly permeated with poetry. Certainly, if you want real poetry, a sense of infinite wonder at the universe, you should not first go to poets. If you ever need to go there at all.

AM: Well, you may resist it; but I detect here a distinct echo of the good old Scottish polymath.

FK: What? The man who claims to know everything?

AM: No. I was thinking rather of the man who'll read absolutely anything, provided it isn't imaginative literature.

FK: Well, few things are more inhibiting to the imagination than imaginative literature. It's true I do read all sorts of stuff, utterly unpredictable in principle. Like life. You can turn up a lot of wonderful books in the second-hand bookshops round here. I've bought things in intellectual areas that I wouldn't normally have even thought of enquiring into, just because I happened to stumble upon them — sometimes quite literally — among piles of dirt-cheap rejects. You find some amazing things. Some of my most prized acquisitions I discovered here.

AM: What about *An Old Guide-Book to Prague?*

FK: Yes; that was one. Twenty pence, I believe it cost. Mind you, that was in the early '80s. When twenty pence really was twenty pence. Those were the days, eh? Most of these volumes have no sale value, you see. They have absolute nothing going for them except their contents.

AM: If I may say so, your book reviews in the *Glasgow Herald* seem to conform to much the same principle — or lack of principle.

FK: True enough. I would hate to know what I was going to be sent next. In a sense they're broadening my education and paying me for it at the same time. I am theoretically prepared to be interested in anything. In fact, at this very moment, I'm actually doing a couple of novels for them!

AM: That shows an impressive broad-mindedness.

FK: I have no shame. I am prepared to learn even from novels.

AM: One last question if I may — though, alas, not a very original one.

FK: Why alter the habits of a lifetime?

AM: Indeed. I blame the environment. Might I enquire what you are working on at the moment?

FK: Yes. I suppose I shouldn't say this, but I am working on a long, episodic work called *The Silence of the Liar*. It is in principle unendable. It ought to go on forever.

AM: I rather wish I hadn't asked. Is it in verse, or in prose — or can't you tell?

FK: It is in prose of heart-breaking quality.

AM: I don't doubt it. I think we'll end there. It is a rare privilege to be allowed to converse at great length with an unquestioned genius.

FK: Yes, it must be. I very much hope that some day you will be granted such an opportunity.

AM: I was just about to say that myself.

FK: I know. Get out.

TOM LEONARD

INTERVIEWED BY KEN COCKBURN

TOM LEONARD is probably best known for his poems written in a transcription of Glasgow speech, but as his "Intimate Voices: Selected Work 1965-1983" shows, his writing also extends to sound poetry, prose and criticism; while his radio play "If Only Bunty Was Here" and his three sketches and monologues have been published separately. A bibliography complete to 1987 can be found in EDINBURGH REVIEW 77. Since then his publications have included the anthology "Radical Renfrew: Poetry from The French Revolution to The First World War by poets born, or sometime resident in, the County of Renfrewshire" (Polygon, 1990), and a new poem-sequence, "nora's place" (Galloping Dog Press, Newcastle, 1990).

The following interview was conducted in written form, at Tom Leonard's request, April 6 - 13, 1991. It is printed in the form requested by Tom Leonard.

QUESTIONS

1. Starting at the beginning: in the introduction to "Radical Renfrew", you describe your childhood love of the public libraries. Who were the writers that first excited you? What about other arts — music, theatre, visual arts — were they part of your growing-up as well?

2. In your first collection, *Poems* (1973), you're already using what you call the kinetics of the poem to generate meaning: for example visual devices, juxtaposition of ideas or rhythmic progressions, rather than descriptive language. What led you in this direction — what sort of poetry scene (if any) were you involved with at the time — were you working in isolation or were you with, or aware of, others involved in similar experimentation?

3. Many of your poems seem to have the shape and 'breath' of a musical phrase, a playing on rhythm, melody, silence — are such phrases found instinctively on your part, or are they based on particular models?

4. A similar question regarding the philosophy poems (I Said, Moral Philosophy, mehta physics) — are they instinctively or imitatively structured?

5. The poems in "Bunnit Husslin" are also short dramatic monologues, with speaker, listener and situation sketched in varying detail. Was there a direct progression from these to your radio play "If Only Bunty Was Here", when you break into dialogue so to speak?

6. In "Bunty", the character Spud Lukacs is described as "a breezy conceptual artist". You've also written a piece called "Four Conceptual Poems". To what extent have you learned from conceptual art, to what extent would you describe any of your other poems as 'conceptual'?

7. Before "Unrelated Incidents", in most of your poems each line forms a complete phrase or sentence. In "Unrelated Incidents", you use more complex sentences but very short lines, so the poem flows down the page in a thin line. What was the aim of this change in the layout of the poem on the page?

8. You started publishing essays on James Thomson in 1985, having undertaken obviously painstaking research into work and his circumstances. How does such academic (?) work relate to your practice as a poet? Is it a chore, or is it similar to research you'd undertake to write a poem or a sketch?

9. Since 1985 you've published a number of essays on poets you particularly admire, as well as critical prose about your experiences while writer-in-residence in Paisley. Does articulating ideas in prose feed back into your poetry directly, say making explicit previously sensed but vague notions?

10. How influential has the work of the Renfrewshire writers you published in "Radical Renfrew" been on your own poetry and thinking? — formally, politically; or simply acting as encouragement?

11. You've described Reznikoff as one of the few poets in whose work "the imagist (of the moment of existence) and the narrative (of the timespan) co-exist". How do you feel the two co-exist / have evolved in your own work, particularly the poem sequences?

12. After your explicitly satirical and political work in the 80s ("Satires and Profanities", "Situations . . . ", "Two Members Monologues . . . " etc), "nora's place" is quieter, more concerned with character and voice, though the same political concerns are evident. What influenced this change of tack? Why did you decide to write a whole sequence from the perspective of a single character (which you haven't done before) who is female?

15. You wrote in 1986 that, for practical and other reasons concerned with an old testament God, you were no longer making tapes for your sound-poems. You mentioned your performance work was continuing — "Lentil Soup Diagnostic", 1989. Perhaps you could describe this and any similar events. Are your performances likely to develop in this way as 'actions', i.e. doing something on stage, rather than an orchestration of written and spoken language?

15. Finally, could you describe your most recent work, on the subject of the Gulf War?

* * *

ANSWERS

1. Dramatic theatre had no part in my growing up at all. The first time I was in a theatre was when I was about 13 or 14, it was in the Empire to see Slim Whitman, whose record "I talk to the waves" I liked a lot. I liked Hank Williams a lot then too. Shortly afterwards I was back in the Empire again, this time Frankie Vaughan was top of the bill. I didn't fancy what he did much at all — "What's behind the Green Door?" was his hit at that time. I was also taken by an uncle, probably about a year or so earlier, to see the Gaiety Whirl in the Gaiety Theatre Ayr when we were down there for a day. I don't remember much apart from the audience roaring and my uncle being a bit embarrassed at some of the risque stuff with a bra. I must have been in my twenties before I was back in a theatre again.

I went to the cinema a lot, though I remember one of my brothers would describe with a screwed-up face a film as being an "E.E." This meant it wasn't worth going to, being an "English Effort". I can see why he felt that way when so many British pictures of the time were full of posh thoughtful detectives and plodding cockneys — if they weren't safecrackers — bogus Scots and virtuous housewifes who talked like the Queen, unless they were "loose" or had a mop in their hand. American pictures at least had none of that baloney, and you could relax with them. My favourite film-maker is a Spaniard called Bunuel. Ask me another.

At home there weren't any books that actually belonged to the house, so the library was everything to me. I'd read most of Dickens by the time I was about 16 but the English novel outside of Dickens never excited me the same way again, what I liked tended to jump straight from Sterne to Beckett very quickly, and both Irish. The Russians and the French seemed the most interesting beyond that, again I think because, certainly with the Russians, you could relax with any character as equally human to you the reader and to the other characters in a way that didn't seem to be part of the English novelists' way of presenting the world. Of the French I liked Gide a lot, and eventually got secondhand the complete four-volume translation by Justin O'Brien of the *Journals*. I had to swap a secondhand set of Waverley novels plus £15 for it as I couldn't afford the asking price, but I was happy enough with the exchange. This was in my twenties by which time I was heavily into Kierkegaard, Gabriel Marcel, Tillich, Pascal and various religious encounterists and dark ruminators, although I had decided that by this time I was an atheist. I hadn't gone to university and I don't think I discussed my reading much with anyone else. I was reading a lot of existential psychology, and a good proportion of the European novels I liked I knew were described as "the existential tradition" though I never got too concerned with the phrase. I later came to realise

111

this tradition included the Hogg of *The Confessions of a Justified Sinner* and the Thomson of "The City of Dreadful Night". Gide did an introduction to the Hogg in the edition I first read.

In poetry I had become interested in Cummings and Williams and various Americans, mainly. How absolutely fascinating.

————

2. I can't be bothered talking about whatever "scenes" I've been in as this is just getting a load of bloody gossip. What does it matter who I knew or what I think I wrote something for? I don't want to be a "personality" or have my portrait under a column headed "People". I don't care who the hell I read between 1967 and 1987, any more. If I've forgotten them I'll read them again if the notion takes me.

————

2 — perhaps. I knocked about with an Art School mob after leaving school. Of visual artists I liked Utrillo and Klee, the latter for his sense of irony in his titles, a sense of ambiguity, balance and movement in his paintings, and his way of bringing in certain ambiguous signs like the arrow in "Mixed Weather" 1929. I quite early got to know about Schwitters and heard Cobbing and Bryon Gysin on the radio; fleetingly but the memory stuck.

At this time also I'd moved very heavily into classical music, it was another alternative universe. Bruckner was my first big love there, though he wasn't so popular then so I'd roam radio waves hoping to pick him up on the continent. I got that way about Carl Nielsen later. In calling my collection "Intimate Voices" there was nothing special about Sibelius's quartet for me, it stood as a sign for music itself. The "intimacy" of the voices, plural, was to do with the book's having nothing to do with the supposedly objective Public Voice nonsense Britain's had to put up with since Clare's time. As for your question about musical phrasing I think I do believe that when a person is being authentic in a specific act of speech there's a shape of authenticity occurs in the structure of their articulation, a kind of shape made with the spaces between the words, and the repetitions. But that's just an "act of faith" or whatever, it's not something I rationalise at any time. But it's where my intuition lies.

7. Unrelated Incidents was different in that it shifted from the first person present tense of previous sequences to third person, Past Tense, reported speech. That had to affect the line as the focus was no longer the present speaker's articulation. It included "story" albeit a bogus story being the subtext masquerading as the text. So it was conceptual rather than naturalistic though in fact a lot of my stuff is on that basis. As far as "drama" goes it's a head talking on its own as if it wasn't on its own; but of course it isn't on its own what with the reader being there, but that's straight into Beckett/Graham country.

4. I don't see any difference between what you call the "philosophy" poems and others in this. All this technical stuff I only serve up because you're asking me. The process of reading has got damn all to do with any of this. The reader either finds it funny, or moving, or interesting — or not. And my interest in writing it has got nothing to do with all this ratiocination either.

————

I look at these questions again and say — If I knew the answers I wouldn't write, and if I thought the answers weren't in the writing, ditto.

————

3. Instinctively.

4. Same again

5. If there wasn't a progression I'm too late to go back and try to squeeze one in.

6. They're all conceptual. See above, somewhere.

7. See somewhere in the mud, above. Again, if the question is necessary then the poem is not working for you. The poem should always carry its own answer.

8. It's not academic in that I don't write for an academic audience, though academics are numbered among my friends, and the Thomson book began as a Ph.D. I see the Thomson book, as I saw the Reznikoff essay and others, as setting out to somewhere whose end I could not conceive, making a shape in response to the shape of another person's work. In Thomson's case that shape will include a readable biography of the man's life with facts discovered; but the end product will be, for me at any rate, primarily a shape.

9. There are different types of essays and prose works. As just stated I've in most of them set out to find out something in the writing, which has either come in the form of an advance in my perception of how a writer's work functions, or in the shape found necessary to arrange the material of investigation. The borders between criticism and creative writing, collage and poetry have become fairly meaningless to me, I don't really care or give a damn about any of these borders. If I've written any poetry that's worth reading it is also a worthwhile piece of criticism, and the kind of "criticism" I am interested in writing is more to do with speculation and engagement than with conclusion and summary. Of course if they all occupy the same landscape then it might dawn on someone that when I'm talking about Copleston on Duns Scotus in one context that might have some kind of relationship with something they didn't "get" before in something like "The Rainbow Of". Or maybe it won't. Whether it does or it doesn't, that's for that individual, not for me to start pointing out.

10. The poets in Radical Renfrew had no influence whatever on me as I only came on most of them four years ago when I was compiling the book, most of them having been out of print for a century or more. If you hold Radical Renfrew up to the light at the front of a cave though you'll find it makes the same shadows at the back as Intimate Voices, if you try the same trick.

11. I couldn't really answer that, at least I wouldn't want to. It's up to the work to answer that, if it can. It's not up to me so start giving assessments.

12. Because I hadn't done something before would seem to me to be precisely the reason for it to be attempted. I don't anyway think *nora's place* is unrelated to other things I've written, but I'm much too close to it to talk about that even should I want to. Though nora is a female name the gender isn't important to me, the name nora seemed right and the rest followed from that. There were various things about passivity going on in *Ghostie Men*. The word "place" has resonances as well. I like having made a structure where the line "I'm just a human being" can appear in it without being sentimental, and that it can say any human being is totally representative. I like also being able to list a supermarket's contents without irony or some kind of game going on, nora is the only thing not named in that place. If poetry couldn't encompass that area of experience I couldn't be interested in it.

13. *Lentil Soup Diagnostic* was a performance event commissioned by the Third Eye to open Mayfest 1989. It began with a stereo tape playing superimposed tracks of typewriters, while on the stage I chopped up carrots onions and turnip to put in a soup pot that already had water and lentils in it. There was so much went on I can't remember it all without looking out and playing a big tape, which I haven't got time to do. There was a multitracked sequence of poems and bits of speech I'd made that got quite noisy, and with which I joined in in different ways, as with other tapes that were played. The soup was put on to cook which made a fine smell throughout the performance. In the middle there was a reading-performance of the "Goggles" thing with Biggles Ginger and Alice (Biggles as a football strip fetishist who goes to confession) given by myself Jim Kelman and Alasdair Gray. I read what I'd written of *nora* at one point, and the *Moderate Members Monologue*. There were two phone calls received — I'd taped them previously — one

113

from someone phoning up to make sure that this was "nothing to do with that City of Culture shite, and to make sure you're not selling out," the other from an old man who thought he was speaking to the Radio Clyde sports phone in programme, wondering whether if Rangers should bring back Kichenbrand to lead the attack, and whether the Scottish Cup should be scrapped since it wasn't a surprise any more for the winners, they should replace it with a small animal or bird, perhaps a budgie. There were various tapes to do with lists of proverbs, collective nouns and so on from a school primer that I responded to in different ways, and the thing ended when Alasdair and Jim came back on stage and sat down to a plate of lentil soup with me to the accompaniment of a blackbird singing which I had taped from the park facing the house at the crack of dawn a couple of weeks before. Small medicine bottles were then distributed to the audience each containing lentil soup with "Lentil Soup, Diagnostic" on the labels.

14. I can't talk about the so-called Gulf War. My pamphlet will have to suffice there.

LIZ LOCHHEAD

INTERVIEWED BY EMILY B. TODD

Liz Lochhead, the Scottish poet and playwright, was born in 1947 in Motherwell, Lanarkshire. She attended Glasgow School of Art where she studied painting and drawing. She then worked as an art teacher until 1978 when she was selected to participate in the first Scottish/Canadian writers' exchange fellowship, enabling her transition to a full-time writing career. Lochhead began writing poems during her time at Art School. Her first collection, *Memo for Spring*, came from Reprographia in 1972, and is included, along with *Islands* (1978) and *The Grimm Sisters* (1981), in *Dreaming Frankenstein and Collected Poems* (Polygon, 1984). Lochhead has also created several dramatic monologues and performance pieces, many of which are collected in *True Confessions and New Cliches* (Polygon, 1985). Her stage plays include *Blood and Ice* (Salamander Press, 1982), a translation into Scots of Moliere's *Tartuffe* (Polygon, 1985), *Mary Queen of Scots Got Her Head Chopped Off* (Penguin, 1989) and *Dracula* (Penguin, 1989). Her latest performance pieces, dramatic monologues, and poems are collected in *Bagpipe Muzak* (Penguin, 1991). Lochhead has written several revues for the Glasgow Mayfest and the Edinburgh Festival Fringe; her most recent play, *Quelques Fleurs*, was performed as part of the Edinburgh Fringe 1991. She has held writer-in-residence posts at several universities, including Edinburgh and Dundee. Liz Lochhead lives in Glasgow, where this interview was recorded in the summer of 1991.

ET: Could you begin by telling me a little bit about your background?

LL: I was born in the west of Scotland, not all that far from Glasgow, but yet it seems quite, quite different. About 15 or 20 miles out. It always says I was born in Motherwell. Yes, I was born in Motherwell, but my main growing up from age of four was in a little mining village about three or four miles outside of Motherwell, so it was on the edge of the moors, which is sort of countryside, but it is very industrially-scarred countryside. Both my parents were Scots, Scots through and through — I suppose, Protestant Scots. They were very unbigoted: they weren't interested in sectarian differences and so on. However, the area was very divided. Catholics and Protestants lived, in many ways, quite separate lives because of the separate schooling of the children. And yet the neighbours were friendly. It was odd. But you had these quite separate institutions, the church and schooling, which, you know, changed things. It's quite odd actually, our village was sort of Protestant, and the next village down was largely Catholic. The main schools and the main church in our village were Protestant. I had lots of Catholic friends — it's just that I didn't go to school with them. Terrible, divisive upbringing. I still think that the Labour Party in Scotland ought to address this problem very seriously.

ET: Did you read a lot when you were young? Did you have any favourite authors?

LL: Not really. I read voraciously; you know, mostly rubbish. Although I was fairly precocious as well. I read all kinds of pony books and school books, but I also know that I read *Wuthering Heights* when I was seven. I remember getting those books, *Wuthering Heights* and *Jane Eyre*: I read them when I was seven. *Mill on the Floss* when I was about nine or ten. I've read them a lot since. I liked them better, even at the time, though I didn't understand them. I liked them better than *Little Women, Good Wives, What Katie Did*. But I didn't read them thinking I was reading anything special — it was just among all the things you read.

ET: You went to Art School and worked as an art teacher and painter before your devoted yourself to writing. In what ways did your years as a painter and art teacher feed into your writing career? Was your time at Art School useful?

LL: Oh yeah. Of course, I didn't go there to learn to be a writer. When I was fifteen, although I read a lot and quite liked writing things, I didn't write anything I wasn't told to write. This was the point, I think. I always tended to do what was asked at school, although I always enjoyed writing once I started. I sometimes couldn't resist going on and on and writing big long things instead of the essays that were asked. But with painting it was different. I decided when I was fifteen that I wanted to go to Art School, and I drew and painted all the time in the way that later, once I was in Art School, I wrote all the time.

ET: So you started to write at Art School.

LL: Yes.

ET: Was there a community of people writing there? Were you there at the same time as Alasdair Gray?

LL: No, no. Alasdair had left. I didn't know Alasdair. I know him well, now, of course, but I didn't know him then. I knew who he was. He was famous for being a genius. And he wrote a play which I remember being on when I was in Art School. And I remember he was a rather exotic figure. I remember thinking, "That's Alasdair Gray. He's a genius," as he walked past on the street. But no, I didn't know him at all. I think it was almost two years after I left Art School, or about a year after I left Art School, that Alasdair became quite a close friend. But no, he finished Art School quite a bit ahead of me. So did John Byrne, who is also a well-known writer. There's other people who went to Art School who have written. . . I can't think off hand right now. But yes, at the time there was another woman called Jean Millington who was writing quite a lot. She was published in magazines like *Scottish International* which were out at that time. In fact, she was sort of a published writer before I was. I remember being sort of slightly envious. She knew people like Tom McGrath and Tom Leonard and Alan Spence, actually just six months or so before I did, but I remember thinking. . . I remember going along to a reading in 1967 or 1968 that they had done. I remember thinking, "I write as well," but I don't know how they were supposed to know. Whenever I began to show any of them my writing, they were totally helpful. Tom McGrath took an interest in my writing — I think that was about 1970 though. While I was at Art School, I wrote a lot. There was a writer teaching at the Art School. Not teaching writing, but he had a little writers' group, and I used to go along to that. His name is Stephen Mulrine. He's a playwright and he is a fantastic critic. He just really is. He used to rip my poems to bits, and I remember a friend of mine saying, "Aren't you offended that he rips them to bits? What does he know? You can write better poems than him?" And I would think, "Oh no," I was terribly pleased because I knew he wouldn't have spent so much time on them if he hadn't liked them. So he used to help me cut things down to half the length that they were the first time I thought they were finished. So, yes, he was in lieu of a literary education.

ET: Was that a period of working on writing, perhaps more than working on painting?

LL: No, no. I did paint, but certainly about halfway through Art School my real love switched to writing. No, I was painting all the time. But it just stopped being what I loved doing. In fact, I haven't really painted seriously, though I still like drawing, since I left Art School.

ET: Did you have any training when you first started writing? Did you attend any writers' workshops of any sort?

LL: Well, sure. There was Stephen Mulrine's workshop — that was when I was at Art School — so that formed. . . you obviously need a bit of somebody critical reading your work, a bit of help, so he gave me that. Once I left Art School in 1970, I couldn't really go to him any more. I suppose I could have actually, but it's not the same. When I finished Art School, I joined a writing workshop that was attached to Glasgow University — it was an extra-mural thing, a sort of writers' workshop, a weekly thing. It wasn't expensive. I went along maybe every week. Some of the people there weren't writers at all, but I went along with the kind of thought. . . it was a poet who takes this group. His name is Philip Hobsbaum. He's been a sort of Movement poet, a

Movement poet in the Fifties. And you know, I thought, "He's a real published poet". . . I'd read his book, I took it out of the library. And I thought, "He'll like my poems." I wasn't sure that he would, but I hoped, "He'll like my poems, and then I'll be discovered." Indeed he did give me a lot of help, and so did the other people in the group. It's often erroneously said that Jim Kelman and I met at that. Though Jim Kelman, he actually went the following year, and yes he (Philip Hobsbaum) did introduce a lot of us to each other. He used to have a little writers' group that met on a Sunday night. Although I was actually only at it twice, you know. By this time in 1972, I had left Glasgow briefly, so I think I was there a couple of times when I was visiting friends for the weekend. But I remember it was Philip Hobsbaum who first showed me a Jim Kelman story which must have been the following year, after I left his group. I must have been in that group in 1970-71, and then I was still in contact with Philip in 1971-72. I remember his showing me a story by James Kelman, "Nice to be Nice," I must say I remember thinking, "What's so terrific about this?", you know, at the time. I liked it, but I didn't really get it. And yes, two or three of us did become friends by that time. Just largely through being asked to read together.

ET: Did *Memo for Spring* grow out of that period?

LL: Yes. Most of the poems in *Memo for Spring* were written while I was at Art School and during the year after Art School.

ET: Was *Memo for Spring* influenced by any sort of feminist awakening?

LL: No, not consciously. Yes, obviously it was, but yes, and I was interested in feminism by this time. But that's not why I wrote the poems. I think in a way if I had read more feminism and had been a bit later, I wouldnt have had to write some of the poems. I think that's the point with writing. Even though ideas are out in the world, if you haven't come across them yourself, you've got to invent and invent a language for finding them. By that time I was. . . of couse I was interested in women poets, you know, quite early on in about '68, I remember being interested in Anne Sexton and Sylvia Plath. They weren't the first poets I was interested in, but I remember kind of coming to them after. The first poets I was interested in were probably Movement poets: Philip Larkin, people like that. I was very interested in Larkin because of the prosaic nature of his poetry while put into this poetic framework. I never was able to do that myself, but I liked the idea of the cliché and the flat language. In fact, I liked Larkin's poetry a lot more then than I like it now. I still like about five or six Larkin poems very, very, very much. But at that time I was very interested in that. I was very, very interested early on in Thirties poets, Auden and MacNeice. MacNeice was probably my first great love. I think the first book of poetry I ever bought was a paperback selection of Louis MacNeice. And of course at the same time, there was something that attracted me about what was happening in Liverpool: there were these poets who performed things. I thought it must be great to say poems to a big audience.

ET: Did you begin performing early on then?

LL: Not very early. 1972. Just before *Memo for Spring* came out was the first real reading. I had read my poems out loud a couple of times at the Art School. In fact, I can remember reading poems, reading my poems, bad as they were, alongside Robbie Coltraine, the actor, reading e.e. cummings. Pretty bad competition. An actor, a brilliant actor as he already was then, reading e.e. cummings against me, reading my first gropings at poems. The first public reading was this thing called Poem '72 which was this enormous poetry festival that was held in Edinburgh. There was a Poem '73, but it wasn't as successful, in a way. Poem '72 was wonderful. This bloke, John Scoffield his name was, just decided to put together a big, big, huge reading event where there would be at least three different things happening at different places. Certain lesser known poets would be performing in smaller rooms while at the same time famous poets, like MacCaig. Oh gosh, I mean there were lots of people came up for it. Peter Porter probably. I can't remember, but, you know, lots of poets — Adrian Mitchell — people who were quite well known came up and read. And alongside that there were lesser known poets going on in different rooms who took the overspill because not everybody could get in. But I was on as a support actor, namely to Norman MacCaig. There was me — I had to do ten minutes, and MacCaig, of course, was doing half an hour. I had to do my ten minutes at the beginning and another poet who died just about a year later, another youngish poet. So that was sort of getting thrown in the deep end of performance, having only performed once before. And at that time I had a long-term lover who was very interested in performance and so on. I remember he made me practice, and I remember thinking, "You don't practice. You'll lose your spontaneity." I remember he made me, the night before, do this reading — made me read into a tape recorder, listen back, listen to how I was mumbling bits. He made me practice speaking out loud. He said, "You know, if you're going to do this, you'd better to it well." And I suppose that was the first realisation. . . I think I see lots of poets even in their 50s and 60s, who haven't taken on that basic message. I don't mean that you perform it as if you were an actor. It's not the same thing at all; but if you're going to do it in public, I think you ought to decide the selection of poems which will be accessible to an audience, you ought to do it loud enough so they can hear you, and you ought to make some sort of communication with them. I've still seen too many poets, some of them wonderful poets, who come on, read a long section of their latest work, or haven't even decided what they are going to read before they do it. I think they should just try and do it well. Of course, the downside of that is that you begin to do jokey poems just especially for reading out loud. Yeah, it's a big danger and, yeah, it's not danger I manage to avoid. But so that interest in performance, which seemed slightly to split away from an interest in writing. . . It feels to me that I write two quite different things, although I don't think other people see these as two. . . I feel as though they are written by two different people.

ET: That you have a person who writes for performance and a person who writes poems for a book?

LL: Yes. Although I like reading the book poems out loud as well, but I tend to feel. . . you know how there is the black book and the white book [laughs]: there's *True Confessions* and there's *Dreaming Frankenstein*. And there are a few poems that overlap slightly like "Smirnoff for Karloff" which belongs in the white book, but is very much a sort of performancy poem. I don't think other people see them as being written by two separate people the way I do. The new book that's coming out [*Bagpipe Muzak* — Penguin, August 1991]. . . I am a bit worried about how that will be received because there is a lump. . . about a third of it, is light verse, just performance stuff, not even the best performance stuff I've written really, in some ways. You know it's very, very, almost. . . agitprop. Most of it was written for a purpose. So there are those. Some of them are parodies. I mean they are all right. I'm not knocking them. I'm quite pleased with them. And there's a third which are voices, some of them in poem form and some of them more lightly dramatic monologues. And then there's a section of poems. There are these three different sections in the book and maybe they are not so different as all that. Maybe they don't need to be apologised for in that kind of way.

ET: You still then consider yourself someone who both writes poems and performances. There hasn't been a transition from being a poet to being a playwright?

LL: No, although I write much less poetry than I used to. But when I do it, it's my favourite thing to do. I wish I wrote more, I hope it won't go away. It's the most satisfying thing to write.

ET: How is writing poems different from writing plays? What makes it the most satisfying thing to do?

LL: I don't know. Certain bits of writing plays are just about as satisfying as writing poems. I think that's the trouble, that writing plays for me usually uses up some of the same energy, so certain speeches in, say *Mary Queen of Scots Got Her Head Chopped Off*, felt like writing poems to me while I was doing them. Just certain speeches. The opening speech gave me the same kind of satisfaction as writing a poem. A little section later on where La Corbie and Mary talk about the Virgin Mary being pulled out of the sky in Scotland, that bit was satisfying like writing a poem. Whereas mostly writing plays is much more structural in a different way. There's a big structure going on instead of a small, intricate structure, like a poem. Also plays are for something. They are for a deadline. A play is something that doesn't exist when you have written it. It only exists when it begins to be performed. Whereas a poem is something that even before you've tightened it up properly, once you've got it finished, even if it's lying under the bed, there it is: it's a thing. So I think that's what satisfies me the most about poetry, that it is not for anything whatsoever and that you don't really do it to order.

ET: When you write plays are you very conscious of the performance-end? Are you involved in the performances of your plays?

LL: Oh yeah. I think really, as a writer, I like to be there during the first rehearsal. Not much interested in being there after that, but I'm there during the first rehearsal period. Not to check up on what the director and actors are doing, not at all for that, to check up on the play, cut it down, get it into shape. Because it's only really a draft you go into rehearsal with, I find. Some don't change much, some change radically, but they all change during the rehearsal. I mean in script, even in ideal script form, some things you change just for that particular production because certain actors aren't getting a particular line through. You know writing for the theatre is so practical, quite vulgar, quite rough. It's a rough trade. It really is a rough trade. Whereas poetry is very much about getting exactly the voice and tone, and tinkering. I mean that's what I love about it. Of course you tinker a lot with speeches in plays, but, you know, you make a version of a play for that particular company to do. And out of that also at the same time, you make your playing version of the piece that will go to other people that are going to do the play and then you won't go. You might go once, just literally to see what you think of what they are doing, so you would only go that once. Whereas the first time you are finding out about your play, you're rewriting it, cutting it down. I've been doing that all last week with the new play [*Quelques Fleurs*, performed in August 1991 at the Edinburgh Festival Fringe].

ET: I want to go back for a minute to the poems. Your poems are full of American details and words. I know you've been to the United States and Canada several times, and I wonder if you are particularly influenced by American poets?

LL: Oh yeah. I think all of us were right from way back in the Sixties. The English poets I liked were very, almost narrative poets, poets who were making something of the demotic voice. I also began to be, in the late Sixties, interested in Scottish writing. I'm very, very keen particularly on Morgan, Iain Crichton Smith and MacCaig. They were just giants as far as I was concerned. Although they are all Scottish poets who mostly write in English. Crichton Smith writes in Gaelic, but he writes in Gaelic and English; he doesn't write in Scots at all. Although there is a Scots rhythm in the way they use English; there's a Scottish sensibility which obviously means a lot to me. So I was interested in them. I was interested in Irish poets like, I suppose. . . definitely, Heaney has always appealed to me a lot, because he gets in the voice, and that voice seemed not at all alien. So I liked Heaney, and I liked Derek Mahon. I like Longley. I was interested in their poetry from, say, the early Seventies. But I wasn't much interested in English poetry. Ted Hughes, yes, it was good to read, but apart from that, mostly the voice of English poetry didn't really attract me. Although I always wrote in English, I don't think I realised how Scottish my English was in, say, *Memo for Spring*. It's standard English, I suppose, sometimes with the rhythms of Scottish speech. And also it's got the rhythms of childhood speech in it, I think. And it was a created persona, even though I didn't necessarily use that word. There was a sense that these poems were being spoken by somebody who was. . . perhaps it was me, aspects of me. But whenever people talk about the confessional, I always knew that was wrong. Of course I was using bits of myself. All writers use bits of themselves. Science-fiction writers are writing metaphorical maps of their own souls and psyches. I think all writers use themselves, but for some reason women writers are always regarded as being autobiographical, and the more you work hard on sounding autobiographical, which I remember consciously doing, even in *Memo for Spring* — I was consciously creating a sort of persona speaking these poems who was perhaps a younger, slightly more dewey-eyed and innocent than I was myself and it was a fairly conscious literary thing. I wasn't sort of a Grandma Moses, which I felt I was getting regarded as, as an interesting primitive.

ET: The spoken voice was then something you cultivated and worked on?

LL: Yeah. It came naturally, and then I pushed it further. I think that's the point. Something is natural to you and you then push it further.

ET: You mentioned Edwin Morgan. I know you have a poem dedicated to him in *Dreaming Frankenstein*, and he wrote the foreword to that collection. What have you learned from Edwin Morgan? Has he had an influence on your work?

LL: Probably not really, or not that I can see. I admire his poetry very much. What attracts me about Morgan's poetry is the way that he can take in all aspects of experience and make a poem out of them. I am interested in the way that he used rhythms of speech and all different kinds of fragments. No, I just admire him very much, but I don't think I'm particularly influenced by him.

ET: What about Adrienne Rich? Is she a poet you read or were influenced by?

LL: No, she wasn't. Yes, once I read her I found what she had to say fantastically useful and true for being an accurate statement of many things that I had subconsciously been feeling and working on for quite a long time. I now like Adrienne Rich's poetry very much. I tend to prefer the poetry before she wrote the wonderful prose in *On Lies, Secrets and Silence*. When I read that, I thought, "Ah yes", but it was quite later on. When I was in Canada, I remember Margaret Atwood saying, "You've never heard of Adrienne Rich?"; it was just in conversation, and she was amazed.

ET: When was this?

LL: Oh, it can't be so long ago. It was maybe about '78 or '79, so yes I did read her in 1980's, but I prefer Rich's poetry when she was working through this stuff — you know things like "Diving into the Wreck" which are just, you know, they are wonderful. I don't enjoy the poetry so much since the wonderful prose, because now it seems to me that she is sort of writing to fulfil the statements that she made. The same thing happened, I think, to Atwood in her prose more, after she had written *Survival*, a book of literary criticism and of thoughts about being a Canadian, about Canadianness and literature, nationalism and literature, feminism and literature. It's a wonderful book, actually, this book *Survival* of hers. But then her novel *Surfacing* was almost like a scheme.

ET: Is Margaret Atwood somebody you spent time with in Canada?

LL: Her husband was the other half of this swap, the Scottish-Canadian writers' fellowship, so I got to know them a little bit and they were very kind to me. They had me out to their farm and stuff like that. But like most writers, when you get together, you talk about money [laughs] and other things. I admire her writing quite a lot. I like her poetry and I like certain of the novels enormously. I think my favourite Canadian writer and probably the biggest influence, though I can't think why. . . the person I would most like to be influenced by, is Alice Munro who is a short story writer.

ET: Have you ever written short stories?

LL: No. The nearest to short stories I've written are these monologues which are in voice. Some of the pieces in the new play, which is monologues. It's not really a play, well it's a play, but the form the play takes is two interwoven monologues and there are different sections in it, so there are parts of it that are akin to the short story. Short stories and monologues — dramatic monologues, differ from each other, even first person short stories, in that the point about a dramatic monologue is the effect it's having on the person speaking it now. In other words, with drama. . . if there's a scene in drama where I tell you a story about my past, interesting story about my past as that might be, the point of it has to be what that's doing to you and me at the moment, whether I'm putting you down by it. They are still different. But I have got a hankering to try and write short fiction. Although why I imagine that I could do it, I don't know. I don't think that I probably would be. But short fiction is probably some of the writing that I find most interesting at the moment. I think I'm probably more interested at the moment in reading short fiction, especially stuff with a strong voice, like Carver and Munro. There are too many short story writers I admire to talk about. Grace Paley has been an enormous influence, the New York short story writer. I remember being influenced by her right from the very first book I read, or wanting to be, because of this sense of voice that she had where the short story was a sort of performance, almost. She influenced even the poems I was writing at the time.

ET: When were you reading Grace Paley?

LL: I first read her in 1969. I don't think she was published in this country at that time. I just found a book, *Disturbances of Man*. She'd been published in America and somebody had it, and from then on I'd always been interested in the way she writes, the sense of voice. So I suppose I'm interested in voice, whether it's in drama, whether it's in poetry, or whether it's in fiction. I'm not particularly interested in poetry in which I can't hear the voice. And I often find with poetry I'm not interested in that sometimes once I've heard the poet read, even if the poet isn't a very good reader, I can then somehow hear that voice back into the poetry. And sometimes that brings it alive for me. I think most poetry I don't understand is because I can't hear the voice in the poem.

ET: I want to ask you about a recurring image in your work. There are several images of mirrors in both your poems and plays — in ''Mirror's Song'' and ''What the Pool Said,'' even in some poems in *Memo for Spring*, and *Dracula* begins with Lucy gazing into a mirror. Are these images deliberate? What do they represent for you in these texts, if they are deliberate?

LL: Well, they are deliberate in that they are chosen. For me to answer questions like this I have to do the kind of job that I don't do in myself to write the poems. I have to become a sort of literary critic of my own poems which is something I'm not terribly interested in doing. I think when I look back at my own poems in the way I don't do when I'm writing them [laughs], or it's not at all the work I do when I'm writing, I would say that these images or mirrors reflect [laughs] my interest in identity. Probably if I think of *Memo for Spring*, it was the idea of forging-out a Scottish and female and working-class and contemporary identity as a writer. I would probably say that was the function of those poems for me. Although I did not articulate this, I just did it.

ET: That was probably the process of articulation. . .

LL: Yes. It was. Well, I think you see the same problem again and again, often in female poets. If you think of Plath, she actually had to invent this language to describe the state she was in because she had internalised all the male and literary and high art models, and she had internalised them so that they were her. I mean that they're not something false. It's something that you own, is this male half. So for me, if I think about it, I had already got a posh, grown-up, male, English voice to write in. Although that wasn't the voice I spoke in. And probably *Memo for Spring* was about articulating that voice into being Scottish, female. And yet I didn't think about any of those things when I did it. And then also I remember at that time being sure that I didn't want to write poems — this was a conscious decision even then — I didn't want to write poetry that was allusive, that was based on Persephones and Penelopes. I just had hated that kind of think in Milton so much. I thought, "Ugh I don't want to write like that. I want to write about here and now." Then of course the next thing I had to do was write *The Grimm Sisters* which was all about archetypes and so on, but by then I was writing about them from a female, inside point-of-view.

ET: So it was ok. . .

LL: I suppose it must have been. I just had to. I didn't know whether it was ok or not; it was just that having decided that I don't want to do this, definitely not, then there was this way in which it was work that had to be done without consciously deciding why. And then later on beginning to write in Scots without particularly having decided to. So I suppose all of these things are about forging an identity.

ET: And finding a voice. . .

LL: If one can articulate, then there would be no need to write the poem. . . if one could articulate the things that the poem is doing for you and therefore for other people, you hope. There's always this sense. . . and I think maybe that's what's wrong with English literature, with English poetry: it doesn't have to do that work itself. Of course it does for individuals. Individual poets are finding out ways to talk about their identity and so on, but in general there is this sense of consensus which I don't think I feel I can write out of.

ET: In an interview last year, you said "the really big split [in Scotland] isn't between male and female; it's between self and other" [*The Guardian,* 8 February 1990, 37]. That remark left me wanting to know more, and made me wonder whether you read contemporary literary theory?

LL: No, certainly not. I don't know what I meant at the time! I guess I would say that the big split in Scotland is between self and other self. In many ways I think that the big theme in Scottish literature is the split, from *Justified Sinner* to *Jekyll and Hyde*, and I think that's natural if you're Scottish where you are half English, really. There's a bit of you who's internalised all of that, so you're English, but you're Scots. So two different halves of you talk to each other which is very similar to the states of the male and the feminine. The Scots is in some ways in the position of being the feminine with regard to Britain. You know the Celt, the other. Once again we split again — in Scotland, the Celt is the feminine, the Scot is the male, the standard. I don't know where that leaves Scottish Celts. They're split and split and split and split. It's probably between dominant cultures and undominant cultures. I would like the split to become between self and other, but sometimes you're so busy defining self that you are talking to other halves of yourself. I don't really think that male and female is the only opposite by any means. I think there's a certain part of art which does aspire towards androgyny. I think the thing is that the female tends to be aware of its difference from the male.

But we were still talking about whether it was American poetry that interested me. I was interested when I was young in, first of all, Scottish and Irish literature, ballads and oral stuff and then Scottish and Irish poetry and the kind of flat, prosaic voice of the Movement poetry interested me quite a lot because it was about the here and now or whatever. And then American poetry. . . well American poetry just interested me enormously because of its use of voice and its energy, its intimacy. It's quite interesting to me that in America, where you have got lots of male novelists, big male, macho kind of novelists, and there are lots of women poets and I think maybe it comes through from Whitman and Dickinson, where the poetry is quite private. Whereas, I think, in Britain, in general, there is a bardic, public-function to poetry. The poems of the grand old men, the kind of boys of the tribe. So here we get women novelists and male poets. I suppose the Romantics are the kind of maximum set of that. . . So American poems had this freedom, this energy. Also there's just this cultural interest in Scotland in America, in an ordinary popular culture way. And particularly Glaswegians tend to think they're American. Because we all liked American films when we were little, because we. . . America seemed a more free influence than say England did because England was saying, "You're not good enough." America seemed to us kind of free and fun and big and brash and exciting. So American poetry. I suppose it was things like the voice in Carlos Williams. There are still poets that I don't understand very well, like Berryman, that I love because just that noise the poetry makes. Berryman, Lowell, Plath and Sexton just interested me enormously, as well as things like Whitman, Ginsberg, Getty, all that Beat stuff, Olson, the Black Mountain stuff. Yes, I mean it was exciting, it was interesting. It made poetry about breathing, about talking. It seemed to me then, and I don't disagree with myself now, that it was more interesting than what was happening in England. I had begun to get rather bored with this sort of democratic posturing of Movement poetry. It began to seem just dull and provincial.

ET: Were there Scottish poets who were doing the same thing, as far as you were concerned.

LL: Yeah. Tom Leonard. Alan Spence, who wrote poetry at that time. Other of my contemporaries who were Brian McCabe and Angus Nicolson. . . He was then writing about Gaeldom in English and now he is writing about international themes in Gaelic. Same difference. Oh yeah. I'm still influenced, in a sense, by everything I read. I think I was probably interested in taking things that I learned from, say, short story writers into poetry. Maybe it's perverse, maybe I should just actually have tried to write short stories. I was interested in a sort of quasi-narrative quality as well.

ET: That's true in *The Grimm Sisters*?

LL: I suppose so. I think more in *Memo for Spring*, like 'The Choosing', the equivalent of the kind of thing a short story writer might do at more extended length. Probably it was quite perverse. I've got no idea why I did decide to write poems and indeed a lot of people have said that I haven't done it yet. I think that's a fair comment. I don't think everybody likes them. I don't think everybody would think that they had enough control and so on. Although all kinds of internal rules grow up for the poem itself. I would be able to explain what those rules were, but only poem by poem and at great length and elaborately. I can't make general statements about what I do, but each one does seem to have a form, even the free ones.

ET: What do you mean that people say you haven't written poems yet?

LL: Some people just think that they are too slack or they are not controlled enough or they are not compressed enough,

ET: Do they feel slack when you are writing them? Is it the slackness that you want. . .

LL: No. I'm trying to get them as tight and formal as I can do while doing what I want to do. That's the tension for me. I'd like to make them more formal and yet more colloquial at the same time. And I'm not working hard enough on the techniques that would be involved in doing that because I'm spending so much time writing plays. You know I'm not putting in the kind of work so that poems still come to me as rare random events in much the way that they did in *Memo for Spring*, therefore I'm inventing a form for each one. Probably a sort of free verse and voice thing is what I should be doing anyway. But if I was really, really, you know, working at my poetry, which I have this big ambition to do again sometime. . . you know, but that would probably be forbidding myself to write plays for a year or something because it does use up a lot of the same energy, finding a voice, but that's for different characters.

ET: So there is a tension between the two forms. They can't co-exist easily. . .

LL: Oh yeah, sure they can, but not easily. I think if I was writing the poems that I'd probably like to write now, I'd probably have been putting my hand at formal. . . things that would make me more supple. I think my painting was the same. It's a sort of struggle against inarticulacy, against clumsiness. It's the finding of enough grace, enough ease to do it, to do the job. Not to be graceful, but just to find enough grace. That seems to be good enough. I'm not trying to let myself off the hook, but I'm just trying to write good enough poems. You know in the same sense that the best thing is for a mother to be a good enough mother [laughs], which can also mean that you are not pushing yourself as hard as possible, but I don't mean that at all.

ET: You once said in an interview, I think in the early eighties, so it may very well be something you don't remember. . .

LL: It certainly might not be something I remember!

ET: You said: "I do feel that my writing — just for me, not for Scottish literature, just for me — is what I want to do more than anything else, so I make space for that" [*Weekend Scotsman*, 12 May 1984, 6].

LL: Gosh, how pompous! You know that's the trouble with interviews: they don't have in the irony or the grace. You know "not for Scottish literature", I think that was probably a joke. I hope. . .

ET: So my question, which may or may not follow from your quote, is have you ever felt that you *do* need to write for Scottish literature, that you need to make a certain kind of contribution, add a female voice:?

LL: No. I don't feel that I have to do it. I feel it has to be done. Yes, sure, the female voice has to exist. It's not a responsibility, no I don't have to do it. If I stop having fun, or if I don't start having more fun [laughs], I'll stop doing it. It's not that you have got a big responsibility. But, on the other hand, if you are writing and that's what you do and that's what you enjoy then, of course, you've got the responsibility to do all you can. You can't take on po-faced crusades in writing. I don't actually have to worry about my writing filling in more of a female voice, because my writing is going to have a female voice. What am I going to do, sprout a penis? Of course, I don't have to say what aspect of female writing I have to bring in: I think that's the trouble with feminism. . . I think it's whenever feminism becomes prescriptive. My friend Dilys Rose put it very well in an interview of hers that I read a few weeks ago. She was part of a sort of collective women's writing group, and it was when they became more interested in criticising what you were writing than how you were doing it that it became impossible for her to keep being a member of it. And I think that's the point. You've got a right to write about anything you want, as truthfully as you want. And if you're a feminist, if you're a woman, of course it will be feminist and female and part of the female voice. Of course it will.

ET: Is there more of a community of women writing in Scotland now, would you say?

LL: Not really. I don't think that there's a community of people writing really. Some of my best friends are writers, but we don't talk about writing all that much. No, there's not really a community of writers. There's a set of friends who write and who don't write and who help one, and are interested in what one does which is very good. But there's not a community of writers. And yet one feels that because there's more work being produced and it's being taken more seriously internationally, of course that's a help and that feels like a community.

ET: I'm curious about your experience as a writer-in-residence at Edinburgh University. Did you do teaching there?

LL: Not really. I just talked to people about their individual poems. We had a group where the group criticised each other a lot. It was fairly tough, you know. We were quite hard on each other. I spoke to people about individual poems they were doing. I enjoyed it a lot. There was a wonderful poet called Angela McSeveney. Her poems are great. She's published in *Other Tongues: Young Scottish Poets in English, Scots and Gaelic* — there's a selection of Angela McSeveney poems, a lot of which I saw. I must say I didn't do anything to them except encouraging her to cut them down a little bit. But no, there they were. It was exciting. So no, it's lovely work that, but it's just very individual. There were quite a few poets. I just heard last week that one of my — I wouldn't call him my student, he just came a lot — one of my friends there who was a student at the time, Roddy Lumsden, has just won a Gregory Award. So that's great, but I don't feel that I helped him particularly. Although I feel having somebody to talk to helped him, just the same as it helped me. It's very exciting, it's great. I love doing detailed work on poems and things as they happen. And I think that kind of contact with the raw materials of it helps your own work. So no, it's great. It's great being a writer-in-residence. It's fantastic. I saw bits of prose and plays as well, but mostly it was poetry that I was tinkering with, helping people to tinker with themselves. It was interesting because there was a sort of movement to write in Scots — very strong — that just existed. That was really, really exciting to find that there it was. A guy named Matthew Fitt came along and he writes very well, I think.

ET: Did your own writing in Scots begin at that time?

LL: It did actually, strangely enough. Well, it had begun just before then.

ET: With *Tartuffe*?

LL: *Tartuffe*, a surprise to me.

ET: How did *Tartuffe* come about?

LL: Well, first a phone call. There was a commission. I had been working with the Royal Lyceum Theatre Company. I had done an adaptation of *Dracula*, a kind of personal *Dracula*. I quite like it actually. I'm quite pleased with that, the first half of it anyway. The first half is good. The second half has problems, but so does Bram Stoker's. And there had been a Moliere on, *The Miser*, and it was a very good Alan Duret translation. And they had done the miser himself as being Scots. You know it was just an accent and to me that wasn't good enough. There had been a version that used Scots, but it was just a matter of this text which had been written for presumably English actors where they just used an accent. And I had an argument with Hugh who directed it, and who had just directed my *Dracula*, a friendly kind of argument about whether or not this kind of thing was possible. And I said I thought you could do a Moliere into Scots. . . not into Scots at all, but into an English for Scottish actors to do in their own accents. I thought that would be taken account of there in the writing. And we decided that the play was going to be *Tartuffe*. I had read it once ages before in the Richard Wilbur translation which is excellent — lovely, neutral. It's terrific. It's very, very good, but it wasn't what I saw in the play. I could see lots of social gradations and things like that, and Scots is a fantastic language for multiplicity of register. There are all kinds of very, very local and particular class and almost gender and certainly geographical divisions which, you know, are mostly about class. Lots of Scots speakers, we have different ways of speaking. You know, I speak differently to my sister from the way I speak to you. And certainly that would be different from how I sort of had spoken to my grandmother where I'd probably fall naturally. . . without thinking I'll now use a different voice. And there's probably a posher voice that I would reach to when I'm talking to the BBC. I'm not talking about putting on voices. I'm talking about voices that are natural to you. I mean this is true of everybody. It's truism. But in Scots that kind of thing is very marked. We're very acutely aware of this sort of thing. Much more acutely aware than so-called received pronunciation speakers are when they think, "Well, of course, I'm just speaking neutrally." We are aware of these things. We use it a lot in our own ordinary, social discourse. It's a wonderful method for comedy, so I decided that I would write this new version of *Tartuffe*. It would also rhyme because the Moliere rhymed. I didn't know I could do it. A whole play in rhyme! God, could I? I just started on it, and, to my great surprise, it was fairly easy. Of course, I would hit terrible patches, where it would dry up for a while. But to my great surprise it was in actual Scots, most of it. It wasn't a decision. It wasn't just English for Scottish speakers. It was Scots, and then that led to setting it in the 1920's. And I used the way that everybody in the play speaks differently at different times, except the maid, who has got this intact Scots which is just natural to her in that she is always honest. She's probably the most honest person in the play. And so her language was intact and everybody else used it in various ways as rhetorical devices. And it was just great fun to do. It was wonderful fun. I started that actually just before I went to be writer-in-residence at Edinburgh. It was what I was working on during my first term there, so it was really strange and coincidental to me that one of the best young poets who came — although I think Matthew might not have come to the second year, but just after that anyway, when some of the poets who were coming were writing in Scots, young people that it just hadn't occurred to them to do anything else. So there seemed to be a sort of resurgence again in Scots writing which had definitely been going through the doldrums in the late Sixties and early Seventies. Donald Campbell, the poet, had done it, but all the other people who had done it, trying to sort of ape MacDiarmid, hadn't seemed to really get anywhere with it, to me.

ET: Is MacDiarmid somebody you look to at all when you are writing in Scots?

LL: Yes and no. I love *A Drunk Man Looks at the Thistle*. There's a sort of meanness of voice in MacDiarmid's Scots that gets me down. I love the small Scots lyrics. They're not any influence to me, but they are just lovely. Lovely, lovely things. A lot of them are in *A Drunk Man*, the small lyrical passages, like "The Rose of All the World." I'm not particularly interested in MacDiarmid's poetry in English. It's probably more Burns and people like that I look to. But once again, it's not actually poetry that already exists which is the nice thing. I don't really write poetry much in Scots.

ET: There's the one in *Dreaming Frankenstein*. . .

LL: Yeah.

ET: Are there any poems in Scots coming up?

LL: Sort of. . . but they tend to be in a voice. I don't really write in Scots much in my own voice.

ET: Do you write in a dictionary Scots?

LL: No. There was a bit of dictionary Scots in *Tartuffe*, but not much. There was this well that I didn't realise was there, of even vocabulary, and definitely thought and rhythm. And then, of course, having had that to my great surprise brought out of me, that was available for *Mary Queen of Scots Got Her Head Chopped Off*.

ET: In *Mary Queen of Scots* you have everything: Scots, French, posh English voices, non-posh English voices. Why that mixture of languages?

LL: Well, it's about Scotland and England, so obviously. . . Everybody in Scotland at that time, even the nobles, spoke Scots. It's very different from *Tartuffe* where you are talking about a time when the middle classes ape England, so what we had was. . . It was terrific. . . Ann Lacey was wonderful playing Mary. She played this person speaking Scots with a French accent. So in other words, Mary didn't learn to speak in English. Mary came to the Scots. She was good. It just came naturally. I don't know if there's everything. There's a sort of cod English that Elizabeth speaks. You know, she's a sort of bad pantomime queen. She had a lot of vigour and fun. I wasn't trying to send her up any more than Mary. The language came out the way it did because of what I had to do. It was great fun, but it was great fun after six months of complete panic and inability to do it. It was all written under pressure. I just kept doing research. I kept. . . I had to work on it, so I kept saying, "I need to do a little bit more research. Research, research, research. . ." Eventually I had to write the bloody thing. But it nearly killed me. I just thought, "Ugh, I can't do it." I remember in May going to Gerry Mulgrew at Communicado and saying, "I can't do this and there's not going to be a play." I was not going anywhere with it. I had only a few scraps. I just kept getting stuck. In other words, for me it's always about inventing a whole language, so therefore it's scary, there's a sort of noise. . . It's true of everybody. You start a new play, or a new poem, it's this new world that you've got to find. But for some people they just have to find the world and the language is already there. I didn't feel that. I didnt know what noise Mary should make, You know the English people had to speak English and the Scots played the Scots. It was just once again, this lovely, lovely language. Probably La Corbie's bits and Mary are sort of the most poetic voice.

ET: Were those voices the most difficult to write?

LL: No, it was the play and the structure, whatever. It's like everything else with poetry: It's not the writing poetry that's difficult, it's the bit before it. It's plucking up the courage to go into doing it.

ANGELA McSEVENEY

TALKING TO CAROL GOW

Angela McSeveney was born in 1964 and brought up in Rossshire, Livingston and the Borders. She attended Edinburgh University. She was awarded a Scottish Arts Council Bursary in 1990 and has published work in the anthology *Other Tongues* with David Kinloch, W.N. Herbert and Meg Bateman (Verse 1990). Her first full collection is *Coming Out With It* (Polygon 1993). The following pages offer an edited version of our conversation in Edinburgh, December 14, 1992.

CG: McSeveney's an unusual name — where does it come from?

AM: It's Irish. My father's father I believe came from Ireland in the early part of this century. He came from Ballymena and settled in Shotts.

CG: Does that Irish background filter through at all? Tell me about your family.

AM: I don't feel at all Irish or that I've any connection with Ireland. I always say — because I'm quite pedantic — that I was born in Edinburgh because I was a caesarean and had to come down to Edinburgh to be delivered and after two weeks Mum and I went back to Rossshire. I was still under five when we left Rossshire. If you want to try to position me socially, when I was born my father was working for the forestry commission as a woodcutter, log dragger and we lived in a tied cottage. He had various jobs — he was a bus driver, a groundsman for the council, a gardener, an electroplater, factory worker, taxi driver, storeman. My mother did mostly domestic jobs — we lived in council housing or tied cottages.

CG: So you started with a rural background?

AM: Fairly rural. Apart from three years in Livingston which was immediately after we lived in Rossshire so it was a bit of a culture shock, especially for my older sisters.

CG: Was there a sense then, that you were uprooted? You would be about five, then, five or six?

AM: Four — I think I remember quite a lot about my immediate surroundings in Rossshire — the croft, the garden, going down to the shore to Loch Carron and also the village, Achmore, because it was such a contrast to Livingston — there was a very clear cut between the two places. It's always a child's memories. I wrote 'Under Five' and 'The Bed and Breakfasts' to put on record my version of Rossshire. I've always been aware of feeling that I don't really come from a particular place.

CG: Do you like that sense of not belonging to a particular place?

AM: Some of it was dreadful when I was a child. When we moved from Livingston I was really miserable. I found I wasn't very adaptable.

CG: How old were you then?

AM: Going on eight. Lots of things happened. I was bullied a bit when I went to my next school — I just couldn't adapt, I got behind with school work. That was when I became short sighted. We were living — my father was a gardener then — in a tied cottage, the sort of big house scene, the gardener, the gamekeeper, Mum went into the big house and did cleaning, so we were living from my point of view quite an isolated existence. I didn't mind that there were no other children there at the weekend and I would go from beginning to end of the school holidays with no-one but myself to play with. This was the beginning of the problems that I had later — I mean you can look back. I'm not going to make a big psychological deal out of it but this was when I began to feel awkward, this was when all the not fitting in, not being good at small talk — it all stems from this horrible school. (laughs) But it was at this school that I began to enjoy reading and tried to write some stories.

CG: So round about seven — it was that uprooting, rather than the one at five, that was the problem for you.

AM: Yes, for me it was a problem. It was just everything. It wasn't till I moved and I started to go to primary school — I was almost ten now — in Galashiels that things started to get a lot better. For about the first term I was in primary five and almost at once I seemed to feel a lot more confident. I think it helped that the playgrounds were separate for girls and boys. I think life was a lot gentler in the all-girls' playground.

CG: You've been quoted as saying you mismanaged your education so well you ended up fitted only for an Arts course in a Scottish University. What were your ambitions — did you have set ideas of what you would do in the future?

AM: I've thought a lot about this. I started to read a lot when I was about nine — I tended to read solid children's classics which were around the house, like Heidi, Pollyanna, the Katy books — I remember trying to read the Swiss Family Robinson when I was about eight — and I had a little go at abridged Dickens but it was just incredibly dull. So I tended to read things like that or trashy children's books, adventure stories, Enid Blyton, some pony books. It wasn't till I was older I realised I'd missed out on the good modern children's books — like Roald Dahl, Judy Blume, the Pippa Longstocking books. I do regret that I missed out entirely on teen books and went straight on to Steinbeck, Lawrence, — very weighty adult books. I think I took literature a bit too seriously. But right from about the age of nine or ten, after reading a particularly thrilling Arthur Ransome book I decided that's it! I want to write!

CG: Was it important that you had a university education?

AM: That's really hard to answer. I have so many regrets about school and university. I think university was a good place for me to be between eighteen and twenty-two because I had to be somewhere and I certainly wasn't ready to go out into the workforce — If I had to go somewhere to sort myself out university was a safe place to be.

CG: Who was writer in residence?

AM: Allan Massie. I'd been writing all the time I was at school, short stories and I'd started to write poetry. I'd discovered Scottish literary magazines on a day trip to Edinburgh. I bought *Words, Chapman*. I must have been about fifteen or sixteen. It was the beginning of my having a real awareness of Scottish literature and modern poetry. When I read *Chapman* I didn't read the Scots poetry — I didn't even look at it — until Raymond Vetesse. That was when I began to read articles about women and writing and became aware that if you were Scottish it was going to be tough, you wouldn't be listened to and if you were a woman you wouldn't be listened to. And if you were a Scottish woman you might as well give up!

CG: What effect did that have on you?

AM: It made me quite nervous. It made me wonder if male editors would take me seriously.

CG: Which writers influenced you in particular?

AM: At school there was Wilfred Owen, Heaney and MacCaig. I did Latin at school and a little bit of Greek so I enjoyed Catullus, and things like *The Aeneid* — solid going, but gorgeous passages, wonderful metaphors. I also like Baudelaire — in translation — again the heavy images. Nowadays, unfortunately, I don't know much about non-British writers — I have a *Penguin Greek Anthology, Poets of the Late T'Ang* and recently I read Anne Sexton and the Finnish writer Solveig von Schoultz for the first time. I really enjoy Les A. Murray's work. I've been a fan of Grace Nichols for years, Ellie Macdonald, Edwin Morgan, Tom Leonard. Recently there's been Wendy Cope, and Jackie

Kay. Last year — Connie Bensley and Susan Wicks. English poets — odd but when I read their work I felt they wrote a bit like me. I won't try to define this — it was just an impression. The first time I read Robert Crawford's *A Scottish Assembly* I had the same feeling. Liz Lochhead. Especially *The Grimm Sisters*. A few years ago I read Kathleen Jamie's work and I was really impressed. Terribly envious that she was doing that so young.

CG: Did you think, well I can do that too — there's a Scottish woman writer. Was it that kind of inspiration as well as the actual poetry?

AM: Yes. It was. I remember when I was sixteen or seventeen hunting out women writers, trying to read Virginia Woolf, the Brontes, Sylvia Plath. I'd never heard of Sylvia Plath but it was a woman, and that was enough. And of course it was a woman who had committed suicide. I didn't know that she was a cult figure.

CG: Has your interest in women writers ever led you to belong to a women's writing group?

AM: I would be interested in that and I've been thinking of doing that lately because I was feeling quite isolated. When I came to university there were writers in residence — Allan Massie in first year but I think I went to see him twice. I stopped writing entirely in first year and didn't start again till the beginning of second year — I just couldn't write, there must have been a block of some sort, so after taking him some things that I'd written at school I just felt there wasn't any point in going back. In second year I began to write again. I wrote an awful lot — very short poems — and I used to take them to Cairns Craig, my director of studies, who very kindly read them and talked to me about them and didn't mind me shoving sheets of poems under his office door — I just foisted myself on him. I suppose I found Allan Massie a bit frightening — I don't want to say that he is a frightening person — it was just that I was such a bag of nerves about everything — tutorials, other students, essays, mixing with people, eating in front of people — that to also go to a writer in residence was all too much. In second year I had a renaissance.

CG: When did you first publish?

AM: My last year at school. I had a little flash in the pan and had two or three poems published which is just as well because if I hadn't I would never have tried again after being blocked in first year and being so nervous and on edge. I was quite ill with it by the second term. I think it was just incredible tension because for a term and a half I had nobody to confide in or giggle with. I also had this sense of not matching up, of not being dressed like everyone else and of not being able to say anything in tutorials and knowing that I was becoming conspicuous — as conspicuous as the people who wouldn't shut up.

CG: So this was a result of all this tension and of not being able to write?

AM: I think not being able to write was a sympton, like the headaches. I did write some really therapeutic bitter stuff when I was in second year. 'The Hirsute Woman' is a very bitter poem.

CG: You can read that poem now and recognise the bitterness. I was thinking about the poem 'Reviewed' where you come across a review of your own work. It can be taken literally but also there's the idea of your reading the published poems and becoming reviewer of your own work. Is there anything that surprises you — are there discoveries that you've made about your own work? I'm thinking here too about 'At the Shrinks' where you talk about 'blurting out some startling truth' — do you ever look at your own work and suddenly see blurted out there some startling truth?

AM: My style changed very dramatically in third year in university. I think you could spot it in the book because the poems are published virtually chronologically from nineteen, twenty, to the very last which was just before the book was published. When my style changed and became very stark and very bare and very stating the facts I was quite ill. Ron Butlin by this time was writer in residence and I'd been taking work to him — bursting into his office with thirty poems.

He was keen on cutting back my poems which we could see benefited a great deal and because I wasn't bursting with confidence I was anxious to please and what he said I did to the letter. I was cutting back a lot. There's a hint of desperation in a lot of the poems because I just got on to the slippery slope and I knew damn fine it was going to end in something awful — which it did. I was very ill by the summer of 1985.

CG: When you read the poems you wrote at that time are they very painful?

AM: I remember writing them and partly there was the excitement of finding a new style — I mean that was thrilling and there was also the feeling that I knew damn fine what was causing the illness and the breakdown. I didn't have a psychiatrist and so I was basically counselling myself. I got to grips with the problems on the page. I wondered are there other people writing like this? Will people feel that I'm being self-indulgent, will people feel that it's just domestic?

CG: In 'The Bed and Breakfasts' you offer 'quaint anthropological studies'. In a way you're treating yourself as an anthropological study in many of the poems — you analyse yourself, looking not just at the physical body — you write about smear tests, about sexual encounters — but the emotions too are analysed on the page and considered. Isn't it the gap between the woman who writes, and the persona who comes on the page — it's the gap between the writer and the woman which creates the persona isn't it it? Because you're treating yourself as an anthropological study?

AM: I'm glad you mentioned that because it crops up quite a lot when people talk to me after readings because they assume that the person in the poem is me always. They think nothing imaginative has gone into it and the poem has just landed flat on the page ready-made. Take 'Bed and Breakfasts' — we never had our photos taken by a Dutch family, we never had the photos sent to us. The 'Bed and Breakfasts' is just a collage of things I've heard my family talking about.

CG: The idea of using material, recording, but at the same time creating something different on the page comes over especially in poems about your own background — the poem about your mother's pregnancy — and 'Nightshift'. There's a line in that poem, 'the curtains in my parents' room were almost always closed'. How important is it for you to find a place in your own creation of self, to create a background as well, and given that the curtains were always drawn, how much do you need to create that for a fuller picture. Is that why you're drawn to it, because you need to fill in gaps?

AM: One of the reasons I've written several poems about my mother or based on things my mother told me is because she is a very good story teller. One thing I will say about the poem, 'The Pictures' — I didn't really write that poem. My mother just said it to me and I wrote it down.

CG: So that in a sense was a 'recording' — creating the space to set it down.

AM: Yes. I mean I was about fourteen when *Gone With The Wind* was re-released into the cinemas and it came round the cinemas in Galashiels and I asked my mum if she'd seen it when it first came out. She just told me the story and the line, 'the worst of it was she didnae faint' — when she said that it just hit me like a brick. I was only fourteen. I was having a different sort of life than her, living in a bigger house, there was no question that I wouldn't go on to sixth year if I wanted to, whereas Mum had had to leave when she was fourteen.

CG: Was it important then for you to give her a voice?

AM: Yes. I just had this sense of it's not fair. And it was horrible to think your mother had gone through that — that sense of there's nothing I can do to change this, there's nothing I can do to stop that this happened to you and that you have to carry this memory with you.

131

CG: In 'Victim of Violence' there's a feeling of guilt because you're not aware that someone is being attacked in the street outside, that it wasn't recorded, if you like, 'witnessed'.

AM: 'Victim' is a bit different. It's based on a true incident. A woman was attacked by two men very close to where I was living. I was really disturbed by it and because of this I got in touch with the Rape Crisis Centre and was a volunteer off and on for two years, until I burned out. 'Victim' was actually an introduction to a series of four poems which I've not actually used partly because once I almost fainted trying to read them and other times I just found my face was shaking uncontrollably and I have never ever been able, even practising at home, to read all four poems one after the other. They're not lurid. I just can't do it. I lose control of my breathing. I've changed facts in them, but at the moment I probably couldn't deal with the questions you get asked after reading them and I wouldn't want to publish them at the moment — it's a bit irritating because one or two of them are as good as anything I've ever written, so Victim, I hope it does work on its own but it actually became the intro to a series of four other poems.

CG: There's a question I was going to ask you later on, but maybe I should ask it now because it ties in with what you've just said. In 'Woman with a Lilac Sash' there's an image of the chaperon sitting just outside the frame of the picture. I wondered if you have a 'chaperon' just outside the frame of your poems — what you've said suggests to me that there are areas that you feel are not ready to be written about, or you can't write about. Is there a chaperon outside the frame?

AM: Yes. Definitely.

CG: Is that a good thing?

AM: Well I wrote a poem which was actually published, read by the other person who was in it and I've not used it since because she was so upset — which taught me a lesson.

CG: Can we turn to another theme in your work, the theme of loss, which is explicit in poems such as 'Myself': 'I am the only souvenir I have of you.' In many ways I think the sense of loss runs throughout so many of your poems — whether it's childhood, whether it's the loss of illusions, a dream, a myth — you go over that kind of ground in lots of ways — in 'Gone Wrong' for example you write 'I read the famous five, kept pets, believed in Santa Claus'. There's a tension between the child that was and the woman, and a sense of something lost. Do you feel that you have let that child down or that that child has let you down? Can you explain the tension in the poem?

AM: I was really pleased with that poem. I felt when I started writing it I was rambling away and I had this idea of how I wanted it to be when I'd finished and I'm not sure how I got there but I think I did it. I did what I meant to do. And it was dealing very specifically with having some sort of breakdown which was caused by realising that I'd the wrong idea about a lot of things. I'd thought certain things were important that weren't so important — losing weight, getting a good degree, worrying because I'd a beard. I never got any other signals except that they were extremely important.

CG: So is it the loss of all that time, that you can't go back and redo?

AM: Yes. I do feel — well I had to stop feeling it, because you just end up going nowhere but I went through a period where I really felt that I'd wasted a lot of time and gone in the wrong direction. 'Gone Wrong' was written about this feeling. It was very frightening to have a breakdown, especially when I was quite a reserved person, not extravert in any way, quite controlled, I suppose repressed. And then suddenly to find that your mind was just breaking down. I can remember thinking this is it I'm going mad and the sheer terror. And then coming out of that and getting better and looking back and thinking why did it happen? How could I have stopped it happening? How can I stop it happening again? I was a failure. How can I have been so stupid. Because as

132

I say you end up at the stage where there's no going back — you've got to crack up before you start again. I remember round about the February of that year really being aware I didn't have a grip on things — not understanding why because potentially third year should have been the best year at university. I look back on all that and I feel quite a lot of compassion for the person who's gone through that, this terribly naive person. I wanted to put the record straight for myself. I was so bloody average when I was little, why did it happen to me, and not to other people?

CG: In a lot of the poems there is this sense of the happiness of the young child and the disconnection that you're trying to bridge between the very young child and the woman who looks back and sees some of the middle part as being full of times when you were worrying about things that now you wouldn't. It's trying to connect with the child but at the same time seeing that the time has gone — there's no way you can go back. If you think about the image of the ponytail being cut and kept and 'still having the auburn highlights your mother loved', the image of severance shows it can't be bridged. In the poem you mentioned earlier, 'Under Five': 'my mother wore summer dresses now back in fashion', the last two lines are powerful because fashions come round again — summer dresses come round again — but for the child, that time never comes round again. The shock of the adult there is every bit as overwhelming as the shock of the bumble bee, the hailstones, for the child. The title is interesting too. It's almost a label — the kind of thing you'd see in Mothercare — 'Under Five' Why did you use that title?

AM: My family often chat away about living in Rossshire. My oldest sister was taught English by Sorley MacLean at Plockton Academy. But I just have little girl memories, child's memories and I was kind of keeping them all together for myself and I don't know if you noticed it all happens in the garden — that was where I was allowed to roam about. I feel I have so many separate memories of those four years that I must have been older when I left, so I just put it down as under five. Memories of before I was five.

CG: There is a sense, though, of the childhood being idyllic — despite these frightening, terrifying discoveries, these are growing discoveries, so there is a sense that that was a time of perfection, something preserved and separate.

AM: The three times I ever talked to a real psychiatrist you knew they were doing you good when you wanted to get up and leave the room because they'd offended you so much. I remember one saying to me 'You don't like children once they become eight or nine because that's when you stopped liking yourself' and I just wanted to get up and leave. This reaction of indignation, and at the same time thinking damn him he's right! I think that's true, round about the time I was twelve, thirteen, I felt my life began to unravel.

CG: That's one of the tensions that I enjoy in your work — you occasionally look from the point of view of the child forward to where things looked set and ordered — in 'Edinburgh Suburbs', for example, there are ideas of little girls in party dresses and buckled shoes on these streets, and later the adult walks there with the unbuckled shoe and with a sense of not being at home there — although in that poem the idea of 'striding' shows confidence — something's been worked out there, there's a new way of being in the world — you've found a new way of being free in that world — different from the way the child projected a way of being. That's a confident poem. There are other poems where the sense of not being at home comes across much more strongly. I'm thinking of 'Second-Hand Dress', the idea of being in the wrong role, with the wrong script on the wrong stage. That's something that you play around with.

AM: A lot of it is unconscious. It must be because it was years after I'd written 'Edinburgh Suburb' that I realised my unbuckled shoe and that the little girls had party dresses and buckled shoes.

CG: The stage set is really the adult world? The child looks forward to finding a part on this stage set, but the adult finds nothing fits. What your poems do, it seems to me, is to redesign a stage on which your persona can tread? In 'Woman with Lilac Sash' — 'You give away nothing but your loveliness' here you have a portrait of a woman who's costumed, the eighteen inch waist, sashed, corseted and confined and seated for the public eye. In many ways it's the antithesis of the persona you've created on the page. The private individual, stripped, rather than costumed. Does that suggest that you're redesigning the persona inside the frame?

AM: Well if I can go back to when I was a student and I started writing very spare, cut-down poetry — 'Exposure', 'My Crime' even 'My breasts walk ahead of me', 'Kirsty', 'Retreat', 'For the Best'. When I was writing them I think it was from a sense of writing on my own, with no particular audience except perhaps for Ron Butlin or Cairns Craig. I had this vague feeling of 'I've never written anything like this before. Is it all right? Will it do?' And at the same time knowing that at some time in the near future I was going to have a breakdown and I just thought it doesn't matter. There's a sense of devil may care — it doesn't matter, to hell with the consequences. There wasn't a psychiatrist and in a funny way he came too late. I mean if I had had a psychiatrist I wouldn't have been writing.

CG: Isn't talking to a psychiatrist a dangerous thing for a writer to do — does it not channel some of that creative energy elsewhere — dissipate it? Was there a danger that you would discuss things with him, and then not have the need to write about them?

AM: Perhaps. The way I wrote when I was twenty-one, twenty two has changed — I wrote an awful lot then and of the poetry I wrote a very high percentage of it I thought was good enough to keep — a very high percentage. I wrote it quickly, it seemed to pop up out of nowhere. I wasn't sure where the ideas came from. I hope people reading this interview don't think it's all very self-indulgent, harping on about one particular set of experiences. I mean I can't overemphasise how important they were, having that breakdown and just realising that all the things that had led up to the breakdown, the constant worry about was my work good enough, was I going to get merit, I didn't look right, I didn't dress right, and I don't want to go into too much detail but I had an endocrinological problem which didn't help my appearance. In fact I worried that I might become a hermaphrodite and one of the reasons I perked up a lot in the second year was I was getting treatment for this and I suddenly felt happy — I felt happy being a woman — getting treatment for a while and feeling that I'd had the pressure taken off me to hide parts of myself and becoming comfortable with myself actually made me think this is a load of tosh. Why should these damn tablets make me one sex or the other? It's all to do with attitude and how you feel about yourself. Taking tablets for a while took a lot of pressure off me, and I think that's why that poem Edinburgh Suburb was so confident — I'm not covered from the neck to the ankles and I'm not having to shave as often. You know I said that just now and I thought Oh Christ! now everybody knows I shave (laughs) I thought I've let the cat out of the bag! (laughs) Then I thought this is ridiculous because I go round with a five o'clock shadow and my boyfriend knows and he's not bothered. But I think women who look like me get a totally different sort of men, men with totally different sorts of attitudes.

CG: And yet if you think about 'A Swim, the Freedom', the idea of taking off your glasses and sashaying into the pool — I loved that.

AM: That's a later poem. Being fat and wearing specs is not a disability until somebody tells you! I feel people's narrow eyes, narrow minds, narrow everything stuff so much crap down other people's lives.

CG: So taking off the glasses is denying all that?

AM: Yes. I'm saying 'Stuff you lot!' I suppose every day you have to set yourself up in front of the mirror, and then go out there and ignore them.

134

CG: The poem 'Vivisection' ostensibly deals with analysis and I think possibly writing poetry must be a bit like that as well. Iain Crichton Smith has said that writing poetry is a bit like opening up your side with a knife — do you find that? Especially since although you're creating you're also drawing on experience as well, things that are very close to you, very important to you. Is writing poetry a dangerous occupation?

AM: The first part of that question — yes. It is a bit like analysis and I definitely used it to work things through. I find it satisfying — in a sense a lot of the poems came out like statements of fact but I was aware people reacted to them very strongly at readings. When I was first writing in that stark style I was getting rid of a lot that had been stored up. I suppose it is dangerous and yes I wrote a poem which really hurt somebody.

CG: The idea of the chaperon outside the frame is tied up with how the poem would affect other people, rather than areas you won't or can't explore?

AM: Yes I think so. That's quite a difficult one because you could be quite happily censoring yourself without owning up to it. I don't want to talk about the poem in any detail, but 'Kirsty' was one which I remember battling away at for three weeks. It is a pity I didn't keep the first drafts because there were reams — that poem went on and on. It's amazing it's only got six lines. It never got finished, and then I just took out six lines which made some sense — one little image out of reams and reams.

CG: Why was it so difficult to get through to the poem you wanted?

AM: Probably because at that point I needed the crisis centre myself. I could just as well have phoned the crisis centre myself. But I didn't. I just jabbered away for three weeks and carried this poem about and was writing it in lectures and not getting anywhere really. I think I worked it all out, began to feel better, and then I suppose the horrible cynical bit of you thinks right I'm going to get a poem out of this. It's a very difficult one to talk about because I don't want to talk about the poem itself.

CG: Let's talk about the two publications you've done. The first one is *Other Tongues* with David Kinloch, W.N. Herbert and Meg Bateman. How does the title refer to your own work?

AM: I wasn't sure why that title was chosen. I thought perhaps Robert Crawford chose that title because there were four of us and we all wrote very differently and there were three different languages. Going way back to the beginning, when I started writing very cut-back poetry I think I was aware then that I was not going to keep quiet. I was talking about not fitting in and feeling glum, and talking in very small detail about myself, such as stretchmarks. I was cataloguing myself but I wasn't going to shut up. That's how I felt when I was writing these poems. I think it's taken me all this interview to get that phrase out — you know when I started writing these poems I had this feeling I'm not going to shut up. So maybe right at the beginning there was that sense but I don't feel like that now. I think I'm back, almost back, to it being a bit like a huge hobby. All that distress and I'm going to have my say whether you like it or not — that feeling has gone away.

CG: The title of the new book, *Coming Out With It,* though, is quite aggressive as well? You're saying you don't have this feeling I'm going to have my say now, but there's still a declaration here. 'Coming Out' — with what?

AM: The poem was written after a friend of mine had confided in me that he was gay. It was quite awkward for me because he was someone I was very strongly attracted to. I think he was the first person I had ever had the courage to begin to say to I fancy you. It was the very same night he decided he was going to tell me. There he was, six foot three, my dream man, but at the same time, it was like instantly I just changed to knowing I would never have him that way. I remember thinking this is good because it means we can be friends forever. So I needed a title for the book and the easiest thing was to use the title from one of the poems because he's coming out — it was a pun within the title — we were both coming out that night. The first time I'd ever tried to seduce someone (backs off from the word, laughs) well yes, seduce! and he was coming out as a gay person, and coming out to me. We were both coming out with what we wanted to say and it was very difficult. He just decided he couldn't live as a cardboard cut-out any more. And it was a good pun on the first book coming out.

CG: What next?

AM: I did have the feeling, especially as I only write poetry, right I've done it, that's it, what next? The rest of my life, what'll I do? I live quite a quiet live — I don't have a career plan so at the moment I have quite a lot of time free this winter, so hopefully working towards volume two.

GLYN MAXWELL

TALKING WITH DAVID KINLOCH

GLYN MAXWELL's first collection, *Tale of the Mayor's Son*, was published by Bloodaxe in 1990. A Poetry Book Society Choice, it established him as one of the outstanding new British poets. This interview was recorded before Glyn Maxwell read with Simon Armitage at the 1990 St Andrews Poetry Festival, shortly before the publication of his collection. In the interview he refers to his essays on Walcott (in *Verse*, Vol. 5 No. 3) and on Auden (*Verse*, Vol. 6, No. 3), as well as to his poem 'Out of the Rain' (*Verse*, Vol. 7, No. 1), not yet collected in book form. The St Andrews reading greatly impressed all those present, including Douglas Dunn and the editors of this magazine; Michael Alexander described it as 'electrifying'.

DK: Perhaps I can start by asking you a bit about your childhood and background. I'm not doing this simply for biographical reasons but because its quite obvious from your first collection, *Tale of the Mayor's Son*, and the essays you've written for *Verse* on W.H. Auden and Derek Walcott, that the nature and long term effects of a certain type of English childhood and education is an important theme in your work. I'm thinking initially of the first poem in the collection where the image of a roundabout is quite important. So can you tell me where you were born and what kind if school you went to?

GM: I was born in Welwyn Garden City, the New Town, the second Garden City in the world, which was built in 1920 something — 1922 I think — I ought to know . . . I'm still living there. I've moved twice in my life. Once when I was one I moved about half a mile and then when I was twelve I moved about 200 yards. Bloodaxe has been trying desperately to find something for their publicity material, something interesting that sets me apart, but when it comes down to it I had a very happy upbringing, very stable, serene — outwardly — I guess. I went to quite a good comprehensive school, not even a rough one! It used to be a grammar school. I was a fairly averagely rebellious teenager who managed to get an exhibition to Oxford where I had what was probably a fairly typical Oxford experience for someone who hadn't been conditioned to think he'd be going there all his childhood. I went through Oxford rather with my eyes closed I think. No, Bloodaxe and I are still trying to find something unusual to say about me and Welwyn Garden City, which is quite a pleasant town, really, that's received quite a lot of stick because it sounds modern and it sounds like Milton Keynes. I always try to defend it when I can because it was planned by decent men who were trying to plan something that people could live in decently. There have been worse efforts than that.

DK: You name sounds Welsh. Is it?

GM: Well, the name Glyn is. My direct paternal decent however is entirely Scottish. My mother is Welsh. Well, now I come to think of it, my father's half Welsh; the other bits are English and Scottish. So it reflects a sort of hereditary Celtic mixture which does something to offset the environmental factors which are entirely Home Counties, South-East.

DK: You don't feel Welsh in any way?

GM: Ah, now that's different. I was thinking that perhaps because I haven't grown up in a dangerous environment or known much in the way of family or domestic trouble . . . no serious political trouble has engulfed the area I live in and is never likely to . . . I wonder, then, if you think broadly speaking about what a bloke is, part environment, part blood, then the hereditary aspects are more important than anything and to me it all seems fairly clear that on the one side, the Welsh maternal side, there was a lot of creativity, a lot of musicality. It was a large family that was very much involved in artistic things.

DK: There were writers among them?

GM: Not exactly writers but people with that Welsh respect for education and literature and achievement in that respect. My maternal grandmother, whom I never knew, could recite reams and reams of English poetry, standard English poetry, and had great respect for that. From the paternal side I think I've inherited a great sense of balance and proportion. I think the best things I achieve in my work are usually where there's an input of musicality and one of balance and form which I suppose displays itself in some of the quite tight forms that I use.

DK: The reason I asked you about the Welshness is simply because from reading your collection you strike me as, in a sense, almost a quintessentially English poet. What you're writing about is the state of England today and if it weren't for what you say now about musicality the word Wales wouldn't have entered my vocabulary at all.

GM: Yes. I don't know if it does extend further than that. When I'm in Wales I suppose I sometimes feel something beating but that might just be fancy. I don't know. When it comes down to it I'm just a guy that has lived all his life in a very quiet place which is however right in the centre of things, of what's going on. Because Welwyn Garden City is now too expensive a place to be interesting in any way — it's uniform, it's psychologically quite untaxing to live in — I've always thought of it as an easel one can paint things on. About the state of England at the moment.

DK: You say that Welwyn Garden City is a 'kind of quiet place'. If I were to describe you as a poet of ordinariness and the apocalypse, that you try to yoke the two together, would you accept that description?

GM: Erm . . . !

DK: I'm thinking of the kind of progression you get when you move from a poem like 'The End of the Weekend' to 'Out of the Rain' [in *Verse* Vol. 7, No. 1]. In the first, the flood of rain comes to confirm and perhaps reproach a certain lack of energy, a rather bleak ordinariness. You write 'No tragedy had struck'. The only event worth talking about and, perhaps even worse, the only thing that seems to activate memory, is the weather. In this poem you declare that 'It was still not all that late'. But then in 'Out of the Rain', to borrow Auden's phrase, 'it is later than you think'. What I find most alarming about these two poems is that they imply that you don't have to be positively evil to get drowned. All you've got to do is lose faith in your ability to be much more than a cricketing party-goer. 'Manzadinka' drinkas don't get to see unicorns! Your Gomorragh is more irritating than evil . . .

GM: Well, let me say first that 'Out of the Rain' won't be in the first collection as it was written too late. I'm still too close to it really to be able to talk very coherently about its implications. It seems to me that, of whatever species it is, its more sustained than anything else I've done and in a way its almost become rather burdensome. I keep wondering what exactly I've done here. I think its something quite worth while but I'm not sure what it is. It's interesting that you should compare it with 'The End of the Weekend' as I hadn't done that. 'The End of the Weekend' is, I suppose, making something musical out of something that is terribly ordinary, the most ordinary thing that can happen in a town like that. And then 'Out of the Rain' . . . well, when I'd finished it I thought: 'well look, boyo, this is it, you've just described exactly what your life in this town is like. Take away the mythical elements, the floods and unicorns and the last part of the poem, that sort of limbo I try to evoke, shows that you can be terribly happy with what you've got except that you haven't really got anything. It is just a limbo. The narrator at the end of the poem has no sense of what is going to happen . . .

DK: He has had a vision of unicorns though . . .

GM: Yeah. I noticed that at the end of the poem he's treated as if he's an old man, as if he's mad. And he is, well, he's drunk a lot of the time! I think we're supposed to understand that contemporary society is aligned with the people looking at the man and saying thats the guy who says he saw unicorns. Whatever structure I've given to this story it ends by mouthing the words of what it's like to be in a situation in which . . . yes, now I start to see what you mean . . . in a way you do have just about everything you want but you know that nothing good will ever come of it.

DK: Its's not enough . . .

GM: Yeah. And you're not entirely sure what you've been left with. I can't be more coherent than that, sorry. It hasn't set in my mind yet.

DK: Could you think about it perhaps in relation to *The Shield of Achilles*? In 'Out of the Rain' you're playing off apocalyptic detail against petty, bourgeois reality. Were you thinking of Auden's poem when you wrote it at all?

GM: No, I wasn't. But that brings out something that is quite clear looking back. That's what *The Shield of Achilles* is. In my essay on Auden I mentioned that what was particularly striking in that poem were the bits of documentary observation. And what I tried to do with 'Out of the Rain' was to show that this is the kind of society we live in. The South East is like this society where things are decided, where a code of how to behave is made. This is how people *will* behave if these unthinkable things happen. This is what your mayors and aldermen and MPs are going to be like if this happens. This is what they *are* like, this is how they discuss the appalling things that go on. You can see a comedy show on BBC 1 which everybody says is great and its about how slow the civil service is and that's made rather amusing. Well, fine, it is amusing but the result of this is poverty and delay and sadness and boredom.

DK: Would you describe yourself as a political poet then?

GM: Yes. Without wanting to tap into the enormous ongoing debate about what a political poem is, isn't all poetry political and so on. The way I think of political is perhaps just expressing the colour of your heart, of indicating what your morals are and that can be expressed in a love poem or a poem about an MP which can be satirical, realistic or fantastical. A political poet on the contemporary scene in comparison with more inward looking people perhaps.

DK: At the end of your poem 'The End of the Weekend' you write: 'And when you tell me things you think you know/Don't tell me what they look like, how they sound,/Tell me what kind they are and how kind'. Could you explain what you meant by these lines and would you wish to relate them to what you've just said about being a political poet or simply a poet with rather high moral standards (laughter) — which is the impression much of your verse leaves me with.

GM: Actually, I was wondering before this interview whether you'd ask me about those lines because I think they stick out a bit. They stick out because I had them before I had the poem, which I hardly ever do. When I wrote the first draft a friend told me that I'd managed to get 19/20ths through a poem without introducing myself and then here we are . . . I clump in in my boots! And say 'This is the way things are!' I think I agree with her actually. All I can say in their defence perhaps is that they are maybe what is needed. Poets since Auden seem to have been shy of taking *a* moral stand or of saying that it is possible to have moral absolutes, to say this man is good and this man is not so good. Although I'm not absolutely convinced that its the right direction to take I don't think I'd scratch that out at this point: those lines, because they're over-compensating for what has been a long period of feeling that poets ought not to take any kind of moral high ground. That phrase itself 'moral high ground' has been dreadfully comandeered by the most immoral of people, by politicians and devotees of hanging, believers in law and order, the great moral imperatives. So perhaps its as simple as thinking that it is actually poets who ought to take the moral high ground, grab it back. And if that sticks out of that poem or of the collection as a whole then thats probably a good thing. If my saying that sound out of tune, its probably good as well because people have to stick their necks out sometimes. Its what I believe and its taken me a long time to muster the confidence to be able to say 'yeah I'm prepared to take a moral stance'.

DK: Perhaps we could go back to your childhood at this point. I didn't mean to leave it quite so rapidly! What books made most impression on you as a child and, in particular, were nursery rhymes important to you? Because one of the things I hear coming quite strongly out of your poetry are the rhythms of an English childhood used to ironic effect. The nursery rhyme is one of the elements you mention in the catalogue of things used to avoid 'The Enemy' in your essay on Auden.

GM: Yes, well, I didn't want to give the impression earlier that my childhood was without excitement. I had that thing which seems to be quite traditional with British writers. I had this fantasy world. My brother and I had a fantasy world which was complex, as complex as the one the Brontës had, although it was probably more self-serving and a little less noble. It was a well organised thing which sustained us for years. It wasn't linked to creative writing or poetry at that stage but I was certainly struck by rhymes. I do remember nursery rhymes and scary ones at that. I know that Auden was really struck by the 'Struwelpeter', those rather nasty German nursery rhymes. I was too. It was a real shock of recognition when I read this about Auden. Because I remember having the life scared out of me by the Scissor Man and the guy who dies of starvation because he won't eat his soup and so on. I want to make it quite clear though that we didn't actually have a nursery! It was toys on the floor, that type of nursery childhood really.

DK: Any other books, any particular authors that interested you when you were very young?

GM: *Alice* and then a long flirtation wth Tolkein. I liked Tolkein because there were strong moral principles and it was endlessly imaginative. It also had a lot of war in it and the fantasy world my brother and I were involved in became quite martial after a while! and then it started to reflect the real world in all sorts of distressing ways. What else? Tove Jansson's Moomintroll series. I loved that stuff. She's a Finnish children's writer who was working in the 40s or 50s. Some of them are really just chldren's books that made me want to write, to try to do that sort of thing myself. So now you mention it, it is quite a traditional English writer's upbringing in that sense. There was time and obviously money. Not a lot of money but enough.

DK: What about the Bible? For a young poet your use of biblical myth and imagery is perhaps a little unusual.

GM: Well, I went to a Church of England infant and junior school. We had a lot of New Testament stuff and I knew all that early on and I have retained most of the things that were really hammered. And then I became interested in the Old Testament for the grandeur of the stories. I've retained quite a lot of biblical feeling about things. Not enough. I ought to have more.

DK: Why?

GM: Um . . . Maybe if there are more myths to be worked, like you work a mine, quarried . . . I was going to say initially: because the language is so beautiful, but I remember now Auden saying 'beware those who read the Bible for its prose!'

DK: You went to an English comprehensive and yet the way you talk about an English boarding school, particularly in your essay on Auden, gave me the impression that perhaps you had gone to one yourself, that you knew the English public school system intimately. And from your poetry you seem to believe that human beings, and perhaps particularly English public school educated ones, do not grow up and mature and that they retain the kind of simplistic ideals and unquestioning credos of their childhood. Many of the human beings that pass through your poems seem to act with the irresponsibility of children. The characters in 'Mandate on an Eighth of May' seem to me to be like this.

140

GM: Well I do believe that really. This struck me forcibly when I was reading about the way Auden's warnings about what might happen changed. He couldn't use surreal images anymore because it was happening anyway. In western Europe today we're not dealing with anything quite as bad as that, but within the last decade things that were once ludicrous, satirical jokes are now White Papers or they're law: the next thing they'll be doing is making doctors compete for patients — Ha Ha! — or soon they'll be privatising water!! That seems to have been a feature of the last ten years. And I happen to think that a large amount of the responsibility for this, and also for keeping this fantasy existence going, is with the English public schoolboys who've remained so. No, I didn't go to English public school but I think you have to say that anyone who's been to a comprehensive or anything else knows an awful lot about English public schools because so much of literature and TV and film has been about it, rather than vice-versa. How much does your average man in Westminster know about what its actually like *not* to go to a public or boarding school? I think that in these places where the sexes are segregated and you're with like-minded people that you're inculcated with things you never really shake off. In a comprehensive where you could be with anybody . . . anybody *could* be there, well, you have . . . options. But this is old ground really.

DK: Old ground, yes. So if I were to be very unkind and describe you as a 1980s or 1990s version of W.H. Auden, how would you react to that? Are you just a re-write of the early Auden? In what ways do you think your poetry is different from Auden's?

GM: Well, this is something I have to deal with, I suppose. I can't deny that he's an influence although he really wasn't at all until about 2½ years ago. Auden said at one point that he'd spent the whole year reading nothing but Hardy and in so far as he meant that literally I could say that I've spent the last two years reading nothing but Auden. I'm still under the shade of that oak tree. I don't know how much longer I will be but I think its a good place to grow, at least in the climate as it is now, politically, morally and also poetically. Nobody else has really decided to beat a path to that door it seems to me! Obviously you have someone like Joseph Brodsky who has said he wants to do that. But that's a different generation. If you need a poet of modern times, a poet for this century, then its like you don't because we've had one and Auden was it. Have things changed enough though for anyone to have the gall to have a stab at those concerns again? To have that talent and that intellectual curiosity and that knowledge . . . nobody has had that. Appearing just in the same paragraph as Auden's name is to make a pygmy of oneself. I think, however, that I do quite a number of things where you can say, yes, there is an Auden influence here but not that Auden would have done this. 'Out of the Rain' or 'The Chocolate Egg' say, are not his style really. Or for that matter 'The Mayor'. His intellectual curiosity was, I think, greatly more outward looking. He takes this bizarre course whereby he *ends up* writing about himself, what's going on inside himself physically, which is the opposite from the track most people take. I think I'm prepared to do more egocentric things than Auden was. It's difficult. To me he's the poet of modern times and there's no need for anyone to have a go at the same things . . .

DK: Isn't there? Surely thats what you're doing . . . ?

GM: Yes, you're right. That was a different voice — mine and not mine — saying why not to do it. No. I'm glad you asked me this because its something I feel I'm always going to have to deal with. Auden is a great country and its going to take me a long time to work through it.

DK: Obviously there's not just Auden. There are a number of very Eliotish figures in your poetry. The woman in 'Aurora' for example: 'Aurora wakes without a kiss and it's not/Sunday it's Monday.' Then there's Mr. Harman and Mr. Gem and his children, none of whom presumably manage to get out of the rain and into your ark.

GM: Well, I read all the standard stuff at Oxford but I felt I wasn't really seeing it. Eliot represents something else to me. He's on his own in a different way. You can vaguely echo Eliot in the names of some characters or in locating them in certain parts of town. But I've never come across anyone who could sound like Eliot in the way that you *can* sound like Auden. There's some quality of Eliot's that just sounds unique and this scared me off, perhaps. Also for political and religious reasons. I have no affinity with him there as I do have with Auden or Frost for example.

DK: Is Larkin important to you? In the sense that he writes about the state of England and Englishness is important to him too?

GM: He was magnificently gifted. But I came across something quite interesting he wrote about Sylvia Plath after her death. He was reviewing her *Selected Poems* and he praised her great technical gift if I remember this right but limited the whole thing by asking at the end to what extent we can revere a poet so much of whose work we can only recoil from in shock and sorrow. There is that sort of limitation with her work and I've often thought that it was the same with him. An appreciation of how great a poet Larkin is technically is slightly qualified by the fact that I've never seen the world as he saw it or said he did and I don't think I ever could.

DK: In your essay on Auden you talk about his 'casual and formal expression of how bad things can get' and that struck me as a good description of your own work. I wonder then if you'd like to talk a bit about the relation of formal to colloquial/casual elements in your poems? Do you choose fairly strict metres because you're writing about chaos and one sets off the other . . . or are there other reasons?

GM: Yes, I think thats a good place to start. Originally I used strong forms because someone told me it was a good exercise and before I'd written anything that was worth anything I did it for practice. The form helped to create something when I didn't have anything much to say. This habit has survived. I still impose quite difficult forms on myself. Or rather I sometimes write a first stanza in a particular form and see how it works and then write all the other stanzas in that metre. I was using form to process chaotic material in my own mind. You're putting a frame around something, putting this stuff on a screen, this absurdly logical, strange behaviour of people in positions of power or people who are deluded, people who are obsessed. Also it's funnier. Using strong forms is funny if you do it properly. In 'Out of the Rain' I really just rhymed where I wanted to, but particularly at the end of sections or scenes or at comic moments which are heightened by the stronger forms. I've never been able to write to no form at all, never been able to write freely. That's not my way to create something that's worthwhile or aspires to anything beautiful. My thought in itself isn't organised, its not intellectually disciplined. I did OK academically, but it was undisciplined work. Metre, form, helps me to impose structure on diverse material and this spirals back I suppose to early Auden again.

DK: The form actually creates the poem for you . . .

GM: Yes. I do believe also there's an aesthetic rightness in using rhyme and cadence at certain moments and also that it's not entirely explicable, that it's mysterious. That really is the mainspring of any joy I get out of it: why certain words taken together sound so good and if you change it just a little bit then it wouldn't work at all.

DK: Do you find that when you get stuck . . . if you get stuck! . . . in a poem, the rhyme or metre will help you get out of it?

GM: Yes, it can do, but, if I find myself grasping, then occasionally I just give up on it but more often move back a bit and recognise that this or that wasn't quite the right route to take. Or I'll go back to the start and see it was good but then that I shouldn't have done that there . . .

DK: In your essay on Walcott you write 'He will be the poet making nothing happen and straight away, as he must do, he begins to describe. Walcott's poems procede from life novelistically described and mercifully free from clearly obvious selection down two roads, memory and metaphor.' Again this strikes me as a good way to describe the way you begin many of your own poems except that you like playing with novelistic conventions, you enjoy drawing our attention to conventions, to rhyme and metre. You love telling stories . . .

GM: Yes. And most times I'm really doing it for the sake of it. Just that: telling stories. That's not something I feel I'd have to defend. Derek doesn't have the same concerns now, i.e. telling tales for their own sake.

DK: Is that what 'A Chocolate Egg' is? A comic tale for its own sake?

GM: No, its not for its own sake. The two or three strong plot lines convey a message, a moral if you like. It's a mock epic, like *The Rape of the Lock*. It's just one tiny, utterly trivial event which you build the whole thing around. Sometimes I do write them for their own sake. I feel I've just got to write something and so I start just to keep ticking over. Often I end up thinking, 'Well, you know, Glyn, this is pretty thin really. You're just jogging here!'

DK: But you like jogging novelistically . . .

GM: Yes, I like that. The aspect of literature I was most interested in at school and university was narrative viewpoints. I was very struck by it at an early age, the complexity of it in Chaucer for example, how beautiful that is: the lenses through which you were seeing things, how one thing said by one person could mean something very different if it was another person telling you he said it. A beautiful box of tricks we don't really deserve, its so limitless in its implications. I never really do it consciously. I don't regard it as an intellectual game, it just happens. A lot of it is play.

DK: You said that Walcott is fond of pressing the claims of the cliché and you are too a bit, aren't you?

GM: Derek used to tell this story about a film he liked. I think it was a James Coburn western. All the bad guys have been shot and the hero is walking out of the town and there's a rose on the ground and a girl who he's had some rough and tumble with nearby. And you think, no, no, he's *not* going to give the rose to the girl! But he does and then you think, well, why shouldn't he?! Clichés are just things that happen an awful lot. Walcott has some very sharp things to say. He has his eyes very open.

DK: And the cliché is something you can use to make the ordinary extraordinary . . .

GM: Yes. I suppose the bloke in 'The Chocolate Egg' — I call him my hero and he is a hero in the sense that he's the hero of this poem — . . . I suppose by writing a poem of that length about whether a guy is going to eat a chocolate egg or not is making him extraordinary without having to do anything else. Because he doesn't really do anything interesting as far as I can remember. Ordinary people who believe something exciting is going to happen to them, like the voice of the character in Walcott's poem 'The Light of the World'. He's the ordinary man. He lusts after these girls and thinks maybe something will happen. Nothing much does. That's the cliché. That's OK, that's OK.

DK: Again, in your essay on Walcott, you say that 'a poet needs no more than a painter to draw a true picture, a colour, a couple of edges a chosen degree of clarity'. I may have picked this up wrongly, but colour seem to be important to you. You seem to see, or pretend to see, primary colours before shapes, colours divorced from objects and this helps you to dislocate the reader's vision and surprise us with the familiar. Perhaps 'Black Song' is an example of this . . .

143

GM: Well, yes, that poem is an orgy of colour. I've always been much more aware of colour than of sound or shape. The sounds of things rather than the sounds of the poem that is. I'm not sure why that is. That might well be from having been impressed by illustrations in children's books. It may be that unlike somebody like Derek, I'm from a place that is predominantly grey and green and not much else. Its like using a calm environment as a grey backround and just dabbing bits of colour on it. I was very impressed by Walcott's 'girl in a yellow dress' in the poem I wrote about. She was just *there*. A two line sketch: perfect. Eliot was great at that as well. I sometimes think I overdo the colours a bit. But to be able to say something like 'a yellow dress' or . . . I don't know if there's anybody alive that could make a red rose come back to life. To attempt to do that and make it come off . . . that's really special. Seamus Heaney can do it.

DK: In your poem 'Tale of the Mayor's Son' you describe some of the things that happen to Elizabeth and the Mayor's son. They go skating and the mayor's son loses his hat and you write 'Hat elsewhere, hat kicked on by a small bully/and ruined by the bully's friend. Once/that would have shelled and reddened my idea,/To see such fun. But nowadays I just/cram it in with all the other eggs/for omelette'. Poem as omelette? What do you mean by that?

GM: That was quite an action-packed clip! That's quite young stuff I think. Its a description of something that's intolerable for a child or could be. It's like saying it's indigestible. And I recall Brodsky saying that the 'omelette makes me vomit'!

DK: Are you talking about the way you write a poem, though?

GM: Yes. What I meant is that the event I describe would once have upset me, now it just goes in with everything else.

DK: Because nothing is really important?

GM: Well it's not unimportant. It's vital. But only as a part of what might be created at the end of it. I wouldn't linger long on those lines though. That's just me having a good time!

DK: To finish off, maybe we could leave the British isles for a moment. What foreign poets do you read, if any, and who in particular do you admire? Do you like Ashbery for example?

GM: There are some moments of Ashbery that I like enormously, but at this stage I feel I'm still catching up on stuff that's really Palgrave stuff in a way. Stuff that I went through with my eyes closed at college. Its as if I'm not ready to play in Ashbery's ball park just at the moment. There's time to look at them later. I feel that there's a lot of American poetry that's very alien to what I do and once I wouldn't have wanted to know about it. Now I do, but I'm much more temperate about it. The Northern Irish poets interest me too. I know Seamus's stuff quite well now but I haven't really got involved with the others yet.

DK: Do you like Mahon's work for example?

GM: I do, yes, what I know of it.

DK: I would have thought that the musicality of a poet like Mahon would be attractive to you . . .

GM: Yes. I can't have read more than about ten but am impressed and sorry too that he doesn't seem to be writing more now beyond translations.

DK: You're about to be published by Bloodaxe and Bloodaxe have a reputation for publishing interesting East European poets . . .

GM: Bloodaxe have a reputation for publishing every poet!

DK: Well, someone like Miroslav Holub for example. Are you interested in him?

GM: Yes, but I haven't read much East European verse except for Brodsky's. There's a slight difficulty for me with reading translations. I'm still very preoccupied wondering what on earth it is that creates a great poem in English and I'm not ready to take things further yet.

DK: But then English doesn't belong to Britain any more. Its a world language and perhaps too translatorese is part of that . . .

GM: Yes, yes, I agree. But when you come across a translation that's really not all that good, you can't know that at the time, you can't know whether its the poet or the translator . . .

DK: But if it works well in English does it matter . . . ?

GM: Sure. I don't know if it does.

DK: You're obviously interested in Brodsky. Is this because of the Auden influence or for other reasons?

GM: I was struck by his use of formal metres and he and Walcott are close. Being taught by Walcott meant being close to what Brodsky did as well. Then I got to read about Brodsky's first visit to Auden in Austria which is all relevant to my interest in him. Also Brodsky dares rhymes in Englsh which an English poet would never dare. Almost like a songwriter would. Brodsky will attempt rhymes that you can actually go past and it will have the effect on you of a normal rhyme and you think, well, why don't people try that more. That's quite liberating. But English poets feel that there are some rules that you don't break. And Douglas Dunn and Tony Harrison. They're right up there at the top for me at the moment in Britain.

DK: Are you interested in the kind of thing Craig Raine's doing, or has done in the past, in the so called 'Martian' school.

GM: No. Not at all. It's natural. I don't have that gift. Raine has it to a great extent and I don't have it at all. It doesn't particularly interest me to see things in that way either. Of course I'm sure Raine wouldn't want to be limited to Martianism now. But I feel it's limiting in the way Larkin limited his outlook. Its a point to make — about alienation — but it's not where I'm playing. A great poet is, I think, like Derek Walcott, who has Raine's metaphorical gift but he can sing and hit all sorts of different notes, really transfigure the world. I came across an excerpt in an American magazine of an epic [Omeros] he's writing and it's intoxicating. It's about colonialism fading away from the islands and what I've read of it is breathtaking. It's just been published now in the US so it will follow on here in a couple of years I expect.

DK: Final question. Where do you go from here? Do you have poems for a second collection ready? Are you thinking about one?

GM: I'm pretty prolific! It really has to be reined back, I think, but I've got just about enough for a second book. But then again as the months pass the number of good poems one's written shrinks. You develop and I'd like to think that only about a third of what I've written will actually survive into a second book. 'Out of the Rain' will be in it and it might be called that in fact. I want to write some short plays too. I'd like to think this is another apprenticeship that I can start?

DK: Without giving any secrets away, do you think it will be a very different collection from the first? Do you think you're still writing the same kind of poems?

GM: A lot of the time I am, but I think it's going to be linguistically more interesting. Everything I do now seems to be kicked off by language, by interesting first lines and I often think that if I've got a good first line then I'm going to end up with something good. Or maybe this is just the sort of little prejudice that helps me work at the moment. It may be slightly less accessible, nothing as knockabout as 'A Chocolate Egg', and more interesting linguistically. It may even get out of the confines of Welwyn Garden City!

DK: Fine! Thank you very much.

EDWIN MORGAN

TALKING WITH ROBERT CRAWFORD

In Britain and internationally Edwin Morgan has become known as a poet of remarkable talent, variety, and experimental energy. Very few contemporary poets have a wider imaginative range. Best known to some readers as a concrete poet, a sound poet, a city poet (especially a poet of Glasgow), or a sonneteer, Morgan has a virtuoso's command of many poetic forms. He is also a prizewinning translator from a battery of languages including Anglo-Saxon, Dutch, French, German, Hungarian, Italian, Russian, and Spanish. Born in Glasgow in 1920, he studied English at Glasgow University and served in the Royal Army Medical Corps in the Middle East during World War Two, before returning to work in Glasgow University where he became a titular Professor of English. His first collection appeared in 1952; also in 1952 he published a translation of *Beowulf*. *The Second Life* (Edinburgh University Press, 1968) won him wide acclaim. *From Glasgow to Saturn* (Carcanet, 1973) was a Poetry Book Society Choice, and was followed by his *Essays* (1974) and *The New Divan* (1977), both published by Carcanet who also published *Poems of Thirty Years* (1982), a widely admired collection of his earlier work. As an editor and anthologist, Morgan is best known for his *Scottish Satirical Verse* (1980). Recently the Mariscat Press in Glasgow has published his *Sonnets from Scotland* (1984) and *From the Video Box* (1986). These, along with other recent poems — several published in *Verse* — will be included in *Themes on a Variation*, due from Carcanet in 1988. The following interview was recorded in his home in Glasgow on 7 January 1988.

RC: Does your childhood matter a lot to you?

EM: It doesn't seem, on the face of it anyway, to mean all that much to me, really. It seems to be something that was just there. Reasonably happy, except with the kind of problems, perhaps, that any *only* child has. I think that if I was married and was wanting to have a family, I'd want to have more than one child. I think there are always some problems about that. But I never felt that it was something that I particularly wanted to write about, and I don't think it comes into my poetry to any great extent at all.

RC: What did you read when you were very young?

EM: Oh, everything. I was very voracious. I read the kind of standard things in the sense that there would be collections of legends or fairytales or children's classics like *Alice in Wonderland* — I remember reading that. But as soon as I was able to choose at all I read a lot of adventure stories of various kinds. Perhaps some of the names are not very well known now. G. A. Henty, I don't know whether you know G. A. Henty's novels? Edgar Rice Burroughs, and, later on, H. G. Wells, Jules Verne, Edgar Allan Poe. Tending to be either adventurous or a mixture of adventure and imagination — Jack London, that was another one I read pretty early — adventure plus strong imagination, shading off towards fantasy and science fiction. Also standard school stories. And annuals, annual collections that would be perhaps in the house. P. G. Wodehouse I enjoyed; I read most of his stories. I tended to pick up some author like Edgar Rice Burroughs or Jules Verne or P. G. Wodehouse — and Dickens also I read very widely when I was in my early teens — and just pretty well go through them, trying to get their books out of libraries, often being disappointed once I'd got hold of the two or three I really liked and found the rest weren't nearly as interesting.

146

RC: Were you attracted to informational books — encyclopaedias and the like?

EM: Yes, indeed so. I was thinking just now in terms of fiction — but, yes, very much so. I often in fact pestered either my parents or grandparents to allow me to get encyclopaedia-type books which were coming out in weekly parts. That was a great thing in the early 1930s especially when I was getting interested in that sort of thing. Almost any subject really. Some were just general encyclopaedias. Others were about, say, nature or astronomy. I loved these, yes, and I enjoyed very much the more general kind where in each weekly part you would get the story being carried on from about a dozen subjects and you'd be flipping from one page of archaeology to the next page of marine life or something of that kind. And I liked the juxtaposition, the idea of great variety of knowledge and I was never somehow put off by this. It always seemed to feed in somehow to what I wanted to get from reading.

RC: Did that feed in to scrapbooks that you kept at the time?

EM: It must have done, because I started the scrapbooks pretty early — about eleven; eleven or twelve. That was just collecting cuttings from all sorts of places and pasting them into these books — little exercise books to begin with, and then they were later collected into larger books. That again was just a collection of pretty well, you might say, anything that caught my eye, caught my interest. There was no selection of subject whatsoever. Just everything that seemed to be of interest to me — in it went.

RC: What sort of speech did you hear as a child — standard English, Scots, or what?

EM: Well, it was a middle-class Glasgow childhood. Both my parents were Scottish — grandparents, the whole family was Scottish and they tended to come from the Glasgow area, so that the speech was what you would call educated Glasgow speech, but with a good many Scottish phrases and words and idioms being used, and I certainly remember these and used them a lot. I've got a poem or a collection of poems called *The Whittrick*. That is a childhood memory of a favourite family word. Both my grandparents were very fond of using the phrase 'As quick as a whittrick'. It just means a weasel, but a weasel of course moves so quickly it's almost like a flash — you don't know whether you've seen it or not. It was a very common phrase. It may not be so common now. There were lots of words like that used in the family without any thought that they were strange, or even Scottish; they were just the way people spoke. In Glasgow itself, of course, moving around — we always used public transport because there was no car (my father didn't drive — we just used trams and buses and trains) — so obviously living in Glasgow your ear is attuned to the broadest kind of Glasgow speech as well as what you're using yourself. I always liked listening to what I heard being spoken in the streets, in buses, and so on.

RC: Do you think that collage of speeches fed into your writing?

EM: I think it may have done, though I didn't think of *using* Glasgow speech until much later. I certainly enjoyed it. I enjoyed different kinds of speech, and I think I was probably thinking about that fairly early. I'm not quite sure how early; perhaps I was collecting different accents and making something of it. I liked speech and language in general, pretty well as far back as I can remember.

RC: When you were an undergraduate at Glasgow University you concentrated on English but also studied Russian. Was that an unusual combination?

EM: Yes, I suppose it was. I took two languages. I took French and Russian, and other subjects like History and Political Economy. When I went first of all I had no real sort of career plans but of course you have to say what your career's going to be. On the form, I put down 'Civil Service'. I think my parents thought 'You might as well put something down, and it's not impossible.' I had no real ambition whatsoever to go into the Civil Service. But, once you had done that, certain things tended to follow. They'd encourage you to do things like History and Political Economy, which I did and quite enjoyed, did well at. But I'd only done French at school; I was good at it and liked it and I thought I'd better do that and another language as well. And the Russian was something that — it was partly political, I suppose, really; but partly also just a purely personal thing. I had a close friend who was doing Russian and who was very far left. He was a Communist. We were talking so much about Russia, I think, that it just came to both our minds at about the same time that we would like to take the Russian Class, and I enjoyed it very much.

RC: Was there any tie-up with the literature of the Thirties in that decision?

EM: Yes, I think so. Because to me at that time starting to — well, I was writing of course even further back (in fact I started at school when I was about ten or eleven) — but at university when I was beginning to write more seriously (about seventeen or eighteen) — yes, the Thirties, the so-called Thirties, poets (everyone always thinks of Spender, Auden, and Day Lewis as being the main names) — yes, these were very interesting at that time and I devoured their books as they came out. Also Dylan Thomas, just perhaps a little bit later, and David Gascoyne and people like that. Yes, there was that Thirties thing of a political poetry which was strong. Though I remember enjoying Auden best because there was more than politics in what he was doing. I loved the obscure menace of his early poetry and still do. To me that still is the most powerful part of his work though the shift in critical opinion has gone towards his later work to a large extent. But I'm still haunted by that early poetry because I liked it a lot.

RC: I suppose there's an Old English presence in some at least of early Auden. I've heard both poets and professional medievalists admire your version of *Beowulf*. What interested you there? Did that come out of what you were doing in that period?

EM: Auden was very much influenced by Old English poetry, that's true. But, no, it came out more from my own English course, I think. I was one of the few who positively liked Anglo-Saxon. It was generally thought to be a hard part of the course and wasn't very popular. But I liked it and fairly soon I suppose got into the way of being able to read the language and to enjoy it. The poetry appealed to me very very strongly. I liked both the melancholy side of it, the elegiac side of it which is pretty strong, but also the heroic side of it. It was the first really convincing heroic poetry that I read as a student and I thought I would like to have a shot at it. I had read various translations, and it didn't seem to me that any of them really met the case, and I thought I would just go through the whole thing, and do it. I did quite a few other Anglo-Saxon poems at the same time, or later.

148

RC: Were you affected at all by MacDiarmid's slogan about getting 'back to Dunbar'?

EM: No, I don't really think so. I suppose I was getting back to Dunbar in a way, but it wasn't really because of that. I think it was more an interest that I myself had in that general medieval and especially early medieval period, because I was just as interested in, say, *Gawain and the Green Knight* and *Piers Plowman* and *Pearl*. I loved that poetry very much; still do, in fact, admire it tremendously. And that in a way abuts on the Anglo-Saxon poetry, and I got into that when I was — but I think it was more as a study of English, what I had just read and learned as a part of my English course than something that came to me from what other people said I should be doing.

RC: When did you first read MacDiarmid's work?

EM: That's something I'm not sure. It's a funny thing, you can't always remember a thing like that exactly. I must, I'm sure, have come across some of his poems here and there in magazines and anthologies before the war, but not to any great extent. He was a name that I hadn't really associated very closely with ideas about poetry. Then, during the war when I was away in the army, people sent me various things and I got into his poetry a bit more then, but it was really after the war I began to discover his poetry more and more. Before the war it was actually quite hard to get hold of, you know. Most of it was out of print. He published with small — 'fugitive' I think is the word — publishers, and the books were very hard to come across. You tended to come across his work in a piecemeal sort of way and not to get the whole picture of what the man had done. It didn't make really a strong impact on me until after the war.

RC: What kind of impact did it make then? How did you react to it?

EM: Well, it was first of all the Scottish poetry. I think the fact that I was away from Scotland during the whole of the war — abroad — gave me stronger feelings about Scotland (looking back towards it) than I might have had otherwise. That was certainly sharpened. I remember writing to people who were still at home and asking them 'Please send me books which had Scottish poetry or Scottish language in them.' I got a very good anthology of medieval Scottish poetry by M. M. Gray sent to me, and that was a kind of revelation; so that immediately after the war I was still thinking in those terms. I don't think I had quite come to accept the idea that what MacDiarmid had done was something that was bound to lead to a wholesale revival of Scots. I don't think that that was an idea that had really either sunk in or, if it had sunk in, had conquered me, because (as you know) the earliest poet probably that I'd got to know well was Sydney Graham; and that was not a Scottish Renaissance thing. That was different altogether. So in my mind what MacDiarmid was doing, when I began to get into it in the late Forties, was *one* thing, but I had also other things in my mind, and the Graham thing was still very strong of course.

From the start, Graham's poetry always impressed me as being so much the real thing. I could argue with him. As you probably know from the *Edinburgh Review* number where I quote from his letters we argued a great deal about this, but I always felt that there was a great energy, a great power in Graham that I went out to, and even if I didn't always like what he did and said so, I always thought there was something very powerful there. It was a *verbal* energy. When I didn't like it, I felt it was too uncontrolled, but when it was controlled I thought it was as good as what anybody was doing at that time. I knew the man of course. It was partly a personal thing. I knew him and liked him and I was impressed by the force of his character, whereas I didn't

149

know MacDiarmid at that time, you see. I hadn't met him. So Graham was a powerful personal presence as well as a writer. Knowing someone well like that when you're in your teens and you're both beginning to write, it is a strong bond in any case, whatever you think of the other person's poetry. He was interested in mine, I was interested in his, and we talked a lot about it.

RC: Though it was another Edwin Morgan who published a small book on Baudelaire in the early Forties, was Baudelaire's work important to *you*?

EM: It wasn't just Baudelaire. It was the whole of the French Symbolist movement that really got under my skin when I was a student, Baudelaire and Rimbaud, but Verlaine too, and others. Baudelaire particularly. I think to me it was a kind of revelation. I particularly admired what Baudelaire was doing because it was classical. If you want a classical poetry, that's it. He had an extraordinary command of regular modes of writing, and yet at the same time he's got a very deep infusion of something you could only call Romantic, even decadently so. And I thought that was wonderful. It made a great impression on me because there was nothing like that in English as far as I know. The great satisfaction of formal elements in Baudelaire coupled with deeply strange, often bizarre subject matter led me on to other French writers who were pre-Romantic, like Racine. We *had* to do Racine. We did *Andromaque,* I remember, and various other plays too in the French Class and I surprised myself by liking this. It still didn't make me like Dryden, Pope, and Johnson, but I admired what they were doing in the French neoclassical style. And even in Rimbaud where you're moving even further from Baudelaire into the modern period — a poet who makes himself a Modernist or an apostle of Modernism — even there there's an extraordinary concern with form that I liked. Except for his prose poems where it's a special genre. But when he's writing in a kind of classical style he also is able to combine that formal control with the most extraordinary adventurousness of ideas and language.

RC: Were you attracted to Baudelaire as a city poet?

EM: Yes. That's another thing which would be a part of it. As in the case of Eliot. It was Eliot's early city poetry that I really liked. The 'Preludes' in particular made a very strong impression. But, yes, Baudelaire and Thomson's 'City of Dreadful Night' and other things at that time — they all seemed to my mind to come together, very much as you were saying in your book in fact, which I've just finished reading. Yes, that was strong. I liked Baudelaire especially, I think, because . . . In fact, I think, I got into him before I got into Eliot and it seemed to me that he was one of the few who had, at a very early date really, the sense in poetry of what was going to be a modern city and I liked that tremendously. I think subsconsciously I had been looking for that and not finding it, but it seemed to be there in Baudelaire.

RC: Have any particular anthologies made an impact on you?

EM: Well, I can think of two. One especially was the *Faber Book of Modern Verse* when it first came out. It was much changed later on. The more recent editions have diluted it. Now it doesn't have any unity, but when it first came out it had unity and was a very striking anthology and I think, for the first time probably, gave me an idea of what was happening in both British and American poetry of modern times, though it went back to Gerard Manley Hopkins. I read that about 1937, I think. Maybe it was '36 when I read it. I'm not quite sure . . . but that I found *very* striking. Introduced me to people like Hart Crane and Laura Riding as well as the more obvious names, and I learned an awful lot from that. So that's a kind of landmark I think.

And the other one is an anthology of foreign poetry, *An Anthology of World Poetry* it was called, which came out about 1930, edited by Mark van Doren, and consisted of — it's a big book — translations from many many languages, very often by poets, and I remember being struck by some of these, from different periods. A lot of the Oriental material in that, which I'd never seen before, made a big impression, and probably chimed in later on when I went to the Middle East and I began to put these sort of things together. Among the more exotic contents of that book I remember being greatly struck by some of the Arabic and Persian and Indian poems, and I think a lot of the Arabian translations by a man called E. Powys Mathers seemed to me to be very good, and they opened up really a new kind of poetry. He, of course, was translating (and also writing about elsewhere) poems from different Oriental countries, but it wasn't just they were presenting a kind of exotic scene that was interesting because it was exotic. Often it was strange storytelling or very powerful erotic imagery that was just that little bit different from what you'd get in Western poetry and yet at the same time was obviously the real thing. It was just as much human experience — even bits he'd translate from the *Thousand and One Nights,* and *Arabian Nights*, have got this mixture of something — you seem to believe it could actually have happened — and yet it's all very highly imaginative at the same time. There was something about that. Hafiz, the Persian poet, also came into that anthology and there was something about that that I think must have struck me a lot, and later on perhaps when I began to write about it probably that was somewhere at the back of my mind: this early anthology which certainly I devoured at the time, just before the war.

RC: When did *you* start writing poetry?

EM: When I was about ten or eleven, I'm not quite sure exactly. I had poems written at school. Some were in the school magazine. Some I just wrote myself. And at the same time I was writing prose, stories, usually long rather strange adventure stories which I suppose — I haven't got any of them now so I can't check on this — but I think they were abutting on, verging on, science fiction; possibly they were science fiction. Not for any purpose. Just because I liked doing them. They were never published anywhere, and probably they were too long to publish. I remember once I finished one and it was about a hundred and odd pages long, and I think my grandfather thought there might be a possibility of getting it published, but it didn't come to anything at the time, and eventually it just disappeared. Round about that time, between ten and fourteen, I was writing a great deal, probably more in prose actually than in verse.

RC: Your first book of poems, published when you were thirty-two, was called *The Vision of Cathkin Braes*. Were you wanting to bring Langland to Glasgow?

EM: I think possibly that there's a bit of the alliterative style certainly in the poem. I'm not sure whether it was as literary a thing as all that. I was living in Rutherglen at the time when I wrote that and very often was actually on Cathkin Braes. I suppose it was a kind of local poem in a way, looking back to ballads and poems of that kind where the dreamer, if you like, goes out into the landscape and has a strange dream and wakes up at the end. Things like that were perhaps there.

RC: Did the 1960s give you a second life?

EM: Yes, I think probably I would say they did for a number of different reasons. It's hard to say it was just one thing. The whole feeling of the decade seemed to me to be very stimulating and liberating and I liked it a lot and found I was able to write more and probably better than I'd been doing before. I didn't like the period before that. I didn't enjoy the Fifties very much at all. I was sort of casting around for different ways to write without really making it. But towards the end of the Fifties, things began to get better; in the Sixties especially. Just the climate of the time just seemed to suit me for some reason.

RC: Did it matter to you to attempt a poetry that was both joyous and Scottish?

EM: Well, I suppose so. I think it's maybe partly a temperament thing and partly a sense of Scottish poetry — I think there has been a good deal of recognition of the comic in the whole Scottish tradition, which I liked. If I was reading Dunbar or Burns or MacDiarmid, comedy was obviously important to all three of them, even though they were serious poets, and I liked that and I think something positive comes through that that attracted me and still attracts me. So possibly . . . well, when I say 'positive' of course a lot of satire's involved too, but satire can have something positive about it. Maybe the energy of language that you get from satire can be in a way positive although you're attacking something.

RC: From 'The Whittrick' through to 'Cinquevalli' and perhaps beyond, are you attracted to mercurial, slightly elusive personalities?

EM: Yes, yes, I think I am, yes. It's partly the great liking I have for energy as a quality. I think that's what attracted me to Dunbar. It wasn't just a 'back to Dunbar' thing. It was loving Dunbar because he's a kind of whittrick, and I find the same with MacDiarmid, and with Burns too. I think the three of them are whittricks. Yes, and Cinquevalli obviously in a physical sense, was a kind of whittrick. Yes, I like this. The risk in liking it is perhaps the risk that you might miss the opposite liking for something that is very solid. But I don't think that that rules out a liking for the mercurial. I think you can see the mercurial in a number of contexts which, like overlapping worlds perhaps, or different spheres of existence, do amount perhaps to something very very solid really because life might be just like that. It might be something that is just as mercurial as it is solid.

RC: Has painting been important to you?

EM: Oh yes, very. From an early age in fact I always liked doing what I could myself in drawing and painting. Art was one of the subjects I did at school. I took my 'Higher' Art at school. In fact, I was going to go to the School of Art, and almost did. University was just a second thought really in the last minute. Yes, I think starting from that, just from my own enjoyment of it and learning a bit about it because I took 'Higher' Art, having to learn a bit about the history of painting for the final exam, got me into it quite strongly. Although I haven't continued to do very much in a practical sense I've always enjoyed painting.

RC: How about film?

EM: Yes, film too. Maybe because when I was growing up it was very much a kind of film-going generation. The cinema was very very popular at that time, in the nineteen-thirties particularly, and I did see a great many films. My parents took me at a quite early age to go and see various selected films, which they thought would be good for me I suppose! Maybe I got the bug then, but yes I always liked the film. And when the Cosmo (the G[lasgow] F[ilm] T[heatre] as it now is — what used to be the Cosmo before the war) was started, that was a great thing in Glasgow because you were able to *see* things that you'd read about — classical film which you would never have hoped you would see before — but now they were able to be seen and I remember going there just before the war and catching up, as it were, with the history of film and being very excited by it. I was very much persuaded by the early theory of film — that this was going to be one of the most important arts, possibly the most important art of the twentieth century. I think I accepted that and was sorry in a way that I wasn't going to be going into film. Though I didn't do anything about it practically, I was *greatly* attracted by the way in which imagery was used in film, even if it was at the expense of words. I was never quite sure about how important language was in films. Although I've been saying before that language was what attracted me right from the earliest years, nevertheless that was qualified to some extent when I began looking at film seriously and learning how much could come through imagery and not through language. You might have a very good film in which hardly a word was spoken; and it forced me to rethink some of my ideas about how the arts worked. But I was greatly impressed by film.

RC: How about music?

EM: Yes, music too. I think I liked all the arts. When I was at school we were taken occasionally to classical concerts in the old St. Andrew's Halls and I got a kind of inkling of classical music from that and got my own favourites coming out of it: Beethoven and Sibelius, mostly. And it was mostly classical music until the period we were talking about, the Sixties, or the late nineteen-fifties anyway, when what is now called Pop or Rock music seemed suddenly to me to become something that I enjoyed listening to very forcefully. Before that, I was brought up if you like, at home on what you would call the popular music of all time — the nineteen-twenties, the nineteen-thirties. We had a gramophone. The most popular records were bought and played on that. Neither of my parents had any particular interest in classical music at all and all the majority was for the popular music of the time. But looking back on that, I think it was just the kind of background of the scenes as it were and although I remembered the songs and they often have a kind of emotional resonance, I don't think probably as songs they were really as good as the songs that began to appear throughout the nineteen-sixties. That made a different kind of impression on me, because it seemed to me this was a new kind of music where there was a sort of poetry in it as well as often very catchy tunes or even interesting orchestration as you got with the Beatles. The Beatles and Bob Dylan, and many of the other groups at that time gave me something from music that I hadn't been getting before and possibly that chimed in with the sense of getting involved myself in the whole creative scene. It added to the enjoyment of 1960 as a kind of liberating period for me.

RC: Your 1973 collection is called *From Glasgow To Saturn*. Your selected translations carry the title *Rites of Passage*. The idea of constant translation — linguistic, cultural, and geographic — seems central to your work as a whole. Do you feel that that's the case?

EM: Translation in all senses! Well, maybe so. I like translation itself as an activity, the challenge of translation, of trying to do it as well as I can. Yes, also I like various kinds of confrontation, I suppose — like going back to these old encyclopaedias that I mentioned, the different kind of subjects being brought together. I like the idea say in *From Glasgow to Saturn*, of living in a place, like Glasgow, acknowledging that as your base, seeing the place where you have your being as it were, but at the same time feeling that you're not by any means bound to be only writing about that; you're quite entitled to think of Saturn or some other place outside our world and as far as you can to have ideas or feelings about it and to bring that into your writing too. And the whole business of communication — I suppose that comes into translation — always interested me a lot and it was partly the difficulties of communication (I suppose that's often a theme in what I write) or even imaginary communication, but again the idea of bringing things together and of giving things a voice through what I write, even if they don't have an actual voice — giving animals or inanimate objects a voice — that attracts me a lot, and I suppose that is a kind of translation in a way. If I write a poem called 'The Apple's Song', the apple is being translated if you like into *human* language. Who knows what an apple thinks! We don't really know — it doesn't give signs of thinking, but because we don't get signs of what an animal or a plant or a fruit really is thinking, I don't think we're entitled to just switch off and say it's not feeling or thinking. I like the idea particularly that in a sense we're surrounded by messages that we perhaps ought to be trying to interpret. I remember in 'The Starlings in George Square' I brought in the bit about "Some day we'll decipher that sweet frenzied whistling," which in a sense I suppose I believed actually — although it seems just a fantastic idea.

RC: Messages from the past and the future also?

EM: I think probably also. Yes, yes, yes. The writer or the poet being in *receipt,* if you like, of messages, just like people listening for stars messages, astronomers listening for that. I think the writer too does that kind of thing. He does his best. He tries to decode, if you like, the messages that he thinks he gets from everything that surrounds him. Nothing is not giving messages, I think.

RC: 'CHANGE RULES.' Does that sentence have a wide significance for your work?

EM: Yes. I think so. Because, I suppose, so much of my work has been about something that is in the process of change, and I like, I think, even the idea of change more than I like the idea of tradition. Obviously tradition exists and you are a part of some kind of tradition, whether you want to be that or not, but it's not something that particularly interests me — I'm more interested in what does change than in what has been and what is constant.

RC: Like the novels of Alasdair Gray, your own work blends ludic fantasy with the sometimes grim depiction of urban life, particularly in the West of Scotland. Again, like Alasdair Gray, you've chosen to live in Glasgow. Do you see many links between your work and his?

EM: I suppose so in a way. I know I remember seeing parts of the work long before it was actually published, and liking it, and going out towards it and wanting to encourage him and so on. Yes, I felt there was something there that was similar. The difference is I suppose that what he's doing is a novel, a large novel [*Lanark*] which presents different problems and different ways of dealing with them from what we get in poetry. But, yes, it was something that I liked a lot. I felt that what he was doing there was what ought perhaps to have been done in fiction a long time ago, but had never been done. He was perhaps the first person to see that Glasgow could be, well 'mythologized' is perhaps the wrong word — but something like mythologized. It had to be a real presence, it was a real place, but at the same time it had to be given a resonating, a reverberating kind of existence that you would expect a big place to have, and he was able to do that.

RC: Embedding parts of your own biography in the text at the same time as going way into the distance strikes me as something that, as a partly subterranean structural device, would again connect you with Alasdair Gray.

EM: Yes, I think that's true. Yes, because his own life is very much embedded in *Lanark*, as my own life is embedded in *The New Divan* and many of the other poems too. I think 'embedding' is the word, because it's not always immediately straightforwardly clear that the life is there, but it is in fact there and various clues are dropped here and there just to make sure that the real person *is* in the poetry. Sometimes people say that it's not a very personal poetry, that it tends to be an impersonal poetry. I don't think it is. You can't talk about your own poetry, obviously, in an objective way in that sense, but I don't think that is really true. I think in fact that it's just as personal a poetry as anybody else's, but the clues are not perhaps as clearly spelt out as they would be in other people's poetry. But I'm quite sure that the personal life, the autobiography if you like, is there, and is there quite strongly in all the things that I do.

RC: Do you think that your own prose — your early essay on Dunbar, for instance, — is bound up with your own poetry?

EM: Yes, I think that probably early things were bound up a bit with what I was doing and what interested me particularly and sometimes even the style of somebody; early essays would fit in with that idea. Yes, I think you're often drawn to subjects that you want to write about for reasons that are not just concerned with critical estimates of writing you're taking up. At the same time, of course, that has to be qualified by the fact that you're *asked* to write this or that. You're asked to review a book or to write an essay on somebody and so you're constantly — CHANGE RULES again — changing your views on certain things or you're extending your views on certain things because of accident. I think that quite often when you're reading an early essay on someone you can tell that it comes from an interest that's of primary creative concern to that person, as being different from what he's been asked to do for some particular occasion.

RC: Looking back, it seems as if there's a strong line in modern Scottish poetry that passes through John Davidson, Hugh MacDiarmid, and Edwin Morgan. Are you happy about being seen as part of any particular position?

EM: Well, with these names, yes, I would accept that that is so, and I like that kind of association. I suppose that (just going back to what I've said about tradition) I'm not myself particularly interested in that really; but yes, I do take this as being something that, looking back, I would certainly feel to be true. I know that when I did come across Davidson, and Thomson — Thomson even more in some ways than Davidson . . . I do feel there's something there that is a kind of link, but it would probably be complicated in other ways. We've already mentioned people like Dunbar, and I suppose they're in the background too. But in so far as it's recent time we're talking about, yes, I think so, and maybe it is a tradition that is not one that's always thought of. Perhaps it should be thought of more.

RC: Like several Scottish poets, including Davidson and MacDiarmid, you're interested in using scientific materials in your work. Why does your science usually take the form of science fiction?

EM: Well, I suppose I was always interested in science fiction. I was interested in the sciences as well, but in a very amateurish kind of way. I remember at school enjoying the American science fiction magazines and, although some of the stories had a good science basis, others were much nearer fantasy. I think probably it was a combination of two things. I liked the idea that, if possible, you should keep the arts and sciences going together; if you had any interest at all in the sciences you shouldn't let it drop if you happened to be an artist of some kind. But I think particularly as far as actual writing was concerned, it had something to do with what was happening in the sciences from about the late Fifties onwards, when especially perhaps in space exploration (but also in biology and biochemistry) the most extraordinary things were happening. With space exploration it was as if for the first time life was really catching up with science fiction, and somehow it seemed to be more of a subject for poetry because in poetry — you could write science fiction poetry before that time, there was some, not very good most of it — but it was really from that time, the time of the first Sputnik, and then the first man in space — the first dog, then the first man in space — it was really from that quite a lot of poets began to feel that you could write *genuine* poetry which would once perhaps have been called science fiction, and perhaps you would still call it that, but nevertheless it has a basis in what is happening in the sense that the area for human operations is moving out, it's extending itself to other places than the earth. And you have there something that is perfectly real and will someday perhaps be even ordinary, and yet at the same time highly appealing to the imagination and to the sense of the adventurous and the heroic.

RC: Has organized religion meant much to you?

EM: No, not really. It was a churchgoing environment. I don't think my parents would be called really 'religious' in the way people use that word, but, yes, there was church and Sunday school every Sunday, so that inevitably you got to know a good deal about it. You got to know the Bible very well, learning a lot of it by heart and so on. So that background is there and I know I often use Bible imagery in what I write — it is simply there — but organized religion as such did not, I think, really mean very much to me and I didn't go to church after about fifteen or sixteen. I think I felt it was something I really couldn't honestly go on doing. So it's maybe a difference between organized religion in that sense of churchgoing, and the sense of getting something from the Bible — which one shouldn't split off from that, but nevertheless one does in many cases. Obviously certain bits of the Bible, and partly the language, I suppose, of the Bible, did make a strong impression and that is no doubt still there somewhere.

RC: Do you have a particular interest in the structural devices which can govern poems?

EM: Yes, quite a lot. Though, obviously, beginning to write poetry when I did, there was a great deal of free verse around and one tended to use free verse a lot — though even free verse has its ways of structuring things. Yes, I've always felt that it's important to find or to have structure, and sometimes it can be a use of existing structures like the sonnet or rhyming couplets which are still available and can be done something with; they don't really disappear. At other times, I suppose in some kinds of concrete poetry, you are searching for new ways of structuring which are perhaps harder to combine with traditional ways of thinking about poetry, but, yes, I think structure has always been important — maybe a structure of ideas, maybe a structure of events, a narrative, or whatever, but yes, I have thought a lot about structure.

RC: Are you interested in randomness?

EM: Yes, yes. That is a kind of structure too I suppose [*laughter*]. But, yes, I think again this was to some extent a kind of nineteen-sixties thing. There was a lot of discussion of randomness and I was reading people like Jackson MacLow in America who made a great deal of this, and of course John Cage was interesting too. I think the question is just how do you do this, and how far you can do this. I suppose in a sense I made use of randomness if you like in the hundred poems of *The New Divan* which are not . . . They have a *kind* of structure. It's not randomness obviously. It has a beginning, it has an end, and I think the one in the middle (the fiftieth one) is of some importance too, but apart from that (if you can say apart from that) it deliberately does use a kind of randomness in the sense that one is not following a story that really goes forward step by step. Characters appear and reappear. You're not certain whether the characters are autobiographical or not. That kind of randomness is something that did attract me. And, if you like, the idea of non-structure almost as a structural idea in itself — in a sense that a good deal of the poetry of the Middle East (which I got to learn something about when I was in the Middle East) deliberately is almost anti-structural and almost in fact thinks that we in the West are too obsessed by structure, and we drive our readers too hard. In Arabic or Persian poetry they're rather fond of the idea that a 'divan' as they call it, a collection of poems, is something that you enter; you move around; you can cast your eye here and there, you look, you pick, you perhaps retrace your steps. But you're not as in, say, *Paradise Lost* being driven from point A to point B, to point C, or being driven perhaps back but then forward again but in a very clearly defined kind of way. That appealed to me. Whether you call it in a strict sense 'structure' or not I'm not quite sure, but it's one way of doing it. The idea that if you were writing a divan, a collection of poems, although it wouldn't be something that a critic could very easily analyse as having structure, nevertheless there would be something that in a more mysterious, subterranean sense would be structure, an emotional structure, a structure perhaps relating to the life of the person who had written it. But you'd have to know something about that life, if you like, to get the key to the structure. So the structure is underground, it's tantalizing, but it may perhaps even — who knows? be there — in a more profound sense than the structure of a very highly organized poem.

RC: Is the idea of a quest important in *The New Divan* and your poetry generally?

EM: I think it is, yes. That means saying, I suppose, that *The New Divan* is not really a narrative structue in the ordinary sense of the term, and very often of course a narrative structure — a story — does have some kind of search in it, but it is a kind of quest poem in many ways, I think. And very often I am attracted by the idea of a quest, partly I suppose because I tend not to start off from having a firm basis of ideas or of belief. There's a search for ideas or a search for belief which is often translated into a search in physical terms, and I like again the idea of coming to something that hadn't been quite foreseen or foretold; maybe that links back with the liking for change itself and the sense of something unknown as something that looms and is worth thinking about even though more immediate concerns are obviously going to be a large part of your life. That has always I think been there, as far back as I can think; and it's partly the feeling that poetry has got to reach out in that kind of way — whether it's science fiction or even a straightforward story, poetry has got to look outwards towards something that hasn't happened yet. It feeds on that, if you like, and it's meant to help its readers to feed on that too. It draws things forward, it draws life forward, it draws people forward. The way in which I like Shelley, for example — of all the Romantic poets probably Shelley makes that appeal very strongly — and I always liked the ideas in Shelley of reaching out to something which you perhaps *cannot* define and the more you could define it the less value it would have. The danger of that of course is that you have the whole thing begining to be something that disappears out of view altogether. But I would hope that, with the other kind of interest I have in the immediate and the real, in the documentary and so on, there would be a check on that, and it would be an attempt if possible to combine the idea of something very immediate in human terms with an extraordinary outreaching hand as it were, outreaching as far as you can think at all.

RC: What do you feel you've taken from American writing?

EM: Oh, I'm sure a lot. I think Whitman was probably the earliest American poet that I really enjoyed, and that goes right back to certainly early university days, maybe even at school I think I may have come across some of his poetry, and I liked him a lot. But also much later when the Beat writers came on the scene — Ginsberg, Corso, Ferlinghetti — I enjoyed them and I could understand what they were doing. That, when I read them (again in the late Fifties and early Sixties)

157

was again part of that sort of liberating process of the Sixties. In America they were deliberately doing this of course as part of a reaction against what they thought of as the over-academic poetry, and they didn't quite catch on in this country in that way. There was perhaps an English and even a Scottish Beat poetry movement, but it was a much weaker imitation of what they were doing across there. But I liked what they were doing, and it seemed to me in a way something that was important to me not in a very direct sense, but it seemed to unlock something in me that I could certainly use; and it also helped to get me into other kinds of American poetry which I hadn't liked before at all. William Carlos Williams had just seemed prosy and dull to me before the Beats, although they were very different from Williams (Ginsberg acknowledged Williams of course and liked him); I got into Williams from them. It seemed to me again that it was a sense that there was nothing you couldn't write about. The thing was just to feel for it and to allow yourself certain kinds of spontaneity that perhaps had been difficult to get before.

RC: Have you learned from Russian and East European writers?

EM: It's probably easier for other people to say what you've learned from. I've enjoyed and read and translated a lot. It must have been influential. The influential must show in some ways. When I took the Russian class at university I remember getting very interested in a lot of Russian poetry. Mayakovsky was probably the first one that made a really big impact, though Pushkin too about the same time in a different way. But Mayakovsky particularly. That was a kind of revelation. That was a bit like the kind of Baudelaire/Rimbaud thing, I think, because they were happening about the same time too, in my first two years as a student. With Mayakovsky what attracted me particularly there — again it was something I hadn't seen before but had perhaps subsconsciously been looking for — it was the combination of a very strong, committed political content and a very adventurous style. He was a revolutionary poet as regards his style, but whereas in Anglo-American poetry the revolution had tended to go with a right-wing view of politics in Eliot and Pound and people like that, this, for the first time for me anyway, was a poet who was committed to the left but being revolutionary in language. I was fascinated by the struggle Mayakovsky had in trying to persuade people, not immediately after the Revolution but as the Twenties went on, that his way of doing it was the only way to do it; that you couldn't in fact constantly dilute your poetry for the popular market just because you were left-wing, or just because you were a socialist, that it must still be good powerful poetry; and the way in which he still kept doing this, trying in various ways to be a good communicative poet but not giving up the sense that an innovative use of language was still very important and must be kept up at all costs.

RC: Someone once said that you represent Modernism at its most acceptable. Do you like that description?

EM: [laughter] Ah! Should I or should I not? Well, I like Modernism. I suppose I always was a Modernist in the sense that, for example, even in the nineteen-twenties I remember being greatly taken by, say, modern architecture. I suppose that's a kind of touchstone in many ways. You tend either to like or dislike what's called Modernist architecture. I always right from the start really liked it, and I remember seeing books which happened to be brought into the house from somebody, showing modern architecture in various countries, mostly the Le Corbusier type of architecture, and my eyes were lighting up at this and I was saying 'Why is Glasgow not more like that?' I did feel that. And I felt the same about the other arts too. When I was doing my art course at school it was quite a good course. They went really quite up to date — far more up to date than they did in the literature department — and I did know about Picasso and Matisse and the Cubists and the Fauves and so on when I was still at school. And there again I was attracted by the modern developments and didn't see them as something that had to be fought against. I felt it to be somehow part of my world and I continued to feel that.

RC: Do you like the idea of a documentary poetry?

EM: Yes and no. Yes, I do obviously — I must to some extent since I've done quite a bit of this. Yes, I like the idea of especially recording things that are not being recorded in other ways. A great deal that happens simply flashes past in the media — whether it's radio, television, or newspapers — often things that are of the greatest interest flash past, and nothing really fixes them. Artists no longer fix them; painters don't fix them any more. Sculptors don't fix them. So it's left, if you like, to the writer. Novelists can do it, of course, in their way, but I think poets also can do something about this and when I was doing the *Instamatic Poems* (which I suppose are an example of that kind of thing) I was, really, I suppose, saying 'Here are all these events being recorded very briefly in newspapers — not followed up, many of them — just there, perhaps even just one day — of great interest whether they're perhaps strange or comic or frightening or bizarre or whatever, but of great human interest. It was always the human story that attracted me. Why should the poet not try to do something with this? The question is 'What?' And there is a problem there, because the more you do use this immediate contemporary material, things that are going past very quickly, the more you may be finding yourself stuck in the position of the camera-artist as against the painter. People will say 'Well, why do it? Is this a poem at all?' Or 'Why are you not adding more to it?' And I was tempted by the idea of opening out all these little *Instamatic Poems* into longer pieces and working them up into various comments about the world that was of that particular year. But I didn't do this, and I felt in the end that perhaps it was best leave it as if the camera had been there and had taken a shot, just to see what would happen with this. Again, it's a bit like the divan idea. Taken one by one in isolation this wouldn't mean very much, but I hoped that a collection of them in a book would in fact add more and that you would see a context for the whole thing. It would be a context of those particular years when this thing happened. It would be a kind of unusual but nevertheless perfectly real picture of what human beings had been up to at that particular time. So it's partly recording things, it's partly documentary, but also it is exploring the whole idea of what a collection of poems can perhaps do which an individual poem can't do.

RC: How did you come to write *Sonnets from Scotland?*

EM: That didn't begin with the idea of the whole thing. It began with the idea of writing one or two, I think as a kind of reaction, probably, to the failure of the Referendum to give Scotland political devolution and any idea of a Scottish Assembly. I think at that time there was a sense of a kind of gap, a hiatus, a numbness in Scottish thinking. There had been such a build-up towards the possibility of not independence, obviously, but some kind of Assembly, and I think lots of people had felt that really it was going to happen. It didn't happen, of course, and there was this great deflation. But the deflation led to (not just in myself but in other people too) a great deal of thinking about it, not necessarily picking over what had gone wrong. I think there was a kind of 'Nevertheless' feeling. We hadn't got our Assembly, and everything seemed to have gone back to square one as it were, but. And it was the but that seemed to be important. I had very strong feelings about Scotland at that time and wanted perhaps to put something down that would make this 'Nevertheless' feeling quite palpable and tangible. Although there's only one of the sonnets about the Referendum itself and the sense of deflation, nevertheless the whole thing is meant to be related to that. It's a kind of comeback, an attempt to show that Scotland was there, was alive and ticking, that people were living there, were thinking and feeling about it and were going to go on writing about it even if political change was at that time cetainly pretty unlikely. It was just a kind of desire to show that Scotland was there and that one mustn't write it off just because the Assembly had not come into being.

RC: What's your attitude to Scottish Nationalism?

EM: Well, in general I approve of it [*laughter*]. That's a kind of very blunt answer. It's become quite a complex subject nowadays really. The family was not inclined that way. My parents were both Conservative — not Thatcherite Conservtive — I suppose they were kind of natural Conservatives. It was their belief that anything that wasn't Conservative was 'political'. If they called anyone 'political' it meant that he was probably left-wing. But when I began to think for myself about these things I tended to do the opposite. I tended to vote Labour, but when it came to the nineteen-sixties I began to feel more strongly about the possibility of some change in the constitutional arrangements and some sense of Scotland's difference from England being acknowledged politically. And I then tended to vote for the SNP without joining it. I never joined any political party, but I would tend to vote SNP, and have gone on doing it. I still do, with lots of doubts about the actual party itself which doesn't seem to me to be a charismatic party at all. But it seems to me to be the only party that is really committed to Scotland as an entity, so I tend to give it my support. I feel Scottish — I suppose it really comes down to something as simple as that on a kind of basic level. You have a passport which says you're UK or British, and you obviously have to acknowledge that in a purely official sense but I don't feel British. I don't feel, certainly, English. I don't feel anything but Scottish. I suppose in that sense, a bit like MacDiarmid, you want the political arrangement to reflect the way you feel about it. I think I go along with him in that sense. So, yes, I would like a Scottish Republic really. That's what it comes down to.

RC: Your next collection will be published by Carcanet later this year. What attracted you to the title, *Themes on a Variation*?

EM: Well, the phrase actually came from a reviewer who had been looking at some of my poems and feeling that what I was doing was not so much variations on a theme, as it might seem on the surface to be, but rather the opposite — that it was really themes on a variation. And when I read this, my ears seemed to prick up somehow, and although it was a strange sort of reversal I began to think about it and thought that there was probably some truth in it. It seemed to me that it did apply (although I didn't want to work it out) — I just liked the phrase. It seemed to me to apply to a lot of the things I had been doing recently, so I just used it as the title.

RC: Are you interested in a sort of 'themes on a variation' in some modern composers — Philip Glass, for instance?

EM: Yes, I am, though I see from the current number of *The List* that Philip Glass is on his way out already — that's pretty quick, isn't it! [*laughter*]. But, anyway, yes, I do enjoy Philip Glass. I suppose I came to it really rather late but, yes, I liked it and I like the way in which he's been able to move. I suppose he had originally a pretty small audience and he thought of himself as a sort of avant-garde composer, to whom it was suggested that he might broaden his scope and write operas. He tried it out and in fact they were successful and probably among his best things. I like the idea — maybe again this is the acceptable face of Modernism — he seemed to me to be able to devise a style that at first seemed to be almost perversely repetitive, and in that sense not having broad appeal, into something that, although it is still repetitive, does somehow unfold very good stories and ideas as well as in his operas.

RC: You spoke earlier of autobiographical 'clues' embedded in your work. In what direction do you want these clues to be followed up? I mean, would you be happy, say, with a biographical reading of your poetry?

EM: I wouldn't object to it. I think this kind of thing can be done and can be useful, can be helpful. I suppose if that had been meant to be the *whole* thing, then the poetry would have been itself more obviously autobiographical. It isn't that. But, yes, I don't see why every aspect of a poem couldn't be investigated and, as, eventually, when you pop off and people begin to wonder about you, perhaps to think about your life, and ask qustions, and trace you up and so on, they *will* go back to the poetry and they will see things that weren't immediately clear perhaps at the beginning. And I think that this can be useful. It probably is one approach, because the other things that you've been asking questions about — the structure, and interest in various subjects and so on, influences from other poets and poetry — that obviously is part of it. So it's only a part of it, but I think that the person in the poem is still an important idea. I don't think critics will ever really get away from it. I know some have tried very hard [*laughter*] and are still trying very hard to get away from it, but I don't think you ever will. I think that the poetry *is* a man's life as well as being whatever else that it clearly would be to an analytical critic.

LES A. MURRAY

TALKING WITH ROBERT CRAWFORD

Les Murray has become one of the most important poets now writing in English. Since the publication of his *Selected Poems: The Vernacular Republic* (1976), his poetry collections have included *Ethnic Radio* (1979), the verse-novel *The Boys Who Stole the Funeral* (1979), and *The People's Otherworld* (1983), as well as two books of essays - *The Peasant Mandarin* (1978), and *Persistence in Folly* (1984). All his books, with the exception of *The Peasant Mandarin* (University of Queensland Press), are published by Angus & Robertson, though a collection will soon be appearing from Carcanet (UK), and a *Selected Poems* was published by Persea (USA) in 1984. From 1973 - 1979 Murray was acting editor of *Poetry Australia*. He has recently edited the *New Oxford Book of Australian Verse* (1986), and has received various awards in Australia and elsewhere. This interview was recorded on 29 November 1985 at St Hugh's College, Oxford, the day before Les Murray returned to Sydney after a reading tour of Canada, USA, the UK, and Denmark.

RC: You were born in 1938, and your home town is Bunyah on the lower north coast of New South Wales. There's a poem called 'Evening Alone At Bunyah' in which you say, 'It can be enough to read books and camp in a house.' Would you describe your childhood as 'bookish'?

LM: No. It was bookish *manqué*. There weren't very many books around, but I read every one I could get hold of. In the country then, we were sort of outside of western civilization in many ways; certainly we weren't contemporary. Radio was just coming in, my parents were quite poor, and there weren't that many books. My mother had brought the books that she won as school prizes with her; she was unusual in her time in having completed high school. She'd then been a nurse. My father completed primary school, and was a timber worker and what we call a 'bullocky' - chap who drives a bullock team in the forest - and then he became a dairy farmer. There was a set of encyclopedias in the house. I read them to pieces, you know, literally till they fell apart. And I borrowed or begged every book around the district. For lack of other printed matter I'd read the Angus Stud Book or Stanley Gibbons stamp catalogue, or anything. It set my mind. It set the way I would go, because I became a sort of universalist. I've always been interested in reading books about everything. I'm not that much of a specialist.

RC: You didn't have any particular tastes when you were a kid?

LM: Well, it wouldn't have mattered if I had, because the books wouldn't have been there, right? Oh, I suppose I had a fascination with military aircraft because it was during the Second World War that I came into consciousness, and I used to help my aunt at the post office as an aircraft spotter - always hoping I'd see a Mitsubishi Zero. But, no, when I got to Sydney University when I was eighteen it was like - I suppose - a bit like a Bedouin finally getting to a place where there was unlimited water. I went into Fisher Library, Sydney University, which had about two million volumes, and I resolved to read the lot. I got through a good many of them. There are books in that library which had been in there uncut since the 1880s, and I cut the pages.

RC: What did you head for first?

LM: Literature of all sorts, in all sorts of languages - including Gaelic. The books I was thinking of just now were in fact a set of Carmichael's *Carmina Gaedelica*, which I cut the pages of. It's disgraceful; Sydney still hasn't got a Chair of Celtic Studies. Despite our history. It's got a fairly good collection of Gaelic books, though, at University Library. But I read everything. I was learning to write at the same time so I was reading poetry in enormous amounts. I hadn't read much poetry before that, and I'd only really been turned on to poetry in the last year at high school. Before that, in common with most boys of my generation, in the bush and the country towns, we were far too tough to be interested in poetry. And it was also fairly unreal because no modern poetry was taught in the schools in those days; poetry was poorly taught anyway - and it was all British. The natural and class ecology of an island off the north-west coast of Europe was pretty remote from our experience. So when I discovered modern poetry I pricked up my ears, and when I discovered modern Australian poetry my ears pricked up so much they've never sagged down again.

RC: Somebody else who reacted quite positively to Carmichael's *Carmina Gaedelica* was T. S. Eliot.

LM: Ah! I wish I'd known that! I resisted Eliot early on. Unfairly.

RC: How did you react to European and American modernism?

LM: With incomprehension, I think, and some scepticism. I saw, for example, fairly quickly that it was cyclic. The same breathtaking breakthroughs were made on a twenty year rotation. We've seen surrealism come round three or four times now, haven't we? And it struck me that surrealism was a bit of a trick: that it can be a kind of chocolate-sauce that you pour over things to make them sound supernally important, deep, and fascinating. It's an effect, derived I suspect in the first place from early psychoanalytic writings. I wrote a poem about that which I had in the *TLS* last year. I also resisted the mandarinizing tendency of modernism, the power it gave to critics, the estrangement from a wider readership, the sort of aspirant aristocracy of it.

RC: You weren't attracted to any sort of synthetic impulse in modernism?

LM: Yes. Very much. That's *the* great thing about modernism. That, and also its administration of a wide range of vernacular speech. It didn't *need* to be a mandarin language. Poetry always tends to revert to being written in mandarin language, and in certain forms of modernism it became extremely mandarin. You have to keep breaking the moulds open, but the freedom of language that it conveyed and conferred was the thing, I thought, was important about it. The dangers were a very imperious received sensibility, and that aristo or *nomenklatura* exclusivism that goes with and demands that sensibility. In which lots of things aren't allowed to be said.

RC: The thing that strikes me most about your poetry is the way it's at once resolutely Australian, rooted in loved specifics, yet global, aggressively wide-ranging in its outlook and impact. Maybe those two impulses are summed up in an image from 'Towards the Imminent Days' when you present

> mortality crumbling down
> till on summer mornings, a farm boy can see through the hills,
> the roots of pumpkin-vines knotting clean under New England.

Are you very much aware of twinning these two impulses, the native and the global?

LM: Yes, yes. I think they both have to be done. My ideology is really what I call 'Boeotian'. It's against words like 'provincial' and 'capital' and 'metropolitan' and so on. The capital of the world is anywhere a good writer is writing. Or, really, anywhere an individual is living! I figure that no-one should be made to feel relegated by mandarin centralisms - and so writing from where I write from is a model for anybody who wants to do the same thing, from, say, Guyana, or Belize, or Zambia, or wherever they like. They shouldn't have to feel as we used to feel that you have to go to London or New York to make a big splash. Nor should they be insulted by anthologies of 'English' poetry which contain only British and American poets' work. 'English' ought to mean either exclusively *English*, or else work from the *whole* English-speaking world.

RC: Did you read MacDiarmid when you were young?

LM: His middle name was Murray! He's related to us on his mother's side. Yes, as soon as I read MacDiarmid I recognized the kind of cross-grained crankiness of my family was in there. And I found him quite fascinating.

RC: When did you start to read him?

LM: MacDiarmid would have been a bit after university, I would think. Somewhere in the 60s.

RC: When did you read Robert Frost and Edwin Muir? Were they important to you in any ways?

LM: I would have started reading Frost in the late Fifties and Muir in the early Sixties. Both were important to me, I think. There are traces of Frost in my early poems, and Muir opened up some areas of style to me, maybe a certain 'timeless' tone. I remember being excited, too, by his fierce rejection of Calvinism. That was a path I'd trodden too, and I was glad to find so clear-minded a supporter. He spoke very intimately to me there.

RC: In several poems — 'Toward the Imminent Days,' 'Walking to the Cattle Place,' 'The Buladelah-Taree Holiday Song Cycle,' and maybe elsewhere in shorter works like 'Physiognomy on the Savage Manning River' — you seem drawn to marrying various traditions in a kind of hymn to Australia, celebrating in an extended poem the Australian landscape and its animal and human inhabitants. Does the desire to write such a poem continually tug at you?

LM: It does a bit, because there's a lot of Australia that has not been assimilated into English yet. There are many plants in Australia, for example, which have only their Greco-Latin botanical names. All that work of hymning the plants and animals and the landscape of Europe has pretty well been done here, but in Australia it's just at the start, you know. They've been hymned in the Aboriginal languages, because for Aborigines Australia is a large network of songs; but in Australian English we're still working on that subject matter. I'm a bit against the received trends in this, because at the time when I came to the city and started trying to write critics were starting to say that Australia was now a Western urban culture and should produce sophisticated urban verse. Sophistication yes, but urban? no, not necessarily, I said to myself; particularly as most of what I knew came from the country - and it's a wild strange country in many ways. It's as much outside of the English language as inside, you know. I said in a poem recently that three quarters of our continent is set aside for mystic poetry. There's nothing much else you can do with it.

RC: In your poems, for instance in 'Aqualung Shinto', different cultural traditions come together: Japan meets the west. Italian, Indian, Gaelic, Vietnamese, Aranda, English - you like weaving these traditions together. Is that because of the nature of Australian society - and something you want to say about it - or are there other reasons?

LM: Yeah. That's part of it, I would say, that although the social impulse isn't all that strong, it *is* such a society. And my approach is more *de*scriptive than *pre*scriptive. It's potentially a new and interesting creole society. At the moment the fashion at home is all for separation of the various strands, a sort of hermetic walling off of various traditions from each other, and I'm rather against that. I think the real identity of Australia which potentially and even actually exists is creole.

RC: Do you want a creole language?

LM: I won't see it in my time, I don't think; except to the extent that it already exists. It's not a very pronounced phenomenon, unless you want to pun on the word 'pronounced.' But when you look at it closely there are hundreds and hundreds of *words* that are different, and differently used. I suppose you could say every word in the English language has a different meaning in Australia.

RC: Do you feel strongly about nationalism?

LM: Strongly ambivalent. As a religion-substitute, it's a monster that demands human sacrifice. But it's also something in us that demands some satisfaction. Human loyalty's a funny plant: it'll grow over just about anything, like morning-glory creeper. I've been involved, rather gingerly in fact, in recent efforts to get the last traces of colonialism out of our culture at home. But some others who want to rewrite Australia entirely in very doctrinaire terms rather frighten me.

RC: Your work uses elements from various religions. Would it interest you to be thought of as a Christian poet?

LM: It does a bit, yeah. I am a Christian, after all, and I do overtly write religious poems, sometimes straight-out Christian and sometimes more generally religious. I think all of my work is fundamentally religious, subsumed by a Christian consciousness, though. I would say that's where the geniality comes from, and a lot of the humour. And it's my sheet-anchor against nationalism.

RC: Would you like to say something about your religious development?

LM: I began moving out of our local Calvinism very early. In adolescence, I was nothing much, just part of that modern no-faith which feels free and easy till you look closely at it. When I did reflect on that it began to horrify me: its arbitrariness, its confusion, its potentials for tyranny - be young and sexy or be relegated, for instance, and the contemptuous bigotry with which just such sensibilities are enforced in the intellectual world! I was drawn to Catholicism as soon as I made contact with it, drawn as much as anything by the mysterious idea of the sacraments. By the congruence of that with my other new religion of poetry.

RC: You have a moving poem called 'Thinking about Aboriginal Land Rights, I Visit the Farm I will not Inherit,' and you use quite a lot of Aboriginal material in your work. Why?

LM: Because it's part of the landscape, it's part of the country, and it's the ancient history of Australia which continues. It's not dead. The names of places are often Aboriginal, the names of small places particularly. My own district, the place is called Bunyah. It lies between two other districts called Coolongolook and Buckenbeeapplebee. Bigger places tend to have English language names - Scottish or English or Irish mainly. Irish names, of course, aren't necessarily in English-language, are they? . . . That's one clue to it. There's a kind of what I call convergence in Australia which is not the same thing as assimilation, that old bad habit of expecting the Aborigines to become exactly like us - which would be a disaster. Convergence is more like a cross-fertilization between two peoples learning things from each other. It's what really *happens*, inwardly, in a culture

165

where there's contact of this sort. I recently wrote a book, for example, on the Australians seasons - it's a prose book - and said that the great Aboriginal season is the Rainbow Serpent, which is their way of expressing mythologically the return of water, which is the biggest climatic thing that happens in Australia. The core seasons at home are an alternation of drought and water; they're drought and flood, really. And in that process all of life in Australia is involved. All the native plants and animals know how to turn on their lives and start breeding as soon as water arrives. They're programmed for it, and I worked out what the mechanism of it was. It was discovered in the 1960s - a thing called petrichlor, which is kind of exudate that comes out of trees, floats in the air, gives the atmosphere a nice bluish haze in hot weather. In cool weather it falls down into the soil, undergoes various chemical changes there and then is washed into the streams. It tells all the living creatures in the streams to start breeding, and start their life-cycle. Out in the desert country it's very noticeable that within a day or two of rain there'll be flowers all over the countryside. Because they're coming up, and they're flowering, and getting their chance to reproduce while there's water. So these facts are just inescapable, and the Aborigines have identified them in mythological language. I mean, to ignore the Aborigines in Australia or try and write in some kind of hermetic bubble sealed off from them is to live somewhere else, is to live in the air, you know.

RC: In using Aboriginal material do you draw mainly on books like T.G.H. Strehlow's *Songs of Central Australia*, or do you get material from elsewhere?

LM: Oh, some of it's from talk, some of it's from working things out, some of it's from books, yes. Particularly for literary material, you know. The great Aboriginal poetry is their own oral poetry which has been passed on from song-man to song-man over thousands of years, really. We don't know how old some of those songs are. Some have been translated into English. I don't know any Aboriginal languages. I've read those translations. I put a lot of them into the *New Oxford Book of Australian Verse* because I thought they belonged there. I put some Aboriginal poetry written in English in there too, including the earliest Aboriginal poem I could find in English - from the 1920s by a chap called David Unaipon; a very interesting piece of work it is too. Strange, though.

RC: What's that about?

LM: It's really about the Fire Spirit, and addressing the phenomenon of fire, saying how strange it is that so great a spirit can be concealed in two little sticks which were rubbed together to produce it. The poem's written in a weird mixture of poetic prose and lines.I like it, so in it went, not by any means merely for historical reasons. It's in there because it earned its place.

RC: Would you like to say something about the importance of Gaeldom to you?

LM: Well, when my family came to Australia in the late 1840s (they came to the Manning River in New South Wales) they were Borderers themselves. My great-great-great-grandmother was born about seven miles inside Scotland. But most of the folk they met on the Manning were Highlanders, and so they got Highlandized a bit, particularly in religion. They became Free Presbyterians, which they had not been before.

RC: What were they before?

LM: Church of Scotland . . . And, em, Gaelic was still used around the place. It's now part of the 'loom of language' as I call it - the way that a language which has disappeared still leaves a kind of afterglow behind it. I mean, Gaelic ceased to be used in Church at home about the year 1900. Possibly because the Minister didn't want it, you know. But I remember scraps of Gaelic in conversation when I was small. Dad certainly remembers them a good deal more. We were never Gaelic-speaking, but the language was around. For the first three generations, I suppose, in Australia our family spoke Scots rather than English; my great-grandfather who was born on the ship going to Australia spoke Border Scots all his life, and his sons would speak it when they were deeply moved, in emotional moments and so on.

RC: A book like Don Watson's *Caledonia Australis* argues that the Gaels inflicted on the Aborigines treatment frighteningly like the treatment they had themselves received in the Clearances. Is there a danger of romanticizing the Gaelic background?

LM: There's a danger of romanticizing anything. I'm certainly not a romantic. I've been called a reactionary and it's because of one belief: that everything has a dark side to it, dark potentials in it. I'm not a Pelagian; I do believe in the doctrine of the Fall. It's natural enough that people who have sufferings in their past will inflict them on others. The convicts, for example, were frightful to the Aborigines. And yet ironically there's an Aboriginal poet in Australia called Kath Walker who is very black *and* a proud member of clan MacCallum, and she said to me once when we were drinking brandy together on an aeroplane that the Scots were always good to the Aborigines, it was the Germans and the English who were bad. And I guiltily thought, 'Oh dear, well, what you don't know won't hurt you!' (*laughter*)

RC: Perhaps we've talked about this a bit before, but I'd like to ask you directly how important is it to you to use a distinctively Australian vocabulary?

LM: I think I wouldn't be sort of chauvinistic and assertive about it, but it's natural to me because I'm from there. That's the vocabulary I know. It's my inheritance. It's not a calculating thing, saying 'This is my difference, I can play on this,' but I think really everyone should have the freedom to use the inheritance they've got and make of it what they can. So it's not a proselytizing effort. My only contention in that regard would be that English is polycentric, and that there are many languages inside English, there are many Englishes. And the ghosts of many other languages. You can't allow their educators to ignore that. As ours have stubbornly insisted on doing in regard to, say, the Celtic side of our past. Of course, this has been a matter of class, and ideology. As a Hanoverian colony, Australia had to be Anglicised, and its elites kept Empire-loyalist.

RC: Your use of language is stunning, as is your presentations of a physical landscape. You've been praised here recently as a great poet of cows. Is there a danger of being typecast?

LM: (*laughs*) No. No, I haven't come back to cows since, I don't think. I wrote a long thing about them in 1971; it's really an etymological sequence as much as anything else. It was sparked off by realizing from linguistic studies that the oldest root we can trace in Indo-European languages is 'cow'. That was from a branch of linguistics called glotto-chronology. I thought, yeah, there are two great cattle cultures in the world: the Indo-European one and the Bantu one. All sorts of haunting survivals and resemblances that I went on the track of over about fifteen poems. What was the first part of that question?

RC: Well the first part was about being praised as a great poet of cows, and I was thinking that your use of language was very stunning in terms of bringing out the physicality of landscape.

LM: Yeah. Well, language is more important to me than most things. It's a family inheritance to some extent, because the relation of mine whom I'm proudest of is Sir James Murray of the *OED*, who was my great-grandfather's first cousin. I've always been a word person. I was fascinated by words as a small child.

RC: Do you read dictionaries?

LM: Yeah, I read dictionaries. I wish to God I owned a copy of James's big *OED* too. I almost got one cheap once. Wish I'd bought it. But I used to recite words to myself for the pure, the sheer music of them when I was three or four years old. I never knew what it would lead to. It just seemed to be a pleasure in its own way. I remember, as a small child, misreading the motto on an OUP book and making a very mysterious, pregnant piece of para-Latin out of it: Dominus Illustio Illumea. It's a sort of mantra I still recite when I'm feeling low. I'm very conscious of the weight and echo of most words, I think - like Tennyson who said he knew the exact quality of every word in the language except 'scissors'. I know 'scissors'. I know the exact quality of scissors. (*laughter*).

RC: How, if at all, were you affected by the time you spent in Scotland?

LM: It was research. It was recovery. It was retrieval. It was confirmation. It was also finding out, as any descendant does, that a lot of what he knows is out of date: that the Scotland that our family belonged to and believed it belonged to no longer so thoroughly existed, though you could still find its traces. I found the kind of dry humour that I was brought up on (the leg-pulling and all that) had not disappeared from the Borders. But realising that many things were vestigial and historic in a country that had moved on, become a modern country. Discovering the physical accompaniments of that culture. Seeing the old towns and viewing the old hills and that sort of thing. Hills which can occasionally be hauntingly similar to home, except there's far more forest where I come from.

RC: Did you meet some Scottish poets when you were there?

LM: Oh yeah. I met Gaelic, and English-language poets. I met Garioch jist before he died. I wouldn't call *him* an English language poet. He was a Scots poet. I think he's a great one. In fact I like his Scots poetry better than MacDiarmid's.

RC: Why?

LM: Oh, just, eh . . . MacDiarmid is a . . . It would be hard to put my finger on exactly why, but I think MacDiarmid's is such a synthetic-sounding Scots in someways. Which obviously it is; he's patched it together from all sorts of sources. Garioch's always seemed to me more integral, and nearer to a sense of a *spoken* language, rather than a mandarin language. I liked them both, but Garioch's language convinced me more. I like an effect of the colloquial, even if it's only a final polish and a throughly artificial diction. It suggests a culture that's secure, with a shared, living identiy, whereas a very idosyncratic diction is apt to sound embattled and isolated, like something that knows it's losing and is desparate to regain, or to gain, power. I also like the sly fun Garioch was able to make of his own diction - though perhaps without MacDiarmid's re-establishing of Scots he wouldn't have been able to write in it! I liked them both, but Garioch's language convinced me more. I went to a reading in Glasgow and I got him to read one of my old favourites which he said he hadn't read for a long time (it was 'Embro to the Ploy'). I had a great night of it. Then only about three weeks later he died suddenly, and so I want to his funeral which is (and I knew it was) a great Scottish occasion. A funeral in our family was pretty well the biggest social event of your life. At Home I remember in 1971 I went to two funerals in a fortnight. One was the funeral of one of our greatest poets, a fellow called Ken Slessor, and he had about thirty-five people at the funeral. It was over in about five minutes, and it was pretty unsatisfying, and we all got miserably drunk after it. Two weeks later I was up at Amright at the funeral of my cousin Hughie Murray. He was known as Johnnie Cope; everybody had a nickname. He was not famous for anything much, old Hughie, except that he'd fallen off his horse once on an heirloom fiddle, and he also used to take lots of live lizards to school in his pockets. That was all he was famous for, but he drew eight hundred (*laughter*), and the party lasted for two days after it, you know. That's how to do it.

RC: That's because of the size of the Murray clan as compaared to the Slessor clan?

LM: (*laugh*) Oh yeah. Well, the Slessors, I don't think they're a clan. They're anciently German. Their name was Schlösser, and in fact Slessor's great-grandfather taught Beethoven music. The Schlössers changed their name in 1914, as many at home did. But he didn't seem to have many relatives. Just a few journalists, and some of his family, and a few poets came along. It was a very quiet little affair. It was said later with some grief that he should have had a state funeral, but somebody else pointed out later and probably rightly that Ken was a purely private man and he would have preferred a quiet funeral, so that's all he had. He just didn't come from a funeral culture, and I do. So I knew Scotland was a funeral culture, and I went to Garioch's.

RC: Have your careers outside poetry been important to your own writing?

LM: Yeah, you learn from everything you do. I've been a civil servant, I've been a translator, I've been a labourer of various sorts - you know those jobs that poets always put into their curriculum vitae to look romantic and identify with the working classes. Storeman-packer, you know, labourer, this kind of thing. Translating was I think the one where I learned the most. That was again a matter of vocabulary. A lot of the time I didn't know what I was translating even when I'd got what all the words were. I was doing scientific and technical translating from Western European languages. And picking up lots of *disjecta membra* of learning around the university. Because one of the ways I like to educate myself is to go to somebody who knows the subject and talk to them. And I had plenty of opportunity there just to go and talk to people; geographers and geologists, and so on. This all comes in handy later on. I think a poet should know everything. (*laughter*).

RC: Could you say something about your work as an editor - of *Poetry Australia*, and at Angus and Robertson, and of the *New Oxford Book of Australian Verse*? What gave or gives you the most satisfaction in these jobs?

LM: What I always look for is the same thing: it's the poetic experience, which tends to be under-emphasized these days in criticism, and I always suspect criticism that under-emphasizes it, because I think that then the door is open to special pleading. I look for a specific experience, which is really an effect of what I call whole-brain thinking. I mean where the quality of dream and the quality of rational thinking are married together in a text. A poem has to be truly dreamed as well as clearly thought, to be a poem. This fusion happens in prose, but it happens more acutely in poetry at its best. I look for that, and I can find it awfully fast if it's there. So I can whizz through a lot of material just using that one geiger-counter. At *Poetry Australia* I tried at once to identify and promote good new poets and to turn that magazine into being something of an important international one. To some extent it was already. But it was held down by a couple of things. It was held down by the large cost of distribution from Australia, and by the small amount of money that it could afford to pay contributors. And if you only pay A$10 a page, you'll get the good people but you won't keep them. You'll get Seamus Heaney once; you'll get Ted Hughes once, you know. But I was slowly raising its quality but then, oh, I guess, Grace Perry who founded the magazine thought that I'd had long enough at it. I think she may have thought I was estranging her magazine from her to some extent, and so she removed me and took the magazine back. Which is fair enough. It's her magazine and she founded it. I was running it for her largely because she was nearly bedridden by disease. I think I accomplished a bit of good there. In the case of Angus and Robertson's, they're the remains of a good old firm which was *the* main publishers of Australian literature from the 1890s onwards, till the 1960s. Then it was bought up by a trucking millionaire who asset-stripped it, sold all its properties in the city and so on, left just about only the imprint and, luckily, the firm's library - which is a major resource. It lost its direction for a while. It became sort of a publisher of ephemera: books like *Origami for the Over-Forties* , in Tom Kenneally's phrase. Tended to have the fatal Australian liking for dim-witted coffee table books. Happily, it has now come up as the flagship of Australian poetry again. It had its bows under a heavy green wave of confusion for a while, but it's sailing again. That's important because it's our only remaining major publisher that's not British-owned. It still doesn't distribute well overseas, so poets who want to reach an international market eventually have to be published with a firm overseas by some arrangement or other. I'm publishing with Persea in New York and Carcanet here. The pity of it is that our publishers just have never managed to overcome their slight fear of the metropolitan market, or their inability to handle it. The Australian branch offices of big British houses, of course, are rarely allowed to feed anything back into the UK. They're often just doing a bit of local publishing for token-goodwill reasons, while pouring in their British titles.

RC: So your books are likely to be more readily available in the shops here and in North America at last?

LM: Yes. At last! Although Persea's smallish it's regarded as a good house. I hope they'll become more readily available here too. It's really just a simple matter, nothing to do with overvaulting ambition or anything like that; it's just a matter of trying to reach the *rest* of the English language market. You don't want to be forever in that late-colonial situation of having books pour into Australia all the time, and nothing get out.

RC: Do you read a lot of poetry from abroad (outside Australia)?

LM: Oh yeah. Oh yeah. Australian poets often are well-informed, because the metropolitan stuff pours in, but it's rare for an Australian poet to be read much outside. Many deserve to be. Slessor, for example, is a major poet of the twentieth century who is not heard of. To some degree Frank Webb is known because Sir Herbert Read put him on a level with Eliot and Pound. I wouldn't have, but he's a good poet. Judith Wright is slightly known in America. Alec Hope is slightly known outside - and that's about the list. You know, there are thirty more poets who deserve to be read beyond our shores, not just in the dual metropole either, but in the whole English-language world.

RC: Your sense of humour plays an important part in your poetry. Would you like to see its role increasing?

LM: (*laughter*) I don't think it has to. I think I've got the mixture about right. It's part of my ideology of making poetry non-mandarin without comprising its quality, reaching a wider audience including people who don't think they like poetry. The terrible crime of modernism has been to isolate poetry from a wide readership. All those enormous readerships of the nineteenth century, like the hundred thousand readers for a new book by Tennyson, disappeared with modernism and I'm trying to recover that ground. I'm interested in retrievals of various sorts; I tried once with a verse novel to recapture for poetry the ground we had lost to the prose novel, and to the film later on. So humour is I suppose, to some extent, a ploy and a technique for reassuring people that what they're reading is not going to snub them. Because you must not compromise the quality of the work on some kind of condescending view that people are stupid and can't understand you. I assume that all my readers are at least as bright as I am (which wouldn't be hard) and that we can go into this as if it were a sort of dialogue. So the humour, as well as having its own pleasures and being the only way to say some things, is a technique for normalizing poetry as reading material.

RC: What are you working on just now?

LM: Well, I'm a bit over half way through the next book of verse, which I haven't got a title for yet, but its finding its way as it goes, you know.

RC: Do you feel anything valuable for you has come out of your recent reading tour of Canada, the States and this country?

LM: I met a lot of good people (*laughter*). You know why I don't write about other places much? Because I think it's too easy to write tourist verse. If you don't profoundly know another culture your poetry that you write in any given other locales will be merely quaint. I've ventured as far as to write a poem about Edinburgh, or really about a snowfall in Edinburgh, on the twenty-fourth of April 1981. But even that's related to an Australian thing, because that's the day before our festival of Anzac Day, which is the festival in memory of the dead of all wars really. I thought 'Ah! I'm going to see snow on Anzac Day!' but it didn't last. But I avoid the danger of tourist verse. I think there are ways of being international and of being universal, global if you like. But they're not that way, through consumerist dropping of heavy place names. That's Peter Stuyvesant stuff, or very often is.

RC: Do you feel that you're in search always of Australian history or histories?

LM: I'm in search of some understanding of human nature and behaviour, really, and commemorating things. Commemorating the world that's human and celebrating it, trying to understand reality and picturing it, and it's not just Australia by any means. Things may have an Australian address and be of universal significance, of universal applicability. We assume this without doubt when the verse comes from, say, America or England.

RC: Could you talk a little, please, about the background to your new poem, '1980 in a Street of Federation Houses'?

LM: Well, that's really a poem about relativities of time and of style. I mean the poem's written in 1985, already five years on from the scene that it's setting. A Federation house is a particular style of house in Australia that flourished around the time of Federation, 1900. It's rather a handsome brick house with lots of bow windows and iron lacework and broad pillard verandahs with tiled floors. It's quite a nice, distinctive style, particularly a Sydney style. There are not that many streets consisting entirely of these, but there are a few. And this man is standing there in a kind of dumb misery of divorce, his life's unplugged. And particularly it's about the relatives that he's already been through, these various periods that he's already been through. He's just caught up in this terrible confusion of what is contemporary, and what is already keepsakes. This is part of the dark side of relativity. The weapon we have used so effectively against religion works effectively against our lives too. It relativizes us. We become obsolete. Every human these days who lives by the terrible modern ideology of interest, or being interesting or else relegated, is threatened at all times by our latest spiritual invention, obsolescence. And at the end of it there is only the new concept, which most people haven't believed until recently, of everlasting death, that faith which the universities proselytize, especially at home. Before you're dead you'll be out of date. So will everything you love.

RC: You use the image in the poem of playing with a tuner on a radio, and moving across history that way, and moving from an account of one time to an account of another, and mixing them up. Are you particularly interested in the way that's possible in the English language because of the way the English language is spread across the world?

LM: The environments it's spoken in? No, I hadn't thought of that connection, or not in writing that poem, but you're right, it certainly is. No, that just came to me as I was writing it - the idea of the years being like the numbers along a radio tuner, stations which you can be tuned into. We do that a lot these days because we don't any longer know in Western culture where the hell we're going. So it becomes almost a consumer thing; you know, you pick your nostalgias with some finesse. It's almost as if you had a kind of tuner for picking the period that you're going to relate to today, you know - 'What'll I be today? I'll be Fifties today.' (*laughter*). It's a sign of profound spiritual drift, I think, of going nowhere. I haven't got much hope for Western culture as it stands. But I haven't got much hope for any other that's offering itself at the moment. We shall see.

RC: Do you see yourself as a poet with a mission?

LM: No, only to decentralize the English language. Which is happening. It's not particularly a thing that I'm leading; it's happening anyway. And in some ways to oppose the mandarin idea of culture. I think that somehow we can't go on having aristocratic cultures, we have to break that cruel fallacy of levels - and yet we *must* not sacrifice the principle of quality. The usual mistake that's made when egalitarianism is brought anywhere near art is of condescension. It's often passionately ignored or denied, but it *is* condescension. We still use the words like 'vulgar'. We must not compromise art, but somehow shift it. I try to show that art can be good and at the same time fraternal, rather than elitist, in spirit. Not just a luxury for the nomenklatura, the intelligentzia or whatever Russian word we're using - those *are* the words to describe the new forms aristocracy is taking in the modern world, after all. My religion demands a different, fraternal ideal from me. And so does my past, all those neglected and rather despised rural people I want to be a credit to.

RC: Thank you.

LM: Thank you.

SEAN O'BRIEN

INTERVIEWED BY R. J. C. WATT

SEAN O'BRIEN was born in London in 1952 and grew up in Hull. He read English at Cambridge. After teaching for several years in a comprehensive school in Crowborough, East Sussex, he spent 1989-91 as Fellow in Creative Writing at the University of Dundee. He now lives in Newcastle on Tyne. A selection of his work was included in the anthology *A Rumoured City: New Poets from Hull*, edited by Douglas Dunn (Bloodaxe, 1982). His first collection, *The Indoor Park* (Bloodaxe, 1983) won the Somerset Maugham Award in 1984. A second collection, *The Frighteners* (Bloodaxe) appeared in 1987. In 1988 he received a Cholmondeley Award. A pamphlet collection, *Boundary Beach*, was published by *The Honest Ulsterman* in 1989. His latest book of poems, *HMS Glasshouse*, a Poetry Book Society Recommendation, was published by Oxford University Press in November 1991. He writes about poetry for a variety of papers and magazines, including *The Sunday Times, The Times Literary Supplement, London Magazine, Poetry Review, The Honest Ulsterman* and *Bete Noire*, as well as giving readings in the UK and overseas and teaching creative writing. His current ambition is to go to the USA and get paid for it. This interview was recorded in Dundee in July 1991.

RJCW: When is the new book, *HMS Glasshouse*, coming out?

SO'B: It will be out in November this year, '91.

RJCW: And do I take it that as well as a lot of new poems it reprints all the poems from *Boundary Beach?*

SO'B: Yes.

RJCW: So in what ways would you say that *HMS Glasshouse* represents a new departure?

SO'B: I see quite a lot of continuity with its predecessor, *The Frighteners*. For example, it is concerned with history and politics, though it addresses them more expansively. At the same time another strain has re-emerged, something to be found in the first book, *The Indoor Park*, a more meditative way of working.

RJCW: You say that it continues the political and the historical interests in your earlier work, and yet it struck me that there is not an obviously, so to speak nakedly, political poem in *HMS Glasshouse* in quite the way that there is in some of your earlier books. I am thinking of a poem like 'Song of the South' or 'Summertime' or 'London Road' from *The Frighteners* which are about the miners' strike, or about the Southern English Tory hypocrisies and complacencies of the 1980s. Are the 1980s a thing of the past in your work?

SO'B: No, but the extent to which you can write directly political ballads in the light of immediate events or political fashions and tendencies may prove to be quite limited. It would not have been wise to continue in that very up-front vein and to do only that, because there are areas of imaginative experience of which that kind of writing naturally doesn't take account. You can write a very bald and furious political poem, but you are also likely to want to write other more secretive kinds of poem at the same time where, I suppose, the concerns are the same but the methods involve a slower release. I don't hold them to be different in kind but different in emphasis, incidentally.

RJCW: And in formal or stylistic terms do you think there is anything that you are trying to develop that is new in *HMS Glasshouse*?

SO'B: It's not really up to me to say, but I think in some ways the new book is clearer about its own methods and in some ways more confident of its ground. I hope, for example, that it is not clotted as some of the stuff in the first book may have been, and I hope that a more lyrical strain is more to the fore as well.

RJCW: Yes, it seems you almost have two distinct manners now: the caustically witty poems are often associated with formal techniques: with rhyme, with regular metres and tight little stanzas, aren't they? And the more free-wheeling, imaginative poems, the ones you just called secretive, tend to be in much looser forms. Why do you reach for a particular form? Are you aware of making that kind of distinction?

SO'B: I resist drawing the distinction you point to. But a ballad, for example on a political subject, has an obvious rhythmic propulsion. It invites clarity and speed of movement over the ground. Satire invites a terse form, perhaps. Other poems seem more immersed in the backs of their own minds and have to find their own way out. In the end both varieties are just as formal and highly-wrought.

RJCW: What else would you add by way of preface to *HMS Glasshouse* or by way of saying how it matters to you?

SO'B: Well, I hope it contains the most interesting work I have done to date. I also think you could describe it as a kind of 'condition of England' book, not in any very programmatic fashion but simply because a lot of the poems are concerned with post-war history, not from a public point of view but from the point of view of a private occupancy of history, the way in which events make themselves felt in the private life. I think that is part of what the book's about.

RJCW: Right, but of course one would immediately have to qualify the phrase 'condition of England' because quite a lot of them are about the condition of Scotland, aren't they? What has the Scottish experience meant for the poetry in that book?

SO'B: I've been fascinated by Dundee. It bears strong resemblances to Hull, my own home town. Both are maritime cities fallen on hard times. Both are strongly working class. At the same time Dundee is completely foreign. It's a bit like waking up in a Hitchcock movie and finding everyone's got different names. There's also a sense of exposure about Dundee which I find hard to describe and will keep trying to get hold of. Architecture, geography, all that stone.

RJCW: Yes, one recalls that quite a number of your predecessors in the Creative Writing Fellowship at the University of Dundee have also written Dundee poems, obviously Anne Stevenson, and Val Warner, and Douglas Dunn; and yet your Dundee poems are not like theirs. I mean Douglas Dunn might be the person you would think of as most likely to draw the same kind of imaginative stimulus from a city if you think back to *Terry Street*, but Douglas's Dundee poems are not like that and yours are, aren't they?

SO'B: Well, I think Dunn's work has become, in certain ways, more pastoral of recent years, partly because he doesn't actually live in the city, but in a very small town nearby. And there has always been a strong pastoral leaning in his work anyway, because of his background. But I'm basically urban. I like the countryside but the city is what preoccupies me, and the idea of the city as a place — without putting it melodramatically — a place of simultaneously extreme pleasures and extreme terrors and extreme miseries interests me more and more.

RJCW: All right, that is what's different between you and Dunn. What about the common ground? After all, you have been called one of the 'sons of Dunn', and I guess from reading your work that you would not utterly reject that description.

SO'B: One of the many things I admire in Dunn's work is his ability to relate the personal and the political, explicitly and implicitly, and to work from the individual life or imagined lives to suggest the history through which people are travelling and by which to some extent they are directed. There is also the fact — no disrespect to Tony Harrison here — that for many readers Dunn invented the working class as a subject for poetry in the late sixties and early seventies, in the *Terry Street* poems and then in *The Happier Life*, which expands and in some ways mythologizes similar material. It seems to me he was trying to depict or dramatise areas of experience which were not then the staple of poetry but which are essential to it. One of my favourite poems is 'The River Through the City' from *The Happier Life*, an exemplary poem in relating place to the concealed larger context. He's also combined realism with an interest in symbolism, both from the French and from James Wright and Robert Bly. That interests me: I think one of the most exciting possibilities for poetry is using the ground-bass of realism but inviting more strangely imagined things in as well. I think that's inexhaustible.

RJCW: Have you seen more of Dunn personally in the last two years than you did at earlier periods?

SO'B: We see each other quite often. There was a period from the mid-seventies to the early eighties when I saw him very frequently because we lived down the street from each other, and he operated as an entirely voluntary, and infinitely patient, adviser to myself and at least half a dozen other poets who were working in the city or had recently worked in the city. And we spent many afternoons with him patiently reading my work and telling me what was wrong with it.

RJCW: By the city, of course, you mean Hull.

SO'B: Yes.

RJCW: Who were those other poets? Do you see them as people who are doing the same things as you, or not?

SO'B: There were basically two lots. There was a slightly earlier lot which includes Tony Flynn, who publishes with Bloodaxe, and also Ian Gregson, who hasn't yet published a book but is quite well known as an academic critic, and T F Griffin as well. And then there was a slightly later lot including myself and another Hull poet, Peter Didsbury, whom I had known for a long time by then anyway. We had been friends for years and regularly exchanged work. And slightly later arriving, another poet, Douglas Houston, who was a friend of Dunn's when they were students. So I have had a lot to do with them. Our work is markedly different from each other's, though I think there are mutual interests in common.

RJCW: Have you just given me a definition of the School of Dunn?

SO'B: Well, it's occasionally been suggested in recent years almost that there is a kind of Hull poetry or that there are Hull poets. I don't agree, because if you look at the work of the people who happen to be living there at the time — and also people that have lived there since — they are all very different from each other. There isn't a strong stylistic consistency among them. I mean, Didsbury is a very post-modernist kind of poet with a strongly experimental wing in his brain. In comparison with him I am probably a more realist poet, though I don't want to be confined by that. Houston is different again. We were all there at the same time, all interested in doing it and Dunn encouraged all of us in various ways; so there wasn't a conformity or a house style attached to it really. We share a concern for detail. Avoiding moral generalities and trying to deal in detailed particulars is probably common to all of us. What we used to call 'actual circumstances' — the idea of poetry as dramatic — was important, too.

RJCW: Yes, in your own work that concern for detail is presumably part of what you mean when you say you think of yourself as a realist. But the reader of your poetry will obviously react by saying 'yes, there is a great deal of very shrewdly observed social detail, geographical detail, physical detail, but there is also the strikingly imaginative, at times exuberantly or even wildly imaginative element in your work'. Is that right?

SO'B: I hope so, yes.

RJCW: How do you see those two co-existing?

SO'B: I don't see them in any kind of competition, but when things get weird, get strange, or the poem goes into overdrive, that seems to me to be the earned surplus of all that realism. It's something more peculiar or, in literal terms, exaggerated or unreasonable. It also has to do with the desire to discern a shape in things, a sort of imaginative energy that seeks out shape.

RJCW: So you don't find yourself consciously having to manipulate the balance between realism and fantasy, or realism and imagination?

SO'B: No, no, the two are aspects of each other.

RJCW: Let's move on to another obvious connection or influence, and again with a Hull connection, Larkin. How would you now sum up that influence on your work?

SO'B: The thing that has always impressed me about Larkin is that at the same time as he seemed to have very strong confidence of being disappointed at all points of the compass, that sense had no dispiriting effect on his imagination, as far as I can see — not until pretty late on. His imagination tends to be rich, ample, specific, suggestive. You know — all the praise words that I would want to apply to the poems I like. He imagines lives in detail. His best poems don't deal in glum moral generalities about the low horizon of our expectations. If they end up reaching those conclusions they do so in a highly imagined way. And I think Larkin's detractors, who appear to have gone into the woodwork for the time being, have tended to forget that. They object to the outlook, and because they don't like the outlook they miss all the virtues of the imagination and the technique.

RJCW: Right. What you say reminds me of Orwell's phrase about Eliot, that the later poems exhibit a 'melancholy faith' and the earlier ones a 'glowing despair'. 'Glowing despair' is something you could almost apply to Larkin in that connection isn't it?

SO'B: Yes. There are, of course, celebratory poems, 'For Sidney Bechet' being a fine example, and there are those poems which seem to play down the left wing of Larkin's imagination. 'Water', 'High Windows'. All the assurances that expectation, training, and habit provide, that things are as bad as they look, are none the less sometimes answered by a purely voluntary imagination at work.

RJCW: Mm, left wing with a very small 'l' and 'w'.

SO'B: Yes, what Americans would call 'left field'.

RJCW: How do you deal with that? I mean Dunn's political outlook is, I imagine, not so very different from your own, but Larkin's is a million miles away, isn't it?

SO'B: I think it was only comparatively late in Larkin's career that a kind of recrudscent Conservatism really made itself apparent in his writing and before that all those options were open. He didn't immediately develop that tendency to confuse dyspepsia with philosophy which characterises his friend Kingsley Amis, and he didn't begin to view unreasonableness or failures of generosity as in some way commonsensical, until comparatively late. I could be wrong about that. It's a shame he wrote 'Homage to a Government', because it's simple-minded.

RJCW: Yes, it does stick out like a sore thumb — on one occasion when he gave a reading and answered some of our questions he said 'This is my one political poem' as if for him too it was at least an oddity if not a turning point.

SO'B: Well, we can see how someone of a deeply pessimistic disposition generally speaking, can take fairly sternly Conservative views as a kind of bulwark onto which to hold while all around is crumbling. Recognition of man's inherent pettiness and evil is something that seems to be common to right-wing thought. Recognition that we're all going to die seems to lead to people thinking, well fair enough, therefore the poor should continue to be poor. It's easy to see how it comes about.

RJCW: We've talked about Larkin and Dunn. What about Auden? There are phrases which could actually be by Auden in your poems, aren't there? For example, these lines: . . . 'waiting for muffled reports / From a neighbouring district, / But if they should come / We'll do nothing.' Now that really could be the early Auden, it seems to me. It's not presumably just the early Auden which is the influence on you, or is it?

SO'B: I was thinking that poem you quote, 'The Era', is more mittel-European than I find Auden to be, but fair enough. I began to enjoy Auden in the late sixties for the same reason people have always enjoyed him — the excitement, the sense of the personal and the larger political context being fused and not hived off from each other, the one being expressive of the other and so on. The obsession I've already referred to. The fact that he could combine the local and particular with the big picture. The symptomatizing tendency. I enjoy the fact that he has access to anywhere he wants to go — the near, the remote, the important, the trivial, the real, the imaginary, the prophetic, the vulgar, the satirical, the elevated. I don't find there's another twentieth century poet writing in English who covers the range with his authority. I was brought up, of course, to feel that this was somehow evidence that he wasn't properly serious. In the aftermath of Leavis, whose teachings were still very influential when I was at school and university, somehow Auden wasn't quite serious in comparison with Eliot. Well, he probably wasn't serious with quite such strangulated finality, but he did put himself about a bit more than Eliot tended to.

RJCW: What's the downside of influence, or as Harold Bloom would put it, 'the anxiety of influence'? Is that something that figures in your mind at all? I mean the supposed need to kill the poetic father, to reject that aspect of influence which might stifle your own work?

SO'B: I don't know that Auden is long enough ago to be the strong father. I had the idea that there has to be an absent generation which has no effect. Auden was still an active and influential writer until the seventies. He's not a remote figure. Much more influential on people having it in mind to write when I was a teenager would have been Eliot. His influence has receded more than somewhat. There was the sense then — and again I have the feeling it was somewhat propagated when I was a student — that here was somebody who was so serious and had gone so close to the heart of things that there was no point in anyone actually doing anything after that. All that was going on was a kind of literary mopping-up operation on a more or less frivolous basis. So Eliot might fit Bloom's model better than Auden, only people haven't so much killed him as abandoned him. Auden's influence is endemic in English poetry. I don't know about Scots poets. You can see touches of it in Douglas Dunn now and again, but in English poetry his influence is endemic: John Fuller being a distinguished poet who is markedly Audenesque and quite overtly and unashamedly so. It has become a lingua franca. Peter Porter, another very distinguished poet, is markedly Audenesque. James Fenton would be inconceivable without W H Auden. But I don't think any of those poets is in any way disabled or disqualified from being themselves by the acknowledged presence of that large language. Again, a younger poet like Glyn Maxwell is also clearly Auden-influenced. In a much more recondite way, so is the Irish poet Paul Muldoon, it seems to me. And so at various stages is the St. Lucian poet Derek Walcott; so is Joseph Brodsky.

RJCW: Let's talk about the Irish or American poets or indeed non-English writers that have meant something to you.

SO'B: The emergence of what's now the middle generation of poets from the North was very important. There's nothing very secret about any of this, is there? I detect occasional resentment over here. I remember at Cambridge I wanted to do my Part Two long essay on Heaney. This

177

would be 1974, when his first two books were out. I got a letter back from the faculty office saying they didn't consider 'Seamus O'Heaney' a suitable topic and why didn't I do R. S. Thomas, 'who, though Welsh, is also a Celt'. Times change, don't they? The one I admire most is Mahon. His economy and musicality. More recently I've admired Carson, and from the South Sweeney and Durcan impress me. As for American poets, I've read and enjoyed a lot without really feeling influenced, except perhaps by Stevens. Unlike a lot of my contemporaries I'm not all that interested in Lowell and Berryman.

RJCW: What about poetry in translation?

SO'B: Again, my generation were lucky because there was Penguin Modern European Poetry in translation, that series. 'Modern' had a very broad definition to it, so at one end of it was Rilke, and there was also stuff that was being written, as it were, the previous week. The one I really admired greatly was Zbigniew Herbert, and I continue to be a great admirer.

RJCW: In what particular respect?

SO'B: Well, he's managed to find a way of making tone of voice stand for detail. I think that's it, where you've got the kind of economy where a vocal gesture brings into play history or an attitude to politics or the weight that an event exerts on hiim.

RJCW: Can we now turn to your own first collection, *The Indoor Park?* I take it the indoor park is a real place in Hull?

SO'B: Well, it is and it isn't. The real location of *The Indoor Park* is the Plant House in Pearson Park in Hull. But it's also that the book is held metaphorically to be the indoor park where the relations of outside and inside are reversed or effaced. I can't quite describe why, but I've always been intrigued by the idea of roofing over the outside, and taking the roof off the inside, as it were.

RJCW: Certainly for the reader a sense of enclosure is very much there. What does that mean, that idea of closing something in like that? Has it got anything to do with the constant sense of limits or boundaries which is in your other books as well?

SO'B: It may well have. The poems in *The Indoor Park* were written between about 1977 and the beginning of 1982 or the end of 1981. The park in question is a Victorian city park attached to a suburb, and therefore, as I guess parks traditionally are, a model of nature, nature used to resemble itself, manipulated to resemble itself. And you can see analogies between that and all kinds of artistic activities. And the idea that one location becomes a model for all others, becomes exemplary for all of us, has applications for all kinds of art as well. This idea is something I don't altogether understand, as if you had a garden indoors. Plant houses, for example, palm houses, conservatories, seem to me to be quite uncanny, because they're there and yet they're not there in some important way. The idea of limitations and obstructions seems to be quite frequently present in the book. A sense of dissatisfaction, imprisonment and so on, which I can't really account for. It just seems thematically to recur, a sense of limits, either in view of the possibilities of experience or limits on political change, ideas of foreclosure.

RJCW: Of course, it's not just parks but beaches and seaside towns and ports which are, I suppose, the predominant settings of a lot of your most distinctive poems; and they're partly closely observed realities but they're also clearly symbolic in some way, aren't they? Why do you choose that particular kind of location again and again?

SO'B: Because they're gateways, I suppose, places where theoretically things can change, where one thing is ended and another is begun. Or alternatively, where the population spend their time watching other people's business ending and begun afresh. Departure, return, transformation, and also immobility — all those are very strongly suggested to me by maritime environments, maritime cities, ports, rivers, water of all kinds.

RJCW: Another characteristic O'Brien landscape would be 'the dead harbour, the pub and the station buffet', wouldn't it? That's from *The Indoor Park*. Where there's a strong sense of finite and circumscribed lives, people stuck there but also with the potential for not being stuck there. After all, they're in a place of transit, so they could go, but they don't actually go, do they, very often?

SO'B: That's true, but at the same time, there may be liberty in being accurate. The way out may involve seeing clearly what you're in.

RJCW: But there is also a historical or ideological dimension to that sense of people fixed, isn't there? You write about people 'condemned to live this script / Until the gestures make you retch', people as the victims of history, or weighed down by history. Where did that sense of history begin for you?

SO'B: The poem you refer to there is one called 'Walking'. It was written a long time ago. It's thirteen or fourteen years old, and it's probably rather too ready to write everything off. But you could say it had something to do with a certain sense of social immobility, unchangingness. Hull is one of those places where we were still in the 1950s until quite recently. And it was quite parochial, you know, there was a sense of constriction and want, not purely economic, but in terms of the imaginative horizon. I think a lot of people may have felt rather constrained in that respect. It's also the idea of finding yourself repeating the lives that you've been studying critically, the lives of previous generations, and the same dissatisfactions recur.

RJCW: I can't remember who used the phrase 'panoramic poetry' to describe your work, but is that a description you'd accept?

SO'B: Well, latterly it may be accurate in some cases. There are poems that try to get a whole landscape — a social, political, geographical, imaginative landscape — and see it intimately and as a whole. Now and again it seems to maybe come off.

RJCW: Certainly! Can we move on to *The Frighteners*? The first section of that book is called 'In a Military Archive', and you seem there to be using images of war as a connection with the present, a map of the present. Would you agree with that? What are those images of the military archive doing in the first part of the book?

SO'B: 'In a Military Archive' itself, which was the title given to the first section as well as to the first poem, was written over a period of about two years, even though the poem's only about eighteen lines long, I think. It was actually written and then set aside and completely reorganised, and it arose from looking at a picture by a guy called Mike Murfin, who does heroic pictures of vernacular subjects, if you know what I mean. It was a painting of three young men standing outside a boathouse holding oars. And Murfin told me the story that this derived from memories of members of his family who went to the war in the First World War, two or three generations prior to him, and died there. That doesn't figure in the poem at all. I couldn't make the oarsmen poem work, but then I got the idea of transferring it to somewhere like the Imperial War Museum. At the time I was reading a great deal about the Great War. Reading Fussell's book and Dennis Winter's *Death's Men* and John Keegan's *The Face of Battle* and all that kind of material, and I became interested in the fact that even though the officer class was allegedly virtually wiped out in the First World War, it was still them who ended up writing the history. Top-down history.

But the war imagery may have something to do with the South too. Although I'd been in the South before — I suppose Cambridge qualifies as being in the South — I'd never actually lived south of the river, and the south-east of England came as a major shock to me because it was a completely different country to the one I had grown up in, with an apparently completely different set of operating assumptions, some of which I found offensive in the extreme. Like the advanced state of materialism and various kinds of encouraged vulgarity and cynicism and ruthlessness,

179

which I suppose could be found anywhere, but seemed to be richly concentrated thereabouts. And this definitely had a politicizing effect on me. This coincides with Thatcherism really coming into effect in the early eighties when not only had she been elected but now was actually laying boldly about her in all directions.Poems like 'Song of the South' were written about that time. The idea that somehow society was divided on a class basis and regionally and economically and in other ways, and that there was a kind of unspoken, undeclared war going on, I suppose. It still holds true, I guess. And this was exacerbated when an actual war broke out, which was the miners' strike, which people don't seem to talk about any more but was the most significant domestic political event in this country since the second war, I think, because it signified the lengths to which authority was prepared to go in order to disempower the working class. I know some people would hold that to be an extreme account of it, but I think that was what was going on. So all those things I suppose, generate imagery of warfare. Imagery of secrecy, imagery of covertness, imagery of trespass, imagery of forbidden territory, imagery of the peremptory and so on, are all to be found in it.

RJCW: Right. I personally think that's one of the strengths and successes of the book, the way that you can use images from wars of the past, or the relics of war, or war's impact on the lives of children, and make them a metaphor for your present concerns, the way that the inherited weight of the past alienates people from the present. But then, moving on, there's the second section of the book which is about Ryan. Now of course Ryan first made his appearance in *The Indoor Park*, but it's the second section of *The Frighteners* which belongs to Ryan, a vaguely threatening, certainly mysterious figure. Does he have something in common with the poet, or with you yourself? Ryan was 'born expecting something quite different', and that's a very strong sense elsewhere in your work; and again Ryan is 'a liar who means what he says'. That could almost be Plato's idea of the poet, couldn't it?

SO'B: Yes. I don't know that I'd Plato in mind at the time, but in fact I think I was taking Plato at his word. Plato's estimate of poets is that they are active rather than accidental liars, for example. If that was what Plato meant, then yes, that's what Ryan's all about. Obviously a persona like that has got to start from somewhere, he doesn't spring fully formed onto the page, but he is heavily fictionalised, because he doesn't actually have a life. All he has is a series of cameo appearances in contemporary history.

RJCW: Quite, but what's his importance to you as a device, leaving his origins out of it?

SO'B: He might be a kind of unifying agent, a way of making sense of apparently disparate experiences. There's the poem 'Ryan at Home' which is — I don't really know how to describe that poem. Some people find it pretty revolting, but it's the dark crossroads where the mind and cities meet, I suppose. It's him trying actually to identify the nature of the society that he's seeing in front of him, and because he doesn't have any manners he tries to go straight for the meat and to view it as a totalitarian condition both outwardly and inwardly.

RJCW: So he's the man from Mars with no preconceptions, who is capable of registering the full astonishment of what we take for granted?

SO'B: Well, he's not innocent, you see, though it's not so much he has preconceptions, rather that he has more than his share of disbelief and contempt. Everything he touches turns to scepticism.

RJCW: Is that characteristic of a period, or of your personality, or where does that scepticism come from? Is it also part of your response to the South?

SO'B: It certainly has something to do with that. You could also see Ryan as the kind of surplus of social and economic relations — everything that's left out of mechanistic accounts, that's not answered for and not accommodated.

RJCW: The bloody-minded human bit?

SO'B: Yes: The unaccommodated part of a personality which hypostatizes itself — makes itself the totality. This is a rather rhetorical way of putting it, but he's also a solipsist who keeps finding that despite all his efforts, external events do intervene and confirm his suspicions. I've occasionally thought since of writing a Ryan poem but the impulse is no longer there.

RJCW: Why not?

SO'B: Well, I think he went through his roster of possible outings. You know, he was born, he lived, he described where he lived. He thought about death. He went to the pub. He attempted to leave, then he threatened to come back. I don't know what else he could do.

RJCW: What about the third section of *The Frighteners*, 'Kingdom of Kiev'? That strikes me as the place where you allow a slightly ampler imaginative activity to come to the fore. Is that how you see it?

SO'B: Yes, I think there's more obvious fun to be had out of some of the poems in the third section because some of them are actually about pleasure.

RJCW: You could have fooled me! But seriously, some of them are also more opaque, aren't they? Or maybe I just don't know enough of the references.

SO'B: Well, 'Kingdom of Kiev, Rios das Muertes', the poem itself, is really what it purports to be, an elegiac celebration of general knowledge and the sense of possibility that the possession of useless information could give you when you were a kid, the sense of the scope of the world.

RJCW: That immediately suggests several of the funniest poems in the new book which are about useless information too, aren't they? Particularly as preserved in libraries, which you would burn down if you get the chance! Can you shed any light on this preoccupation with useless information and your wish to possess it and also to destroy it by burning it down? There are three library poems in the new book, aren't there, or is it two?

SO'B: Three. Well, libraries characteristically make me very uneasy. Despite the fact that obviously my life is largely occupied with books one way or another, the place where you get them, the library, causes me great unease. There is a tendency quite frequently in me to think of the next door as leading into another zone where things cease to be metaphors and become actual. There's a poem called 'Hatred of Libraries' which proposes an infinite recession of further and further galleries and sets of stacks, at the imagined centre of which is to be found *the* definition; which is a joke, because we in the poem, as it happens, are not the ones who are going to get there, and even if we did what we would find would be the rather dispiriting instruction that you can't smoke. The subtext of the poem is also that if you are a smoker, libraries can be a bit of a torment anyway. I know it's my fault, but hours in a library, in the Victorian sense, are not often possible to me. Half hours in the library perhaps.

RJCW: And where does the fascination with useless information fit in?

SO'B: When I was a kid, my Dad used to buy me lots of comics, and they were the kind that had writing in them rather than just pictures, like *The Wizard*, which was largely written stories, and they were full of very suggestive bits of information, things which don't lead anywhere, except further into themselves. Such as: the airline co-pilot had been to the dentist before the flight set off and the dentist had accidentally left a bubble of air in one of his teeth. This was before the cabins were fully pressurised, I guess. So the air inside his tooth expanded, and his tooth exploded in his head — which I just thought was a tremendous story. The fact that a goalkeeper in Norway hadn't let a penalty in for three years I thought was tremendous.

181

RJCW: What was it about the fifties? Why did we grow up that way?

SO'B: The decade in which I was a child seems to me to have been very much inclined to retrospect. Everything took its definition from the war. People were trying to understand what it meant and where they'd ended up. Labour's eventual defeat and so on. I was dimly aware of the internal strife in the Labour Party, of which my father was a member, in which he was passionately involved. You know the child's sense of time: last year is infinitely remote. I used to look in his suitcase, which was full of what seemed ancient pamphlets — 'Forward with Labour', that kind of thing. All this seems important, but I don't understand it yet.

RJCW: Can we continue with your early life? Despite your name you are in fact English rather than Irish? Where were you born?

SO'B: I was born in London.

RJCW: Did you spend your childhood there?

SO'B: No, when I was a few months old my parents moved to Hull where my mother's family lived and that's where I grew up. I spent my time there till I went to University.

RJCW. Which was at Cambridge.

SO'B: Yes.

RJCW: How would you describe your class background?

SO'B: I find it quite difficult to describe really. My mother's family were working class, people who were typically public servants of one kind or another, or they had army connections, back to Crimean times, other ranks variety. They'd been at the Crimea, they'd been at the Indian Mutiny, they'd been at Mafeking. There were journals about some of these events. And my mother's generation of the family tended to become teachers and nurses so they would eventually I suppose enter the middle class. My Dad was a more or less self-educated Irishman. He was schooled by the Christian Brothers which taught him that if you want to find anything out you'd better find it out for yourself. He did a variety of things, especially in middle life, and later was unemployed for spells or unsatisfactorily employed. So our economic position was an odd one, I think. It's difficult to determine what it was. It wasn't middle class particularly, it wasn't really working class, but lower middle class doesn't seem to quite suit the bill. Ambiguous. I had quite a privileged school education from the age of about eight onwards. So I don't really know — 'neither nowt nor summat' I think would be one way of putting it.

RJCW: In a Northern phrase. But you'd see yourself as, whatever else, a Northerner rather than a Southerner?

SO'B: It only became apparent to me that this could be of any significance when I actually went to live in the South. When I went to University, matters of accent suddenly became important to some people. It didn't matter a light to me but it seemed to matter to them. And then latterly when I worked in the South, where you were from began to signify something to me. So now, yes, I'd guess I'm a good deal more Northern than Southern. Now that I'm living in Newcastle I'm probably not Northern enough for the Geordies, of course.

RJCW: What about religion? It seems to me that in your poetry, religion is exempted, by and large, from the crimes of the other State apparatuses, not part of the authoritarian nexus. Is that right?

SO'B: I can't think offhand if it figures all that much in the poems, but I was baptised a Catholic and the first Infant School I went to was Catholic. I was there until I was about seven. After which it was C of E or nothing in particular. But I'm technically, probably residually, a Roman Catholic with a lapsed card.

RJCW: Another thing which is perhaps conspicuous by its absence from the poems is the quite considerable length of time you spent as a school teacher.

SO'B: No, there aren't many poems about teaching, partly because those there are were unprintable!

RJCW: And yet you were writing at that time, weren't you?

SO'B: Yes, I finished one book and wrote the whole of another and perhaps the first third of the third book while teaching full time, teaching English in a Comprehensive.

RJCW: In Brighton?

SO'B: Well, it was a town called Crowborough in Sussex, near the Kent border, but I was living a lot of that time in Brighton as well. I didn't write very much about teaching, partly because sometimes things you're right in the middle of are invisible. I did write one or two satirical ballads about it, but I didn't in the end incorporate them in anything I published.

RJCW: I suppose in talking about your early life I was really interested in trying to understand your idea of Englishness, which is so prominent in everything you've written, isn't it? It's there in each of the books, a preoccupation with England as it is — you talk somewhere about an England 'just left here, and what's to be done?' And at times you're a very trenchant, very fierce critic of some of the things that have been done in the name of England. But I take it you also have a good deal of affection for the place, or for the country in which we live.

SO'B: Yes. I except Scotland. When I refer to England, I mean England. Because I don't know enough about Scotland, I haven't spent enough time in it, so I can't really comment adequately at large about Scotland. I am interested in England and Englishness because I find the subject fascinating. The more you think about it, the less you know, the less confidently you can speak about what it is to be English. My passport is British, I am a British citizen, I've lived all my life in England but I'm kind of half Irish as well, so again, there's a slightly exterior view as well as the interior one, which is fruitful in some ways. But I don't know what it is to be English. It depends whereabouts in England you happen to be. The English in Derby, where my partner comes from, are very very different from the English in Tunbridge Wells and likewise the English in Hull are very different from the English in, I imagine, Bristol, and the Geordies are different again. What common ground do the English have except certain historical allegations that are made on their behalf?

It's a subject which is being written about a bit at the moment. For example John Lucas has written on it but I've yet to read the book in question. There are certain things which I hold to be somehow English, but they're all inventions. They are largely cultural products, works of art, or forms of entertainment, often of a propagandist nature.

RJCW: That sounds to be as if you are about to say something about films.

SO'B: Yes. I watch with great interest British films, of sometimes the thirties, but usually the forties and the fifties, which trade as part of their vocabulary of assumptions on an idea of England. For example, recently when David Lean died they re-showed a number of his films, including 'In Which We Serve' which is about the Ship of State, as it were; we're all in it together and we all have a collective purpose and our sense of this effaces or abolishes any differences of economic or class fortune between us and we submerge our identities for the greater good. Which is a collectivism by other means, which I think the Conservative Party has quite a stake in, traditionally. I'm interested in that, and also in what people mean when they speak of an English landscape. I think they mean Kent and Sussex. I think that natives of Kent and Sussex do feel themselves to be particularly English — they feel that's the place. Sussex, according to Kipling, is the land God gave to England.

RJCW: Is there anything consciously cinematographic about your poetic technique, do you think?

SO'B: Not by direct analogy but, as will be apparent I think, visual data are important in my poems. I hope other kinds of data are important but I would like the things I'm on about to be visible to a reader. There are people who think this is the besetting sin of English poetry, this preoccupation with seeing at the expense of writing in other ways, but my imagination is strongly disposed towards what can be seen. And I think the best examples of British film show what can be done with this too. I mean, one of my favourite bits of film, or several of my favourite bits of film, are found in Olivier's *Henry V* where realism, people walking about, and something that's evidently theatrical, run into each other. So the use of mediaeval perspectives, for example, in landscape, is allied to realist use of landscape, the Irish landscape used for the filming of the Battle of Agincourt. Or the use of models and so on, the way in which the visual doesn't have to rely on realism, but can be about other things too. The fleet, you know, that sails across the Channel, from Southampton, I think it is, which is obviously a model fleet, never fails to fill me with awe, precisely because it is a model. It's much more interesting to me than if they'd gone to the trouble of using proper ships and filming it like that.

RJCW: I always put that down to wartime economy, you know, a film made in 1944. That's fascinating.

How would you sum up your views on the place of politics in poetry, or in the context of English poetry?

SO'B: I occasionally get an uneasy feeling in conversation or when reading criticism of a certain kind that there is for many people a safe assumption that poetry always has its mind on higher things and that these higher things don't include political life. The conception of political life that would involve is not one I share, and I suspect you might feel the same way. I don't know anything that's not, at root, political in human affairs, and therefore I think it's the proper place of poetry to talk about politics. Some of the best poems of the language, let's face it, have been manifestly political poems. The idea that if you have decided political commitments your art will be somehow contaminated — it strikes me that there is a kind of cheapness to the vocabulary there which does neither part of the equation a service. So I'm interested in poetry which tries to deal with these matters.

I'm also interested in the fact that if we look at the decade of the eighties you will not find all that much at the level of public audibility in English poetry which is really talking about the times we are living through. Now there might be good reasons for that, in the sense that people prefer to reserve judgment and to write in a considered way: that's fine. But it might also be that there is an evasion going on, and if you get past a few pretty familiar names like Douglas Dunn (who is of course a Scot!) — and he wrote about the eighties prophetically, he wrote about them in the seventies — Ken Smith in a variety of ways, Carol Ann Duffy, Tony Harrison, beyond that there aren't all that many people known to the non-specialist reader who were actually addressing those topics. There was more urgency in the theatre than in poetry. That might have to do with the marginalisation of poetry, but I wonder whether poetry is a bit 'polite-ified' on the one hand and mythologized on the other, to the point where it has no place in the everyday. So I'm interested by writing that does try to get a sense of what it's like to be here now. It's often argued that poetry takes place *sub specie aeternitatis*. Well, possibly; it's hard to know without the advantage of hindsight. But a lot of the things that we're interested in in poetry were written from specific experiences and occasions and historical moments, so I don't think that argument stands up either. Even Kenneth Baker admits the existence of history.

RJCW: But then there's also a contention over what constitutes the everyday itself, with different parties claiming it for their own, isn't there? After all, there are one or two phrases in your poetry which are rather like the kind of ways of seeing which I associate with the Martians. For example:

'Chestnut trees / Are fire-damaged candelabra' or 'The goldfish . . . rehearsing blasé vowels at the sun'. Now, both admittedly from your first book. But one could find something very similar in Raine at that period, and yet it seems to me that the use you make of that kind of imagination applied to the everyday object is the reverse of Raine's, because he wants us to enjoy his attempt to make the familiar seem very wonderful, and thereby ultimately he is inviting us to accept the way things are, take joy in what we can find around us and in the way the world actually is now. Whereas you seem to be much more subversive than that. Is that fair?

SO'B: I read Craig Raine's remark somewhere that he's politically a sceptic, which I find interesting. I shouldn't think politics is all that sceptical about him. As Fredric Jameson puts it, we can be confident that history will not forget us. That it will want something to do with us. I think Martianism is not a term much used these days, anyway. But there are only really two people who are significantly Martian in poetry, Craig Raine himself and Christopher Reid, whose work in both cases has developed to some extent away from that original device and habit of the imagination. It may be that they like to think of the imagination as a realm of freedom, which by some means escapes any shaping influence and has no obligation and no blind spots. If they do, well fair enough; I'm not convinced of that. I think the imagination is historically shaped. Claiming liberty is one thing, proving it is another.

RJCW: It's only quite recently that certain kinds of literary criticism have tried to break free of the idea which was dominant for a long time that poetry had nothing to do with anything so mundane as real events and real people and real lives. Do you think poetry is in advance of that or lagging behind? Do you see any prospect of it breaking free of that rather smoothly constructed myth of the eternal verities?

SO'B: Well, I think there are plenty of examples currently that suggest that poetry is more various than some imaginary person trying to describe an orthodoxy, or trying to enforce one, would be happy with. There's poetry from many kinds of people who wouldn't previously have been publishng poetry. There's a lot of poetry coming out of the North of England which wouldn't have got much of a look in twenty years ago; a lot more poetry published by women and by black people and Asian people and people of mixed nationality who happen to be writing in English. It's internationalised and taken away from central dominance. The metropolis is not significant as the producer. It may be significant as the publisher. It may be significant editorially to a degree, but the emphasis on a kind of Oxbridge quietism you might at one time have suspected, isn't the most significant thing that's going on in poetry any more. Exciting work is being written by people from all over the place and written for all kinds of reasons. And, just to take one example, a young poet I enjoy a great deal and admire is Simon Armitage, and Armitage's work proceeds very confidently from the assumption that there is no battle to be won about where he comes from — he is a generation on from Tony Harrison — this battle has been fought and won and it's not something he has to concern himself with. As Kavanagh says, 'gods make their own importance'. Where you live is not significant, it's what the imagination makes of it that matters.

RJCW: That's like Joyce's injunction to Heaney in *Station Island* where he says that battle's an old battle, already fought and won, take it for granted, get on and do your work.

SO'B: Yes I think that that is something Armitage may have taken to heart.

RJCW: So the state of poetry in English is healthy, as far as you are concerned?

SO'B: I think there is a lot of good work being done, but obviously you can never say in the present what's going to seem worth reading twenty years hence. I think the way in which it's discussed in the media, to the extent that it is discussed, is completely wrongheaded. It's too much based on names, it's too much based on prizes, it's too much based on those poets who've got their head over the parapet of literary notice, out of the ghetto of poetry — who are nearly as well known as some novelists! I think that's the problem the media creates. I don't know what poets can do about that.

RJCW: In twenty years' time, what do you hope to have achieved in poetry? What kind of poet would you like to have become by then?

SO'B: A good one! What I would like to avoid, and I hope it won't take mortality to avoid this, is hitting a flat patch in middle age. I'd like to go on doing interesting work through middle life, which is proverbially rather difficult.

RJCW: Obviously the fear of hitting a flat patch is partly a matter between you and your Muse, but it must be sharpened up by the fact that you make your living out of your writing, to a large extent, one way or another. Is that a congenial mode of existence, or do you hanker for the nine to five?

SO'B: No, not at all. I've spent a long time wanting not to have a proper job. I don't think many poets actually make a living off selling books and so on. I think to the extent poets make a living it's from doing reading, teaching courses, reviewing, and all the other bits and pieces that go with it. It can be very vexing to have commitments to do things that are taking up time when you want to be writing poems, but there are worse situations to be in. Like being so knackered by teaching, for example, that you can't get any work done of any kind. Economically it's not great but the opportunity is there to do the work you want.

SHARON OLDS

INTERVIEWED BY SUE STEWART

Sharon Olds was born in San Francisco in 1942, and now lives in New York. She published three collections of poetry — *Satan Says* (1980), *The Dead and the Living* (1984) and *The Gold Cell* (1987), which Secker & Warburg have now brought together under the title *The Sign of Saturn* (Secker, London, 1991). The poems are about sexuality, power and the idea of family. As part of the Secker promotion a national tour was organised, with a final reading at the Poetry Society, London. Sue Stewart met Sharon Olds there to arrange the following interview, which was conducted by post in the Summer of 1991. From the long list of questions sent to her, Sharon Olds then selected the following answers.

1. Your poetry is very much in the confessional style, and has attracted large audiences during your English tour. What reactions have you had from them?

It was a delight to tour with Roger McGough and C. K. Williams. The first time I had read in Great Britain, in October 1990, I had felt a bit overawed: the land where our language had come from. Keats' *home*. But gradually, on this tour, I began to feel that maybe our countries weren't so entirely different from each other.

I have a rather old-fashioned sense of language, and I like to use the word *confessional* to refer to sin. What is sometimes called "confessional poetry" I think of as *apparently personal* poetry. (We don't really *know* that the details in a poem are factually accurate).

The various audiences we read to in England and Scotland were quite different to each other, as different American audiences are. On the whole I found U.K. audiences perhaps in general quieter — and yet uninhibited in their laughter about things sexual. I felt myself in the presence of very careful and what felt like very generous listening.

2. Did you read different poems for English than for American audiences?

As one reads to an audience, one often thinks (perhaps quite wrongly!) that one is getting a sense of who they are — then one may, for the second half of the program, select accordingly. In the States, I'll read a different program at a small rural college from what I'd read at New York University — in Scotland and England I tried to figure out where I was, and then read accordingly. I tended to be fairly conservative at first — feeling that I had no idea where I was, really — but by the end of the tour I felt that audiences there and here were not so very different.

3. You don't give introductions to your poems at readings. Are you suspicious of the entertainment value of introductions — or do you simply want the poems to do all the work?

I want each poem to have all its body parts, to be complete. Sometimes afterwards I like talking a little about a poem. I suppose I feel a great separation between conversation and poems. Many poets don't feel that — Roger McGough read some poems whose introductions were an essential part of the poem. And we saw the rapport and affection between Roger and his audience.

4. Would you argue that what is personal is also political?

I wouldn't have, years ago. I did not see, then, that some apparently personal poetry, which is about power, perhaps in a family, is political in that it's looking at power, at the small body politic. And there is apparently political poetry which is, at its roots, personal, probably. I admire poems of fairly recent times which take on and embody the large world — the poems of Muriel

Rukeyser, Denise Levertov, Philip Levine, Galway Kinnell, Gwendolyn Brooks, Robert Bly, Adrienne Rich, Etheridge Knight. I was ashamed for a long time of my own inability to write about "the real world." Gradually I developed a sense of who apparent strangers might be.

5. Is there anything too personal to write about?

When I first read poetry, it seemed that it was dedicated to language, and to the line, and to experience — to love and death, for instance — to absolutely intimate experience shared by everyone. The personal seemed to be universal.

6. Do you feel poetry should primarily educate, challenge or offer succour?

I'm not sure what I feel poetry should do. (Though my ear and my foot (my sense of rhyme and meter) want to vote for *offer succour*!) I think that a poem forms in me — I suppose in my subconscious (though I feel that it happens behind my breastbone — in the lungs, in the borrowed air) — like a cloud in a cloud-chamber, and by the time I notice it, and begin to write it, it is already pretty much formed, though I cannot see it.

The writing of a poem would then be my effort to get it out of me and onto the page without distorting it — like a very, very over-easy egg out of the pan onto the plate without breaking the yolk.

And the dance that goes on between the language and the line and the idea or narrative if the poem works, it embodies something. I see the body likeness (as if in a mirror):

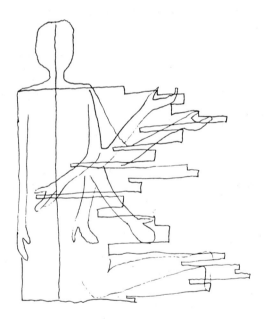

the left-hand margin is the still left arm; the caesura is the mid-line of the body (the spine); the right-hand margin shows the right-hand's freedom.

When I am writing a poem, it's true that I am often hearing it, my lips move, but I am also, in a way, *dancing* with it.

7. Can you tell us about your childhood?

It may be (it seems to me) most fruitful for a writer to keep the public and the private separate. What I most care about, in the new poems I see at N.Y.U. or at Goldwater Hospital, or in my own notebook, is whether the poem feels alive. It is that life which matters to me. And it seems possible to me that more of that life might come to us if we try, in our dialogue about poetry, to protect the poems from the people, and the people from the poems.

8. What did you read as a child?

Before I read, I heard the Psalms, and The Book of Common Prayer, and the hymns from the Episcopal hymnal. Once I could read, I read *The Gold Book of Fairy Tales* (and The Pink, and The Rose), *The Scotch Twins, The Irish Twins, Mary Poppins, The Secret Garden, A Child's Book of Christian Martyrs*, and Nancy Drew.

9. When you write, do you have an imagined audience in mind? Or do you write, like most writers, for yourself, and think about audience later?

While one is actually writing, one is too absorbed, I think, to imagine an audience. One is wrestling with — dancing with — the creature of language and the creature of experience. But probably the unconscious has some imagination of audience. . . I ask people sometimes to try to formulate whom their unconscious might "think of" as their reader: does this reader have a sex? An age? A race? A sexual preference? Is he/she/it born yet? Already dead?

I don't think I write for myself. Maybe I write for anyone, myself as one of the anyones.

10. You've lived for 23 years in New York. Do you enjoy the charge of the city?

When Reagan put a large percentage of New York State's mental patients out on the street, and radically cut social services, people unable to provide for themselves began living in the subway. One sees vividly in New York what kind of government we have — maybe what kind of people Americans (or humans) are. The city is charged with grief and ruin. And it's my home. I've lived here 27 years, 23 of them in the same building. And the beauty I see sometimes seems as extreme as the suffering: the river, the setting moon and sun — occasional egret, cormorant, rough-legged hawk, great blue heron, peregrine falcon.

11. When did you first begin to write?

I was amazed to remember, on this tour, that one of my first poems was written in the persona of someone missing Scotland — having left her true love there. On the streets of Glasgow or Edinburgh the poem came back to me, almost whole! (I recited it to Charlie who raised his eyebrows and smiled.)

As a child and teenager I wrote as much fiction as poetry. But my fiction was full of wishful thinking, and of self-pity and melodrama — I mean *packed* with them, *made* of them. The form of a poem seemed to exert a kind of moral force over me, to help me not lie. Poems had not just sentences but the line; its rod and its staff comforted me.

12. Who influenced you as a poet — Plath, Ginsberg, Sexton? Did you study with any poets, or apprentice yourself to anyone? What advice did they give you?

When I was a teenager, I read Kahlil Gibran and Keats, Dylan Thomas and Shakespeare; Walt Whitman, Emily Dickinson, Edna St. Vincent Millay, James Weldon Johnson, Ezra Pound, W. H. Auden, and Allen Ginsberg.

In my twenties I came to know the work of the poets about half a generation ahead of mine. I heard many of them first at a poetry reading against the Vietnam War: Muriel Rukeyser, Philip

189

Levine, Adrienne Rich, Robert Bly, Etheridge Knight, and Galway Kinnell. Many of them wrote personal as well as political poetry. Many had been praised on the quatrain and the sonnet, the old *reusable forms*, and had gone on to find their own *exploratory forms* (the phrases are Denise Levertov's). Ruth Stone was another of these essential poets. Some of them wrote about children, even about birth. I spent my twenties trying to write poems without sentences, with a lot of white space in them, and much of the time I was too stunned and wretched about the Vietnam War to write. But when I came back to something like my own voice, when I was thirty, the work of the poets at the protest was stored in me, and had been gestating.

Plath's work, like Lowell's, I had read and admired, but not been terribly drawn to. Sexton, too, I had read, but somehow what she gave wasn't just what I needed. I needed poems of Vietnam and of children. I wanted *out* of the self, and I didn't know how to get there. (The bridge turned out to contain many little I-beam girders: I, I, I (oi, yoi, yoi).)

13. I know you teach now, but what sort of work did you do on the road to becoming a poet?

From age 9-13 I put out a two-page family jelly-graph newspaper. I had 45 subscribers — one in a distant place called Saigon. I had recipes (candle salad — the maraschino on top of the half banana is its flame), a serial story, editorials, ads. I liked having work, a desk, a reporter's hat.

I have worked as a secretary, a waitress, and a driver for the Red Cross. In the early 70's, a group of us figured out how much the services of a full-time caretaker of babies and young children would cost if the services were professional. I think we came up, twenty years ago, with $30,000 a year — that's, what, £20,000, by now probably it would be £30,000. I realized that the labor of love that childcare was was a *job*, one which many people didn't want, but which for someone on the road to becoming a poet might be a luxury, an apprenticeship.

14. How do you see your role as an American poet?

I guess each poet's task and joy and luxury is to write the new poems, to try to follow one's vision where it leads — not because it is a good vision, but because it is what one has, it is one of the many human visions, perhaps someone else's too (as other's are often like one's own).

15. If you were to be known to future generations by one poem only, which would you like it to be?

One I haven't written yet, which is truer and more complete than what I have! But if it has to be a done one, then I guess ''I Go Back to May 1937,'' which is in a way a little manifesto (womanifesto).

16. Who do you show work-in-progress to?

Having, like many poets, an imitative ear (I see us as having not an anxiety of influence but a gratitude for nourishment), I used to be afraid that I would lose my voice, start sounding like someone else. I didn't want that, even if it meant I could sound like one of the ''real poets.'' So I never showed my work to anyone before it was published.

About five years ago, Galway Kinnell invited me to teach with him for a summer week in a new kind of workshop: everyone, us too, would bring in a new first draft every morning. There was no living poet whose work meant more to me. I was honored and, of course, anxious. That was the first year of this new version of the Squaw Valley Community of Writers poetry conference. For seven days each of us read a brand new poem to twelve people.

When the week was over, I missed that energy of exchange. Sometimes I'd show Galway a new poem to see what he thought. His comments were so interesting — nothing I could think up myself. And he clearly didn't want me to sound less like myself. And he clearly wanted me to tell him exactly what I thought about his new poems. I now realize that virtually all poets have the good fortune of one or more poetry friendships.

190

I feel it's helped my new poems very much — sometimes virtually drawn them out of me — to sense that there is, out there, a reader who wants for me what I want for myself, new poems that are actually new for me. And he saved my new book (*The Father*). I had wanted it to be a love book, but its soul was more complex than that. The poems often used the word *love* inaccurately — to stand for *hate*, or *fear*, or *longing*. Galway would ask me about these words. At N.Y.U. he's a famously kind, unbossy teacher. He would just ask. It was a powerful experience. I wrestled with *The Father* for a year — "polishing" (*love loathe adore fear love see*). Now I feel the book is pretty much where it should be. I learned that what matters is that the poem become its true self — not that I am the only one who touches the poem.

17. What advice would you give to a very young poet?

I think of what Muriel Rukeyser said years ago: "Write about what burns in you, what you can't forget." (Of course what burns in one might be an idea, a beauty, a national or town history.)

18. You teach at New York University and Goldwater Hospital — can you tell us something about this?

N.Y.U. is one of the largest Creative Writing Program's in the States (with about ninety students). For three years I was its Director; now I am on the faculty. It is a great pleasure to be a colleague of E. L. Doctorow, Jean Valentine, Philip Levine, Mona Simpson, Peter Carey, Toi Derricotte, Galway Kinnell, Michael Harper, Gerald Stern, Michael Burkard, Thomas Keneally, and many others. Our students are often remarkably gifted as writers and as human beings. I love this contact with another generation of poets, and I love to see them forming their poetry friendships, which will keep them company and challenge and enrich their work.

Goldwater is a 900-bed New York City public hospital for the severely physically disabled. The writers in the workshop there are in wheelchairs, and most do not have writing use of their hands. Several are non-speaking as well as non-moving, and communicate with various devices whose materials of construction range from laser beams to cardboard. I've taught here for six years, and now a set of graduate students teaches with me each year. The Goldwater writers are our friends and spiritual teachers and we are their friends and transcribers and contacts with some of the outward manifestations of the poetry world.

Poetry workshops can be vital presences in hospitals and schools and hospices and prisons and teenage-pregnancy homes and homes. . . Poetry is the art in which one being calls out to, whispers to, sings to, one other being, in the most intimate way. Our species needs it, perhaps, to survive.

19. A recent review of your work compared you to Plath, saying that she wrote "brilliant, self-destructive poems" whereas you write, "brilliant, self-affirmative ones". Would you agree with the distinction?

I am honored to be compared to such a gifted poet, a genius really. But I don't know if I feel that her poems were self-destructive. There is a truthfulness in many of her poems which seems to me to affirm the human. I would imagine (I don't know) that her poetry might have been a force keeping her alive — a force that in the long run wasn't strong enough, wasn't stronger than the other forces.

20. What would be your Desert Island Disc? Book? Luxury?

Stranded on a desert island. . . I would take the book in 8,000,000 volumes, in the inflatable rubber edition. . . the one whose volumes are attached to each other — and I would head out along it toward the nearest habitation — maybe the Manhattan island with its 8,000,000 inhabitants, many of them stranded. I want to get poems — free broadsides — into the check-out lines in supermarkets. I'm afraid poetry *is* stranded on a desert island. And people dying every day for lack of it.

DON PATERSON

INTERVIEWED BY RAYMOND FRIEL

Don Paterson was born in Dundee in 1963. He left school at the age of sixteen and moved to England in 1984. He now lives in Brighton. His debut collection, *Nil Nil* (Faber) is the summer 1993 Poetry Book Society Choice. In 1990 he was the recipient of a Gregory Award and in 1991 he won third prize in the National Poetry Competition, with the poem "An Elliptical Stylus". He reviews regularly for *Poetry Review* and is a member of the jazz/folk band Lammas. Raymond Friel met Don Paterson in Kettner's restaurant, Soho, on November 30th, 1992. The ideas raised at that meeting were subsequently elaborated in this postal interview.

RF: You've lived in the South East since 1984. To what extent do you still consider yourself to be a Scottish writer?

DP: My Scottishness wasn't something I was aware of until I'd actually left the place; I think in my late teens I'd harboured some woolly notion about being British, or European, or something. I was disabused of these almost immediately my feet had touched the platform at King's Cross. I get by down here by pretending I'm on some kind of extended sabbatical, or a school outing that went horribly wrong, and that I'm coming home tomorrow. I've every intention of returning to Scotland, though not to Dundee, unless I'm getting paid for it. It doesn't do any good to think of yourself as a writer at all, since, like murder, it describes an act, not necessarily a permanent disposition.

RF: Do you have any interest in writing in Scots?

DP: Inevitably, being Scottish -— *well* Scottish, i.e. a Nationalist and someone who can relax into an accent strong enough to be incomprehensible to anyone outside St. Mary's, Dundee — infects my writing, though not, I hope, to a self-conscious degree. It's this self-consciousness I object to in a lot of contemporary poetry in Scots. My own interest in, or use of Scots, doesn't go beyond the basilect, that's to say a tongue my mother was anxious for me not to speak; a fine tongue for rough communication, for cursing in, telling jokes in, being ill in, for describing flora, fauna, bodily functions and terrible weather in, but bog all else. On the other hand, you couldn't order a pint in "literary" Scots, or if you did, God nows what you would get. The middle way doesn't exist, the tongue in which intelligent Scots could discuss politics, or culture, or whatever; and it *can't* exist until we reappropriate a classical vocabulary, something long denied to us through our political and cultural disenfranchisement. The top-down approach that literary Scots adopts alienates more people than it wins over; it's an entirely separate, hieratic diction, one that means absolutely nothing to the vast majority of the population. The way forward is through discussion groups, that sort of thing; until we can talk Scots among ourselves I don't see how we can write in it. The trouble is you're still dealing with an essentially rural vocabulary and a certain kind of linguistic perversity manifests itself, mainly in the form of post-MacDiarmid lexomania, when you try to bend it to accommodate more sophisticated concerns or abstractions, for which it's ill-suited. There are other limitations — I find it difficult to conceive of an erotic literature, say, in a language that has fifty-three different words for "cough". The urban vocabulary — pletties, polies, closies and cribbies — is very poor by comparison, simply because there's less to describe. My feeling is that a language and its associated concerns, as opposed to jargon, have to be earthed to a particular geography before it can claim any kind of authenticity. I often try to imagine this place where auld wifies are scrapping in the sub post-office about Frank O'Hara, and the ploughboy is stopping for his piece, a big Forfar bridie in one hand, Olson's *Maximus* poems in the other . . . Literary Scots is too inclusive and self-reflexive to be grounded in anything but itself; it's a romantic tendency, not a pragmatic one. Don't get me wrong: something like Bill Herbert's "Cormundum" would still be a fine poem even if it had been written in Esperanto; I'm just glad that Bill seems to be publishing more stuff in English, as about a thousand times more people will be able to recognise how good he is.

RF: Several of the poems in *Nil Nil* refer to Fife and Dundee. Do you feel you have anything in common with writers *like* Bill Herbert, and Douglas Dunn, who are either from the area or have something to say about the place?

DP: Dundee and Fife are, for me, very much the primal territory, and this wealth of personal association makes it impossible for me to put it in any kind of political or historical perspective, though Herbert doesn't seem to have that problem; I find Dundee far more recognisable in his work than in mine. Douglas Dunn, and Robert Crawford, are better qualified, I think to say what makes Dundee and Fife distinctive as a place, since they come from a different part of Scotland. My own tendency to mythologise increases in direct proportion to the physical distance I am from the place. Dundee and Tayport are now populated entirely by fairies and demons and bogey-men; even my own family have been driven from their homes by some sinister Disney-types. Most Dundonians have this highly ambivalent relationship with the city; the position it occupies on the Tay estuary is roughly equivalent to the prostate, or the quasi-mythical G-spot, depending on which way you look at it; it can look like the worst place on earth, but also the shining city of God — admittedly, this is usually just a trick of the light and distance, but a very good trick, as any Dundonian will verify. *Duende*, sure, but also *Undeed*; the city that saw the invention of the reverse gear, but also Sandy Kerr's anti-gravity machine. Sandy Kerr, from what I gather, is now working somewhere in the middle of the Australian desert, as opposed to a toolshed in Barnhill . . . his research is being funded by the American military; they moved in after Dundee University, with characteristic vision, pulled the plug after a month or so. You have to laugh.

RF: At a recent poetry reading you said that you don't like going on about being working class because your audience is based largely in the South East and is, presumably, largely middle-class. Is this some kind of marketing strategy and are you not concerned that some people might accuse you of a lack of integrity?

DP: They might do, but it's just paranoia on my part; the poem ''An Elliptical Stylus'', which I was introducing when I made those comments, was intended as a deliberate inversion of the current practice of inviting the audience to ''share'' the experience; I'm terrified some well-heeled wee bugger will come up to me afterwards and tell me how much he enjoyed it. I think there are some grudges that have to be renewed annually; poetry is a good way of making palatable things that should remain indigestible, making certain kinds of crime easier for both the perpetrator and the victim to live with. There are a lot of sub-Harrison types about who see their poetry as lending dignity to the working-class experience, as commemorating it in the proper fashion, when what they're really dealing with is their own embarrassment with their social origins, and their awkwardness in using the language of their superiors. It's depressing to see the working-classes patronise *themselves* in this way. But I do worry about talking too openly about this sort of thing — even brilliant poems like Dunn's ''The Come-on'' and O'Brien's ''Cousin Coat'' worry me; part of me thinks, no, no, you're telling the bastards too much, this should be circulated between ourselves, as in-house memoranda or something . . . paranoia, like I said. I suppose the Elliptical Stylus poem is really about my own inequality to the task, masquerading as frustration with the form.

RF: I'd like to ask you about your childhood. It would appear from poems like ''Amnesia'' and ''Heredity'' that yours was a very strictly religious, Calvinist, upbringing, and one which you rejected early on, at least privately. Did this have any effect on your poetry? Does this double life early on explain your fascination for doppelgangers?

DP: It wasn't really all that strict, just a matter of being booted out to Sunday School in a kilt for five years. My grandfather is a minister in the Free Church, and still preaches; in his incumbency as Moderator of the General Assembly he had something of a reputation as a liberal, though I suppose it's all relative. I suppose I got involved in the charismatic movement as a rebellion against all that, though it would have been far healthier, in the long run, to have opted for a spell of vandalism and solvent-abuse. I've really no idea what effect it's had on the poetry, except perhaps reinforcing the interest in matters eschatological. I don't know where the doppelganger thing came from either, though there should have been a brother between me and Steve, who died after a couple of days, and possibly I'm waiting for him to turn up.

RF: These poems strike me as being extremely candid, either courageously or foolishly so. What do your family think of them? Or are they entirely fictional?

DP: They're probably a little more candid in tone, though not in terms of any basis they might have in reality. It's a tremendously liberating day in a poet's life when you suddenly realise *you can make it all up;* the idea that poetry involves a fidelity to one's own experience and emotions is much more deeply engrained than you suspect — it operates almost as a moral imperative, so the first time you put words into someone's mouth, or kill off an aunt or uncle, it feels deliciously sinful. Novelists do it all the time, though. This approach is also a good way of covering your tracks — if you're a known liar, it actually gives you the freedom to tell the truth, since no-one will ever believe you. If you read Michael Donaghy's poetry, you've no idea how much of it is true, since it *all* sounds utterly candid and sincere; at the same time, you know it must be 95 per cent lies, but you've no way of knowing which 95 per cent. Foolish these poems may be, but I don't think courage is a word that should be applied to literature at all, unless you're talking about Primo Levi. That's very pompous, but I get annoyed when I hear work being described as "courageous" or "ambitious" when what's intended is "embarrassing" or "too long". It never does to let myself forget that, however hard it feels, writing poetry is usually a doddle compared with real work, or real confrontation. My folks like them fine, though they don't read poetry. My Dad reads a lot of fiction and had pioneered this speed-reading technique for pulp novels where he can get through a 500-pager in one visit to the toilet, by reading down the centre of the page and ignoring all the descriptive passages and gratuitous love interest.

RF: The Faber blurb says that you left school at sixteen. Was it you who wanted to highlight this fact? Do you think it's been an advantage or a disadvantage not to have gone through the Eng. Lit. process? Many academics *are* poets. Do you think this shows?

DP: I suppose it's my plebby response to the usual "gained a double first at ---, completed his --- at --- on --- under ---", etc. Admittedly it sounds like special pleading, but at least it has the merit of being strictly autobiographical, whereas a list of your academic qualifications reads like a guarantee of the intelligence, if not the quality of the verse. Since poetry has the knack of making nearly everyone who tries to do it look completely stupid, you'd be as well mentioning your Cycling Proficiency Award and membership of the fucking Tufty Club for all the relevance it'll have. Okay, I won't do it again. I just thought it might be politically useful to signal, to other people with background similar to my own, that it's possible to aspire to a condition of semi-literacy without a university education. I think poets are poets despite, not because of things — it's only a peculiar oversensitivity to the weight and texture of words, and has little to do with whatever other talents you might possess. There are plenty of academics who are fine poets, but the two are unconnected. When people start thinking they *are* related, they usually stop being fine poets. My main grouse about academics is their elevation of chancers like Ashbery to near god-like status, just because he happens to be ideal thesis-material; the nearer to sub-conversational rubbish he gets, the more commentary he requires, which is where the boys come in. People even have the nerve to talk about the "humour" in Ashbery's work — I recently read a review that quoted "I've had so many identity crises in the last fifty years/I've lost count" as a great example of his comic timing, though after four pages of Ashbery I'd be desperate enough to laugh at the pagination. Paul Merton, now *he's* funny. Clive James. Again, I can't say if having missed out on university has been an advantage or a disadvantage, though never feeling properly qualified to do anything leads swiftly to a thorough acquaintance with your own ignorance, which isn't the same as having a proper education, but it's the next best thing. The bigger danger, though, is the rediscovery of the cliché; one of the best ways to guard against it is always to opt for the weird and outlandish solution, which admittedly might not always be the best one.

RF: When and why did you start writing? Who were your main influences?

DP: I started writing around '85, for much the same reason I started playing music, i.e. the rather obscure notion that it might impress women. Pathetic, but still better than doing it out of an overwhelming desire to express yourself, which is about the worst qualification you can have to do anything. I wasn't expecting anyone to be moved by it or anything, I just had this vague idea that some girl might be bowled over by my iron control of the iambic line. As usual, it didn't occur to me that this might not be the sort of girl you'd want to impress in the first place, but by then it was All Too Late. I strongly suspect that for a lot of men, and probably the same number of women, sex, money and fame — which is just the promise of sex and money — are among the primary motivations for writing poetry; I know that sounds heretical, hilarious even, and that the poetry is ultimately its own reward — but we all have egos to placate. Sean O'Brien sees poetry as a kind of historically detached activity; he's right, of course, but we all want to be loved in *this* life, not the next. The first poet who really affected me was Tony Harrison — I saw him on TV in about 1984; he was reading some of the poems from "Continuous". It was a terribly moving performance, and I can honestly say I would never have thought of writing poetry if it hadn't been for that. In the last few years "he has become himself to the nth degree", and my allegiance has waned somewhat . . . I'm all for doom and misery, but you have to crack the odd joke here and there, if only to keep people listening. I saw him read "Loving Memory" on the box recently — it's a lovely, yearning, delicate poem, but he delivered it like the last rites, with a frown like an axe-wound. After that, it was Paul Muldoon; the thing I admire about Muldoon more than any other is the way he tries to take the top of your head off with every poem he writes; but he's a terribly dangerous influence. All his stylistic tics, like Auden's, would be absolutely fatal in a lesser talent, yet there are still quite a few people around playing Cliff Richard to Muldoon's Elvis — they've perfected the hip-swivel and the curled lip, but somehow you just can't buy it. I think I can sense the Muldoonery in my own stuff disappear with every poem I write, almost like a stain does in successive washes, and I think I've kept most of it out of the book, but his cadences are so seductive, his style of poetic closure . . . you sometimes just don't want to let it go. Then there was MacNeice and Auden; I suppose, forced to make the choice, it'd be MacNeice I'd take to the desert island. Then Elizabeth Bishop, Derek Mahon, Douglas Dunn, Michael Longley; as secular apostles as much as poets, really . . . I think if you read any of these poets closely you do come away a little wiser as to how to live decently and humanely. The same's true of Larkin, even though as a man, at least the side of himself he revealed in the *Letters*, he was thoroughly unadmirable. But whenever I forget how poetry goes, I read Heaney. I read Heaney a lot.

RF: What about the forms and metrics in your collection: there's a lot of sonnets, and triple metre in the longer poems like "The Alexandrian Library"?

DP: The triple metre thing I definitely contracted from Sean O'Brien. Anapaests are the poetic equivalent of herpes, really; just when you think you've got rid of them forever, there's this sound of thundering hooves in the distance, and you're off again. It's very good for sustaining momentum over long stretches, though, partly because it's technically easier to let the sentence run on than it is to finish it. For a while I couldn't write anything over sonnet length, so it was a solution to that, really, a way of writing something that was narrative or rhapsodic for a change. I learnt a tremendous amount from Sean; he made me think very hard about things that would never have occurred to me in a million years . . . how you can make the poetic voice sound more authoritative through syntax, what happens when you stick the verb at the end of the line, what happens when you mix Guinness, red wine and Kentucky Fried Chicken.

RF: Apart from poems which are very much of a British tradition, there are other poems in the book, like ''Morning Prayer'', which have their roots in a Continental tradition. What attracts you to this?

DP: I'm attracted to the idea of the Continental tradition, rather than by the reality, because I'm a hopeless linguist. Most stuff in translation isn't much good unless a) there's hardly any figurative language, e.g. Zbigniew Herbert, or b) it's been translated by a poet of equal stature, like Mahon's versions of Jaccottet. I mean I don't know if it's anything like Jaccottet, but it's great stuff. There are a thousand and one factors that determine the sort of poetry you think you should be writing, a lot of them cultural and environmental, peer-pressure and what have you . . . it's just interesting to speculate what kind of poetry would arise in their absence, or their substitution for others. To be *able* to write a poem without any figurative language, or a poem about a sunset. ''Morning Prayer'' was just an excuse to make some melodramatic Gallic gestures, although part of the inspiration for writing the poem was reading a translation of ''Oraison du Soir'' where the last line was rendered as ''I receive the approval of the great heliotropes''.

RF: I'd like to turn to Lammas, the band you're in. The one album I've heard blends several traditions together: jazz, folk. Is this analogous in any way to your writing? Or do you see the two activities as being unrelated?

DP: As disciplines, yes, they're entirely unrelated, though they *do* inform each other by analogy; but this would be true of poetry and pottery, or poetry and scratching your arse . . . the only good reason for putting the two together is to get paid twice on the same gig. In terms of content, I find them totally unrelated . . . music's very much the last bastion of innocence in my life, whereas poetry had fallen to the infidels long before I'd even started writing it. If nothing else, my experience learning music led me to approach poetry fairly pragmatically; there was never any ideological conflict between form and expression because in music they mean exactly the same thing . . . so I didn't spend four years writing rotten free verse about Infinity, or not getting off with Tracy Johnston. I wrote rotten formal verse instead; I was besotted with the form, so my approach was idiotically practical — I read the dictionary, a book about prosody, and as much poetry as I could lay my paws on. Compositionally, yes, there *are* precise poetic analogues for parallel dissonance, and musical ones for pararhyme, but they'd be meaningless to anyone else, even someone doing the same things . . . that sort of dialogue is probably fruitful, but hopelessly subjective.

RF: What about the theology of the poems? There's not much sign of any redemption. There are several references to coins in palms and in the mouth; there's the ferry and the doppelganger. You seem to be very preoccupied with death . . . and the underworld.

DP: Yes. I mean, it's not a fashion thing, or anything, I really am, and always have been. I found this word the other day: Hadeharia, the constant over use of the word hell. Partly it's just that hell is so much more interesting to describe — look at Dore's crap etchings of Paradiso; I think Heaven for a lot of poets, not just Dante, is an opportunity to walk through Hell unscathed; it's a morally indefensible practice, what with all the real suffering in the world, and all the real suffering that's probably yet to come my way. Also, I find the longer a poem goes on, the more likely it is it'll end horribly . . . though there are a couple of short, ecstatic poems in the book that end just before gravity, or Freddy Kruger pulls them through the floorboards.

RF: Mind you, you did beat yourself at pool fairly convincingly in "The Ferryman's Arms". Do you feel lucky, then? Or just talented?

DP: Jammy, definitely. I tried to read that poem from memory recently, and ended up potting the white ball, which would have been an existential catastrophe, though the audience didn't seem to notice. It's true, incidentally, though it's not a feat I've since managed to replicate. I hope to postpone the return match for another forty years or so.

RF: There's a great deal of *body* in these poems; a very somantic vocabulary: "the peristaltic wave", "the subcutaneous itch" and so on. Do you feel weighed down by necessity, the corporeal? Do you believe in the soul at all?

DP: I'm a terrible hypochondriac; the only person I've ever met who's worse is Matthew Sweeney, who seems to have had half-a-dozen barium meals in as many years, which'll kill him before anything else does. Yes, completely weighed down, which is why I'm obsessed with the great lighteners — drink, books, sleep, sex, trains, death, sport. I do believe in the soul, but I doubt if God or Nature will be too interested in what I believe, so we'll have to wait and see.

RF: Similarly, the unconscious: In "The Ferryman's Arms" you have " . . . the skin of the water, stretching/as black as my stout, from somewhere unspeakable/to here . . . " Also, "The Alexandrian Library" (see *Verse*, vol.9, no.3) has a surreal, subterranean, divagatory atmosphere in which you're being stalked by this minotaur-monster. What's your interest in the unconscious, in dream activity?

DP: This stuff about dream-life and dream logic . . . it's like it reverses the tenor and vehicle of the organising metaphor . . . Muldoon operates smack in the middle, with analogues, not metaphors, one object or situation mapping another point for point, so it's impossible to say which of the two is the real subject of the poem; both are defined in terms of each other. I think it might be possible to rotate the picture through another 90 degrees; usually the concrete details or action of a poem is in the service of some higher abstraction some context or emotion or idea to which it stands in a metaphoric or metanymic relationship. With the dream-logic thing, the whole thing is turned on its head because you're dealing with an irreducible sub-text, something that ultimately defies any kind of interpretation or analysis. It ends up being about the innate mystery of objects and situations — they're imbued with the flavour of these higher abstraction but are no longer operating in their service . . . I'm not putting this too well, and it'll be a while, I suspect, before I can . . . but you know that sort of vague numinousness that adheres to everything in John Burnside's poetry; his approach is quite static and contemplative, but very beautiful. "The Alexandrian Library" was an attempt at that sort of superrealism; I was trying to stuff it with details, clues, anagrams, red herrings and what have you to suggest something of the infinite textual depth and complexity you get in a lucid dream, but the story was only the story itself. The search for some kind of absolute autochthony, something I'm pretty obsessed with, becomes exactly that — a very physical, very daft journey to this Pictish enclave . . . then when that's failed, when it's discovered that there's only this wee black hole at the centre of things, the focus of the search becomes the lost library, for continuity; in real life these activities would be sublimated in some other activity, and then discussed in terms of returning to the womb, or the collective unconscious — but the physical and the concrete have their own integrity, something that's no less mysterious; like when Jung says that a hole dug in a tribal ceremony may well be a representation of the vagina, but primarily it's still a hole . . . in the poem, the labyrinth — though it's always invoked as a metaphor for the brain, memory, and god knows what else — is primarily just a horrible place to get lost in, which is what it was long before we decided it was something else. I just feel there's a balance to be redressed, and that it's partly the job of poets to reinstate some of the mystery that reductive thinking destroys. Put like that, it all sounds like a lot of pretentious shite, but I did try to make the poem as interesting, funny and scary as I could.

RF: Who are you reading at the moment? Who do you most admire on the current scene?

DP: Apart from the people I've already mentioned, I think O'Brien, Donaghy, Duffy, Crawford, Duhig, Armitage and Sweeney are the pick of the bunch at the moment, all poets I read and re-read and probably steal from. Hugo Williams is a fantastic poet. What's really encouraging are the number of women poets coming through — Fleur Adcock's anthology was an admirable attempt to build a canon around Moore and Bishop and the good bits of Edna St Vincent Millay, but now, in the half-generation below Lochhead and Duffy, you've got Maura Dooley, Jo Shapcott, Lavinia Greenlaw, Eva Salzman — okay, I live with her, but I still think she's dead good — Anne Rouse, Elizabeth Garrett and loads of others. More worryingly, there's the current trend of providing subtitles for the thick, in the name of democratisation; with some poets, only the emotional signposting is left, the landscape of the poem having disappeared altogether. You're left with poetry that's easy to negotiate, but pointless, ideal for people who were attracted to the idea of reading a book of poems as some refined, fragrant activity, or as some form of therapy, a legitimisation of their own suffering, or vicarious pleasure in someone else's. Worse still is the perception that John Hegley and Benjamin Zephaniah are poets of any kind, an idea sometimes encouraged by people who should know a whole lot better; sorry, I'll stop moaning.

RF: Finally, if I could turn to your poem "Beltane", which I gather is the name of a Celtic festival of some kind, as is the name of your band, "Lammas". Is your interest in the pagan a reaction against your experience of Christianity?

DP: Some kind of pagan animism strikes me as a far healthier response to the world than the invention of the Great Bearded Inscrutable, or whatever it was whoever it was called him. I'm still religiously inclined, though Christianity, I'm afraid, has blown its chance. Like most people, I use religion for medicinal purposes and tend to swear by whatever god worked last time. I do buy the idea of poetry as a kind of shamanistic, or rather since Kenneth White has sullied that word, alchemical practice: Ultimately, a means by which fairly specific emotional changes can be effected in the sensitive reader. That's why I get annoyed when people talk about prosody as if it were some hopelessly dry, redundant area of study, like log-tables, or something . . . it's the means, one of them, by which we calculate those nuances of sound and rhythm that will hopefully register those emotional, visceral changes. I suppose, like harmony, it *is* dry, unless you understand what it can do. I don't think anyone else should be allowed to learn it, though; if we kept it a secret, it would make it special, magical again . . . it's not so long ago that the composition of poetry was considered an occult practice, something that got lumped in with astrology and entrail-reading. An understanding of prosody might help the non-practitioner to "appreciate" Milton'a genius, but I doubt if it will help them experience the poems more intensely, any more than understanding the harmonic structure of a tune will leave you any more moved, or the chemical constitution of a cough-bottle feeling any better.

RF: A final word on "Beltane"?

DP: It's a poem about two kinds of fire festival, one very old, one very new. It's interesting that poems about nuclear holocaust are suddenly a bit passé, as if we were desperate for them to become that way.

ROBERT PINSKY

TALKING TO SCOTT ANDERSON

Robert Pinsky's new verse translation of Dante's *Inferno* will be published later this year by Farrar, Straus & Giroux. His books of poetry include AN EXPLANATION OF AMERICA (Princeton), THE WANT BONE (Ecco) and HISTORY OF MY HEART (Ecco), awarded the William Carlos Williams Prize of the Poetry Society of America. His collection of essays, POETRY AND THE WORLD, was nominated for the National Book Critics' Circle award in criticism. He is also co-translator of THE SEPARATE NOTEBOOKS, poems by Nobel Prize winner Czeslaw Milosz. In 1989 Robert Pinsky joined the graduate creative writing faculty at Boston University. This interview was recorded at the poet's home on 28 February 1993.

SA: . . . the first and obvious question is, "Why Dante?"

RP: It might be nice to say that this project has to do with some deliberate spiritual reach. But it began as a craft matter, and the appeal of Dante's subject has emerged for me as I have been engaged in the craft struggle of trying to make an *Inferno* in readable English that approximates some of the formal excitement of the original.

The project began more or less by chance, with the assignment to do one canto, and what first caught me was the hook of the technical problem: a problem in metrical engineering, you might call it. It became clear to me that in my previous readings of the poem I had underestimated how very powerful a position Dante occupied between lyric on one side and narrative on the other. I believe that this powerful position has everything to do with *terza rima*, a form that is uniquely propulsive in one way and uniquely clinching or conclusive in another way. And certain inventions I had been forced to devise for myself while working on Milosz translations made me feel I could approximate that *terza rima*. So it was a technical matter, at first.

As I became preoccupied by the *Inferno,* absorbed by it, I felt deeply drawn to the mixing of low material and language with high: the quality that makes Dante call the whole poem his *Commedia* (with the adjective *"Divina"* added by others, later). That comic or mixed quality let me feel that possibly an American poet, or the kind of American poet I am, might have some qualifications for translating Dante: some affinity that might compensate for other qualifications I lack. The mixing of high and low moved from having a technical meaning to having spiritual and political meanings for me.

SA: Another thing that I know you've spoken about a lot, to quote from one of your lectures, is the idea of poetry as "an ecstasy rising out of the body of ordinary discourse." Dante is writing in demotic Florentine Italian . . . did that attract you as well?

RP: Very much. That is another polarity related to the lyric/narrative polarity: in the *Commedia* Dante writes of mysteries, of ecstasy, going above the quotidian world; but he is also scoring points off specific people he feels have ruined his life in quite personal, definite, worldly ways. And the speech of the *Inferno* particularly, among the three *cantiche*, is earthy and plain — part of the mixing that is quite attractive to me.

SA: I suppose the most developed question I have about Dante, technically, is your use of rhyme. You use rhyme very much as Derek Walcott does in his *Omeros*, which is to effect rhymes off things as slight as dental consonants and so forth.

RP: For me this began with working on Czeslaw Milosz's sequence *The World.* In Poland, children learn to read from rhymed verses; the Polish primer is little naive rhymes. *The World,* composed during World War II, under the Nazi Occupation, is subtitled ''A Naive Poem,'' and is written in these meters . . . not quite Stevenson's *A Child's Garden of Verses*, not quite Watts, not quite anything in English — certainly not Mother Goose, which is often not naive but Gothic or allusive. In rendering these poems in English, I found myself using feminine rhymes a lot; in Polish, virtually every rhyme has a feminine ending — that is the norm. In English, the feminine rhyme is so egregious that it is potentially comic, as in limericks or Gilbert and Sullivan. The feminine rhyme sticks out so much in English that even if it is based on assonance it still is awfully prominent . . . ''feather'' and ''bother'' is really quite a lot of like sound, even though the vowel is different — or, er, ''burden'' and ''garden''.

And I found, in trying to balance the sing-song or naive quality of *The World* with the fact that the sequence is, after all, a profound and moving meditation on innocence and history — one of Milosz's greatest works — that hearing a different vowel with the same consonant sounds was very attractive and useful. One finds it quite a lot in Yeats and in Hopkins, a way of expanding the possibilities or rhyme in English, as Derek [Walcott] also does in his poem.

SA: There's no doubt that the Slavonic languages, especially Polish and Czech, offer many more opportunities for rhyme than English. You've spoken elsewhere about the idea that ''all translation is a compromise''. Do you think your translations of Milosz with Robert Hass changed your ideas enough to attempt the Dante?

RP: I think that work broke down some of my own puritanism about translation, including in that term ''translation'' from languages one does not know — in the case of Polish, it was *tabula rasa*: we just didn't know any Polish. We worked as part of a committee, with the author himself as a member of that committee; Bob [Hass] and I used to say that we were not translators, we were consultants in English idiom and rhythm. Czeslaw and Renate Gorczynski, the fourth member of our team, are bilingual — quite good at English. But syntax and idiom: they are such delicate, important, subtle instruments in English, which relies on word order and preposition-tricks to accomplish gestures languages like Polish or Italian might make with inflected endings. And the Brodsky path, which so often consists of ignoring idiom and syntax, and even rhythm, in order to achieve the hard rhyme at the end of the line, sacrifices a lot, in my opinion.

The challenge is to see what proportion of the original you can achieve, maintaining the fabric of English with its habits of word order and expressive cadence. And idiom — and prepositions things like ''can you put up with this translation,'' and ''can you put me up overnight'' and (laughter) ''let me put it to you this way,'' but ''please don't put it down,'' and were you brought up not to bring such things up, and so forth.

SA: It seems as if your work on translations in the last few years, along with your travels to Poland, France and Ireland have widened the perspectives of your own poetry; if you compare ''Avenue'' (*Best American Poetry of 1992*) with a poem from your first collection like ''Beach Women'', there's a widening of the idea of place — it's not just New Jersey anymore, or even America . . .

RP: I did spend my first twenty-one years almost entirely in New Jersey, mostly in one small seashore town: a distinct geographical limitation, a provincial place. The longer I live, I hope, the more able I am to perceive that place in a social and historical way, whereas at my outset the place was invisible to me because it was everything. I can see that the poem ''Avenue,'' which begins with the third-person plural — ''they do this, they do that,'' although signifying everyone on earth by ''they'' — also signifies the lower-middle-class merchants of Long Branch, my town: my father and my grandfather and their friends. That world my brother and sister and I grew up in, the seashore terrain, the people who sold eyeglasses or alcoholic drinks (as my father and grandfather did, respectively) — my ambition would be not to abandon that world, or lose it, but to understand it as part of history, in its relevance to, say, Dante, and not only as part of New Jersey.

SA: In an interview in 1981 you said " . . . my subject is America, middle class Americans and all the things they see and do." Do you think that is still the case in your poetry? I'm thinking particularly of your use of myth in the most recent work, and how that seems to be moving away from the specifically American.

RP: I am a believer in the circular, in the gesture of coming back to where one started. And when I said that, twelve years ago, thinking of *An Explanaiton of America*, I wanted to accomplish a spiral: to circle back to origins, but further in some direction. And I do feel that anything I can say about ideas or history will have authority only to the extent that I can infuse such material with the rhythms created when those ideas or historical realities touch a certain kind of life.

SA: A line that comes to mind from your poetry in this connection is "the impossible field of the present," where you're talking about the difficulties of dealing with experience . . . I wonder if your recent use of myth in many of the poems in *The Want Bone* is another way of trying to come to terms with the difficulties of the present in your writing?

RP: Well, for example, the word "Jesus" is interesting to me primarily through what it has meant to me through the historical forces of my lifetime, and I have to understand the history of that word as best I can in all its ramifications. I must learn what I can and attend to what I can. But my first deep attachment to the word, and my first deep revulsion for the word, have to do with immediate experience, its uses within my lifetime. And "Jesus" was indeed a powerful word in my childhood; it was both foreign and domestic, threatening and attractive, mine and not mine.

SA: In the earlier work, like "Discretions of Alcibiades," it seems to me that myth is used almost as a trigger, whereas in the recent work myth is its own field of exploration, as America was in the 1979 volume *An Explanation of America*.

RP: An interesting comparison. Alcibiades is not an important figure to me in the way that Jesus was. He is a fascinating figure, a powerful *character* or person or personage who seizes the imagination, a great story — but as a word: I couldn't give a damn about Alcibiades in that sense, I hadn't heard of him until I went to college. Whereas Jesus is a sound like "mm!" or "ow!" One hears about Jesus almost before learning to talk. Alcibiades is someone else's strong, electric story; Jesus is myth in the fullest, most commanding sense of the word. He is part of one's own experience.

SA: Recently, there's been a lot of use of the Greco-Roman myths by writers like Heaney and Brodsky and Walcott, from *The Cure at Troy* to Brodsky's Odysseus to Telemachus and Walcott's epic. Whitman wrote about our "overpaid accounts to Greece and Rome" — you seem to use antiquity, even if it's as recent as Dante, whilst shying away from the Greco-Roman axis.

RP: I suppose that for me it needs to be comic. If I am involved with anything Greco-Roman, there'll be a comical aspect to it, in a way that someone else, possibly a European writer, could treat the same material with a straight face. I think some of the funniest lines in *An Explanation of America* are in the Horace epistle embedded in it. "Alcibiades" has to do with the comic aspects of shape-shifting. In this country even using too much of a Latinate vocabulary . . . what does Whitman call it?

SA: "Overpaid accounts to Greece and Rome."

RP: Right. Why is there something in that heritage which is repellent to the national cults? We were founded by Neoclassicists, after all. And Pound's vision of the Classics in America. But it is as if our national Gods don't like it if you are involved too much in Greece and Rome. I suppose that for the generation of Hawthorne, that learning was itself a form of rebellion, as much as Whitman's shrugging it away — for Hawthorne, or later James, it was a rebellion against vulgarity or rawness, maybe. From within each different historical experience, these things are different; for me, there is a comedy of juxtaposition in relating my experience to what I find in Horace or Homer or Ovid. Or as with "Discretions of Alcibiades," Plutarch.

SA: Were you aware of being against the grain of confessional poetry in 1975 and 1976, when you were publishing your first book of poems and writing *The Situation of Poetry?*

RP: That term never meant much to me. But the title poem of *Sadness And Happiness* — and the title itself, in fact — were consciously resistant to some fashions of the time. I suppose I operate partly by thinking of what one is expected or supposed to do, and trying to find a way to deflect such expectations or resist them. The two big, banal abstract words for emotions — maybe the idea was to resist an expected idea of the personal. The poem "Sadness And Happiness" is deeply autobiographical: my early failures in school and socially, my sense that I didn't do anything very well, my thorny attachment to Long Branch, love and gratitude toward my wife, sexuality, nostalgia, anxiety, about making a mark in the world — those are the materials, but they are very decidedly not treated in anything remotely like the Lowell or Plath or Berryman way. There's an interesting book by the poet Alan Williamson, *Introspection and Contemporary Poetry*, that treats these ideas, that very intelligently avoids and criticises the term "confessional."

Of course, "Sadness And Happiness" also resists expectations about the "impersonal" — two words like that instead of an image. In this sense, maybe it was a somewhat literary book, like many first books — very much aware of defining itself against a background.

SA: There is a feeling of a minor revolt against the confessional school.

RP: Really, it is never poetry one resists, but clichés about poetry. Or unexamined habits. Before Lowell's *Life Studies*, it is very hard to find an elegy for a parent in English poetry — from Chaucer to 1962! Then, from the mid-sixties on, it is hard to read a book of poems without encountering an elegy for a parent, it is a contemporary genre, containing some great poems — but it was invented, its time came around, and when the material — any material, any mode — is treated in a stale or received way it is dreary. It is *habit* that one resists.

SA: Some of the most appealing poetry for me in that first collection — "Old Woman," for example, and "First Early Mornings Together" — is an almost purely descriptive poetry which you chose not to develop, fusing it with a deeper exploration of theme in the later work.

RP: Well, when I was in California, working with Yvor Winters and knowing people like James McMichael — well, there was a Western or Californian standard of attention to nature, something like going out and sketching, writing lines of very sharp physical description that could stand on their own, like the American Indian poetry Winters admired very much. It was a good discipline for me, I think, becoming more aware than I had been of the names for plants and birds and natural features. And by extension parts of artifacts, the names of the parts of a building. And how the bird or building works, how it is put together physically, in detail. Though it was not finally a project that came to seem mine.

I guess it is amusing that two poets in my generation I have felt close to, whose work I have read devotedly, are opposites in this regard: McMichael's poems, where natural detail and attention to the physical are tremendous, and Frank Bidart's, where these elements are minimized.

SA: In your most recent work, poems like "The Want Bone" of "Ginza Samba", you use descriptive language almost as a kind of rhythmical or formal tag.

RP: Hm. Maybe if I hadn't had that period in California I would not have written those poems. "The beach had scrubbed and etched and pickled it clean." Those three verbs — perhaps I was aware of that old standard, of trying to see the thing, and of trying not to rely on adjectives, but to look at the object and ask what processes or actions are visible in it or upon it. That Pound-Winters idea of physical precision. And yes, on some level such things are as "pure" or formal as "Hey-nonny-nonny" or "Baby-Baby."

SA: The latest book, *The Want Bone*, ranges over all kinds of geographies and mythologies while including many of the experiences of the first book. This comes back to the question about experience we discussed at the beginning. Does the kind of specificity you've outlined help you move from experience to poem? Your poem "Shirt," for example?

RP: It is nearly a religious principle for me that the material for a poem is at hand, in front of me — that I don't need to seek far to find something that is worthy of art, that though I may read and ponder or even travel to get the work done the *material* is here, because everyone's experience is exactly as noble or ignoble as anything that happened in Troy, or at Tintern Abbey or in Baudelaire's Paris. I just have to understand it properly. "Shirt" is almost a lecture on the subject: if I can understand this garment, I will see in its meanings something precisely as human or inhuman, as glorious or terrible, as a man dragging his enemy behind him, or questioning a leech-gatherer . . . if I could do it right, if we could see the myths and objects at hand.

SA: There's an uneasiness in all your work about definition or absolutes. In *An Explanation of America*, you write: "Countries, like people/Cannot be told or known in final terms." Yet there is a politics in the poem, however personal and lower-case.

RP: Is it a politics? There are certain attachments: to a certain civic idea, to small-scale domestic arrangements, to something cosmopolitan, peaceable and cautious rather than, say, nationalistic, fierce and heroic. And there are prejudices. Regionalism and agrarianism are held suspect: immigration and cultural variety are approved. The threat of fascism — old-fashioned, exalted, Romantic, nativistic, supra-rational, atavastic fascism — is taken seriously. And of course, it is a Vietnam book.

SA: It might be a good introduction to the country for an immigrant, partly because it is refreshingly unpolemical, unlike much American writing from the 60's and 70's.

RP: I am thinking about the Vietnam period here — the frustration and tedium of protests, the rhetoric of debate, carrying signs, teach-ins, a kind of infatuation and exasperation with political change, the boredom and exaltation as well as the anguish of those days. A lot of it was ritualistic, monolithic. In 1979, when *Explanation* was published, the reaction to that had become so strong that it was unusual, even ungainly, to refer to Vietnam at all.
There is maybe a kind of Carter-era wistfulness about it, as if to say, "This is just another country" — but doubting it, too, tempted by the dangerous ideas of destiny and so forth? — that make it feel "unwilling to take sides" to you.

SA: How do you feel about the idea that the main impetus for the world's cultural blend is coming from America, and specifically from the America of Coca-Cola, movies and blue jeans?

RP: Maybe that is one sense in which our mass culture presents a model for poetry and art: the way it expresses and includes the glory of our immigration, which is to say more history, more culture, more past, than a more homogeneous or stable or "pure" America might have.

I'm proud and tolerant and indeed sentimental about the energy and inventiveness that are an element in the mass artifacts you name. There is an American folk culture distinct from the corporation culture even though they overlap, a folk culture that is constantly being created at an intuitive, individual, democratic level, and constantly being co-opted and distorted and packaged at the corporate level, whose artifacts are then raided and improvised upon and revised by the folk culture. That may be too rosy a picture: no doubt at some point commercialization and homogeneity are sinister. But I believe so much in mixing, eclecticism, synthesis, a process of irrepressible creativity in people, that I'm not sure that there is a corporation or government in the world powerful enough to defeat the forces of the imagination.

SA: To end on a grand question . . .

RP: You mean that wasn't a grand question?

SA: Just wait! . . . an American poet once wrote that "The poet in America has a peculiar relation to his public: to them, he is non-existent." [laughter] What's your view of this situation?

RP: I think that is true only in comparison to Coca Cola and TV and blue jeans — imaginative works whose whole point is scale, immense numbers, ubiquity. The point of poetry is nearly the opposite: this is an art whose medium is words coming one at a time from one human body, in a certain order. Not small numbers in the sense of an elite, but in the sense of an art of individual meditation. Like American jazz, American poetry is simultaneously a demotic art and an elite art. Like jazz, it is in constant interchange and dialogue with the mass forms. It comes out of individuals, and it harks back to no particular European-style aristocracy or European-style folk culture.

In Europe, I think there is still some snob value to poetry and to art in general. Here, we do not have cab drivers yelling as an insult the words, "You have no culture!" There are a fair number of Americans, mostly quite well-off, who find social value (not to say snob value) in owning original works of art. There are a small number of Americans who find some such value in being aware of trends in contemporary American imaginative writing, so-called serious fiction and poetry; but I think the proportion of such people is smaller than in France, let alone some poor deprived country like Romania, where people would say, when I admired the quality of their bookstores — the art and philosophy and poetry in the window where we would have books about golf or movie stars or wonder diets — "Culture is a drug for us; we don't have your abundance."

Perhaps our abundance leads us to think in terms of huge numbers, which is a foolish way to think for an artist, in my opinion. Why compete with the numbers involved in a brilliant thirty-second television message for Levis? It is a different magnitude and a different sort of pursuit. And it would be still worse to go in the other direction, and think of fabricating an aristocratic tradition. How dreary it would be if we still had Harvard mandarins in possession of poetry!

So, compared to the Levi's jeans advertisement on television I have no public; or compared to the aristocratic traditions of the Russians (ably exploited in the Yevtushenko sort of phenomenon), I have no public. But if one ignores those models, how extremely well-treated and attended to and applauded I am! Interviewed by visitors from the UK! I get on an airplane and visit some distant state, where I am paid to read my poems aloud to an audience. I get an occasional letter about something I have published in a book or a magazine — what more do I need in order to do my work? What more is there to ask?

Some sense of audience is probably a helpful thing for a writer, I think — though great poems have been written without that help. And I suppose that too much awareness of audience could become a distraction from getting on with the work itself.

And in our contemporary culture, there is always the possibility of a brilliant, unexpected hybrid or category-defier, exploding or bridging the distinction between mass culture and high art. These come not from high-minded entertainers or from foundations or government agencies, but from strokes of genius, like Art Spiegelman's *Maus*, which might be described as a heartfelt, personal, highbrow work brilliantly executed in a mass culture form. Another kind of *Commedia*. The possibilities, as they say, are endless.

MATTHEW SWEENEY

IN CONVERSATION WITH C. L. DALLAT

Matthew Sweeney, one of the more individual voices in contemporary writing, was born in Donegal in 1952 and has lived in London since the mid-seventies apart from a period in Germany where he studied at the University of Freiburg. His publications include *A Dream of Maps*, (1981), *A Round House* (1983), *The Lame Waltzer* (1985), *Blue Shoes* (1989) and *The Flying Spring Onion* (1992). His latest collection, *Cacti*, came out from Secker and Warburg in Autumn 1992. He has held various writing fellowships, has won the Prudence Farmer Prize in 1984 and a Cholomondeley Award in 1987, and is a member of Aosdana, Ireland's academy of leading artists.

(The following largely-unabridged conversation was recorded on a Sunday in May, 1992, in the Diwana Bhel Poori vegetarian restaurant in Drummond Street, near Sweeney's London home: the text has been edited solely to eliminate the rattle of cutlery and thalia, the hubbub of diners, opening of beer cans, discussions with the restaurateur, inane leading questions, exhilirating sitar and tabla musak and the gentle buzz of a heavily-policed but otherwise orderly Anti-Nazi-League protest in the street outside. The recording starts in mid-sentence; Sweeney is talking about his early poetry. . .)

MS: . . . so, as well as the business of picking influences from here, here and here, I remember in the early days being completely, even ridiculously dismissive of realism, of writers such as Larkin, say, and much of that has to do with the fact that I was studying German at the time and the writers whose work I really admired were German writers who tend to move much more easily in and out of realism. Kafka would have been the most significant and I loved the kind of alternative, distorted realism you find there — the idea of waking up in the morning as a beetle — but he manages to tell it in a tone of voice as if he was waking up with a hangover. That was a very powerful influence. I suppose at the same time, though, I was guilty of throwing out the baby with the bathwater, in terms of this rejection of realism, because what I didn't understand then was that to write as someone like Kafka does, you have to have, first and foremost, a supreme command of realism. Indeed on looking again at Kafka's work in extremely non-realist territories and those techniques are what enable the reader to suspend disbelief and that's vital. You need some kind of very controlled realism to achieve that level of success.

CD: So how much has that changed, that initial rejection, in your later work?

MS: I suppose I see my first book as too early, although there are a few poems in there that I would stand by: one of them, ''Last Supper'', was in the Field Day book and I remember the feeling distinctly — as if a switch had been clicked. I remember feeing — ''This is my voice; no-one else could have written this.'' I remember precisely, it was the 6th October 1980.

CD: So when was the first book? Was that *A Dream of Maps*?

MS: Yes, that was 1981, so there are a whole lot of poems in the first book that I would have obviously felt worked at the time but that in retrospect tend to seem like part of an apprenticeship. . . But my main feeling about that book, apart from the fact that a lot of it shows the influence of other writers, is that it was over-ambitious, that I was trying to do things then that I couldn't yet handle fully, that I wasn't ready for. The book after that, *A Round House*, was — probably having realised some of the limitations — was coming right back — very small ambition altogether in that second book. It was a real ''learning'' experience. . . That may be putting it all a bit too strongly, putting down the earlier work too much in favour of the later stuff. . .

CD: I think so! Certainly rereading *A Round House* and trying to gauge the transition between it and *Blue Shoes* in terms of poems like "Leaving the Surface" or "The U-Boat" which are marginally in the same territory as "Imagined Arrival" or "Preparation for Survival" in the earlier book — I get the feeling of a much sharper, much sparer language — almost word-free language, uncluttered. . .

MS: OK. That's precisely what I'm getting at. I mean a lot of my early work seems to me — apart from the occasional poem that would deserve a place in an eventual "selected" like a false start or like a working-out of ideas that were only to be fully achieved at a later stage, when I had more experience, but that initial instinct, that distrust of being too lazily realist — which is the extension of the old maxim that the poem needs a fresh angle — that is the instinct that is still at work. I probably hadn't worked it out fully in theory or in practice — I know I hadn't — but it did come back later and *The Lame Waltzer* was a step further in the right direction. That's a book I still have a considerable affection for, in its entirety, whereas in the others I tend to like things here or there within a book but tend to wish, at times, that the book hadn't been printed.

CD: It's that serious is it, looking back at your starting-out and seeing the imaginative leap, the gulf between then and now in terms of an almost-total rejection of the earlier work?

MS: Yes, if you want to progress, to achieve something, you have to be able to see that progression and to see the earlier work in its context. In *Blue Shoes* there is much more clarity, as you say, but along with the real world there is a world that is sometimes twisted, out of kilter, or certainly the way in which you are let into the reality, the angle you approach it from is twisted. In poems like "The U-Boat" or even in less-obviously distorted angles as in the title poem or in "On My Own", it's approaching the level of allegory or fable.

CD: What I'm after here is where this unusual angle comes from, how much its to do with place, with different backgrounds, different influences. You started off doing Chemistry at University for instance. . .

MS: Chemical Engineering, actually. . .

CD: So how did that lead to the writing? Had you written at school, at University?

MS: There was no encouragement at school: and at University it was a combination of things, going to readings, getting to know some of the writers, giving up the science thing. . .

CD: And what caused that?

MS: Oh, among other things, a field trip to a site that used to be known as Windscale. . . but the writing really started when I was in London. . .

CD: And the decision to take an English degree then?

MS: English and German actually, because of the writers I've talked about, which is how I ended up in Freiburg and all that must have had some influence. . .

CD: But specifically on the science thing, how much did that bring to bear on the poetry? I'm thinking here of my own interests and of writers as diverse as Miroslav Holub, Primo Levi, William Carlos Williams, Tom Matthews, William Peskett or Michael Foley, all of whom came from a scientific background? Given the last few it may be a very North-of-Ireland angle. But it's very much there in the almost-science-fiction scenarios — Ballard or Bradbury, maybe — which permeate your work and in a certain cold vision you bring to the everyday.

MS: It's hard to answer that exactly except to say that it must be there and that it must be different from the influences on someone with, say, a straight English degree. There's the old story about Auden, when he was Professor of Poetry at Oxford, advising a would-be poet to abandon his English degree and take up science to get the wooliness out of his thinking.

CD: How much are your influences other poets then, and how much are they above — beyond — outside the poetry millieu; say, the novel, contemporary film, music: I notice you talk a lot about American novelists such as McGuane, Richard Ford and so on and I've heard you say that "A Couple Waiting" had its origins in the work of a German feminist film-director?

MS: My favourite writer always has been and always will be Kafka but its a very dangerous influence so you can't let it run away with you. That sort of writing isn't something that can be done very easily in this time we're living in or in this language even. I feel Kafka's much more effective in German than in English. One thing that everyone will tell you that is lost in the translation is the humour. Kafka is a very funny writer which doesn't detract for one minute from the seriousness and the blackness but the whole phenomenon where humour coexists with and enhances seriousness can go a bit further in German as, for example, when you mention Kafka in England people only think of gloom whereas when Kafka went to a writers' group with his friends in Prague and they used to read each other's work-in-progress, not only would the others be in stitches when he'd be reading to them from *The Trial* or the stories, but he himself would be so overcome with laughter that he'd have to keep stopping and starting and it's harder to imagine that if you read him in English.

CD: So the influence of American writers comes a poor second?

MS: Well, I really like a lot of what's going on there with the fiction writers you mentioned and with poets such as CK Williams, Dobbins, Simic, Mark Strand, Sharon Olds, Thomas Lynch. . . What I think the Americans can do — I said this in a review of CK Williams recently — is that they can crack the world open and that they can let in the things that matter — let in more emotion, but in a good way. The danger with that is that it can get sentimental and this is why some Americans are not as popular here as they might be, but the best of these, they don't get sentimental and the reason they don't is that they tend to let the emotion in by "showing" — again a little bit like an allegory, like a parable. For example, Williams' poem about the dog that can't shit — and all that he's evoking through that image — owes something to cinematic technique — and I think it goes back to Frost and maybe to William Carlos Williams in a poem like the wonderful — "The Last Words of my English Grandmother".

I'll give you an example. Last year in Hereford and Worcester I had a series of readings to organise, twenty poets in all, and because it was a project involving getting poetry across to a whole county rather than the residencies I've done in safer places like universities where there would, in theory, be more interest, I had to pick very carefully the people who read in the sense that the poetry had to be accessible enough to get across to an audience. Three of the people I invited to read were CK Williams, Sharon Olds and Thomas Lynch and they were electric — the audiences loved them. Thomas Lynch is a good one to focus on in that he hasn't published in this country yet — Secker are bringing him out next year — and so people didn't know his work at all. He had thirty books with him which he intended to take to readings around the country and all thirty books went on that one night. I think that gauges as much as anything how effective the reading was and how directly his work spoke to people.

CD: But there's something else going on in America as well, isn't there? It seems that there's a large section of writing that is dominated by academic cliques and the people you're picking up on are largely outside that circle.

MS: I know what you mean. The poetry I will always like best is poetry that lets the real world into it. Even though another thing I like is when you fracture that world and it goes off in another direction. It's still the real world, though, and the "going off somewhere else" makes you see it more clearly — as in Kafka. Its not some arcane private world he's writing about, but his angle of writing makes you see it in a different way. I would never be drawn to writing that seems to me to be miles away from reality. I mean, it can be very gratifying to get a good review in a magazine you respect by a writer or critic you value but it's also as rewarding to have someone come up to you after a reading and say something along the lines of — "I've never been to a poetry reading before — I only came along because my girlfriend wanted to come — and you talked to me about the world I'm living in — I didn't think poetry would do that".

CD: So you've moved from that earlier rejection into a concentration on realism — not head on — but from your own distinctive tangent?

MS: Well the realism is certainly in there, it's certainly important, but it can go beyond that. The new book that I'm bringing out is different from *Blue Shoes*, I think, in the sense that parts of it are maybe more personal statements — but parts of it take that fracturing of reality one step further and I think *The Flying Spring Onion* is part of the reason for that. Ruth (Padel) said to me when I was writing the children's poems in that book that they would have a liberating effect on my other poetry. I think they have had but also interestingly, the more I write, the more closely I come to the kind of writing that I wanted to do at the start but could only do in a half-assed way so that a long, long time later I can recognise where I'm coming home to.

CD: That whole part of the process baffles me, not just the access to, the ability to write, poems for children which are also, in a way, adult poems. . .

MS: Many of them are. . .

CD: But it's that area of crossover, of neither one thing nor the other. . .

MS: I mean a poem like "Gold" — the one about the ship on the seabed — which is certainly as subtle as anything I've written and a few people have already been picking it out in that book. I go along with them and the question has to be asked, what it's doing in that book — and it's not the only one the question could be asked about. Basically I was fed up reading books that were patronising to my kids.

CD: I can understand that. But there are precedents, in terms of Roger McGough's work and Kit Wright's although in both there's a change of register, of discourse, of formal skills between the "adult" and the "children's" writing. How much have you consciously tried to obscure those boundaries, to avoid the different "tone". . .

MS: I think what Kit and Roger McGough have been doing is very important because they're both very good in that field and there aren't many who are that good. I don't know if I've ever consciously taken from them or how much I've learned from them but I've always taken account of the fact that they were there.

CD: As I see it the difference is in your refusal to be witty or jolly — the humour is somehow darker, malevolent, as in, say, "Johnjoe's Snowman". . .

MS: But stop there — children have a lot less problem with the humour in that poem than you do. When I read that in schools they find it funny and I think that's because they go much more easily across the borders between realism and non-realism than adults do. Take those cartoons where the Roadrunner gets flattened and gets up again — children are just not as literal about life. . . Again you see that in the new book, *Cacti*. It starts off realistically enough and then it goes into a sequence about the imaginary break-up of a marriage and the disintegration of the man involved and some of those poems aren't just realism — they're closer to fantasy. Then towards the end, some of the other poems, "The Desert", say. . .

CD: This is *rim bel terfass* is it? That takes me on to another question. What exactly is *rim bel terfass*?

MS: What is it? It's a stew of gazelle meat and Saharan truffles.

CD: Right. I just wanted to use that as a link into another question. Why, if it's generally agreed that poetry is supposed to be about sex and death, is your poetry so obsessively about food, sex and death? I mean is there a thesis here waiting to be written about the equation of food with sex and its use in literature as sublimation or substitute?

MS: I like food. And I happen to think it's an important part of the world we live in.

CD: Most people like food — but its only a very small number of writers who have taken it on board as you have, particularly the more exotic items — raw fish, melon, pumpkin soup, shark fillets: is it the legacy of rural Ireland — or simply being a good cook — or is it the desire to look outside the society we're living in to the more exotic? I remember discussing with you a poem by Maurice Riordan, a tempting litany of successful and less successful fish dishes and the whole unrequited desire for the perfect meal — you were very quick to cut across and see the whole thing as a metaphor for a relationship. . .

MS: Well of course it's metaphorical — both real and metaphorical — these things work best when the metaphor is first and foremost absolutely successful at a real level, where there's a very focused attention to detail rather than simply being introduced for the sake of "metaphor" as such. I mean the poem we were talking about is clear, "He wanted *rim bel terfass* and nothing else. . ."; he was totally fed up with his life, wanted to have something completely different, completely outside that frame of reference, something he'd never experienced. In "Artificial Blood", (in *Cacti*), a poem that was prompted by a recent Japanese invention, a man undergoes that weird change, this transfusion, and then goes onto a diet of raw fish, which is symptomatic, symbolic of the change. Food is often working like that in the poems. The book opens, for example with a poem call "Sugar" — more everyday, less exotic perhaps, but in an exotic setting — then goes on to really tangential things, the graveyard piece, the stuffed monkey and the well-oiled Luger. . .

CD: Another question then, do you see yourself as a political writer? I mean, I tend to see you in that light, obviously, but then that may have more to do with my reading of the poems than the poems themselves. I'm thinking of "political" here not as "partisan" but in the sense of the root meaning of the word, the *polis*, the city — which figures largely in your work — the state, the health of the body politic? It's one of the aspects that I find particularly attractive in your work, maybe more so because it's so apparently understated.

MS: I would put it this way — I think that if you're going to write about the world, going to let the real world in, you can't keep out the social options, the social elements, and even when you write personally about one individual, even obsessively about one individual, it will seep out in the widest sense as having a political slant. I used to know someone who was a painter who was a committed Marxist-Leninist so he would never allow anything other than Socialist Realism into his work. I remember finding the idea of that extremely limiting. If that's what a political writer is, then I'm not one. But I think that I have written political poems and they may not be that few and far between. . .

CD: I'm thinking of one poem in particular, "Beeches", about being in Potsdamer Platz as the wall was coming down, which I heard you read at the end of 1989, about a month after the event itself. Few people then seemed willing to accept the slightly chilling note of caution sounded against the otherwise over-simplistic welcome, yet a year later even the heavyweight journalists were castigating a liberal consensus — themselves included — that had failed to envisage any of the less wholesome consequences in terms of "none of us could have imagined. . ."

MS: Of course there are more immediate political poems — and some less obviously about "politics" — such as the King's Cross poem, so the question has to come down to a definition of the political. What I'm interested in is where I get to from here, how I connect those poems

210

which may be more overtly political to something like "The Desert" or a number of other poems which may seem whimsical or fantastic to some readers but which, to me, are still essentially about how we live, together or separately, how life affects us; even it it's in an existentialist way, it's still another view of society and the individual.

CD: One of the aspects of the poetry that I've been thinking about — not just from the political angle — are those poems which encompass, say, personal tragedy, "Where Fishermen Can't Swim" or the "Annie Denny" poem where a drowned fisherman is brought up from a ledge and how those contrast in their simplicity with the classic disaster poem from, say, Hardy through to Richard Murphy whose "Cleggan Disaster", in the early fifties, seems to take the traditional ballad mode unaltered — unlike, say, Durcan, who turns it on its head — whereas your view is much quieter, closer to home, less soaring and altogether more persuasive.

MS: Sean O'Brien, in his review of *Blue Shoes* in *Poetry Review*, talked about those two poems together, the King's Cross piece and the fishermen one — and he talked about them in those terms, that possibly in both cases the *ur*-poem was Frost's "Out, Out" and he could be right — I remember being knocked out by that poem for exactly the sort of reasons you mention, and thinking, "This poem is not rubbing my nose in anything. It's simply letting a situation unfold as it would in real life."

CD: That's another point. . . how you respond to reviewers who do and don't understand what you're doing?

MS: A good illustration of that is *A Round House* which was reviewed twice in *PN Review* — one was okay, neither a rave nor a put-down, found some good things and so on. The second one was something of a surprise — and I've not had a book reviewed by *PN Review* since, although the later books have had plenty of reviews, but what was interesting was the way the second reviewer took the book to task partly for dealing with subjects such as hitch-hiking and dope-smoking, saying these were things that poems should not deal with. Of course you have to judge the review on where it appears, on who the critic is and what preconceptions of "what poetry is" or "what poetry should be" are at work here, so even a not-too-enthusiastic review has to be seen in context. In the end, it comes back to who's reading the books, who comes to the readings, how they react to the work and who you can interest in poetry, your own or others that you're interested in, and what that poetry says to them — and most of all what you want your poetry to achieve.

(The conversation ends in a courteous disagreement over who's paying the bill as the remains of beer-cans, mutter paneer, dhosa and paratha are cleared away and interviewer and inteviewed forsake interior darkness for blinding mid-afternoon sunlight.)

JOHN TRANTER

INTERVIEWED BY JOHN KINSELLA

John Tranter (b. 1943) is widely regarded as a leading Australian poet whose work has affinities with American writing, not least with the New York School. His many collections include *Under Berlin* (1988) and *The Floors of Heaven* (1992). He edited the influential anthology *The New Australian Poetry* (1979). Most recently he has co-edited with Philip Mead *The Penguin Book of Modern Australian Poetry*, published in Britain as *The Bloodaxe Book of Modern Australian Poetry* (1994). This interview was recorded and revised between 1991 and 1993 in Australia.

JK: Could you talk about your early years?

JT: I was born in 1943 in the little town of Cooma in the south-eastern mountains of Australia. My father taught in a one-teacher school in the nearby village of Bredbo. It's high country around there, long rolling grassy hills, and pretty much unpopulated; similar to Nebraska, I guess. I remember my mother saying that a hot wind blew all summer long, full of dust; in the winter a bitter cold wind, and sometimes snow. We moved to the coastal town of Moruya when I was about four; the climate there was more Californian.

A peculiar thing happened on that drive to Moruya, late at night. On a bend in the dirt road the passenger-side door fell open by accident. I had been asleep in my mother's arms. I fell onto the road and bounced through the blackberries into a ditch. I can still remember staggering to my feet, covered with blood from the gash in my head, and seeing the tail-light - the car was a ten-year old Chevrolet sedan - disappearing around a bend. It took them a moment or two to realize what had happened, and stop the car. For those few endless seconds it felt very lonely there in the dark.

My father bought a farm, and I grew up there, learning to drive tractors, to plough and sow crops. Later he started a carbonated drink factory, and I drove one of the delivery trucks. He'd been affected by the poverty he saw in the Depression, and he virtually worked himself to death; he died when I was nineteen. He was a decent man, and people liked him.

By the time he died I'd moved to Sydney and started an intermittent career as a university dropout. I managed nearly a year of Architecture at Sydney University, and some Arts subjects. Then I went to England on a passenger ship and worked at menial jobs in London for a year, then hitch-hiked back to Australia across Europe and Asia - Turkey, Afghanistan, Pakistan, India - with my girl-friend Lyn, exploring the hippy trail and having various adventures. I was only twenty-four, and Lyn twenty-one. We're still together. I finally took a B.A. degree in 1970 and became a publisher's editor in Singapore.

JK: Why poetry? When did you develop an interest in poetry?

JT: I guess most people start writing poetry in adolescence; it has as much to do with hormones then as anything. In my last year of high school a teacher gave me some poetry to read - D.H. Lawrence, Hopkins, some Chinese poetry - and suggested I submit something to the school yearbook magazine. I won the prize for the best poem. Mind you, the competition wasn't that tough; this was an agricultural high school, a state-run boarding school, and most of the kids there were expecting to go on to a career in farming, God help them. This was a few years before the bottom fell out of the Australian farming industry.

It took me about five years to work out what poetry was really about, and to catch up on enough reading to know the areas where I should be putting my energy. Rimbaud was my first real discovery. I latched onto him through a pulp novel based on his life by James Ramsay Ulman titled *The Day on Fire*. Ulman has him heterosexual, for goodness' sake, writing love-lorn poems to a beautiful but remote girl, when he wasn't busy exploring the coffee-shops of Paris with his poet pals. I guess that's one way of explaining the poems. Then I found the Enid Starkie biography of Rimbaud, and then the Penguin Rimbaud with its sparkling translations by Oliver Bernard, and I was away.

JK: You're not thought of as following a particularly French line.

JT: Well, no, my interest shifted to the Americans, to the poetry coming out of the USA in the fifties and sixties; all the flavors and varieties from Nemerov to Kerouac and back again. That period in the States - say the forties through the sixties - seems to me a time of extraordinary energy in English writing, like the Elizabethan age, or the Romantic period.

But I was also reading twentieth-century French poetry in translation - Supervielle, Desnos, Reverdy, Michaux - and the German poet Hans Magnus Enzensberger. I've discovered with some dismay that few American poets have heard of Enzensberger. He has a profoundly ironic and richly poltical view of things; that's a dimension sometimes lacking in the US, I suspect.

JK: Critics sometimes mention Ashbery's name in connection with the supposed difficulties of your work.

JT: Of course I've read Ashbery; I found his writing refreshing and liberating. I came across it first in Donald Hall's anthology *Contemporary American Poetry* published in 1962. That combination of lyrical beauty with violent formal and thematic disruption was exhilarating. His sheer intelligence is daunting too. He's almost Elizabethan, isn't he? It's no accident he borrowed a title from Marvell.

But Ashbery also spent a decade in Paris, on and off, and that interest does tie in with my early liking for French poetry. I think you can make out a line of influence that weaves back and forth: from Poe to Baudelaire, then through Rimbaud, Mallarmé and Laforgue back into English through Eliot. Then another later strand, from Desnos, Reverdy and Raymond Roussel back to Ashbery and O'Hara.

It begins with the Gothic, and ends up with Ashbery. But Ashbery has a gothic mode too: I sometimes detect an Edward Gorey tone around the edges.

JK: What about O'Hara?

JT: Frank O'Hara's as good a poet, though perhaps because he's less obviously 'poetic' and more apparently colloquial, he's less discussed by the critics. He's hard to draw energy from directly, because his style was so intimately attached to his speaking voice, his wit, his accent, his milieu, the brand of cigarettes he smoked. Getting his writing separated from who he was as an actual person is like trying to separate Siamese twins.

Actually there's a lot to learn from quieter poets like Elizabeth Bishop and James Schuyler, I feel. And there's so much range, so much variety in American poetry, you hardly know where to begin reading.

JK: You have said that you want to write new and interesting types of poetry, and you work in a very diverse number of forms. Is there a specific reason behind this?

JT: Naturally I want my writing to be lively; I think it's an offense against good taste to be uninteresting.

The culture I grew up in was a provincial one. It's better now, but in the fifties it was awful. Australia began as a British convict colony in the late 1700s, and it's taken a long time for us to relax and learn to be ourselves. You know, the dead hand of the past. I responded to that aggressively; it was the only way to break away and be myself. Part of my interest in finding new forms had to do with that.

Also, on a smaller and more personal scale, I want to keep developing as a writer, from book to book, from year to year. I don't like to see my style settle into a rhetorical stiffness like an old bowl of jelly. I enjoy challenges.

JK: Do you see a necessity to create the New?

JT: Well, now, what exactly is 'the New'? When I was young, loose forms were new. But for an older me, a few years ago, the Sapphic stanza was new, and that's a stubborn metrical form that's been around for thousands of years. I've used the haibun, from seventeenth century Japan, adapting that to my own purposes. Now I'm fooling around with pantoums, an old Malay form. Where will it end?

Something new is usually interesting because it's new; and then when it's no longer new - so soon, so soon! - it's no longer interesting. It's unfair, isn't it? I think it's more important to do something that's interesting because it engages with something vital in human life and society. Its relation to the passing wave of fashion is not so important.

But there's nothing intrinsically evil about fashion, and it's refreshing to see new things being done. It's salutary to notice how many really excellent poets - from Callimachus to Catullus to Rimbaud to Eliot to Stevens - were regarded as excessively 'new' when they began. Catullus and his friends were contemptuously labeled the 'Neoterics', that is, the 'Modernists', in their own time.

JK: Do you see yourself as an 'Australian' poet?

JT: When I was younger I made a big thing out of my liking for international writing, poetry from other cultures. Then about twenty years ago the Australian poet and novelist David Malouf pointed out to me that I would always think like an Australian, and write like an Australian, whether I meant to or not. He's right, of course. I feel easier with that idea as I've grown older and seen more of the world.

JK: In that case, as an Australian, how do you see Australian poetry relating to world poetry?

JT: It's part of English-language poetry; a younger branch of the family perhaps. I see it as part of a diaspora of linguistic energy from the center of empire to the periphery. The British Empire, that is. The US belonged to that empire once, of course. But the other British colonies are part of that too: Canada, New Zealand, India, Singapore, Jamaica.

You see the same thing in Ancient Greece: like Sydney, Alexandria was a polyglot city-port founded as a colony and situated far from the center of empire. The figures are interesting: in the fourth and fifth centuries B.C., 25 authors were born in mainland Greece and twelve in other Greek colonies. After 300 B.C. (Alexandria was founded in 331) only five authors were born in Greece proper, while 24 born in the colonies.

JK: What are some influences on your work drawn from other Australian writers?

JT: I haven't ever felt part of a tradition of Australian writing, though of course whether I like it or not I am, even in saying that.

I suppose Francis Webb is our most brilliant poet, and Sir Herbert Read is right to say that Webb is (from a British viewpoint) unjustly neglected. I mean, he's as good a poet as Patrick White is a novelist, and White, partly through having won the Nobel Prize, is a well known name world-wide. Webb's poetry, for all the respect it has in Australia, is unknown elsewhere. But that's part of the problem of being a poet: you're never going to be that well-known *anywhere*.

We don't seem to have produced an original talent with the power or genius of say Auden, Pound, Williams, Stevens, or O'Hara. Perhaps you need an older, a larger and a more confident society to do that.

JK: How central is Sydney to your work?

JT: Until recently I hadn't thought it was that imortant to my writing, but in my new book of long narrative poems it seemed to take over, almost as a character, or a kind of weather. People define themselves against the background of their towns or cities, almost as much as their nationalities, though of course city loyalty is provisional.

Sydney affects you because of the space, the bright daylight, the sudden torrential storms, the weather - it's unusually sunny and windy, with the scent of the sea in the air. We have twenty-seven beaches in Sydney where the sand is actually the color of pale gold - and of course the harbor, defined by its bridge and the white sails of the Opera House. Melbourne - with a cooler climate, and a more bourgeois past - Melbourne is the other major Australian city, and that has its charms too, of a quieter kind.

JK: Do you have a program of poetics? Is there a particular kind of poetry or an approach to poetry that you would like to see generally adopted?

JT: No, no. I like plenty of variety, the way it is. I used to think I had the answers when I was younger, but that was just the vanity of youth.

I try to stay open to new ideas. And I try to fill out my knowledge of old ideas, which is perhaps more imortant, seeing there are more of them. I discovered Callimachus only ten years ago. I have yet to read Shakespeare thoroughly, or the Arab writers.

Then with my writing from day to day I just do the best I can, like any writer. I like to keep pushing the envelope, as the test pilots say.

JK: How do you work? How does the way you live compare with the way English or American writers live?

JT: Some people have regular hours. I wish I could do that. I have to push myself to write, plodding through sketched lines and ideas and bad drafts until I get sick of it and stop, or until I allow myself to get distracted by the mail, or the phone, or lunch with a friend, or maybe there's some shopping I just have to do . . . Sometimes a draft will come alive and I get a burst of energy, and things go right for a while. Then two or three times a year I'll get caught up in a long run of work, writing maybe ten or twenty poems in a few weeks, some of which survive their further draft transformations. I rewrite a lot. Many, many drafts.

I seem to be creative, in a free-associational kind of way, early in the morning, when I get up. Often trains of words will wander through my mind in the shower, but nothing seems to come of that. I have to be writing things down, either with a pen or on a computer screen, for them to develop into a poem. I like fountain pens, but it's hard to find a good one, and it seems impossible to find a good permanent waterproof ink that doesn't attack the plastic part of the pen. Better plastics, that's what we need.

I've always felt easy with computers, and I've used one as a word-processor since the mid-eighties. I had a typewriter before that; first an ancient manual, then a beautiful old 1956 Smith-Corona portable electric. I still have that. It has a nice touch, though the motor's a bit noisy.

I should say that full-time employment, especially creative or demanding work, kills my poetry. I need plenty of daydreaming time to fill up the reservoir, and I've been extremely lucky to have been given so much writing time through the fellowships offered by the Literature Board of the Australia Council, and also most recently by the Australian Artists Creative Fellowship scheme. I've had about a dozen years of subsidized writing time, and it's meant a lot to me.

I've been writing for more than thirty years now, and the twenty or so years I've spent either studying or earning a living working for other people were useful to me. But the writers' fellowships are vital.

The Australian government is remarkable in that way; there have been few societies that have treated their creative artists so well in terms of fair, democratic, generous hands-off, long-term support. We put Henry Lawson, a working-class poet and fiction writer who died of drink, on our ten-dollar note.

JK: That confidence about high culture, and support for the arts, that's a comparatively recent thing in Australia, isn't it?

JT: Yes, for many years we internalized a British view of ourselves: we believed what they told us, that we were a simple-minded bunch of colonial hedonists with awful accents, good at golf and tennis and not much else. We're now beginning to see how self-serving that caricature is for the British; how it allows them to feel superior to what is after all a more energetic society, a society with a future, rather than a past.

As far as literature is concerned, it's a fact that we buy and read many more books and literary magazines per capita than the English or the Americans.

I have many friends in England and in the United States who are writers. Some of them have support from universities or from arts grants and foundations, but it's not an easy life for them. They have to work hard to survive in what seems to me to be an uncaring society, and they don't have that much energy left over for their art.

America's tradition of patronage is different. It works through philanthropic foundations: the Lannan, the MacArthur, the Lila Wallace-Reader's Digest, these organizations have helped writers greatly, but not as a matter of government policy. In Australia it's done with the support of all the Australian working people, taken from their tax and given to those who need and deserve it. In the US it's more chancy; as a writer you depend on someone's generosity.

JK: I'd like to turn to a concern that many writers and critics seem exercised by at present: postmodernism. Do you think a knowledge of postmodern theory is necessary for a contemporary writer?

JT: No, not really. Of course it's a good thing to be aware of the philosophical currents of the time, particularly when they deal with how art and theory are created and consumed, but it isn't necessary for the art. I mean, it doesn't tell you how to make better art.

JK: I agree.

JT: Perhaps architects have to be more aware of it, because architecture is a fashion-driven trade, like interior decorating - could we call architecture 'exterior decorating'? - and postmodernism is the current fashion. Well, that's not quite true; the geographer Jane M. Jacobs was talking to me recently in Melbourne about the new fashions in building design in Europe, the work of architects like James Stirling, who strongly denies he's a postmodernist, and Norman Foster and Nicholas Grimshaw, who appear to be driving away from postmodern trends towards something else. Their work sounds to me a little like a return to the Bauhaus; back to the future with machine modernism and functional design. But then, that would be a postmodern strategy too. Is postmodernism inescapable? It seems so.

JK: There's a lot of talk about the borrowing and mixing of styles in postmodernist works. Pastiche, that sort of thing.

JT: Well, architects use pastiche - it sounds like a brand of glue, doesn't it? - then movie-makers use montage, writers and artists and primitive shamans use *bricolage* - gluing things together. The word 'collage' is from the French word for 'glue'.

You see it for example in James Joyce's *Ulysses*, where Joyce borrows forms - the stage play, the music hall, the romantic novelette. In a sense he's parodying them, but he's also using them. And you see it in Eliot's *The Waste Land*, and in Pound's *Cantos*. It's a tactic of classical modernism.

JK: And postmodernism - what are its tactics?

JT: Well, I think postmodernism is perhaps more a way of *viewing* and talking about the production and reception of art, and the way art-making strategies developed over the last century, particularly since classical modernism lost steam around the time of the Second World War. I can't see it relating much to a way of *making* art. Few of those who do make art or literature care much for the theories that hang around the edges of postmodernism, and they're often hostile towards intellectual theories anyway. People who make things usually work with concrete nouns. People who make theories usually work with abstract nouns, and there's no way the two dialect groups can understand each other.

Let's look at Pound, Eliot and Joyce - now they may have known exactly what they were doing in, say 1922, the year in which both Joyce's *Ulysses* and Eliot's *The Waste Land* were published (and Wittgenstein's *Tractatus*, for that matter); after all, they were presenting the signal works of the modernist project in literature to a bewildered audience. They knew what modernism felt like down in the engine-room: they were stoking the boilers.

But did they know where the ship was headed? I doubt they would have been able to understand the terms we use today to talk about modernism. I mean, in some ways Eliot's great critical contribution to the twentieth century was his rehabilitation of John Donne and Virgil, for goodness' sake! Could Picasso have seen Pollock on the horizon in 1922? Or Stravinsky, John Cage? No way. Those people were each more concerned with the making of individual works, and the politics of publishing in the magazine of the time, and how to respond to late Victorian and Edwardian art forms, and the need to get a job and pay the rent, and so on. And they didn't know that they were creating the signal works of the modernist project in the way we understand that project now; Eliot was trying to get a poem published, Joyce was thinking about his next book, and a pair of boots he'd asked someone to send him from England.

JK: Is there quality in a work of art that we can call 'postmodern'?

JT: I'm not sure that it's *in* the work of art - hovering behind it, perhaps, or glowing like an electrical spark in the air, jumping the gap between the work of art and the consumer. I suppose that 'postmodernism' might simply be the quality - almost magical, almost invisible - that tells the theorists among us that certain artworks or cultural constructions - television game shows, for example - are responding to the postmodern condition of the world; or of the art world, or the world of intellectual discourse.

I guess it's an issue, just how 'responsive' a wellbehaved art work should be to the condition of postmodernity; or how 'willingly' a good art work should present itself for scrutiny of this sort, which is often derived from a Marxist analysis of society and culture.

JK: Does that relate to so-called 'language' poetry? Some of the thinking behind that seems allied to Marxist analysis.

JT: It seems to me to be a mixture of linguistics, Marxism, Gertrude Stein and French literary theory. It's perhaps the first time a literary movement has been invented by university-trained critics who have written the texts the theory calls for. Perhaps that's why so many readers find the texts boring. Some of the theory can be useful when it explodes and exposes how value in poetry is constructed by the people who consume it, and then how this ideological process is denied and concealed by the consumers.

But the desire for poetry is difficult to analyze in a Marxist sense as a 'commodity'; it functions outside the relations of capital in many important ways, unlike say architecture, which is linked to capital by an intravenous tube with a pump at the other end. So a critique of 'commodity fetishism' can't say much that's useful about how poetry works - how it has functioned since the bronze age.

Critics don't seem to deal well with 'role' in that sense. I'd like to see a theory of poetry that talked not about 'value', or 'voice' or 'stance', but 'role' instead: drawing on Erving Goffman's work in *The Presentation of Self in Everyday Life*, perhaps. That kind of theory could usefully look at Browning, at Auden, at Sevens, at some of Frank O'Hara's games with 'I' and 'you' and role-shifts and reversals.

217

JK: Would you accept that you've written some of the more important Australian postmodernist texts/poems in the last few years? Especially in your 1988 collection of poems *Under Berlin*, in *The Floor of Heaven* in 1992, and the material published in journals since then?

JT: Picasso is supposed to have said that one should not be one's own connoisseur. It's not for me to talk about the importance of my work; that's up to other people. I guess though that my writing seems to have been responding to the postmodern condition, for what that's worth.

JK: But I gather it wasn't conceived as being postmodernist when you were writing it?

JT: When I started writing, postmodernism had hardly been invented. Back in 1964 a friend said I should read Ferdinand de Saussure, the linguist whose lectures in the early years of the century more or less started the fashion for structuralism among French academics. I tried, but I found it too dry and technical, and as far as linguistics went I was more interested in Benjamin Lee Whorf and Sapir, who were on a linguistics course I was doing. In my own writing - and in the reading I did to discover how to write - I was interested in exploring European modernism, which believe it or not felt like a daring new thing in Australia back then, and in Freud and Jung, in relativity theory, in movies, in various other new types of poetry.

I would also say, as a minor point, that postmodern writing appeared in Australia in the late sixties and through the seventies as a result of our trying to come to terms with some of the strategies of late classical modernism. In other words, by the time modernism arrived here to any real effect, it had transmuted into postmodernism.

JK: I dislike the expression post-modernism, but don't you think in your recent long narrative poems collected in the book *The Floor of Heaven*, you're setting up a straightforward construct in terms of dialogue and monologue and then you're stretching it, making it taut? Is the term 'post-postmodernism' relevant here? And do you think you can be humane, or humanist, and post-modernist?

JT: Yes, I suppose *The Floor of Heaven* could be seen as a post post-modernist project, but I didn't set out to do that. I just do what I do, and when I turn around and look at it afterwards, that seems to be a category that might fit.

As for incorporating humane, or humanist values, in contemporary writing - that seems a worthwhile challenge. I think it's always true that writers need to do work that's interesting in itself as craft and art, in terms of where the art has developed to, as well as having something of human worth to give people. You should be able to do both; why settle for less? You only have one chance at it. It's not compulsory, but I think the best artworks give you both a fresh handling of materials, the techniques and themes of the contemporary world, and at the same time they give you a little more - a glimpse of human fate and destiny that the reader can project back into the work. We each have to die, and that's important; and no amount of theory will mediate that.

JK: Let's talk about *The Floor of Heaven* for a moment. It's almost like a collection of four novellas, isn't it, adding up to around a hundred and forty pages of blank verse. They're mainly about strong women characters, although there are some interesting men as well. Now despite the language of those poems - those narratives - being somewhat removed from everyday life, it still operates on a humane and familiar level, wouldn't you agree?

JT: I wanted the language to be reasonably naturalistic, though perhaps a little feverish. And because it constructs 'believable characters', then I guess it is operating on a level where you can talk about humane values and so forth.

JK: From one angle *The Floor of Heaven* seems almost naturalistic fiction, like Dickens perhaps. Are the characters fictional?

JT: Yes. Most first novels are thinly-disguised autobiography, aren't they? Well, *The Floor of Heaven's* different. The characters are fictional, they're not based on me or my friends.

JK: What about the violence, the extreme emotional states, the tides of passion that seem to wash back and forth through the stories? Are we dealing with melodrama here?

JT: It's funny, some critics have read the poems as critiques or parodies of classical melodrama, if you'd allow the oxymoron. I'm not so sure it's as cynical as that, or as simple as that. I confess the action is sometimes lurid, and the emotional currents rather high-voltage, but I wasn't consciously setting out to parody that style of narrative, really. Perhaps I'm not as subtle a writer as some people think. I wanted to jump into the action and get moving, 'in medias res' as the poet Horace says. And the characters - well I've never been interested in pale, self-questioning nerds like the Bloomsbury set, sitting on the terrace in the twilight sipping cups of tea and talking about spiritual experiences. I like characters with a bit of bite, who have a rage to live, to quote a Suzanne Pleshette movie title.

You see, the story is built on narratives, on spoken monologues, so the people speaking have to have something pretty compelling to say, or the reader is going to lose interest. I used to work in radio - radio plays - and one rule in writing radio plays or features goes like this: you have to grab your audience right at the start, and keep them interested. If you lost the listeners in the first five minutes, you'd lost them, period.

JK: Could you discuss the correlations between narrative in your poetry and that in film?

JT: Film always works through narrative. Well, there have been exceptions; I'm thinking of a color short titled 'NY, NY' back in the sixties, a piece about half an hour long that featured distorted reflections of New York, reflections in hub-caps and rippling pools of water, with a jazz sound-track; and of course there's Bert Stern's *Jazz on a Summer's Day*, a documentary of the Newport jazz convention in the late fifties. But film depends, in terms of economics, on audiences of a certain size, and they have an appetite for narrative, and essentially narrative that embeds characters in a plot; a plot that constructs the responses of the characters. So most movies are rather like novels; long and narrative.

I think most contemporary 'lyric' poetry is more like that short film I mentioned, 'NY, NY' - selective, colored, distorted, without a linear time-frame, and with a few small but intense points to make.

Those long narrative poems in *The Floor of Heaven* - they're perhaps more like conventional movies, in terms of scale, duration, narrative approach. You can read most contemporary lyric poems in about five minutes - you get one quick thrill, and that's it - but 'Rain' is forty pages long, and it has characters and a storyline, and scenery - and even a sound-track, if you listen closely. I love the way the language of the film can be so lurid, yet seem so natural. And with the advantages of a sound-track, good-looking actors, makeup, lighting - any poet would be envious of that grip on the audience. Sometimes I think that my poems are my attempts at film.

JK: What about video? Is it the medium of the future?

JT: I've sometimes thought that the reason there isn't a strong new generation of young poets around just now might be that they're making videos instead. Perhaps that's the literary form we should be watching.

But then the medium's soaked with the values of advertising. To make an arresting video clip you have to make it look and sound like a good television commercial. Commercials have the qualities of a good hooker. Look at Madonna: it's all a come-on, and the energy derives from greed. Who wants that?

JK: Looking at the reception of your work generally, how do you feel about the notion that your work is going to be interpreted in a theoretical context, as opposed to the lyrical mode, in which most poets have been examined? Do you see academic-based theoretical analysis as an appropriate way of looking at poetry?

219

JT: Well, on the one hand I can't do anything about that, so what I feel about it doesn't matter. It will happen anyway, and that's fine. On the other hand, I think that what I write will test the critic as much as the other way around. So I find that interesting too. And as for lyricism, while I'm emotionally drawn to it, there's so much opportunity for fakery and bullshit in that mode, that it's a good thing to see it tested by theory.

JK: With some poets like Yeats, say, there is an over-riding concern with the notion of vision. You on the other hand seem more concerned with the possibilities of language as a thing in itself.

JT: Not really. In my early work I was very interested in the idea of vision. My first book was titled *Parallax*, a word that relates to camera viewfinders and binocular vision. On a more complex level, language itself constructs the way a person perceives and constructs the patterns in the world around them. Gestalt theory still has important things to say. Language is obviously the crucial factor in a piece of writing, and I've been interested in it from a linguistic point of view, and from a philosophical point of view, and peripherally from an anthropological point of view. I'm naturally interested in language; it's what poems are made out of.

JK: What about 'vision' as a metaphysical concept?

JT: I've always had a religious tendency, though I don't usually talk about it that much. In my twenties I read widely among the world's religions, and put some years of study and practice into Zen Buddhism. I respect Zen as a philosophical and psychological system, and the general Buddhist theme of compassion seems a good thing.

Wittgenstein said that 'of that which we cannot speak, we must remain silent'. What he didn't realize - apparently he didn't come across any Zen teachers - was that such things have meaning, are vitally important, and can be communicated. At a certain level, you have to go beyond language. In fact it's the dualistic nature of language that's the problem with the way we perceive the world, which in itself is not dualistic.

There's an old saying that those who know do not speak, and those who speak do not know. Somehow writing poems about these delicate and paradoxical matters seems not only stupid - logically stupid - but tainted with vanity and bad taste as well.

JK: Les Murray is a slightly older colleague of yours, a fellow Australian whose poetry is available now in the USA. How do you view his work in terms of the way it uses its language?

JT: Oh, Les has a strong linguistic talent, a real way with words. In his writing I think he tends to take the solidity and denotative abilities of language for granted as a tool he can put to good use. Not for him the modernist doubt and angst of Beckett, say, or *Finnegans Wake*. He just gets on with the job, describing a landscape, or two farmers talking, or an animal's interior thoughts. In some ways I think of him as having the combined talents of an Edgar Lee Masters and a James Dickey.

Then there's another decorative and riddling way he uses words, rather like Craig Raine's 'Martianism', where you get things displaced into metaphors and made strange, and you have to guess what it is he's describing; rather like the mystery sound effect in old radio shows. It's an example of what Viktor Shklovsky called '*ostranenie*', a process of deliberate 'estrangement'. It's also related to 'kenning', an ancient Scandinavian poetic device, and quite attractive in small doses.

Readers who like Les's work tend to invest in the general belief that if a writer says a particular thing memorably enough, invoking 'literature' to authenticate the poet's 'voice' and vice versa, then the words take on an almost magical weight, a gravity, that guarantees the broadly moral values underneath the statement. I tend to think with Saussure that words are a little more fragmented and arbitrary than that. And then there's the dangerously circular nature of that 'vice versa'. You can end up authenticating yourself, endlessly.

220

But then Les and I are more alike than different. We're both contemporary Australian poets, with Scottish ancestry, from coastal country farms, who both attended Sydney University during the sixties, married during the sixties and had children, studied Arts, failed some subjects and dropped out, and came back a few years later to complete our degrees.

JK: Some reviewers have called your early work remote, or cold. Cavafy removed himself from the immediacy of his own life through his use of myth and history. Do you think you've done this in an intellectual way, through language?

JT: Perhaps I have. Cavafy had to withdraw a little from his material for all sorts of reasons. He was writing at the turn of the century in Alexandria in Egypt. He was often unable to be frank about what he was discussing - male homosexuality, much of the time - but also I think there was a natural reticence that heightened the intensity of the experiences underneath or behind the poem, and that's what I like about his work. I'm a naturally shy person; I can relate to that, that kind of double effect where you say: 'I'm not really affected by these things', and yet the way you say that implies that actually you are. I think you get a stronger response from the reader.

I've always disliked gush. Perhaps in my early work I went too far the other way; I don't know. I did the best I could. Something I've realized only lately is that every writer does the best she or he can. There's no use saying 'Oh, I wish Graham Greene would stop going on about his Catholic angst', or 'I wish Henry Miller would stop writing about his dick'. They were doing their best.

JK: How close is your poetry to your life?

JT: Uh - fairly close, but it depends on the poem. Occasionaly I write drafts of poems that are based on linguistic play, and that might turn out to have some interesting material. I develop them a little more, and if I like them I publish them. With some other poems, I find I'm writing about experiences like the ones I've had in my own life that are important to me. And so, some of my poems are deeply personal; while others are quite impersonal. And some - the best, perhaps - are a little of both. It just depends on the individual poem. I write so many different kinds of poems. It must drive the critics crazy.

I was influenced at an important stae of my development by T.S. Eliot's theoretical writings as well as his verse. He talked about the removal of the personality from the poem. Frank O'Hara talked about the same thing. And they're both right. O'Hara's poetry is personal, and it has a lovely touch - like the touch of a good pianist - because it is apparently impersonal, and he manages to do that trick of having his cake and eating it too.

JK: Another tangent. Do you have any admiration for the compression of image? How do you respond to the idea of 'deep imagism', the sort of thing you see for example in the work of the American poets Robert Bly and Galway Kinnell?

JT: I learned a lot from Bly. Poems like 'Awakening', 'Driving toward the Lac Qui Parle River', and 'Sleet Storm on the Merritt Parkway', these are classic works already, and immensely seductive: passionate, yet cool; thrilling, yet beautifully articulated. But I don't know . . . they seem to take the concept of the lyrical moment for granted, like Cartier-Bresson's idea of 'the decisive moment' in photography. If a master does it, it seems to be true; and Bly and Cartier-Bresson are masters.

Yet when you analyze that remark of Cartier-Bresson's, there's no theory there at all, just a simple classroom skill. If you're using a camera, of *course* you wait for the decisive moment - or for the next decisive moment, if you miss the first one; what else would you do?

Whenever I think of Galway Kinnell's audience I think of constructions that are strangely insincere. Not that he is, or that his poetry is: he's a very earnest man. I'm talking about the collective representations created in the space between author and reader, a kind of cultural hologram, created by the desires of the consumers. It seems that a lot of middle-class middle-aged Americans have a belief that if a poem appears to come from an intense and profoundly stirring experience, like fighting to the death with a grizzly bear, then it's a deeply meaningful poem, which will recreate in themselves a corresponding emotional state. They consume *National Geographic* magazine or movies like *Dances with Wolves* for a similar reason: to enjoy a kind of anthropological tourism. But perhaps I'm letting my natural Australian cynicism corrupt my responses. I like Galway's poetry. He has a great verbal talent, but his work sometimes seems to be acting out a role that fulfills a set of audience expectations that I would find somewhat confining.

JK: You've written at least three long sequences of poems, including the 24-poem sequence 'Sex Chemistry' that appeared in 1986. Would you like to talk about the composition of 'Sex Chemistry'? The style of some of those poems seems strange and rather fractured.

JT: You're right. I discovered that I could use the computer to manipulate lines and phrases of texts on a page - on the screen, that is. I had a lot of text stored in the machine: letters, notes, drafts, and so on. I dragged some of this material up onto the screen, chopped it up, rearranged it, and then looked at the mess I had left and tried to make a poem out of it, rewriting it to pull it towards meaning. It seemed to work. I did another one; it worked too. Writing like that is tiring; you seem to be cranked up tight all the time. In ten days I'd written twenty-four poems.

JK: When people talk about poetry they often focus on shifts in tradition, or style, or form. The formalist debate is strong in the US now. Where does content come into this?

JT: I think that content is an important unexamined problem of modern poetics. I think Gertrude Stein tackled it, I think Ashbery was addressing it in a different way in his early book *The Tennis Court Oath*. That's the book so many people, including me, find hard to read, but that's the point in some ways. You could say that the Iowa Writing School poets take it for granted that there's no such problem; the so-called 'language' poets take the problem as their main focus. Form and content are traditionally supposed to work together to create meaning; but we're now beginning to see that meaning is constructed by the reader as much as by the writer, and that it's constructed by the society, and by the complicated and powerful traditions of writing, editing, publishing and marketing, as much as by the individual reader. And then there are the writing schools!

Recently I've been interested in a text-generation computer program called 'Brekdown', which reconstructs a piece of text from any sample you might care to feed into it, using a statistical analysis of letter-group frequency arrays. It's too technical to explain here, but the programme can imitate the texture of a particular writer's work, without imitating the meaning in any way, by reconstructing a text with the typical *sequence* of letters the writer tends to employ. The content is - well, there isn't any, it's a blank, because nobody *meant* any of it; nobody wrote it. The computer merely assembled it. So you can have style - style so pure you could say it's been sterilized - uncontaminated by any considerations of content. And yet as a reader you're constantly scanning for meaning, for content. That's what makes writing readable. Fascinating.

JK: What about the long narrative poems that make up *The Floor of Heaven*? Did they begin as computer experiments?

JT: No, I wrote them as straightforward narratives. In fact my adventures with narrative verse began as prose, as drafts for a chapter of a novel which I never went on with. I seem to do that every five or ten years.

JK: You completed *Under Berlin* in 1988. What did you work on after that?

JT: I worked on the long narrative poems for about five years, I guess. At the same time I was writing quote normal unquote poems from time to time. I compiled them into the collection *At The Florida*, a book which is due to appear in late 1993. It contains a mixture of things, including a sequence of thirty 'haibun', which are poems each about a page long. I was looking for a new form, trying to wade out of the tar-pit of habit, at the same time as I was looking for a way of avoiding the patterns of meaning that the forms of verse themselves impose on a piece of writing. The 'haibun' was developed in seventeenth-century Japan, and consists of prose and verse mixed; traditionally a short prose passage is followed by a haiku. I first came across the form of John Ashbery's 1985 collection of poems *A Wave*, where half a dozen *haibun* appear. In Ashbery's hands the form is more or less traditional and consists of up to a page of prose followed by a single-line haiku. I have inverted and re-engineered the form for my own purposes, settling on a twenty-line stanza of free verse, followed by a paragraph of prose up to half a page long.

Then there are fifty or so pages of various pieces. Oh, and two rather long poems in Sapphics, a particularly obstinate form in English though no doubt it works fine in classical Greek; one has appeared in the *Paris Review* and one in *Parnassus: Poetry in Review*.

JK: Semantically, how do you view language structure in your poetry? I'm particularly interested in the new, shorter forms you are using and how this implicates content in a theoretical context.

JT: With modern poetry there's always a tension between the older formal structures - it's amazing how much energy the sonnet and the iambic pentameter still have in English, and alliteration is perennially energetic - and newer looser structures, particularly demotic and colloquial forms.

With my 'haibun' poems, I guess a reader would find a simple tension between the twenty lines of free verse which make up the first stanza, and the prose that makes up the second. They have different rhythms, different densities. And in a sequence of them, you might find a tightening and loosening effect as the verse and the prose alternated, like the waves on the ocean. Then in those poems there's a different tension, between varying kinds of content: old-fashioned content on the one hand, where meaning lies in description or argument or tone, and an apparent denial of content on the other, where meaning seems to be contradicted, disrupted, fragmented and eventually denied.

JK: As well as writing your own poetry, you've also done a lot of other work in the field of anthologizing, compiling books and radio programs . . .

JT: Yes, I worked as a radio producer with the Australian Broadcasting Corporation at various times over the years, producing programs on history, archeology, a documentary on carnival workers, interviews with poets and critics, and radio anthologies of poetry from Sir Thomas Malory to Frank O'Hara and John Ashbery.

The latest print project I'm excited about the *Penguin Book of Modern Australian Poetry*, which adds up to nearly five hundred pages. I worked on that with Philip Mead as my co-editor for two or three years, and it's been published here in Australia now, to mixed reviews. I think its most interesting feature for the reader is the inclusion of all the poems of 'Ern Malley', a hoax figure concocted by two young conservative poets in the 1940s as an attack on the pretensions of the experimentalist and Apocolyptic schools in Australian verse. It was a nice surprise to discover that John Ashbery took an immediate interest in those poems when he came across them in the late 1940s.

JK: You've been involved in two other anthologies as well, *The New Australian Poetry* in 1979, *The Tin Wash Dish* for ABC Books in 1989. What are your views on the poet as anthologizer?

JT: Well, for a start, anthologies are always acts of criticism, and that's interesting, because criticism at its best is a dialogue, a way of talking about the art form that invites responses. The word 'anthology' comes from the Greek, and means a collection of flowers; the corollary is that you leave the weeds to wither. Sometimes readers need a little help in picking the flowers and leaving the weeds aside. (I'm joking.)

Anthologies also preserve poems. So many poems simply disappear into the maw of the past, and anthologies are perhaps the best way of preserving them for future generations. We'd have no Callimachus and no Sappho if other people hadn't anthologized, quoted and argued about their work.

JK: You've said that you've always been interested in writing from overseas, and you've done some reading tours overseas yourself. Do you plan any more of those?

JT: I did two long solo tours through the States and Europe in 1985 and 1986, reading at around seventeen or eighteen venues each time, from Cody's bookstore in Berkeley to the Universities of Stockholm, Oxford, Heidelberg and Regensberg. That was wonderful fun, but it sure tired me out.

My last trip was in early 1992, when I visited the United States for some ten weeks. It was my sixth visit, I think. I had a residency at Rollins College, a lovely little college in Florida, and I did some readings in Chicago and San Francisco, and attended a conference of the American Association for Australian Literary Studies in Eugene, Oregon, where I gave a talk and a reading from the Penguin anthology. I may visit the States or Europe again in late 1993; I don't know for sure.

I miss my family, with all that travelling. And the distances are hard to believe. It can take more than 24 hours to fly from Sydney to New York, and that's in a 747! I fly Quantas whenever I can; they're safe and reliable, and they have a very nice red wine.

I would like to thank Philip Mead and Lyn Tranter for their helpful comments. J.T., Sydney, 1991-92

Note: The first draft of this interview as recorded in Sydney 1991 by John Kinsella, and expanded and developed later by both participants.

GERARD WOODWARD

INTERVIEWED BY RICHARD PRICE

Gerard Woodward was born in North London in 1961. He studied painting in London and Falmouth, and is currently in his final year of an anthropology degree at the London School of Economics. In 1989 Sycamore Press published his pamphlet *The Unwriter*; he subsequently won a Gregory Award. His debut full-length collection, *Householder* (Chatto & Windus), was a Poetry Book Society Choice for 1991. He lives in Gillingham in Kent. This interview was conducted in The Troubador café in Earls Court, London, on 17th April 1991.

RP: I suppose the first thing I am interested in is your general background. You've moved about a bit. Is your's a 'South-East sensibility,' if such a thing exists?

GW: Well, no, I moved from London to Falmouth in Cornwall when I was eighteen to study painting for two years, and then I moved back to London for about three years, then back to Falmouth again for another year, then to Manchester, then to Gravesend, and then to Gillingham in Kent which is where I am now. So the majority of my life has been spent in London (I was only in Manchester for a year) and in Falmouth — for three years.

RP: Is Falmouth quite a draw then — you went back to that?

GW: No, there was a sort of practical reason — that my wife wanted to finish her degree course. We both dropped out of art college at the same time, and having only done two thirds of the course after a three year break my wife decided she wanted to go back and finish her degree. So I followed her. I didn't finish mine. (Laughter). So that's why we went back. I did like the place as well. I would have liked to stay there, really. I would like to live in that sort of environment. It's attractive, exciting.

RP: In what way?

GW: A visual, sensual way.

RP: Surf on the rocks, that sort of thing?

GW: Yeah . . . wildness. Not that I'm, I mean I'm happy anywhere really. I just like places, whatever they're like.

RP: Does Kent provide anything like that?

GW: Not much wildness. (Laughter). Well not that sort of wildness. Kent's a funny sort of mixture. There's the part we're living in of sort of declining industries, and of sort of rural tranquility. It's a nice sort of contrast I think. On the mouth of the Thames where we're living it's not exactly run down, but there's the feeling that everything's just been washed down from London and the debris has been washed up on the coast of the Thames at Gillingham. It's not quite as bad as that.

RP: Is it very much that you are getting away from London when you go home? Is London a good place to study?

GW: Well I like to get away from it. I wouldn't want to live here really. The idea of living where you were brought up, or where I was brought up — I don't want to carry on living in that particular environment. I always feel that I'm trying to escape London, but it drags me back all the time. Like I found myself at the LSE having made a break, and then through going to the LSE I'm being dragged back to London again, in spite of myself. When I applied to go to art school my first two choices were Newcastle and Falmouth which were the two furthest art schools from London in England. There is quite a desire to get away from it.

RP: What's the connection between painting and anthropology? Is there one? Is there a useful connection?

GW: I haven't really thought about anthropology in art terms, though it was at art school that I became interested in it. There was a tutor there who had been trained as an anthropologist who had changed to being an artist, and I was interested in the way anthropology seemed to have influenced her work. And probably at the back of my mind from then I was thinking about a relationship between anthropology and art. Obviously there is an anthropology of art but thinking of the relationship between two practices I think is rather difficult.

RP: Something that strikes me (and I have to say my anthropology begins and ends with *The Golden Bough*), something that strikes me with your poetry is that it is to do with *ritualising* things, finding rituals for very ordinary things. I don't think finding ordinary things are rituals, but rather [placing] a very kind of artistic ritualising sheen on them.

GW: That would be a way of thinking about art as something studied by anthropologists. Art as ritual, or poetry as the ritualisation of life, and the control of cultural relationships through ritual. But I was taking your question as: can anthropology and art have a sort of intellectual relationship with each other? I find it difficult to think just off the top of my head because I haven't thought about it before — how visual art, at least, could be related to the practice of anthropology. Although there are truisms that you could say — that anthropology is making the strange seem familiar, and poetry is making the familiar seem strange. I mean they are both ways of trying to understand the world, but anthropology is very specific in its objectives and art and poetry less so, I suppose.

RP: It's good that we've come on to objectives, and you've declared instantly that they're unspecific. You were talking about cultural control. In one of your poems you mention — there's a lot of floral and gardening imagery — and you mention that although gravediggers and gardeners rub shoulders professionally, they should be kept distinct for the safety of society ['Forbidden Food'], to paraphrase terribly. And in another poem, 'The Flower Murders', they have merged, that's almost exactly what's happened. I don't know if that's a question . . .

GW: That 'Forbidden Food' was one attempt to make an anthropological poem, which was just trying to confront the question of the place of death in society in poetry. Making a poem about this anthropological question, really. So I was just using a lot of anthropological material I've come across in considering the place of death as seen through the practice of cannibalism. Flowers are interesting because they are used in all these transition rituals, in weddings and death. I've subsequently written poems which explore the nature of the flower. So I seem to be saying I used poetry as a form of anthropology quite a lot!

RP: We were talking earlier, before the interview, about your painting. How would you describe your painting?

GW: Mad, I suppose.

RP: Mad! (Laughter).

GW: The most recent paintings I've done — the ones I wanted to use for this cover — are of kitchens and I was trying to use my imagination more in paintings rather than observations. At art school you're trained to observe, observe all the time, and not to invent anything and I was trying to let myself go. I devised this character who appears in a series of paintings in this domestic environment and just has fun in it really. Plays with the things in the kitchen, uses the kitchen as a sort of nursery. That doesn't really say what the paintings look like. (Laughter). It's difficult to describe. I used to think of my painting as being like a combination of Stanley Spencer and Egon Schiele.

RP: What's your palette, your favourite palette range?

GW: I got really interested in this colour called Payne's Grey, which is a very deep bluey grey colour, and I got interested in a colour called Alizarin Crimson and most of these paintings are those colours. Those paintings tended to be quite dark. I have this problem of when I paint: people who know my poetry when they see my paintings they tend to think that they're done by a completely different person. They're sort of miserable and sort of tortured (laughter) and not really what I want.

RP: I find some of the poems a bit mordant . . .

GW: Yeah, it seems that I can control that with poetry. If I want to be mordant, if I want to be celebratory, I can be. With painting I always seem to be you know, mordant. It's probably only the paintings I like.

RP: In a poem like 'Woman coming in from the rain' you seem to be celebratory right up until the last two lines — which are a major put-down of the man in the poem. And possibly through all the poems there is a sense that this is a wonderful bountious world, and suddenly there's that little jibe . . .

GW: In that poem, I was just interested in the wet and the dry. I can't really think of any moral dimensions to it.

RP: Would you like to have your paintings up against your poetry?

GW: Yeah. The first reading I gave, in Manchester, I used some of my paintings as a backdrop. That was when I was doing the two things simultaneously, but I haven't painted for about three years.

RP: Any reason?

GW: Really I just want to concentrate on writing because it really has taken over. I keep wanting to paint but last summer when I had a lot of time I tried to divide my time between painting and poetry but it just didn't work out. I had to spend more time writing. It's a shame really. I would like to be able to do both at the same time.

RP: Do you think you'll find time when you finish your course?

GW: Yeah, well, it depends after that. I don't know what I'm going to do, what's going to happen to me. (Laughter). Nothing horrible I hope.

RP: I'm interested in small presses, and I'm interested in how *The Unwriter* as a sequence for a small press came about.

GW: Oh, I just sent some poems to Sycamore Press. You know, without thinking too much about who they were or what they did. I didn't realise John Fuller ran it. And he's liked my poetry — he was on the Gregory panel that gave me an award a few years ago — and it was just a chance really that it came about. [Pause].

RP: There's a Philip Larkin poem about 'if I had a religion I'd make it out of water'. Do you feel that in some ways that's what you're doing with this collection?

GW: Yeah. What happened in those water poems — I had that poem in the back of my mind. It's a poem I've always — I first read when I was very very young, and in the novel I've just written this personality considers making a religion out of water, or rather he makes a religion out of kitchens, and he has these plans to build a cathedral that incorporates all the images that you find in a kitchen. So that the altar would be the kitchen table and the font would be the toilet or the sink, just an ordinary sink with taps.

RP: Are you trying to place the novel somewhere?

227

GW: Yeah, I am. I just finished it last year, last summer.

RP: What's it called?

GW: *All the Rooms of the House*. It follows quite closely the themes that come up in the poetry. It was written at the same time as most of these poems were written.

RP: Do you read much poetry?

GW: Yeah. Not as much as I should probably. Not as much as most people seem to.

RP: I hardly read any! (Laughter).

GW: I read a lot when I was very young, not very young, in my teens. I think they had quite a bad influence on me really.

RP: In what way?

GW: Well, just the poetry I wrote in my teens was very bad. I was reading Dylan Thomas, T S Eliot.

RP: Was it imitation, or problems of rhythm . . .

GW: I didn't really know what to do with poems when I was writing them, so I was just using them as models and the result was appalling. And after I tried consciously to shake off those influences I didn't really know what else to do — to be engaged in strict forms and trying to make poems out of rhyme schemes. I tried to write a poem that followed the rhyme scheme of 'The Whitsun Weddings'. I'd do things like that.

RP: So Larkin was pretty important?

GW: Yeah. Only because he was around the house. My father read him.

RP: What did your father do?

GW: He was an art teacher. But he was very literary as well. So I had problems with influences really.

RP: Are these poems a reaction to that? They come over as tight, not in very formal terms. I admire that. That's how I want to write when I grow up.

GW: It was a reaction in a way I suppose. These poems I was talking about were so bad that they put me off writing for about five years or so and the way I got back into writing was through reading Peter Redgrove. Suddenly his poems really sort of hit me and I felt I could write poems when I tried. I don't really know how these poems came to be how they are. The poems started coming very fast and spontaneously — the ones that sort of just proceeded the ones that you see here [in *Householder*] came roughly one a day for a week and all in a prosaic form, semi-prose, and they were gradually honed down.

RP: Is that how you work — you write very fluidly and you begin to find a natural form?

GW: Yeah, I start with a mass of fairly spontaneous material and just extract from it what I can.

RP: Peter Redgrove would be a catalyst, then. Are there any other contemporaries which you admire?

GW: Not in that same way, no.

RP: I wondered about Craig Raine in a kind of peripheral way.

GW: Well, I enjoy his poems but I just can't engage with them deeply. They're delightful rather than enlightening. You don't feel as if you've had a very good experience reading them. That sounds like a terrible thing to say! (Laughter). I find it monotonous really, I mean reading a book of his poems is like listening to something repeating itself — not in terms of ideas. It's like hearing the same tune over and over again.

RP: Having said that, this book comes over as very cohesive. I wonder where you're going to go now, because the voices are very strong but it's the same voice. I wonder if you've got any ideas about how you're going to develop that.

GW: No, really.

RP: It's almost like one of one's favourite albums which have a kind of studio sound. I don't know if you have the same feeling but it's something you'll return to again and again because that particular voice, one you liked at the time, is consistent. You know what I mean?

GW: Yeah — monotonous. (Laughter).

RP: No, I don't mean that. I don't get that from Craig Raine. I think there's a lot of meat here which Craig Raine doesn't seem to have. What about the structure of the book?

GW: That was largely — we collaborated quite closely on it, Mick Imlah and I. I had a mass of poems which I really didn't know what to do with. I could see lots of themes but I didn't know how to relate them all together. Mick had the idea of the chapters of related poems, and it seemed like a good idea. Mick was quite keen to give me that sort of structure.

RP: I wonder about the last chapter, 'Suffolk Interior'. What's that about? It seems to be saying 'this is autobiography.' Is that more true than for the others?

GW: Yeah, probably. I mean most of them are childhood . . . memories really. Mostly about my mother. And it seemed a nice idea to put them at the back rather than at the front where you'd expect to find them. And to have this window-breaking opening and a more quiet note at the back.

RP: Do you like poetry from overseas? What are your favourites?

GW: Yeah. Wallace Stevens. And a lot of Americans — American poetry generally. Derek Walcott. I think *Omeros* is a very good book. It's so sort of lyrical, in the way he uses those three line stanzas.

RP: Are you in awe of people who seem to have mastered formal techniques?

GW: I wouldn't say in awe, no. It's not something I want to do — that's just because of my bad experiences with it when I was younger. I particularly admire someone like Tony Harrison, and James Fenton particularly — I think his use of rhymes is superb. But no I'm quite happy to let other people have a go at that.

RP: I think that's all I want to say. Is there something you are desperate to get out, and you definitely want to say, that this is your statement that you can't let me get away with?

GW: No!

RP: Good, well, er, do you want to eat?

GW: Yeah.